Piercing the bamboo curtain

Manchester University Press

Piercing the bamboo curtain
Tentative bridge-building to China
during the Johnson years

Michael Lumbers

Manchester University Press

Copyright © Michael Lumbers 2008

The right of Michael Lumbers to be identified as the author of this work has been asserted by him in accordance with the Copyright, Designs and Patents Act 1988.

Published by Manchester University Press
Altrincham Street, Manchester M1 7JA, UK
www.manchesteruniversitypress.co.uk

British Library Cataloguing-in-Publication Data is available

Library of Congress Cataloging-in-Publication Data is available

ISBN 978 0 7190 9669 3 paperback

First published by Manchester University Press in hardback 2008

This paperback edition first published 2014

The publisher has no responsibility for the persistence or accuracy of URLs for any external or third-party internet websites referred to in this book, and does not guarantee that any content on such websites is, or will remain, accurate or appropriate.

Printed by Lightning Source

Contents

Acknowledgements		*page* vii
Abbreviations		ix
	Introduction	1
1	Staying firm: John F. Kennedy's China policy, 1961–63	12
2	Holes in the dam: French recognition and the Chinese nuclear test, 1963–64	53
3	In Vietnam's shadow: the reaffirmation of US China policy, 1964–65	85
4	The irony of Vietnam: the emergence of a two-pronged China policy, 1965–66	137
5	Bridge-building in limbo: the impact of the Cultural Revolution, 1966–67	177
6	Testing the waters: an aborted policy review and closing moves, 1968–69	213
	Conclusion	240
	Bibliography	260
	Index	274

Acknowledgements

Nothing gives me greater pleasure knowing that Andrew Humphrys will see this work appear in print. This book is based on a doctoral dissertation completed at the London School of Economics under the supervision of Odd Arne Westad, whose name seems to appear in the acknowledgements page of every book written on a topic relating to the Cold War. He read the entire manuscript, offered encouragement and helpful suggestions throughout a gruelling process, proposed a rather inspiring title for the project, and, perhaps most importantly, eventually instilled in me an acute aversion to paragraphs that are three pages long. Nigel Ashton and Steven Casey, both from the LSE, kindly read portions of my work and took out time from their taxing schedules to discuss various ideas or provide other assistance.

I am enormously indebted, personally and academically, to Robert Accinelli. He has endured countless self-pitying monologues, engaged me in hours of stimulating conversation about American politics, read and commented on everything I have ever sent, and helped me to develop and refine my ideas. He has spent even more time encouraging, reassuring, inspiring, pushing, and guiding me. If the true measure of a great professor is the ability to transfer his own passion for learning onto others, then he is unquestionably in a class of his own. No one is better: past, present, or future. Here's to you, Bob. Thank you.

This project could never have been completed (or attempted) without the invaluable financial assistance provided by Mom and Dad, the London Goodenough Association of Canada, the Lyndon Baines Johnson Foundation, the John Fitzgerald Kennedy Foundation, Universities UK (Overseas Research Student Award), and (without their knowing it)

Intercon Security. The bulk of the research was undertaken at a number of American archives. I must single out for praise and gratitude the Lyndon Baines Johnson Library in Austin, Texas. There is obviously no better place to indulge one's interest in surely one of the most fascinating and formidable political personalities in American history. LBJ, whose competitive streak was legendary, can rest easy that his library has more than earned its reputation as the nation's leading depository for presidential papers. The staff are knowledgeable, courteous, and efficient. Moreover, they all seem to be genuinely interested in their jobs. Mike Parrish and Shannon Jarrett were especially helpful. My research also profited from interviews with former Johnson officials Walt Rostow and James Thomson, both of whom were very generous with their time.

An earlier version of chapter 4 was published as "The irony of Vietnam: The Johnson administration's tentative bridge building to China, 1965–1966" in *Journal of Cold War Studies* 6:3 (Summer 2004). An abbreviated version of chapters 5 and 6 was published as "'Staying out of this Chinese muddle:' The Johnson administration's response to the Cultural Revolution" in *Diplomatic History* 31:2 (April 2007). I am grateful for permission to reprint portions of these articles in revised form.

I would be truly remiss if I did not acknowledge my family. Ken is the only person on this planet who understands my sense of humour. Despite being a brother, he is a tremendous friend who is dearly loved. If subjected to painful interrogation, he would probably admit the same of me. It is beyond my capacity to express what my mother and father mean to me. I could never love anyone as much as I love them, even though I have a bizarre way of showing it. I dedicate this book to my parents and, with a heavy heart, to the beloved memory of Buffy, the most wonderful little friend I'll ever know. "Not only is it the last show of the tour, but it's the last show that we'll ever do. Thank you."

Abbreviations

ACA	(Office of) Asian Communist Affairs
CCNE	Chinese Communist Nuclear Explosion
CCP	Chinese Communist Party
ChiCom	Chinese Communists
CIA	Central Intelligence Agency
CINCPAC	Commander in Chief, Pacific
CRG	Cultural Revolution Group
CWIHP	Cold War International History Project (Washington, DC)
DRV	Democratic Republic of Vietnam (North Vietnam)
DSB	Department of State Bulletin
EA	Bureau of East Asian and Pacific Affairs, Department of State (from November 1966)
FE	Bureau of Far Eastern Affairs, Department of State (1949–October 1966)
FO	Foreign Office
FRUS	*Foreign Relations of the United States*
GRC	Government of the Republic of China (Taiwan)
INR	Bureau of Intelligence and Research, Department of State
ISA	Bureau of International Security Affairs, Department of Defense
JCT Papers	James C. Thomson Papers (JFKL)
JFK	John Fitzgerald Kennedy
JFKL	John Fitzgerald Kennedy Library (Boston, Massachusetts)
LBJ	Lyndon Baines Johnson
LBJL	Lyndon Baines Johnson Library (Austin, Texas)
NA	National Archives (College Park, Maryland)

NIE	National Intelligence Estimate
NLF	National Liberation Front
NSC	National Security Council
NSCM	National Security Council Meetings
NSF	National Security File
OH	Oral History
PKI	Indonesian Communist Party
PLA	People's Liberation Army (PRC)
PPC	Policy Planning Council, Department of State
PPP:LBJ	Public Papers of the Presidents: Lyndon B. Johnson
PRC	People's Republic of China
PRO	Public Record Office (Kew, London)
RG	Record Group
SNIE	Special National Intelligence Estimate
TIM	Thailand Independence Movement
UN	United Nations
WPB Papers	William P. Bundy Papers (LBJL)

Note on transliteration

Chinese names and places are rendered throughout the text in the Pinyin system of transliteration, except where they occur in different form in quotations, or where familiar names might be confused if changed.

Introduction

A few years following his voluntary departure from government, James Thomson, a frustrated mid-level China hand who had served in both the Kennedy and Johnson administrations, speculated that the 1960s would be remembered as "a period of drearily sustained deadlock" between Washington and Beijing. Notwithstanding his own misgivings over the priorities and leanings of his superiors, Thomson noted with bittersweet pride that some of the seeds of the thaw that unfolded during the Nixon years had been planted in the preceding decade, thus warranting this period "a chapter, or at least an extended footnote, in the history of the Sino-American relationship."[1] Of the voluminous literature on America's encounter with the People's Republic of China (PRC) produced in the interim, however, the Kennedy-Johnson years have received by far the least attention.

This apparent oversight has been in part a function of the obstacles that historians of US foreign relations must endure in waiting for the declassification of relevant archival sources. As records from the Truman and Eisenhower presidencies emerged in the 1970s and 1980s, scholars focused their attention on exploring the origins of Sino-American tension, the question of whether or not there existed a "lost chance" for an early reconciliation, the Korean War, and the Taiwan Strait crises.[2] Implicit in the relative neglect of the 1960s, however, is the sense that "nothing happened;" both the incentives and opportunities for a breakthrough appeared to be few as Democratic administrations, acutely sensitive to charges of "softness" on Asian communism, endeavored to contain Chinese expansionism in Vietnam and became confused onlookers to the cataclysmic Cultural Revolution. General surveys documenting the

American opening to China ignore this period and continue to take 21 January 1969 as the logical starting point for discussion, much like the fall of the Berlin Wall signifies for most the end of the Cold War.[3]

Some historians have questioned the tendency to attribute the shift in US attitudes and policies almost solely to the political and geostrategic calculations of Richard Nixon and Henry Kissinger. Such an approach, the pioneering Rosemary Foot writes, "leads to a focus on relatively short-term events and obscures broader currents of change that were taking place in the period after 1949."[4] Just as Truman's and Eisenhower's papers offered a fresh perspective and forced a rethinking of conventional wisdom about both administrations' dealings with the mainland, the massive flood of documentation from the 1960s has had something of the same effect. Indeed, perusal of John F. Kennedy's China record has yielded valuable findings. Building on a reserve of existing scholarship and incorporating new primary materials, Noam Kochavi's aptly titled *A Conflict Perpetuated*, the first and only full-length account of the subject, reveals a President prone to alarmist interpretations of Beijing's motives and hostile to policy reform. Beneath the surface, however, an agenda that foreshadowed the sweeping changes of the Nixon era was articulated by a growing chorus of US officials lobbying for a reappraisal of existing policies, particularly those efforts aimed at ostracizing the PRC.[5]

Lyndon Johnson's China policy awaits a similarly comprehensive treatment. Early assessments, written without the benefit of archival research, invariably painted a decidedly bleak portrait, focusing on the ill will that Vietnam engendered among US decision-makers toward their Chinese counterparts.[6] Nancy Bernkopf Tucker, a leading authority on Sino-American relations and one of the first historians to utilize sources from the Johnson Library, confirmed the primacy of the war in determining the administration's attitudes toward Beijing and cited it as the chief impediment to fresh thinking. Charging the Johnson team with a lack of "energy and imagination," she concluded that Washington's fixation with Vietnam and its misunderstanding of China's role in the conflict, as much as the disruption and chaos provided by the Cultural Revolution, precluded movement toward normalization.[7]

Without disputing the centrality of Vietnam or the marginal advancement in US China policy, an embryonic revisionist school of thought has recently offered a more nuanced perspective of the Johnson years. Championed by Foot and corroborated by subsequent works, this view holds that significant alterations in the domestic and strategic context of American diplomacy in the mid- to late 1960s created a more auspicious setting for the Nixon opening. Images of an expansionist Chinese menace were gradually superseded by the example of Chinese caution in Vietnam and the implosion wrought by Mao Zedong's Great Proletarian Cultural Revolution. The steady depoliticization of the China issue at home, coupled with intermittent outbursts of popular and congressional pressure for a more flexible stance toward the PRC, provided a politician even as deliberate as Johnson with both the leeway and motive for offering feelers to the mainland.[8]

This work affirms that the Johnson presidency did not represent a period of stagnation, and that senior officials contemplated significant departures from long-standing China policy more than was recognized at the time. Parting from available accounts, however, it directly links evolutions in perception and policy to events which scholars have hitherto taken to be a cause of deadlock between Washington and Beijing: the Vietnam War and China's Cultural Revolution. The specter of renewed Sino-American hostilities moved the Johnson team to extend modest yet tangible overtures to the Chinese – a relaxation of the travel ban, the promotion of expanded contacts, and a shift toward conciliatory rhetoric – that went beyond the conflict management tactics of the Eisenhower-Kennedy years, while the internal upheaval occasioned by Mao's political machinations gradually instilled guarded hope among China watchers and US decision-makers that a new era of relations with the mainland's moderate elements, presumably inclined toward reconciliation with the outside world, was in the offing. As official attitudes thawed, attention increasingly turned to speculating on what orientation a post-Mao regime might assume and whether or not the US could facilitate this transition by further policy reform. In short, this period witnessed the establishment of many of the perceptual preconditions for the Sino-American rapprochement that unfolded during the Nixon years.

The purpose of this book is fourfold. First, as the only full-length analysis of the Johnson administration's China record, it makes the most extensive use of the considerable documentation now available and carefully traces the personalities, ideas, and events that shaped approaches to the PRC during these years. Existing literature on this subject has appeared either in the form of short essays or portions of projects with a longer time frame. A concentrated focus on the

Johnson era provides much-needed context to the Nixon opening and allows us to consider questions critical to our understanding of Sino-American relations in the 1960s and on which still very little has been written. How did US policy evolve? What accounted for the tentative bridge-building that characterized the Johnson team's approach to China? What factors precluded bolder initiatives at this time? Who were the key decision-makers? To what extent were their actions guided by strategic, ideological, or political considerations? How did US officials view the intensified Sino-Soviet schism, and what were the ramifications for China policy?[9] How did the administration interpret and respond to the Cultural Revolution?

Second, this study explores the complex interplay between the Johnson administration's dealings with China and the Vietnam War, a dynamic for long obvious to scholars of Sino-American relations yet one that has never been adequately explained. Only by placing this topic within a regional framework can the subtle twists and turns of China policy during the Johnson years be understood. While the findings presented here offer yet another example of the centrality of Vietnam in shaping the contours of American foreign policy in the 1960s, perusal of newly declassified materials also reveals how perceptions of the mainland's intentions in turn shaped the administration's decision to commit forces to a ground war in Southeast Asia and its subsequent conduct of the fighting. As such, this book contributes to a wider contextual history of Vietnam. More than recent literature has stressed or recognized, Washington devoted considerable effort to anticipating Beijing's response to US military moves against its North Vietnamese ally. LBJ's fear of Chinese intervention contributed handsomely to his eschewal of the more provocative war measures advocated by many of his advisers in the spring and summer of 1965. As the mainland became enveloped in revolutionary fervor, US officials wondered how this turn of events would affect Beijing's willingness to come to the aid of Hanoi, a contingency that was pondered at some length as the administration debated the merits of expanding the war in the spring of 1967. The Johnson team's downgrading of the strategic threat posed by China likely made it easier for them to ponder de-escalation of the war effort in 1968. In short, consideration of the "China factor" broadens our understanding of many of the pivotal US decisions in Vietnam.

Third, while the focus of this project is overwhelmingly on American perceptions and actions, it seeks to flesh out the discussion by incorporating the steadily growing volume of secondary literature on Chinese foreign policy. Few areas of Cold War history over the past decade have benefited more from the opening of archives. While access to Chinese papers remains regrettably limited, much light has nevertheless been shed on a host of issues with which Johnson officials grappled: Beijing's reaction to American intervention in Vietnam, the prospects of its own military involvement in the war, its evolving relationship with both Moscow and Hanoi, and the effect of the Cultural Revolution on its diplomacy.[10] Armed with this Chinese perspective, the intelligence facet of the administration's China policy can now be accurately appraised. How sound was the information that US decision-makers received from the field? Could producers and consumers of intelligence distinguish between China's intentions and capabilities? Questions even more far-reaching can be broached. Based on what we now know from Chinese archives, would a more forthcoming American attitude during the Johnson years have been reciprocated by the PRC's leadership? Was there a "lost chance" for Sino-American reconciliation in the 1960s, just as some historians have bemoaned one for 1949–50? Nixon's historic visit to Beijing, coming as it did in just his first term in office, renders such a query valid.

Fourth, examination of a relatively untapped element of Lyndon Johnson's foreign policy opens up a new dimension to the burgeoning debate over his diplomatic stewardship.[11] LBJ retired from office in January 1969 with his reputation in ruins, leaving in his wake a stalemated Asian conflict that had cost the nation dearly in blood and treasure, the worst domestic unrest since the Civil War, and a fractured Democratic Party that still has not recovered its footing. His first biographers mercilessly portrayed him as a shady wheeler-dealer whose only guiding principle appeared to be the acquisition of power for its own sake. Johnson hardly fared better in samplings of public opinion throughout the 1970s and 1980s, consistently ranking near the bottom in a broad range of categories that are typically used to grade presidents.[12] The passage of time and the proliferation of released material from Austin, Texas, particularly the endlessly fascinating recordings of telephone conversations that Johnson personally authorized, have offered a different perspective.[13] LBJ is now rightfully remembered not only as the man who led his nation into Vietnam, but as a politician of uncommon drive and vision, the architect of a far-reaching program of domestic reform – the Great Society – that was surpassed perhaps only by Franklin Roosevelt's New Deal, and a leader who played as large a role as any in extending civil rights to millions of disenfranchised African Americans.[14] As a reflection of this reversal in fortunes, a poll of ninety historians conducted by C-SPAN in 2000 ranked Johnson a very respectable tenth overall among US Presidents, placing him first in the category of Congressional relations and second in the pursuit of equal justice.[15]

While Johnson's standing as a domestic leader and political operator has soared, his foreign policy record remains an issue of pointed controversy.[16] The massive declassification of Johnson-era documents in the early 1990s inspired an outpouring of scholarly volumes dedicated to his diplomacy. Much of this literature confirmed long-standing criticisms of his statesmanship, concluding that those same qualities enabling Johnson to excel as a legislator – the ability to bridge differences and find common ground – were particularly ill suited for the fine art of foreign relations. His assertiveness and effectiveness at home were unfavorably contrasted with his passiveness and ineptness abroad. Johnson emerged from this research as an unimaginative Cold Warrior with little knowledge of, or interest in, the outside world, and whose overriding objective was simply to execute the commitments undertaken by his predecessors and espoused by his seasoned advisers.[17] The Texan's "appreciation of foreign relations was shallow, circumstantial, and dominated by the personalities of heads of state he had met," Waldo Heinrichs noted rather condescendingly. "Lacking a detached critical perspective, he was culture-bound and vulnerable to clichés and stereotypes about world affairs."[18] Vietnam, unsurprisingly, continues to dominate the historiography. Recent studies have faulted Johnson for transforming his predecessor's limited commitment to helping Saigon defend itself against a communist insurgency into a full-scale war, for reasons owing to insecurity, vanity, machismo, impulsiveness, stubbornness, and truculence.[19]

A handful of historians have mounted a vigorous counter-defense on behalf of the embattled LBJ. Robert Dallek, Johnson's most prominent biographer, contends that his elusive and infinitely complex personality has lent itself to constant misinterpretation of, and confusion over, his motives. Moreover, scholars' fixation with Vietnam, seminal though that conflict was, has precluded a definitive, more even-handed understanding of Johnson's role on the world stage during a crucial stage of the Cold War.[20] Heeding Dallek's call to look "beyond Vietnam" and diverging sharply from conventional wisdom,

Thomas Alan Schwartz has recently concluded that Johnson's policies in Europe stand as one of the crowning achievements of his presidency. The groundbreaking *Lyndon Johnson and Europe* portrays a subtle and savvy leader engaged with the delicacies of policy, deftly handling the prickly Charles De Gaulle, and preserving the solidarity of the Atlantic Alliance even as centrifugal forces threatened to pull it apart.[21] Concurrent studies, while less effusive in their praise, have also discovered a "new" Johnson. Bemoaning a Cold War mindset that tended to mistake essentially local conflicts in Vietnam and the Dominican Republic for a monolithic communist challenge to American credibility, Mitchell Lerner nevertheless contends that LBJ's calm response to North Korea's seizure of the USS *Pueblo* in 1968 and pursuit of a peaceful solution bespoke a leader who had matured by his final year in office and developed a knack of sorts for the subtleties of diplomacy.[22] John Dumbrell's look at Soviet–American relations during the Johnson years finds an enigmatic character whose personal contradictions precluded consistent and coherent decision-making, yet who also made some headway in advancing the post-Cuba era of détente with Moscow.[23]

This book offers a balanced assessment of Johnson's contribution to China policymaking. The evidence presented here confirms several of the shortcomings traditionally associated with our protagonist, all of which stood in the way of greater advances on the China policy front: a penchant for Cold War orthodoxy, a wariness of departures from past practices, a hostage to Vietnam, and a short-sighted concern with parochial political maneuvering. Still, this book also highlights many attributes that have only just surfaced. Johnson ultimately emerges as an attentive and well informed leader who dominated the foreign policy process, intellectually flexible, adaptable to changing variables at home and abroad, an adept conflict manager with an ability to empathize with the concerns of the other side, and mindful of the limits of America's capacity for shaping events to its liking.

This study is organized chronologically. Chapter 1 sets the stage for our discussion by providing a broad overview of America's approach to China prior to November 1963, focusing primarily on the Kennedy years. The second chapter takes a look at how China figured in Johnson's worldview as he assumed the presidency, and the events in 1964 – French recognition and the Chinese nuclear test – that steadily undermined the policy he inherited. The next two chapters analyze how the Johnson administration's entanglement in Vietnam governed its relations with Beijing, first sharpening senior decision-makers' hostility to policy reform as they escalated America's military role in 1964–65, then providing the impetus for tentative bridge-building in 1966 as they worked to head off the threat of Chinese intervention and disarm critics of the war by burnishing their peace credentials. Chapters 5 and 6 examine how the outbreak of the Cultural Revolution influenced perceptions of the PRC and the process of bridge-building. A concluding section summarizes the study's findings and highlights the implications for the historiography of both Sino-American relations and Lyndon Johnson's role in US foreign policy.

Notes

1 J.C. Thomson, Jr, "On the making of US China policy, 1961–9: A study in bureaucratic politics," *China Quarterly* 50 (1972), 220.
2 For an overview of the historiography of US China policy during the Truman and Eisenhower administrations, see R.J. McMahon, "The Cold War in Asia: The elusive synthesis," in M.J. Hogan (ed.), *America in the World: The Historiography of American Foreign Relations Since 1941* (New York: Cambridge University Press, 1995), pp. 506–12; N.B. Tucker, "Continuing controversies in the literature of US-China relations since 1945," in W.I. Cohen (ed.), *Pacific Passage: The Study of American-East Asian Relations on the Eve of the Twenty-First Century* (New York: Columbia University Press, 1996), pp. 218–26; E. Goh and R. Foot, "From containment to containment? Understanding US relations with China since 1949," in R.D. Schulzinger (ed.), *A Companion to American Foreign Relations* (Malden, MA: Blackwell Publishing, 2003), pp. 257–61.
3 For example, see R.S. Ross, *Negotiating Cooperation: The United States and China, 1969–1989* (Stanford: Stanford University Press, 1995); J. Mann, *About Face: A History of America's Curious Relationship with China, from Nixon to Clinton* (New York: Vintage, 1998); P. Tyler, *A Great Wall: Six Presidents and China* (New York: Public Affairs, 1999).
4 R. Foot, *The Practice of Power: US Relations with China Since 1949* (Oxford: Clarendon Press, 1995), p. 1.
5 N. Kochavi, *A Conflict Perpetuated: China Policy During the Kennedy Years* (Westport: Praeger, 2002). See as well J. Fetzer, "Clinging to containment: China policy," in T.G. Paterson (ed.), *Kennedy's Quest For Victory: American Foreign Policy, 1961–1963* (New York: Oxford University Press, 1989); G.H. Chang, *Friends and Enemies: The United States, China, and the Soviet Union, 1948–1972* (Stanford: Stanford University Press, 1990), pp. 217–63; Foot, *Practice of Power*; W. Burr

and J.T. Richelson, "Whether to 'strangle the baby in the cradle:' The United States and the Chinese nuclear program, 1960–64," *International Security* 25:3 (2000/01), 54–76.

6   F.R. Dulles, *American Policy toward Communist China, 1949–1969* (New York: Thomas Y. Crowell, 1972), chs. 13–14; W.I. Cohen, *Dean Rusk* (Totowa, NJ: Cooper Square, 1980), pp. 280–9.

7   N.B. Tucker, "Threats, opportunities, and frustrations in East Asia," in W.I. Cohen and N.B. Tucker (eds), *Lyndon Johnson Confronts the World: American Foreign Policy, 1963–1968* (New York: Cambridge University Press, 1994), pp. 99–111. The quote is taken from p. 99.

8   Foot, *Practice of Power*; A. Waldron, "From nonexistent to almost normal: US-China relations in the 1960s," in D.B. Kunz (ed.), *The Diplomacy of the Crucial Decade: American Foreign Relations During the 1960s* (New York: Columbia University Press, 1994); R. Garson, "Lyndon B. Johnson and the China enigma," *Journal of Contemporary History* 32:1 (1997), 63–80; V.S. Kaufman, *Confronting Communism: US and British Policies toward China* (Columbia: University of Missouri Press, 2001), chs 7–8; R.D. Schulzinger, "The Johnson administration, China, and the Vietnam War," and R. Foot, "Redefinitions: The domestic context and America's China policy in the 1960s," both in R.S. Ross and Jiang Changbin (eds), *Re-examining the Cold War: US-China Diplomacy, 1954–1973* (Cambridge: Harvard University Press, 2001); A.I. Dodds, "The China Opening in Perspective, 1961–1976" (PhD dissertation, Cambridge University, 2002); E. Goh, *Constructing the US Rapprochement with China, 1961–1974: From "Red Menace" to "Tacit Ally"* (New York: Cambridge University Press, 2005), pp. 17–98.

9   While Chang's *Friends and Enemies* nominally encapsulates the Johnson years, the overwhelming bulk of its research concentrates on the Truman-Eisenhower-Kennedy years.

10 J. Garver, "The Tet offensive and Sino-Vietnamese relations," in M.J. Gilbert and W. Head (eds), *The Tet Offensive* (Westport: Praeger, 1996); Qiang Zhai, "Beijing and the Vietnam peace talks, 1965–68: New evidence from Chinese sources," Cold War International History Project (hereafter CWIHP) Working Paper 18 (1997); R. MacFarquhar, *The Origins of the Cultural Revolution, Vol. 3: The Coming of the Cataclysm, 1961–1966* (New York: Columbia University Press, 1997); B. Barnouin and Yu Changgen, *Chinese Foreign Policy During the Cultural Revolution* (London: Kegan Paul International, 1998); Chen Jian and D. Wilson (eds), "All under the heaven is great chaos: Beijing, the Sino-Soviet border clashes, and the turn toward Sino-American rapprochement, 1968–1969," *CWIHP Bulletin* 11 (Winter 1998–99); Qiang Zhai, *China and the Vietnam Wars, 1950–1975* (Chapel Hill: University of North Carolina Press, 2000); Chen Jian, *Mao's China and*

the *Cold War* (Chapel Hill: University of North Carolina Press, 2001); Li Jie, "Changes in China's domestic situation in the 1960s and Sino-US relations" and Gong Li, "Chinese decision making and the thawing of US-China relations," both in Ross and Jiang (eds), *Re-examining the Cold War*; Y. Kuisong, "Changes in Mao Zedong's attitude toward the Indochina War, 1949–1973," CWIHP Working Paper 34 (2002).

11 Goh's *Constructing the US Rapprochement with China*, hitherto the most extensive account of the Johnson era, focuses on the evolution of US policymaking groups' images of China, and sheds little light on LBJ's contribution to the policy process.

12 R. Dallek, *Lone Star Rising: Lyndon Johnson and His Times, 1908–1960* (New York: Oxford University Press, 1991), pp. 3–6.

13 Many of these conversations, at least from 1963–65, have been transcribed. See the volumes edited by M. Beschloss, *Taking Charge: The Johnson White House Tapes, 1963–1964* (New York: Simon & Schuster, 1997) and *Reaching For Glory: Lyndon Johnson's Secret White House Tapes, 1964–1965* (New York: Simon & Schuster, 2001). A third volume is apparently in the works.

14 For Johnson's renaissance, see L.L. Gould, "The revised LBJ," *The Wilson Quarterly* (Spring 2000), 80–3.

15 www.americanpresidents.org/survey/historians/35.asp (accessed 15 February 2005).

16 The C-SPAN poll of historians ranked Johnson a poor 36th in the category of international relations. See ibid.

17 W. Heinrichs, "Lyndon B. Johnson: change and continuity," in Cohen and Tucker (eds), *Lyndon Johnson Confronts the World*; David Kaiser, 'Men and policies: 1961–69,' in Kunz (ed.), *Diplomacy of the Crucial Decade*, pp. 12–13; H.W. Brands, *The Wages of Globalism: Lyndon Johnson and the Limits of American Power* (New York: Oxford University Press, 1995), pp. 28–9; D. Fromkin, "Lyndon Johnson and foreign policy: What the new documents show," *Foreign Affairs* 74:1 (1995), 161–70.

18 Heinrichs, "Change and continuity," in Cohen and Tucker (eds), *Lyndon Johnson Confronts the World*, p. 26.

19 For example, see M.H. Hunt, *Lyndon Johnson's War: America's Cold War Crusade in Vietnam, 1945–1968* (New York: Hill and Wang, 1996), p. 78; K. Bird, *The Color of Truth: McGeorge Bundy and William Bundy, Brothers in Arms* (New York: Simon & Schuster, 1998), p. 275; F. Logevall, *Choosing War: The Lost Chance For Peace and the Escalation of War in Vietnam* (Berkeley: University of California Press, 1999), pp. 389–99; D. Kaiser, *American Tragedy: Kennedy, Johnson, and the Origins of the Vietnam War* (Cambridge: Harvard University Press, 2000).

20 R. Dallek, "Lyndon Johnson as a world leader," in H.W. Brands (ed.), *The Foreign Policies of Lyndon Johnson: Beyond Vietnam* (College Station: Texas A&M University Press, 1999), pp. 6–9, 17.
21 T.A. Schwartz, *Lyndon Johnson and Europe: In the Shadow of Vietnam* (Cambridge: Harvard University Press, 2003).
22 M.B. Lerner, *The Pueblo Incident: A Spy Ship and the Failure of American Foreign Policy* (Lawrence: University Press of Kansas, 2002), pp. 236–7.
23 J. Dumbrell, *President Lyndon Johnson and Soviet Communism* (New York: Manchester University Press, 2004).

1 Staying firm
John F. Kennedy's China policy, 1961–63

The logical starting point for an examination of Lyndon Johnson's encounter with the PRC is January 1961, when John F. Kennedy assumed control of the White House after eight years of Republican rule. The significance of Kennedy's China record for our discussion is twofold. First, Johnson's self-image as the custodian of JFK's legacy at home and abroad and his considerable regard for the views of the slain President's staff warrants a more than cursory glance at Camelot's approach to China; the overlap in senior national security personnel and their perceptions between the Democratic administrations of the 1960s was truly unique. JFK inherited a frozen Sino-American relationship plagued by mutual mistrust and antagonism, sealed in blood by the agonizing stalemate of the Korean War. Kennedy's advent to power inspired anticipation in some quarters that a new, presumably forward-looking team would advance fresh initiatives toward the mainland. The Kennedy years ultimately provided little basis for such high hopes. China policy during this time remained faithful to the line of containment and isolation that had governed America's posture since the founding of the PRC, in large part a product of both JFK's political caution and of his profound suspicion of the communist regime. This resistance to policy reform occurred amidst agitation for a reappraisal of attitudes from several mid-level officials and their sponsors. The proposals and rationale for change articulated by this camp, a second reason for the devotion of a chapter to this period, intermittently won the interest of members of Kennedy's entourage and adumbrated the modest innovations of the Johnson years.

This chapter begins with a very broad overview of America's halting engagement in China prior to the 1960s; a long-term perspective provides context to the breakdown in Sino-American contacts following the communists' victory in 1949 and insight into the prevailing Cold War mindset of US decision-makers. Attention then turns to China policy-making during the Kennedy years. The administration's handling of Chinese representation in the United Nations (UN), food relief, and Beijing's nuclear weapons program is covered in some detail, each case study illustrative of both the wide spectrum of official opinion on China and the well-entrenched aversion to policy reform at the highest levels of government.

America's approach to China, pre-1961

Almost from the inception of the American republic, China – vast, mysterious, ancient – loomed large in the imagination of merchants eager to tap into its fabled markets and missionaries in search of new converts. Springing from an idealized faith in the American experience as a model to the outside world, for long a central tenet of US foreign policy thinking, these groups viewed their activities on the mainland in largely altruistic terms, as beneficial to China's economic and spiritual well-being. This rather condescending notion of American goodwill and Chinese gratitude proved enduring, attracting adherents among the public at large and successive generations of US leaders.[1] Yet the considerable gap between rhetoric and reality would have momentous long-term consequences. The US government never shared the enthusiasm of trading and religious communities for extensive engagement in China; Washington's often hollow professions of friendship contributed in no small part to Chinese disillusionment with their "patron." The false comfort provided by the assumption of a "special relationship" blinded US decision-makers to many of these grievances for over a century, thus exacerbating their sense of betrayal when the intensely nationalistic Chinese communists assumed power in 1949 with the intent of reversing a long record of international humiliation.

The modern history of US officialdom's involvement in China can be dated to the last decade of the nineteenth century, when a host of economic and strategic factors compelled Washington to extend greater support to the American community on the mainland than it had hitherto contemplated. The closing of America's famed frontier and a concurrent economic depression stirred interest in finding foreign markets for the country's burgeoning industrial output. As attention increasingly turned abroad, the opportunity for commerce across the Pacific seemed to be narrowing as the predatory Europeans and Japanese carved the crumbling Chinese empire into spheres of influence and established discriminatory trading privileges in their respective zones. This imperialist activity in turn alarmed those officials who viewed a sovereign China as essential to a functioning balance of power in Asia, an important consideration in the wake of acquiring the Philippines during the Spanish-American War.[2]

The McKinley administration's response, a series of Open Door notes issued in 1899–1900 appealing for the respect of equal trading rights in the country for all nations, would subsequently be hailed as further evidence of America's friendship for the hapless Chinese. In truth the policy was narrowly conceived, undertaken without consulting the presumed beneficiary, and solely aimed at safeguarding US commercial interests at minimal cost. Recognizing their finite capacity for projecting power or influence on the Asian mainland, the authors of the Open Door never envisioned using, or even invoking the threat of, force in defending their access to China's markets.[3] As an articulation of Washington's heightened interest in mainland developments and as another example of a new willingness to play a role on the world stage more commensurate with US economic might, the Open Door initiative was noteworthy. Measured as a departure from the traditionally aloof posture toward China, however, its impact was less dramatic. As they had since the Opium Wars of the 1840s, US officials looked at China's persistent vulnerability with some scorn and resisted the efforts of Chinese authorities to recruit them as allies against the encroachments of the imperialist powers.[4]

Its disdain for the machinations of the Great Powers notwithstanding, Washington's reluctance to play a more assertive role in Chinese affairs was reflective of a sense that US interests in the region were not of an order that mandated a major commitment of resources. This calculation remained unchanged as Japan's influence in Asia soared following its victory over Russia in 1904–05. As Tokyo pressed its claims on Manchuria, successive American administrations effectively stood aside. The appeasement of Japan reached a culmination in the 1930s when its designs on China took on a blatantly belligerent character. Preoccupation with an economic crisis at home certainly conditioned Franklin Roosevelt's unwillingness to contest Japanese aggression, yet this non-interventionist stance also comported with a long-standing inclination to concede Tokyo's dominance over its neighbor. The simultaneous challenge posed by Nazi Germany, moreover, struck policymakers as considerably more worrisome and was further cause for the diversion of attention from events across the Pacific. It was only when British and French possessions in Southeast Asia came under attack and Tokyo allied itself more formally with Hitler's empire in the fall of 1940 that the Roosevelt team shifted course and applied increasingly greater economic pressure against Tokyo, seeing the outcome of Sino-Japanese hostilities as tied to the all-important struggle in Europe. Even then, the President's advisers were sharply divided over how far Japan could be squeezed without precipitating an irrational response; all agreed that the objective was deterrence rather than participation in the Asian conflict.[5]

While the attack on Pearl Harbor served as the immediate catalyst for America's entry into the global struggle, Hitler's almost simultaneous declaration of war against Washington spared the administration the unpalatable obligation of satiating a ravenously anti-Japanese public with an Asia-first policy. It was in Europe where US elites continued to believe their most vital interests were at stake and where the configuration of the post-war order would be determined. China's fight against the hated Japanese evoked considerable sympathy from the US public, yet beneath the surface familiar dynamics dashed the hopes of both sides for greater Sino-American cohesion. FDR's intermittent musings on the mainland's role as one of the "Four Policemen" in a post-war settlement, resting in part on the complacent belief that an indebted China would faithfully support the US position, were tempered by doubts of the viability of Chiang Kai-shek's Nationalist regime. Most Americans serving in the region during the Second World War regarded Chiang with barely disguised contempt, seeing him primarily as an incompetent autocrat more preoccupied with vanquishing Mao Zedong's Chinese Communist Party (CCP) than with repulsing the Japanese. Having welcomed Pearl Harbor as his salvation, Chiang was soon disappointed with the Roosevelt administration's apparent neglect of his needs and irritated by Washington's attempts to condition greater aid on a more vigorous Chinese war effort.[6]

Like their predecessors, leading officials of the new Truman administration took notice of developments in China only when viewing them in a wider context. Whereas the scenario of Japan's control of Chinese resources had excited concern in the early 1940s, the spectre of Soviet preponderance in the region after the Second World War occasioned Washington's halting engagement in Chinese affairs.[7] The overriding objective of President Truman and his advisers during the Chinese civil war was not so much providing what aid they could to Chiang's discredited regime as preventing the Soviets from exploiting CCP gains in North China. To this end, Truman dispatched General George Marshall to China in late 1945 to arrange a cease-fire between the Nationalists and communists and to organize a coalition government under Chiang's authority. The Generalissimo's obstinacy and insistence on fighting Mao's forces infuriated Marshall, who returned home from his failed mission believing that Chiang's actions would only drive China into ruin. When he assumed his new role as Secretary of State in January 1947, Marshall was inclined to avoid a program of major military assistance to the Nationalists that would only divert scarce resources from more vital Cold War theaters in Europe and the Middle East and possibly encourage a more active Soviet role in the conflict on behalf of the CCP. Convinced that a communist victory in China would redound to the Kremlin's advantage, however, and with an eye toward pro-Nationalist sentiment in Congress and the media, he could not contemplate a complete American withdrawal. It was hoped that limited aid would avoid the pitfalls of an open-ended commitment and maximize US leverage over the headstrong Chiang.[8]

When Dean Acheson succeeded Marshall in January 1949, few believed that the Nationalist cause could be salvaged. Yet the increasing likelihood of a CCP-led China in and of itself was not seen as a crippling blow to US security. Acheson sympathized with the view expressed by George Kennan, head of the State Department's Policy Planning Council, that the political orientation of this relatively insignificant nation mattered "only as a possible adjunct of Soviet politico-military power." Rather than investing all of their energy into preventing or overthrowing a communist regime, many of Truman's closest aides insisted that the US should instead direct its attention to driving a wedge between Stalin and Mao.[9] Once Chiang's forces had been driven off the mainland and relocated to Taiwan, Acheson sought to manage the administration's disengagement from China's internal conflict. The Secretary persuaded Truman in early 1950 to forgo any military responsibilities for the protection of Taiwan, knowing full well that the communists would eventually assume control of the island; intervention in China's civil war would only galvanize Chinese opinion against the US and undermine any chances of fostering discord between the Soviet Union and Mao's new regime.[10] Some historians have discerned in Acheson's prudent conduct a tacit wish for an accommodation with the PRC, a lofty aim that was derailed only by subsequent fighting in Korea.[11]

More recently, scholars with access to Chinese documents have convincingly debunked the notion of a "lost chance" for an early reconciliation between Washington and Beijing. Acutely suspicious of American intentions toward the PRC, intent on maintaining the internal momentum of the revolution, and in search of security ties with the Soviets, Mao and his comrades were not inclined to reciprocate any US overture.[12] Yet it is also apparent that the Truman team's interest in disentangling themselves from the Chinese morass did not translate into any coherent policy of offering olive branches to their Chinese counterparts or bargaining with them in an even-handed manner. Deluged by stinging criticism from Chiang's vocal supporters at home for having "lost" China to the communists in the fall of 1949, US decision-makers would have found it exceedingly difficult to sustain any domestic consensus for a conciliatory approach to the PRC.[13] Moreover, most senior officials thought that the US need not rush into meeting the People's Republic half-way. His sporadic contemplation of recognition and limited trade notwithstanding, Acheson was susceptible to the traditional view of the Chinese as a backward people in perpetual need of American largesse and rather arrogantly assumed that the US had ample leverage over the communists. It was taken for granted that China's new leadership would be faced with myriad economic difficulties, forcing them to turn to America for assistance that the USSR could not hope to provide. As historian Melvyn Leffler has aptly noted, this was "not a strategy of accommodation ... it was infused with ideological antipathy and designed to force the Chinese Communists to appear as supplicants."[14] Attitudes toward Beijing hardened with the signing of the Sino-Soviet alliance in February 1950. Concluding that Mao had cast his lot with the Kremlin, frustrated Truman officials held that only an unyielding US posture would compel him to see the error of his ways.[15]

The consequences of the Truman team's disregard for Chinese sensitivities and capabilities were felt most profoundly on the Korean peninsula. In light of what is now known about Mao's strong inclination to send troops to Korea, Washington's failure to anticipate this contingency is striking.[16] Even before General MacArthur's successful counter-offensive against North Korean forces in September 1950, senior US authorities found the idea of a military thrust across the thirty-eighth parallel intoxicating. Overthrowing the communist regime in Pyongyang and unifying all of Korea under pro-Western leadership, many of the President's civilian and military aides posited, would remove the lingering threat of another communist attack against Seoul and, more importantly, deal a decisive setback to the Kremlin's ambitions in Asia while deterring Soviet-inspired aggression elsewhere. Those with misgivings about a move to cross the parallel warned that Moscow might feel its eastern flank sufficiently threatened to join the fray. Curiously, it was not believed that China's leadership would be unduly alarmed by a military operation against their neighbor and ideological kin. The PRC was thought too weak and wrenched by internal turmoil to counter any US action against North Korea. Reverting to the long-held view of China as little more than a pawn of Great Power rivalry, Washington concluded that a bid by the Chinese to rescue North Korea would only come at the behest of Moscow. Thus once it was assumed that the Kremlin did not think its relatively limited interests in Korea were worth the risk of a potential world war, the administration felt empowered to strike north.[17]

Coming on the heels of the CCP's ascension to power, Beijing's entry into the Korean War in November 1950 triggered profound outrage among Americans. The ensuing stalemate on the battlefield crystallized a popular image of the Chinese communists as a bloodthirsty adversary and transformed what had hitherto been a vocal yet loose and relatively small coalition of politicians, journalists, businessmen, and missionaries calling for increased aid to the Nationalists into a formidable lobbying machine. General indifference among the public to Chiang's fortunes gave way to widespread support for his regime, even enthusiasm for the idea of assisting a Nationalist assault on the mainland. When pressing for the eschewal of political or economic ties to the PRC and firm opposition to the communists' admission to the UN, the China Lobby was consistently buttressed by public opinion polls. Anti-Chinese sentiment could not be ignored by US decision-makers during the 1950s or forgotten by the Democratic administrations of the 1960s, even as elements of Congress and the press gradually came to voice misgivings over Washington's intransigent position.[18]

Aside from stirring popular resentment and boosting Chiang's lobbying efforts in the US, Beijing's actions dramatically magnified Washington's antagonistic interpretation of Chinese intentions.[19] The immediate impact of Korea on China policy was to accelerate and deepen a process of hardening already under way. Officials at Foggy Bottom had briefly toyed with the idea of offering limited trade and aid to the PRC before settling on a more restrictive embargo against strategic materials in late 1949. China's intervention triggered an altogether less nuanced response, a total international economic embargo to punish its behavior and hamper its performance on the battlefield.[20] Infinitely more offensive to Beijing was the administration's move to order the Seventh Fleet into the Taiwan Strait.[21] While designed to head off an expansion of the Korean conflict by discouraging both the communists and Nationalists from attacking the other, this action occurred against the backdrop of growing US hostility toward the PRC. A number of officials in both the State and Defense departments had questioned Acheson's apparent complacency over Taiwan's fate throughout the spring of 1950 and examined means by which the island could be defended against a takeover by the mainland. The Seventh Fleet decision reflected the strategic and politico-psychological value that US policymakers assigned to the preservation of a non-communist Taiwan.[22] Washington's expanded commitment to this objective in the wake of Korea yielded a concerted campaign to safeguard Taipei's hold on the China seat at the UN while preventing Beijing's membership in that organization.[23]

The broad parameters of the policy of containment and isolation remained intact during the Eisenhower years. As with so many other facets of this administration's foreign policy, however, its approach to the PRC was not nearly as rigid and dogmatic as its harsh rhetoric suggested.[24] To be sure, Secretary of State John Foster Dulles authorized the purge of several China hands and assigned high-profile Asian posts at Foggy Bottom to ardent supporters of Chiang, yet much of this posturing was not so much an indicator of his personal convictions as it was a shrewd effort to protect his right flank from the feared China Lobby and avoid the political fate of the much-maligned Acheson.[25] And while both President Eisenhower and Dulles valued Taiwan as a bastion of anti-communism in Asia, they were persistently suspicious of what they regarded as Chiang's duplicitous attempts to entangle the US in a fanciful scheme to return to the mainland. After stalling on Taipei's repeated requests for a mutual defense treaty, the administration finally relented in the fall of 1954 during the first offshore islands crisis, yet not without first covertly securing the Generalissimo's pledge to seek American approval of any major assault on the PRC. The Eisenhower team's attempts to contain Chiang's adventurism reflected their wish for a peaceful and stable Asia, which would enable them to concentrate their resources and attention on Europe. It was also an implicit recognition that Mao's regime, however unsavory, was a fact of life. Eisenhower and Dulles were ultimately willing to acquiesce in a "two Chinas" arrangement, perhaps to be recognized formally by the UN.[26]

A review of the documentary record has also revealed that, contrary to impressions at the time, Eisenhower officials were sensitive to signs of Sino-Soviet tension and sought to exploit these to their advantage. Seen in this light, the administration's reluctance to alter the inherited line of containment and isolation has struck some historians as a deliberate strategic ploy rather than a manifestation of knee-jerk anti-communism. As Dulles explained to one skeptic, "the best way to get a separation between the Soviet Union and Communist China is to keep pressure on Communist China and make its way difficult so long as it is in partnership with Soviet Russia. Tito did not break with Stalin because we were nice to Tito ... It seems to me that if China can win our favors while she is also working closely with Moscow, then there is little reason for her to change."[27] According to this logic, a "closed door" policy would increase Beijing's dependency on Moscow for its security. When the Soviets proved unwilling or unable to help, the two allies would become increasingly estranged from one another.[28] Even more intriguingly, Eisenhower periodically voiced misgivings with this approach and wondered if the Chinese could instead be lured away from the Soviets by the promise of trade. While political considerations at home precluded any modification of the US economic embargo, the President acquiesced in the decisions of some allies to relax trade restrictions against the mainland.[29]

This stark dichotomy between nuanced perceptions and uncompromising official pronouncements was lost on most contemporary observers: domestic critics, exasperated allies, and, most importantly, the Chinese. Scarred by the political bloodletting over the "loss" of China, the Eisenhower administration discerned few advantages in departing from post-Korea China policy and chose to project unambiguous resolve. Yet Eisenhower's militancy cannot be solely attributed to crude political calculations. The President and the Secretary evidently shared the intense animosity toward Beijing that the traumatic experience of Korea had engendered among most Americans. At the heart of their distaste for the PRC was the sense that Mao and his comrades were implacable revolutionaries who sought to overturn the regional status quo. This image crystallized in the latter half of the 1950s as US decision-makers pursued détente with the Soviet Union, giving rise to unfavorable comparisons between the perceived prudence of their counterparts in the Kremlin and the bellicose Chinese.[30] Eisenhower and Dulles worked to build positions of strength and to "create a regional Asia Pacific structure in which American advantages would be maximized while China's role and opportunities would be dramatically curtailed."[31]

Thus a "closed door" policy, besides preserving harmony within the Republican Party, served as a tool of coercion, designed to secure any eventual reconciliation with China strictly on American terms by withholding recognition and trade until the Chinese had learned how to "behave." The consequences of this heavy-handedness were considerable. Eisenhower's brinkmanship during the 1954–55 offshore islands crisis, particularly his threat to utilize America's nuclear arsenal, alarmed China's leadership and played no small role in their decision to acquire the bomb.[32] The administration's refusal to compromise its ties to Taiwan most likely contributed to the radical orientation of China's foreign policy in the late 1950s. After the inconclusive outcome of the 1954–55 crisis, Beijing shifted course and announced that it was willing to resolve Taiwan's status by peaceful means. The objective of sowing discord between Washington and Taipei remained unchanged, yet Mao now hoped to elicit US concessions on Taiwan by presenting a more conciliatory face.[33] The Chairman's disillusionment with this stillborn initiative, most notably the failure to achieve a constructive dialogue with the Americans at the ambassadorial talks launched in Geneva in August 1955, fed his growing opposition to Nikita Khrushchev's pursuit of détente with the US. Mao found the idea of Soviet collusion with an adversary that continued to obstruct his dream of reunification both unconscionable and unsettling.[34] Eisenhower bequeathed to his successor a tense Sino-American relationship that was nearly as prone to confrontation as it had been eight years earlier.

Camelot looks at China: "two Chinas" derailed

As the Kennedy team prepared to assume the reins of power in January 1961, speculation abounded that there would be a concerted attempt to reverse this grim state of affairs.[35] Part of this impression, no doubt, can be attributed to the successful efforts of the charismatic leader and his aides to project a veneer of dynamism and openness to innovation, an image that was only magnified by the seeming drabness of the departing Eisenhower administration. Long after the young President's assassination, his apologists insisted that, despite a record suggesting the contrary, Kennedy would have used a second term in office to forge new approaches to the PRC.[36] Expectations of new China initiatives were fuelled as well by the fact that several prominent members of the incoming administration, namely Adlai Stevenson (who was named ambassador to the UN) and Chester Bowles (appointed as the Undersecretary of State), had expressed impatience with existing strategy toward the mainland. While no less susceptible to alarmist interpretations of Chinese behavior than Eisenhower officials, they contended that an emphasis on isolating Beijing had alienated allied opinion and foreclosed any possibility, however remote, of arriving at a mutual understanding with the PRC. Both believed that the effective containment of China required the cooperation of regional partners, which could only be secured by discarding the more rigid and unpalatable elements of US policy and shifting the blame for Sino-American hostility. With precisely this consideration in mind, Stevenson and Bowles found much to recommend in adopting a "two Chinas" position at the UN (whereby both Beijing and Taipei would be offered a seat).[37]

John Kennedy was neither politically nor ideologically predisposed toward policy departures as he entered office. For reasons owing to a combination of conviction, the need to distance himself from his father's controversial isolationist views, and a desire to advance his political standing on a national level, JFK had consistently advocated the vigorous containment of international communism throughout his congressional career.[38] As a Democratic congressman in 1949, he immediately recognized the political opportunities that the triumph of the CCP presented to Republicans and the pitfalls associated with appearing "soft" toward the new regime. To insulate himself from the resultant political firestorm, Kennedy joined the throng of those condemning the Truman administration and the State Department's Sinologists for "selling out" the Nationalists.[39] His instinctive caution on China could only have been reinforced by his slender margin of victory in the 1960 presidential election; the new President reportedly carried a slip of paper bearing the small plurality of 118,574 votes as a constant reminder of his limited room for maneuver.[40]

Moreover, Kennedy had based much of his campaign on the premise that America needed fresh leadership to regain the initiative in the Cold War. While his promises to "pay any price, bear any burden" in stemming further communist advances were stirring enough, they had the unfortunate side effect of narrowing his options in foreign policy, as a premium was placed on demonstrating firmness and resolve abroad.[41] Parting words from Eisenhower during the transition in January 1961 may well have contributed significantly to the new administration's trepidacious approach toward experimentation in the China policy sphere. Whether Eisenhower in fact warned his successor that he would come out of political retirement should the PRC be recognized or seated in the UN remains somewhat uncertain,[42] although Kennedy frequently referred to this threat in conversations with foreign leaders.[43] In later years, his Secretary of State, Dean Rusk, left no doubt that political considerations dominated the President's thinking on China. He recalled in his memoirs a private meeting in May 1961, during which Kennedy alluded to his "razor-thin victory" as a factor militating against a change in policy. "Fearing the issue might divide Congress and the American people," Rusk wrote, "he decided the potential benefits of a more realistic China policy didn't warrant risking a severe political confrontation."[44]

If political timidity constituted a major impediment to policy reform during the Kennedy years, so too did high-level hostility toward the Chinese communists. Indeed, Kennedy's concerns about a Chinese menace predated his ascension to the Oval Office. A tour of Southeast Asia in the early 1950s left an indelible impression, alerting him to the opportunities afforded to Chinese penetration by the region's social and economic maladies. The young congressman subsequently developed an enduring fascination with strategies of counterinsurgency and the cultivation of non-communist elites.[45] As a Senator, Kennedy tenaciously lobbied for aid to democratic India, maintaining that the outcome of its "development contest" with China would go some way in determining what political and economic model would prevail in the Third World.[46] JFK's sense that an East–West struggle for the allegiance of the developing world would be one of the defining foreign policy challenges of his presidency was confirmed by a speech Khrushchev delivered on 6 January 1961, in which the Soviet Premier declared his support for "wars of liberation or national uprisings." Kennedy anticipated a stepped-up communist effort to infiltrate those nations struggling to emerge from colonial rule or that had just attained independence.[47]

Suspicions of China's role in Asian wars of national liberation were rampant within Kennedy's inner circle.[48] The early months of Kennedy's presidency coincided with what US analysts recognized as a period of acute economic upheaval in China, as the country coped with the disasters wrought by Mao's Great Leap Forward.[49] Somewhat paradoxically, however, it was judged that the mainland's internal troubles did not diminish the threat it posed to its neighbors. A November 1961 Special National Intelligence Estimate defined the Chinese challenge as primarily politico-psychological in nature, asserting that the country's rulers eschewed overtly confrontational tactics and sought instead to expand their influence abroad "at far less cost and risk through the techniques of Communist political warfare." Rather than engage the Americans or their Asian allies directly, the Chinese provided materiel assistance and guidance to local communist forces seeking to overthrow Western-backed regimes.[50] Believing that these movements took their inspiration from Beijing, Kennedy encouraged his aides to read Mao's writings on revolution and guerrilla warfare.[51]

Impressions of China were colored as well by evidence of growing Sino-Soviet friction. While the administration's initial assessments of the schism tended to err on the side of caution, officials even at this early stage interpreted the dispute as arising out of clashing worldviews. One of the intelligence community's first overviews of the global outlook for the Kennedy team predicted that the Kremlin would "stick to its present policy of seeking to win victories without incurring serious risks, and of alternating or combining shows of anger and bellicosity with poses of reasonableness and compromise ... [and] a recognition of some areas of common interest with the West." The PRC, by contrast, could be expected to press for "a more militant bloc policy" and oppose moves toward détente.[52] According to this view, which had been prevalent among Eisenhower officials, the Soviet Union had evolved into a mature power that accepted the inadmissibility of war in a nuclear age and sought regulated superpower competition.[53]

Haunted by memories of China's intervention in Korea and repelled by the mainland's reversion to a radical line in foreign policy by the end of the 1950s, US policymakers were struck by Mao's apparent indifference to the implications of his bellicose rhetoric. As

George Kennan, the eminent Kremlinologist recruited by JFK to be his ambassador to Yugoslavia, remarked, "We have much more difficult problems with the Chinese than with the Russians. The latter have much more in common with Western civilization."[54] Beijing's uncompromising public posture in early 1961 only exacerbated Kennedy's inherent distaste for China's leadership. It seemed that "the Chinese Communists were just as hostile to the new administration as they were to the old, and were attacking him personally already," he complained to New Zealand's Prime Minister Keith Holyoake. "Their attitude indicated that they did not wish to be on better terms with us but preferred to maintain an intransigeant [sic] position."[55] Kennedy's sense that the PRC represented the more dangerous and unpredictable of the communist giants sharpened over time, to the extent that he hoped to foster the Kremlin's interest in containing its nominal ally.

Kennedy's first sustained engagement with China policy in 1961 illustrated the primacy of domestic political considerations in the decision-making process. Washington's success in isolating the mainland throughout the 1950s rested in large part on mobilizing sufficient international support. This had often been secured by grudgingly tolerating its allies' interests in establishing economic contacts with Beijing "in exchange for [their] adherence to a policy seen as more vital – that of non-recognition and support of Taiwan in the United Nations."[56] The Eisenhower administration deferred consideration of any motion to unseat Taipei and admit Beijing as the sole Chinese representative by offering a moratorium resolution when the issue came up for debate each year. By 1961, however, the proliferation of newly independent African nations and allied impatience with American rigidity had rendered this approach almost untenable.[57] Rusk, Stevenson, and Bowles recognized the pressing need for a shift in tactics if Taiwan was to retain its UN membership.[58]

One of the more ambitious efforts to provide a strategic rationale for a new policy on Chinese representation came from Robert Komer, a senior aide to National Security Adviser McGeorge Bundy. Like most officials in the new administration, Komer did not foresee any relaxation of Sino-American hostility in the near term; Beijing's inherent need for an external bogeyman around which to rally domestic support for the regime would continue to stand as the primary obstacle to a new era in relations. All the more reason, then, for softening the harsher edges of America's posture toward China. Komer pinpointed Washington's reliance on the moratorium procedure as a decidedly contentious matter among allied capitals, who for long had accepted the PRC as a legitimate political entity deserving of UN membership. Demonstrating moderation on this question would prove particularly useful in appeasing sentiment in India and Japan, whose cooperation was deemed critical for the long-term containment of China.[59] As Komer framed the stakes for Kennedy, adopting a "two Chinas" stance was "not just one of our acceding to the inevitable ... but of using greater flexibility on the UN issue to secure greater Free World support for preserving the GRC [Government of the Republic of China – Taiwan]."[60]

The President's concerns were more parochial. He confided to British Prime Minister Harold Macmillan that "it would be best from our standpoint if Red China were not admitted this year ... from a purely domestic political point of view it did not look good for a new administration to have allowed Chinese Communist admission so soon." The problem, as he saw it, was to "find a formula for keeping them from wanting to get in."[61] Rusk addressed the latter point in a memorandum he prepared for Kennedy at the end of May. Arguing that the moratorium was no longer a viable option and that a majority in the General Assembly would vote to admit Beijing over Taipei as the occupant of a single China seat if presented with such a stark choice, the Secretary advanced "two Chinas" as a solution to the administration's problem. It would most likely "result in the continued exclusion of the Chinese Communists[,] who have been strongly opposed to a "Two Chinas" concept. It should also serve to shift the onus for their exclusion [from the UN] to the Chinese Communists themselves."[62] Betraying his persistent fears of a domestic backlash, Kennedy tentatively endorsed the idea, but insisted that the US "should not take the lead" in guiding such a motion through the UN and that "a good discussion with key political figures in the US" was required before a final decision could be made. He worried that an aggressive push for the measure could "adversely affect the foreign aid bill and other objectives of his Administration."[63]

Kennedy's lukewarm support for a "two Chinas" approach was soon shaken by his reading of domestic and international developments in the summer of 1961. There seemed to be little indication that US acquiescence in such a formula would receive support at home. Rumors of an impending change in UN policy yielded a unanimous Senate resolution opposing any variant of "two Chinas."[64] Public opinion was barely more receptive; a Gallup poll taken in September revealed a majority of 65 percent against the PRC's admission to the world body, with only 18 percent in favor.[65] Moreover, deliberations over Chinese representation occurred against the backdrop of a particularly troubling period for Kennedy's foreign policy leadership. The humiliating failure at the Bay of Pigs, the retreat in Laos, Khrushchev's harsh treatment of the President at the Vienna summit, and his brandishing of the Berlin ultimatum all instilled in Kennedy an acute aversion to another diplomatic debacle. In this context, he was concerned that US acquiescence in a move to seat Beijing, even if it was expected to fail and prolong the status quo in the UN, might convey an image of weakness. "Such a success for the Communists – when we face them in Southeast Asia and Berlin," he remarked, "would give impetus to their prestige at a difficult and important time for us. It would be a very damaging blow to United States prestige."[66] Nor could discordant noises from Taipei be ignored. Bundy reported to JFK in early July that "the Chinese Nationalists are more disturbed about their relation to the US than at any time in the past five years." In part the product of Taiwan's bias toward presumably friendlier Republicans, Bundy noted that suspicions had also been stirred by the possibility of US support for a "two Chinas" resolution. Ominously, he speculated that Chiang's disenchantment could trigger "dangerous adventures ... up to and including a suicidal landing on the mainland."[67]

Attention soon turned to finding a less unpalatable alternative. At a White House meeting in late July, the President and his senior aides decided to push for an "important question" formula, which would raise the bar substantially higher for the mainland's admission to the UN by requiring a two-thirds majority vote in the General Assembly.[68] The motion passed by a comfortable margin in December. Even more momentous was Chiang's success in securing from Kennedy a secret pledge to use the American veto if necessary to prevent Beijing's entry.[69] JFK's willingness to grant what his predecessor had refused stemmed from the need to discourage the Generalissimo from sabotaging Outer Mongolia's admission to the UN, a move which would have triggered similar Soviet action against Mauritania's simultaneous bid for membership and a wave of French African resentment against the Nationalists.[70]

Kennedy's ambivalent flirtation with "two Chinas," his opting for the "important question" measure, and the secret veto pledge were all determined by the same factor that had poisoned Sino-American relations for over a decade: a fierce resistance to compromising the alliance with Taipei. Agitation for a change in UN tactics had been propelled only by the sense that Taiwan's hold on the China seat could no longer be secured by traditional methods. It was assumed by the President and his aides that "two Chinas" would be spurned by Beijing, thereby safeguarding Taiwan's status and shifting the blame for the mainland's isolation away from the US. In short, any contemplated departures from long-standing China policy at this time were, as Noam Kochavi has observed, "undertaken chiefly for reasons other than seeking to bring about a rapprochement with the PRC."[71] Kennedy's deference to perceived public sentiment and his persistent hostility to Mao's regime, so fundamental to his China mindset at the outset of his presidency, derailed even this defensive initiative and would continue to define the parameters of his China policy.

Stillborn initiative: food for China

A horrific famine on the mainland, largely induced by the Great Leap's utopian effort to expedite China's economic development through mass mobilization, introduced new strains into the Kennedy team's already prickly relationship with Taipei and was occasion for further consideration of a new approach to Beijing. Reports of China's domestic crisis, which peaked in 1960–61, only whetted Chiang's appetite for a military landing across the Taiwan Strait. In separate meetings with Roger Hilsman, Director of State's bureau of Intelligence and Research (INR), and Averell Harriman, Assistant Secretary of State for Far Eastern Affairs, in March 1962, he conveyed his impression that recent events afforded a unique opportunity to exploit popular discontent with the CCP and advance his dream of reunification. The Generalissimo assured Hilsman that the administration's role in a military operation need not be substantial, asking only for its "tacit consent to this course of action plus covert logistic support."[72] US officials were hardly convinced. Intelligence reports agreed that mass suffering and resentment were widespread on the mainland, yet even these miserable conditions were not seen as conducive to a GRC attack or a popular rebellion; the regime's monopoly on the country's instruments of coercion would enable it to ride through the current storm with little threat to its rule.[73]

Haunted by the Bay of Pigs fiasco, Kennedy harbored no thoughts of acquiescing, let alone participating, in any adventure to overthrow the PRC. Like Truman and Eisenhower, JFK's unstinting political and diplomatic solidarity with Taiwan did not translate into any unqualified backing for its wilder ambitions. Yet Chiang's perceived capriciousness seemed to dictate an ambiguous reply from the administration, lest an outright refusal of his request triggered an irrational response.[74] During a meeting with Central Intelligence Agency (CIA) Director John McCone, the President inquired "what Chiang would do if he were told flatly that the United States would not support him in any military operation against the Mainland. It was agreed that Chiang might then 'go it alone.'"[75] Accordingly, the White House directed its envoys to handle the Generalissimo's probes evasively, gently reminding him to honor his obligations to consult with the US before opting for an attack.[76]

The administration's studied ambiguity became increasingly difficult to sustain, as Beijing grew alarmed over Taiwan's thinly veiled intentions. In June 1962, more than 100,000 Chinese troops were deployed to the coast to prepare for the contingency of a Nationalist assault. While a vocal minority of US officials interpreted the maneuver as a possible prelude to a Chinese strike on the offshore islands, Kennedy's inner circle concluded that Mao's actions were primarily defensive.[77] They determined that defusing yet another crisis in the Taiwan Strait depended, as it had before, on alerting the PRC's leadership to America's readiness to repel aggression against Taiwan or its offshore possessions. More importantly, however, the Kennedy team also moved to disabuse China of its impression of US hostility by utilizing a variety of diplomatic channels at their disposal. Through the Soviets and British, Washington signalled that it had no intention of supporting an attack on the mainland.[78] Ambassador John Moors Cabot relayed the same message to the Chinese during an exchange at the ongoing ambassadorial talks in Warsaw, highlighting the significance of this forum as a tool of crisis management.[79]

A nuanced reading of Beijing's intentions and sensitivity to its security concerns contributed handsomely to the administration's resolution of the affair. Some officials interpreted China's relatively prudent conduct during the brief crisis as evidence that the regime had been chastened by the severe economic fallout from the Great Leap. Hilsman speculated in July 1962 that these conditions "may well encourage it to focus on domestic concerns and contribute to the adoption of a more moderate line in foreign policy during the 1960s."[80] There was in fact some indication that elements of the

Chinese hierarchy supported such a course. In a conversation with a senior British diplomat that same month, the contents of which were forwarded to Washington, Foreign Minister Chen Yi explained that his government "wants international peace so that it may be left free to get on with the vast tasks of improving the people's standard of living and of national development ... since they must mobilize all their resources for internal development, they do not want to get involved in any wars, big or small."[81] Chen's remarks had been foreshadowed the previous summer by Ambassador Wang Bingnan in Warsaw, when a conciliatory appeal for a modus vivendi of sorts was issued to his American counterpart.[82] US analysts had viewed this overture with some suspicion, thinking it nothing more than a public relations ploy or perhaps another effort to exacerbate tensions between Washington and Taipei.[83] Rusk authorized the embassy in Warsaw to reciprocate Wang's sentiment, yet the refusal of either side to discuss concessions over Taiwan failed to produce a breakthrough.[84]

Nevertheless, these hints of Chinese moderation were seized on by a handful of Kennedy officials as an opportunity for modifying America's economic embargo against the PRC. The most persistent members of this camp were Chester Bowles and Walt Rostow, who became head of State's Policy Planning Council (PPC) in November 1961 after briefly serving as Bundy's deputy. While they pressed their case without any apparent coordination, both shared "a rather expansive sense of China's susceptibility to American power and solution."[85] The core of their argument was that Beijing's grave troubles, more specifically its dire shortage of food, could be used as a source of US leverage over Chinese behavior. Despite "Chicom [Chinese Communist] verbal toughness," Rostow wrote the President, "they are in such bad trouble at home ... that they may be seeking a limited accommodation with the West." He suggested that the administration exploit its position of strength and consider offering grain to the mainland in exchange for a curtailment of its subversive activity in Laos and Vietnam.[86]

A similar recommendation for lifting restrictions on the sale of foodstuffs and medicines appeared in a major October 1961 study authored by Edward Rice, a mid-level China hand at the PPC who had somewhat miraculously emerged unscathed from the McCarthyite purges of the 1950s. Unlike Bowles and Rostow, he believed America's capacity for shaping events in China was limited, yet the vast array of policy proposals outlined in his report were no less ambitious and were a source of inspiration to sympathizers throughout the administration.[87] Rice took as his starting point the idea that "the bulk of our China policy ... is related not to the mainland directly but to measures for the support and defense of the Free World countries and areas around China's periphery." By focusing solely on containment and isolation, previous administrations had made "no perceptible progress toward a Communist China with which we can live." In canvassing policy options, Rice rejected both a course of "maximum pressure," which promised only further to estrange the US from world opinion without effecting a commensurate decline in Chinese power, and one of "accommodation," which would be tantamount to an admission of defeat in a vital region of the world.

The most innovative feature of his call for a "new look" was the contention that demonstrating US flexibility and openness toward Beijing, besides tarring the Chinese in the eyes of the world with the charge of obstinacy (a consideration which had initially recommended "two Chinas" to JFK), held out the possibility of appealing to younger, pragmatic elements of China's ruling circle who had become accustomed to American hostility. The means by which long-term reconciliation with a new generation of leaders could be set in motion read like a shopping list of items that would be deliberated for the duration of the decade: the permission of trade in non-strategic goods, removal of the passport ban, avoidance of unnecessary provocations, disarmament talks, enhanced dialogue in Warsaw, and closer examination of the conditions under which non-recognition and Chinese exclusion from the UN could be reassessed.[88]

The advocates of food relief for China in 1961 were hampered by their minimal access to Kennedy or his most trusted aides. The senior rank of both Bowles and Rostow belied their inconsiderable influence on the foreign policymaking process and lack of rapport with their superiors.[89] When an idea for providing wheat to the PRC through Burmese intermediaries came up for discussion in November, it was struck down by the same considerations that had thwarted a new approach to Chinese representation. A State Department cable approved by Rusk asserted that the proposal was "bound to create an extremely sensitive political problem for this country." Furthermore, any food assistance was simply out of the question when Beijing appeared to be "splitting even from Moscow in pursuance of a more aggressive policy, and when our own contacts with the Chinese

Communist authorities show no indication or desire on their part to lessen the threat or reduce tensions" in Southeast Asia.[90] A meeting of National Security Council (NSC) staffers similarly dismissed any food program as too "politically risky."[91] A brief paper drafted by State's INR bureau in January 1962 highlighted the strategic drawbacks associated with any change in the economic embargo. It advised against an initiative at this time, as assistance at a moment of great peril for China might spare the regime from making difficult choices, such as diverting its expenditures from heavy industry and armaments to agriculture and restricting its regional activism. The implication here was that Chinese moderation would be best brought about by letting the country stew in its own juice.[92]

Ironically, Bowles and Rostow's cause was given something of a lease on life after a bureaucratic purge in November 1961 (the so-called "Thanksgiving Day Massacre"), of which they were the primary victims, Bowles losing the second most powerful post at Foggy Bottom for an ineffectual role as a roving ambassador and Rostow moving from the White House to the PPC.[93] With some consequence for China policy, one beneficiary of this changing of the guard was Averell Harriman, the formidable Washington power broker who had steadily gained Kennedy's trust. Elevated to head of the Far East bureau, he recruited Edward Rice as one of his deputies, thereby ensuring that revisionist thinking would get a fair hearing.[94] Indeed, Rice's appeal for cultivating more accommodating Chinese elites evidently resonated more among senior policymakers as they debated the merits of food assistance in the spring of 1962 than the Bowles-Rostow thesis that Chinese subversion could be tamed by the offer of food relief. By early April, general agreement within the State Department had been reached on using the Warsaw channel to inform the Chinese that Washington was willing to reconsider its embargo against the shipment of food grains if adequate supplies could not be secured elsewhere.[95] Harriman found much to recommend in the idea, as "Evidence that the US would be willing to play a part in moving our relationship away from one of implacable mutual hostility might strengthen the hand of any elements [in China] which might favor doing so, now or later."[96] This theme figured prominently in a briefing paper used by Rusk to discuss the subject with the President on 29 May.[97]

While Bowles' numerous memoranda on the advantages of food for China ensured that Kennedy had been exposed to this view, his own thoughts are difficult to trace. He may well have been favorably influenced by Michael Forrestal, who was appointed as an Asian hand on the NSC staff in early 1962. Forrestal's cordial relationship with both Kennedy and Harriman effectively "eased communications" between the Oval Office and the Far East bureau.[98] One may surmise that JFK acquiesced in State's proposal, as the embassy in Warsaw was alerted the day after his meeting with the Secretary that it might be instructed soon to raise the offer of food in a "normal and low-key manner" (thereby alleviating any Chinese suspicions that it was a propaganda ploy) at a future ambassador's session.[99]

This bridge-building gesture, the first of Kennedy's presidency, was soon overtaken by a confluence of external events. The sudden escalation of tensions in the Taiwan Strait in June distracted the attention of US decision-makers.[100] The sense that the moment might be ripe for sending a signal to certain factions of the CCP's hierarchy gave way to an acute hardening of attitudes. An especially significant catalyst for this shift in perception was China's mounting conflict with India, a country whose fate many in Washington, including the President, assumed would be decisive in determining the allegiance of much of the developing world.[101] Only a few weeks after endorsing the idea, Rusk doubted "how food from outside could have much effect on the general situation in China" and thought it would be "essential ... to have some indication from the Chinese communists that they were relaxing their tactics of pressure on India and elsewhere in order to get it through the Senate."[102] When a brief Sino-Indian war erupted in October, the Kennedy team's most alarmist preconceptions about China's belligerent and aggressive tendencies were corroborated. William Bundy, then working in the Pentagon, recalled the widespread impression, New Delhi's share of blame for the conflict notwithstanding, that "China was thrusting to become the dominant power in the area, that it had now shown considerable cohesion and capacity for sophisticated pressure-type action ... the central policy conclusion was reached ... that it was more than ever necessary to 'contain' Peking as a real threat."[103]

While the mainland's role in the simultaneous Cuban missile crisis was much less direct, senior US officials interpreted Beijing's vitriolic condemnation of Khrushchev for "capitulationism" in removing Soviet missiles from the island as further evidence of its recklessness. Some came to believe that the Kremlin had been goaded into action in the Caribbean by the militant influence of the Chinese.[104] These events made an indelible impression on Kennedy, who contrasted the Soviets' ultimate willingness to step away from the brink with China's seeming disregard for the utility of international compromise. "We would be far worse off," he concluded, "if the Chinese dominated the Communist movement, because they believe in war as a means of bringing about the Communist world."[105]

This resurgence of high-level animosity toward the PRC, following a brief reprieve occasioned by the imperative of conflict management in the Taiwan Strait and by the hope of nurturing potentially moderate factions disenchanted with Mao's failed Great Leap, not only relegated China policy reform to the backburner. It also spurred the President's obsession with pre-empting the mainland's acquisition of nuclear weaponry, a national security priority for which he was willing to work in concert with Moscow.

"A more dangerous situation than any we face": JFK contemplates a nuclear China

The notion of a Soviet-American identity of interests in checking Chinese ambitions had in fact been an article of faith for many US officials since the advent of the Kennedy administration. Barely settled into office, two of Kennedy's most senior advisers on Soviet affairs, George Kennan and Llewellyn Thompson, pressed him to develop relations with Moscow as a means of exacerbating Sino-Soviet tensions and encouraging the Kremlin's apparent drift from Beijing's hard-line. This same logic was repeated in several memoranda prepared for the President in the weeks leading up to his Vienna meeting with Khrushchev in June 1961.[106] The intelligence community agreed that the USSR was by far the more moderate and amenable of the two communist countries. A lengthy CIA report in April documented the steady decline in Sino-Soviet relations since the 1950s, attributing this major development in large part to sharp differences over how best to confront the US. Khrushchev's groping for détente with Washington had aroused Chinese suspicions of a superpower condominium working against their interests and ran counter to their insistence on a revolutionary offensive. The PRC's "adventurism," in turn, was viewed with some concern by the Soviets, who were decidedly reluctant to be drawn into unwanted conflicts. Despite the pressures straining the communist alliance, however, this report and others stopped short of predicting a definitive rupture. While

Sino-Soviet relations would remain cool and at times hostile for the foreseeable future, competition with the West mandated at least some semblance of cooperation.[107] Even as they closely followed the troubles plaguing the Sino-Soviet bloc, the Kennedy team were initially reluctant to acknowledge publicly the existence of a split or to tilt decisively in favor of either side, a caution borne out of uncertainty over the durability of the feud and apprehension that any American action might unwittingly prompt a reconciliation.[108]

The administration's passivity was increasingly challenged as new evidence pointed to an aggravation of the dispute. A January 1962 meeting of State Department principals, presided over by Rusk, provided one of the first forums for sustained discussion of the topic. The participants concurred that Moscow and Beijing had reached an impasse, which seemed to offer long-term advantages for the US, yet consideration of an appropriate response was deferred.[109] An impetus to policy revision came with a new National Intelligence Estimate (NIE) produced the following month. Discarding the hedged analysis that had hitherto dominated official deliberation, it rather starkly concluded that "Sino-Soviet relations are in a critical phase just short of an acknowledged and definitive split. There is no longer much chance of a fundamental resolution of differences ... the chances that such a split can be avoided during 1962 are no better than even."[110] Embracing this thinking, Rostow's PPC responded with a detailed list of recommendations. Asserting that there was no longer any need to "inhibit ourselves from action because of fear of driving Moscow and Peiping together," the paper covered familiar ground, calling for intensified efforts to search for "areas of overlapping interest" with the Kremlin, specifically the containment of China's nuclear program and its subversive activity in Southeast Asia. More innovatively, it advocated a two-pronged strategy toward the PRC, combining firm declarations and military pressures to deter Chinese aggression with a fresh focus on establishing "new lines of communication" with the mainland. The latter would be undertaken in the hope that Beijing might be "interested in bettering its relations with the West so as to be independent of bloc pressures" and with an eye as well to "moderating the attitudes of the post-Mao generation of Chinese Communist leaders."[111]

As on the issue of food relief, however, Rostow's was a minority view. A more influential school of thought, articulated by the administration's senior Kremlinologists (Kennan, Thompson, Charles

Bohlen), held that February's NIE had underestimated the potential for a temporary accommodation between the two communist powers and overestimated America's ability to influence the relationship; "in view of the insufficiency of our knowledge of the real factors in operation between these countries," Bohlen cautioned, "we certainly should not predicate any policy on the fact of the Chinese-Soviet dispute."[112] Rusk evidently agreed. He shelved Rostow's proposals, save for a modest idea to exploit the conflict psychologically via the dissemination of information concerning its development.[113]

Had he been alerted to Rostow's proposal of a multifaceted approach to China, it is doubtful Kennedy would have been receptive. His own views of the Sino-Soviet relationship, which he had tracked since the early weeks of his presidency,[114] were a decisive consideration. He tended to side with those who favored a discreet public posture, thinking it "unwise for the United States to talk about a matter over which we have only limited control."[115] Privately, however, the President was less impartial and neutral, ultimately hopeful that he could cultivate a mutual Soviet-American interest in thwarting China's nuclear program. When he raised the prospect of a nuclear PRC during a tense session with Khrushchev in Vienna, however, he was rebuffed.[116] The Soviet leader's reticence appeared to confirm the view that Moscow was unwilling to imperil its leadership of the international communist movement for the sake of acting in collusion with the "imperialists" against Beijing. Even as intelligence reports pointed to an intensification of the Sino-Soviet rivalry in the aftermath of the Cuban missile crisis,[117] several officials opined that the Kremlin's sensitivity to China's stinging indictment of "peaceful co-existence," which was increasingly resonating among Asian communist parties, would continue to tie its hands and complicate East–West dialogue on a host of issues.[118]

Kennedy does not seem to have been discouraged by this advice. Having just barely averted a nuclear catastrophe in the Caribbean, he believed that future crises could best be contained by reining in the arms race and discouraging the efforts of other powers to acquire weapons of mass destruction.[119] His push for Soviet-American détente in 1963, culminating in the signing of the Limited Test Ban Treaty in August, was determined in no small part by mounting concerns over the PRC's nuclear program. In January 1963, McGeorge Bundy asked McCone for a new estimate on China's nuclear progress, explaining that "the President was of a mind that nuclear weapons in the hands of the Chinese Communists would so upset the world political scene it would be intolerable to the United States and to the West."[120] JFK's fear of a nuclear China was intense and long-standing.[121] His interest in obstructing or postponing this development sprang from both a general aversion to nuclear proliferation and, more importantly, animosity toward Mao's regime. Expounding on the nature of this threat during a press conference, he drew attention to a "government [that] is not only Stalinist in its internal actions, but also has called for war, international war, in order to advance the final success of the Communist cause ... And then you introduce into that mix, nuclear weapons." The potential acquisition of these weapons by an inherently bellicose leadership amounted to "a more dangerous situation than any we faced since the end of the Second [World] War, because the Russians pursued in most cases their ambitions with some caution."[122]

Kennedy's apparent willingness to contemplate military action against China's nuclear facilities, including the possibility of a joint Soviet-American strike, remains a point of controversy. Some historians and former aides have insisted that the President merely engaged in "speculative contingency planning" and was not irrevocably committed to the radical pre-emptive option.[123] Nevertheless, JFK's sustained consideration of this alternative (even if speculative) provides much insight into his China mindset during his last year in office, his perceptions of Sino-Soviet differences, and how he hoped to exploit these to America's strategic advantage. He had all of this mind when he pressed for the conclusion of a test ban agreement with Moscow during a January 1963 meeting of the NSC. "Our primary purpose in trying to get a treaty with Russia is to halt or delay the development of an atomic capability by the Chinese Communists," he explained. He thought this feasible since "the Russians are believed to be as concerned about [this] as we are."[124] The considerable faith invested in a treaty rested not so much on the expectation that Beijing would willingly accede to its terms as on the hope that the Kremlin could be recruited as a partner in applying pressure on the mainland to desist from its nuclear ambitions.[125]

Kennedy evidently believed that this pressure could assume any number of forms: political, economic, and, if necessary, military. He hinted at the latter when he personally instructed Harriman, his envoy to the Moscow test ban talks that started in July, to "elicit Khrushchev's view of [the] means of limiting or preventing Chinese nuclear development and his willingness to take Soviet action or to accept US action aimed in this direction."[126] Harriman likely did not explicitly raise the topic of a joint strike, Soviet acquiescence in a US attack, or coordinated pressure of another sort; once the Soviet leader refused to concede concern over the prospect of a nuclear China, even after gentle prodding from his American interlocutor, the issue had been settled.[127] While a Soviet-American initiative seemed to have been taken off the table, the option of unilateral US action against the mainland's facilities was still being considered at the time of JFK's assassination and was one of many outstanding issues that would have to be resolved by his successor.[128]

High-level enmity toward the PRC in 1963 co-existed, as it had throughout the Kennedy presidency, with pressure from below for a reappraisal of attitudes. Just as Harriman's appointment to State's Far Eastern bureau in November 1961 had lent considerable momentum to the administration's discussion of a food initiative, the promotion of Roger Hilsman to the same post in April 1963 spurred a renewed outburst of pro-reform sentiment in government circles.[129] Brash and impudent, the West Point graduate ruffled the feathers of many, with the notable exception of Kennedy, with whom he shared a fascination with counterinsurgency.[130] Striking a dissonant note, Hilsman assumed his new role with a nuanced reading of Chinese intentions and capabilities. He surmised that Beijing's warlike oratory belied tactical caution and that its threat to US security interests had been exaggerated. The decision to attack India, for example, had been in part a "rational" reaction to New Delhi's provocative construction of military posts on its border. Criticism of Khrushchev's move to remove the missiles from Cuba had arisen from "an opportunity ... to assault the Soviets for what Peiping considered a clumsy handling of the crisis" and was therefore not an accurate indicator of "what the Chinese would themselves have done under similar circumstances." Indeed, Hilsman believed that China's instinctive wariness of rash military action, which had for long been conditioned by fear of an American reply, would only be strengthened over time by doubts about Soviet backing and by the overriding need to focus on economic reconstruction at home.[131] Intelligence analysts generally affirmed this image of a risk-averse China, particularly when speculation that Beijing might lash out in reaction to its growing isolation following the successful test ban talks in Moscow was convincingly dismissed.[132] Similarly calm assessments of the implications of a Chinese nuclear test appeared late in Kennedy's tenure and helped shape the Johnson team's handling of this issue.[133]

Hilsman's sober reflection on the Chinese challenge fed his interest in revising America's traditional approach to the mainland. He came to favor a "policy of contact as well as containment: contact to break down the Chinese isolation and containment to prevent any further Communist aggression." Ultimately an emphasis on the former would "hasten the changes which domestic economic pressures and international problems will force on Peiping."[134] This thinking was strongly influenced by a core of State Department China hands, men such as James Thomson (who had served as an aide to Bowles before moving to the Far Eastern bureau) and Marshall Green (the Consul General in Hong Kong), who held that there was a compelling short- and long-term rationale for projecting moderation toward the PRC. While it was conceded that gestures of goodwill would most likely fail to elicit a positive Chinese reply, they would at minimum serve the purpose of burnishing America's peaceful image. Reviving an idea that had been discussed in Edward Rice's October 1961 paper, these officials also recommended that attempts be made to encourage a more favorable impression of the US among those younger leaders, presumably disillusioned with the excesses of Maoism, who would succeed the Chairman and his comrades.[135] Only by "broadening as far as possible our present tenuous lines of communication into Communist China," Green posited, could Washington hope "to counteract Peiping's hate campaign [against the US], to establish a better long-range basis for rapprochement, and to abet already discernible tendencies toward moderation and realism within certain elements of the Chinese Communist bureaucracy."[136] Hilsman departed from the China "doves" in placing the burden on Beijing for an improvement in relations,[137] yet the policy review undertaken at his direction firmly ensconced him within the reform camp. He alerted his superiors to the dearth of Chinese expertise at Foggy Bottom and successfully lobbied for the creation of an Office of Asian Communist Affairs (ACA) in the Far Eastern bureau.[138] By late 1963, proposals for a relaxation of trade and travel restrictions, and for China's inclusion in disarmament talks, had been prepared.[139]

The most notable product of this bureaucratic ferment was a landmark speech delivered by the Assistant Secretary on 13 December. While carefully worded, paying due lip service to popular images of an expansionist China and offering a rationale for the continuation of its containment, the address was path-breaking in two respects. First, in a highly significant symbolic gesture, Hilsman explicitly acknowledged what policymakers had for long implicitly recognized, that the communist regime on the mainland was not a passing phenomenon. Second, reference was made to a "second echelon" of Chinese leaders possibly inclined to rapprochement with the outside world. With this faction in mind, he called for an "Open Door" policy based on "strength and firmness, accompanied by a constant readiness to negotiate." By announcing an American willingness to reciprocate good behavior, he hoped to alert Mao's successors to "the prospect that the way back into the community of man is not closed."[140] As such, the speech represented a subtle critique of ongoing efforts to isolate the PRC from the world community. Explaining his motives in a subsequent letter to Adlai Stevenson, Hilsman asserted that there was a need to justify the divergence in US relations with the major communist powers. Détente with the Soviets, he reasoned, had arisen from both US resolve in facing down the Kremlin and an openness to responding in kind to signs of Soviet moderation. His hope was that, in signalling the administration's readiness to reward prudent Chinese conduct, a similar state of affairs could emerge with the mainland.[141]

Had Kennedy been converted to this embryonic line of "containment without isolation" on the eve of his death? Those answering in the affirmative have cited an oft-quoted remark of the President's at his last press conference: "When the Red Chinese indicate a desire to live at peace with the United States, with other countries surrounding it, then quite obviously the United States would reappraise its policies. We are not wedded to a policy of hostility to Red China."[142] This interpretation, of course, falls short on several fronts. It exaggerates the significance of a policy review that, by late 1963, had not advanced beyond the mid-ranks of the bureaucracy.[143] Moreover, it attributes to Kennedy a view for which there is no empirical evidence; given his propensity for confidentiality and off-the-record discussions, it may well never be known whether he had been kept fully abreast of Hilsman's project or, if he had, where his sympathies lay. The most authoritative account of JFK's China record, sensibly, does not arrive at any firm conclusions as to his disposition in the fall of 1963.[144] Yet if the dynamics that had clearly prevailed through the summer – a conservative reading of his political mandate in general and of public attitudes toward the mainland in particular, a sense that the extension of any olive branch would only be spurned by Beijing, and a pronounced concern about China's behavior and the progress of its nuclear development – are to be taken as any guide, then one could plausibly surmise that the President was not prepared to launch new China initiatives, most certainly not before the 1964 election. There appears to have been little of the ambiguity in the China policy sphere that characterized most other aspects of John Kennedy's legacy.

The scarcity of policy innovation and continued deadlock between Washington and Beijing notwithstanding, it does not follow that the Kennedy years marked an inconsequential or even stagnant phase in the Sino-American relationship. A particularly noteworthy theme that emerges from an overview of this period is the sustained agitation for new approaches to the mainland voiced by several Kennedy officials. The rationale employed to advance their case varied. Perhaps the most common refrain, to which even Kennedy occasionally subscribed (as when he conditionally accepted a switch to "two Chinas" and appeared to signal his approval of a food initiative), was that the US needed to divest itself of much of the heavy baggage associated with the "isolation" component of its China policy and thereby deflect the blame for continued Sino-American friction. By evincing an openness to expanding contacts with Beijing, and exposing the mainland's rigidity in the process, Washington could stem the loss of international support for Taiwan and bolster its justification for containing the PRC.

The more enthusiastic advocates of policy reform certainly agreed with this defensive logic, yet they also maintained that America could favorably influence China's orientation. The most ambitious reformers (Bowles, Rostow) harbored what were surely misplaced hopes that the country's expansionist designs could be reined in by the offer of American largesse, a grandiose idea that won few converts and was largely abandoned even by its most vociferous proponents in the aftermath of events in India and Cuba.[145] A more modest and enduring school of thought (Hilsman, Rice, Green, Thomson) asserted that the first generation of Chinese revolutionaries in power, while more cautious and risk-averse than prevailing assumptions among US decision-makers allowed, were inherently opposed to accommodation with Washington. Long-term trends in China, however, offered reason for hope. A younger faction of leaders, more pragmatically inclined to focusing their energies on consolidating political and economic order at home, would eventually assume responsibility. Relaxing the more obdurate and antiquated aspects of US policy, particularly the trade and travel embargo, would signal restraint to these elements and possibly set the stage for a new era in Sino-American relations. In short, as international acceptance of the PRC gathered steam and conditions on the mainland evolved, so too did attitudes and perceptions in US government circles. Both what might be called the "defensive" and "activist" rationales for policy revision, having taken root in the early 1960s, would be pressed with greater frequency during Lyndon Johnson's presidency.

The short-term legacy of Kennedy's antagonistic dealings with China was, of course, decidedly negative. Recent literature has confirmed that Beijing bore its fair share of blame for the Sino-American impasse at this time. JFK's tenure in office coincided with a period of profound anxiety for Mao, whose fears of growing collaboration between Moscow and Washington were overshadowed only by the sense that the revolution at home had been hijacked by Soviet-style revisionism. As the Chairman turned his attention to turning aside the threat of capitalist restoration, he saw a radical line in foreign policy as a natural complement to this project and a catalyst for domestic mobilization.[146] Maoist rhetoric, particularly the espousal of revolutionary upheaval throughout the Afro-Asian world and hostility toward Moscow's search for "peaceful co-existence" with the West, made a deep impression on Kennedy. It served only to confirm the deeply ingrained image of a militant, expansionist China with no regard for American conceptions of international order that he had harbored before occupying the Oval Office. It is doubtful he ever parted from this preconception; its most dramatic manifestation came late in his presidency as he and his most senior advisers seriously considered taking action to disrupt the PRC's nuclear program. Kennedy's steady resistance to new approaches to the mainland, cultivation of détente with the Soviets, and staunch diplomatic solidarity with Taiwan undoubtedly unnerved his Chinese counterparts and contributed to their growing sense of encirclement. Camelot's record also cast an imposing shadow for an insecure successor set on hewing as close as possible to the inherited line in foreign affairs.

Notes

1 M.H. Hunt, *The Making of a Special Relationship: The United States and China to 1914* (New York: Columbia University Press, 1983),

pp. 299, 311; S.I. Levine, "On the brink of disaster: China and the United States in 1945," in H. Harding and Yuan Ming (eds), *Sino-American Relations, 1945–1955: A Joint Reassessment of a Critical Decade* (Wilmington, Del: SR Books, 1989), p. 7.
2 W.I. Cohen, *America's Response to China*, Fourth ed. (New York: Columbia University Press, 2000), pp. 36–9; Hunt, *Making of a Special Relationship*, p. 151.
3 Cohen, *America's Response to China*, pp. 42–3.
4 For the spurning of various Chinese entreaties in the latter half of the nineteenth century, see Hunt, *Making of a Special Relationship*, ch. 4.
5 Cohen, *America's Response to China*, pp. 55–81, 105–25; R. Dallek, *Franklin D. Roosevelt and American Foreign Policy, 1932–1945* (New York: Oxford University Press, 1995), pp. 144–313; D. Reynolds, *From Munich to Pearl Harbor: Roosevelt's America and the Origins of the Second World War* (Chicago: Ivan R. Dee, 2001), pp. 58–62, 87–92, 158–66, 177–8.
6 Cohen, *America's Response to China*, pp. 125–34; R.L. Messer, "Roosevelt, Truman, and China: An overview," in Harding and Yuan (eds), *Sino-American Relations, 1945–1955*, pp. 65–7; N.B. Tucker, *Taiwan, Hong Kong, and the United States, 1945–1992: Uncertain Friendships* (New York: Twayne, 1994), pp. 11–16.
7 Levine, "On the brink of disaster," in Harding and Yuan (eds), *Sino-American Relations, 1945–1955*, p. 11.
8 M.P. Leffler, *A Preponderance of Power: National Security, the Truman Administration, and the Cold War* (Stanford: Stanford University Press, 1992), pp. 127–30, 168–70, 246–51.
9 Shu Guang Zhang, *Economic Cold War: America's Embargo Against China and the Sino-Soviet Alliance, 1949–1963* (Washington, DC: Woodrow Wilson Center Press, 2001), p. 20. For the basis of Washington's hopes for a split between the Kremlin and the CCP, see J.L. Gaddis, *The Long Peace: Inquiries into the History of the Cold War* (New York: Oxford University Press, 1987), pp. 161–4; Wang Jisi, "An appraisal of US policy toward China, 1945–1955, and its aftermath," in Harding and Yuan, (eds), *Sino-American Relations, 1945–1955*, p. 291.
10 Leffler, *A Preponderance of Power*, pp. 336–7.
11 N.B. Tucker, *Patterns in the Dust: Chinese-American Relations and the Recognition Controversy, 1949–1950* (New York: Columbia University Press, 1983); W.I. Cohen, "Acheson, his advisers, and China, 1949–1950," in D. Borg and W. Heinrichs (eds), *Uncertain Years: Chinese-American Relations, 1947–1950* (New York: Columbia University Press, 1980), pp. 32–52. For an opposing view which holds Truman and Acheson responsible for institutionalizing Sino-American tensions, see

A.A. Offner, *Another Such Victory: President Truman and the Cold War, 1945–1953* (Stanford: Stanford University Press, 2002), ch. 12.

12 For further discussion, see "Symposium: Rethinking the lost chance in China," *Diplomatic History* 21:1 (1997), 71–115; Chen, *Mao's China and the Cold War*, pp. 50–3.

13 Some scholars have argued that Truman deliberately opted for a hardline toward the PRC, as a conciliatory approach would have contradicted ongoing efforts to mobilize domestic opinion in favor of unprecedented military and economic commitments in Europe. See T.J. Christensen, *Useful Adversaries: Grand Strategy, Domestic Mobilization, and Sino-American Conflict, 1947–1958* (Princeton: Princeton University Press, 1996), ch. 4.

14 Leffler, *A Preponderance of Power*, p. 293.

15 Chang, *Friends and Enemies*, p. 64–72.

16 The best account of Mao's decision for military intervention in Korea is Chen Jian, *China's Road to the Korean War: The Making of the Sino-American Confrontation* (New York: Columbia University Press, 1994).

17 Shu Guang Zhang, *Deterrence and Strategic Culture: Chinese-American Confrontations, 1949–1958* (Ithaca: Cornell University Press, 1992), pp. 79–88, 102–6, 116; W. Stueck, *Rethinking the Korean War: A New Diplomatic and Strategic History* (Princeton: Princeton University Press, 2002), pp. 94–102.

18 Foot, *Practice of Power*, pp. 85–95.

19 For the emotional current underlying American hostility toward the PRC, see D. McLean, "American nationalism, the China myth, and the Truman Doctrine: The question of accommodation with Peking, 1949–50," *Diplomatic History* 10:1 (1986), 25–42.

20 Zhang, *Economic Cold War*, pp. 20–31.

21 Gong Li, "Tension across the Taiwan Strait in the 1950s: Chinese strategy and tactics," in Ross and Jiang (eds), *Re-examining the Cold War*, p. 144.

22 R. Accinelli, *Crisis and Commitment: United States Policy toward Taiwan, 1950–1955* (Chapel Hill: University of North Carolina Press, 1996), pp. 17–33, 255.

23 Foot, *Practice of Power*, pp. 30–1, 54–5.

24 For a conventional indictment of Eisenhower's China policy, written well before the opening of archival records, see Dulles, *American Policy toward Communist China*, chs 9–11.

25 N.B. Tucker, "A house divided: The United States, the Department of State, and China," in W.I. Cohen and A. Iriye (eds), *The Great Powers in East Asia, 1953–1960* (New York: Columbia University Press, 1990), pp. 36–41, 55.

26 N.B. Tucker, "John Foster Dulles and the Taiwan roots of the 'two Chinas' policy," in R.H. Immerman (ed.), *John Foster Dulles and the Diplomacy of the Cold War* (Princeton: Princeton University Press, 1990); Accinelli, *Crisis and Commitment*, p. 113.
27 Quoted in Chang, *Friends and Enemies*, p. 85.
28 Gaddis, *The Long Peace*, pp. 174–87.
29 Qing Simei, "The Eisenhower administration and changes in Western embargo policy against China, 1954–1958," in Cohen and Iriye (eds), *Great Powers in East Asia*.
30 Chang, *Friends and Enemies*, pp. 143–4, 160. Expressing a racially tinged view prevalent among senior US officials, Eisenhower thought the Chinese were "completely reckless, arrogant ... and completely indifferent to human losses." M.H. Hunt, *Ideology and US Foreign Policy* (New Haven: Yale University Press, 1987), p. 164.
31 R.W. Pruessen, "Over the volcano: The United States and the Taiwan Strait crisis, 1954–1955," in Ross and Jiang (eds), *Re-examining the Cold War*, p. 99.
32 Shu Guang Zhang, "Between 'paper' and 'real' tigers: Mao's view of nuclear weapons," in J.L. Gaddis, P.H. Gordon, E.R. May, and J. Rosenberg (eds), *Cold War Statesmen Confront the Bomb: Nuclear Diplomacy Since 1945* (New York: Oxford University Press, 1999), pp. 198–202; J.W. Lewis and Xue Litai, *China Builds the Bomb* (Stanford: Stanford University Press, 1988), pp. 22–40.
33 Chen, *Mao's China and the Cold War*, pp. 170–1.
34 O.A. Westad, "The Sino-Soviet alliance and the United States," in O.A. Westad (ed.), *Brothers in Arms: The Rise and Fall of the Sino-Soviet Alliance, 1945–1963* (Washington, DC: Woodrow Wilson Center Press, 1998), pp. 174–5, 181; Zhang Baijia, "The changing international scene and Chinese policy toward the United States, 1954–1970," in Ross and Jiang (eds), *Re-examining the Cold War*, pp. 51–2.
35 L.A. Kusnitz, *Public Opinion and Foreign Policy: America's China Policy, 1949–1979* (Westport: Greenwood Press, 1984), pp. 95–6.
36 R. Hilsman, *To Move a Nation: The Politics of Foreign Policy in the Administration of John F. Kennedy* (Garden City, NY: Doubleday, 1967), pp. 347–8; A.M. Schlesinger, Jr, *A Thousand Days: John F. Kennedy in the White House* (Boston: Houghton Mifflin, 1965), p. 479; Thomson, "On the making," p. 221. See as well Marshall Green's quote in N.B. Tucker (ed.), *China Confidential: American Diplomats and Sino-American Relations, 1945–1996* (New York: Columbia University Press, 2001), p. 192.
37 The best discussion of the incoming Kennedy team's views of China is provided in Kochavi, *A Conflict Perpetuated*, ch. 2. For references to

Stevenson and Bowles, see pp. 29–31. See as well Chang, *Friends and Enemies*, pp. 218–19.

38 For Kennedy's pre-presidential foreign policy views, see R. Dallek, *An Unfinished Life: John F. Kennedy, 1917–1963* (Boston: Little, Brown, 2003), pp. 148–9, 158–68, 183–7, 221–4, 288–90.

39 Kochavi, *A Conflict Perpetuated*, pp. 38–9.

40 R. Reeves, *President Kennedy: Profile of Power* (New York: Simon & Schuster, 1993), p. 18.

41 J.N. Giglio, *The Presidency of John F. Kennedy* (Lawrence: University Press of Kansas, 1991), p. 45. An excellent, if somewhat overstated, discussion of the sources of Kennedy's foreign policy is provided in T.G. Paterson, "Introduction: John F. Kennedy's quest for victory and global crisis," in Paterson (ed.), *Kennedy's Quest For Victory*.

42 For further discussion, see Kochavi, *A Conflict Perpetuated*, p. 56.

43 For example, see Memorandum of conversation, 24 February 1961, *Foreign Relations of the United States* (hereafter *FRUS*), 1961–1963, vol. 22, p. 15; Memorandum of conversation, 3 March 1961, ibid., p. 21; Memorandum of conversation, 5 April 1961, ibid., pp. 42–3.

44 D. Rusk, *As I Saw It* (New York: Norton, 1990), pp. 282–3.

45 Dallek, *An Unfinished Life*, pp. 165–7.

46 N. Kochavi, "Limited accommodation, perpetuated conflict: Kennedy, China, and the Laos crisis, 1961–1963," *Diplomatic History* 26:1 (2002), 101; R.J. McMahon, "Choosing sides in South Asia," in Paterson (ed.), *Kennedy's Quest For Victory*, p. 200.

47 L. Freedman, *Kennedy's Wars: Berlin, Cuba, Laos, and Vietnam* (New York: Oxford University Press, 2000), p. 287.

48 Fetzer, "Clinging to containment," in Paterson (ed.), *Kennedy's Quest For Victory*, pp. 181–2; Kochavi, "Limited accommodation, perpetuated conflict," pp. 100–1.

49 Special National Intelligence Estimate (SNIE) 13-61, "The economic situation in Communist China," 4 April 1961, *FRUS*, 1961–1963, vol. 22, pp. 40–1; CIA Memorandum, "The situation in mainland China," 27 July 1961, National Security Files (hereafter NSF), Countries, Box 22, folder "China General: 7/21/61–7/31/61," John Fitzgerald Kennedy Library (hereafter JFKL).

50 SNIE 13-3-61, "Chinese communist capabilities and intentions in the Far East," 30 November 1961, *FRUS*, 1961–1963, vol. 22, p. 173. See as well CIA memorandum, "The chances of a Chinese communist military move into Southeast Asia," 11 May 1961, enclosed in Walt Rostow to JFK, 12 May 1961, President's Office Files, Countries, Box 114, folder "Communist China: Security, 1961," JFKL.

51 Fetzer, "Clinging to containment," in Paterson (ed.), *Kennedy's Quest For Victory*, p. 196.

52 National Intelligence Estimate (NIE) 1-61, "Estimate of the world situation," 17 January 1961, *FRUS, 1961–1963*, vol. 5, pp. 18–19.
53 For example, see Telegram, Moscow to Department of State, 1 February 1961, ibid., p. 53.
54 Record of the Policy Planning Staff meeting, 8 February 1961, ibid., p. 63.
55 Memorandum of conversation, 3 March 1961, *FRUS, 1961–1963*, vol. 22, p. 21. For Beijing's early views of the Kennedy administration, see MacFarquhar, *The Origins of the Cultural Revolution*, vol. 3, pp. 130–1.
56 Foot, *Practice of Power*, p. 80.
57 Tucker, *Taiwan, Hong Kong, and the United States*, pp. 48–9.
58 Kaufman, *Confronting Communism*, pp. 150–1; Cohen, *Dean Rusk*, pp. 164–6.
59 "Strategic framework for rethinking China policy," by Robert W. Komer, 7 April 1961, NSF, Countries, Box 22, folder "China General: Strategic framework for rethinking China policy, 4/7/61," JFKL.
60 Komer to JFK, 3 April 1961, NSF, Countries, Box 21A, folder "China General: 3/61–4/61," JFKL.
61 Memorandum of conversation, 5 April 1961, *FRUS, 1961–1963*, vol. 22, pp. 44–5.
62 Dean Rusk to JFK, 26 May 1961, ibid., p. 68.
63 Memorandum of conversation, 24 May 1961, ibid., p. 64.
64 Kaufman, *Confronting Communism*, p. 151.
65 R. Garson, *The United States and China Since 1949: A Troubled Affair* (London: Pinter, 1994), p. 81.
66 Memorandum of conversation, JFK–Ch'en Ch'eng, 31 July 1961, NSF, Countries, Box 22, folder "China General: 8/1/61–8/10/61," JFKL.
67 McGeorge Bundy to JFK, 7 July 1961, *FRUS, 1961–1963*, vol. 22, pp. 89–90.
68 Memorandum of conversation, 28 July 1961, ibid., pp. 99–101.
69 M. Bundy to Ray Cline, 11 October 1961, ibid., pp. 154–5.
70 Kochavi, *A Conflict Perpetuated*, pp. 66–7; Tucker, *Taiwan, Hong Kong, and the United States*, pp. 49–50.
71 Kochavi, *A Conflict Perpetuated*, p. 55.
72 Telegram, no. 620, Taipei to Department of State, 8 March 1962, NSF, Countries, Box 23, folder "China General: Return to the mainland, 1/1/62–5/6/62," JFKL. See as well Telegram, Taipei to Department of State, 15 March 1962, *FRUS, 1961–1963*, vol. 22, pp. 195–6.
73 SNIE 13-3-62, "Probable consequences of Chinese Nationalist military operations on the China mainland," 28 March 1962, *FRUS, 1961–1963*, vol. 22, pp. 200–1; NIE 13-4-62, "Prospects for Communist China," 2 May 1962, ibid., p. 222.
74 Freedman, *Kennedy's Wars*, p. 252.

75 Memorandum for the record, 18 June 1962, FRUS, 1961–1963, vol. 22, pp. 246–7. Harriman and Hilsman expressed similar concerns. See Memorandum for the record, 31 March 1962, ibid., pp. 204–5.
76 JFK to Averell Harriman, 9 March 1962, ibid., pp. 192–3; Memorandum for the record, 12 March 1962, ibid., p. 194; Memorandum to Ray Cline, 31 March 1962, ibid., p. 206; M. Bundy to Cline, 6 March 1962, NSF, Countries, Box 23, folder "China General: Return to the mainland, 1/1/62–5/6/62," JFKL.
77 Kochavi, *A Conflict Perpetuated*, p. 117.
78 Memorandum of conversation, 22 June 1962, *FRUS*, 1961–1963, vol. 22, pp. 268–9; Telegram, Department of State to London, 22 June 1962, ibid., p. 270.
79 Telegram, Warsaw to Department of State, 23 June 1962, ibid., p. 274. For a brief discussion of the utility of the Warsaw talks in resolving this crisis, see S.M. Goldstein, "Dialogue of the deaf ? The Sino-American ambassadorial-level talks, 1955–1970," in Ross and Jiang (eds), *Reexamining the Cold War*, pp. 228–9.
80 Roger Hilsman to Rusk, 9 July 1962, NSF, Robert W. Komer Series, Box 410, folder "China (CPR) 1961–1963 (2 of 3)," JFKL.
81 Telegram, Department of State to Taipei, 28 July 1962, *FRUS*, 1961–1963, vol. 22, p. 296. Divergences over the future direction of Chinese foreign policy emerged among Chinese elites in 1962, with momentous consequences for the duration of the decade. This is discussed in Chapter 3 of this volume.
82 Telegram, Warsaw to Department of State, 30 June 1961, ibid., pp. 87–9.
83 Office of Current Intelligence Memorandum, "The signs of Chinese communist friendliness," 17 July 1961, NSF, Countries, Box 22, folder "China General: 7/15/61–7/24/61," JFKL; Hilsman to Walter P. McConaughy, 17 July 1961, ibid.
84 For Rusk's instructions to Cabot, see Telegram, Department of State to Warsaw, 13 August 1961, FRUS, 1961–1963, vol. 22, pp. 118–19.
85 Kochavi, *A Conflict Perpetuated*, p. 248.
86 Walt Rostow to JFK, 22 November 1961, NSF, Countries, Box 22A, folder "China General: 11/1/61–11/26/61," JFKL. See as well Chester Bowles to JFK, 6 February 1962, James C. Thomson Papers (hereafter JCT Papers), Box 15, folder "Food for China 1/62–2/62," JFKL; "US policies in the Far East: Review and recommendations," by Bowles, 4 April 1962, Arthur M. Schlesinger, Jr Papers, White House Files, Box WH-3a, folder "Bowles, Chester, 4/62," JFKL; Bowles to JFK, 27 June 1962, JCT Papers, Box 15, folder "Food for China 6/62–7/62 and undated," JFKL.
87 Thomson, "On the making," p. 223.

88 "US policy toward China," 26 October 1961, JCT Papers, Box 14, folder "S/P 61159: US policy toward Communist China 10/26/61," JFKL.
89 W.I. Cohen, "Kennedy's China," *Diplomatic History* 28:1 (2004), 157.
90 *FRUS*, 1961–1963, vol. 22, p. 175, n. 5.
91 Fetzer, "Clinging to containment," in Paterson (ed.), *Kennedy's Quest For Victory*, p. 191. Even Robert Komer, generally sympathetic to an overhaul of China policy, posited that grain sales could have an "unfavorable side effect" on the administration's concurrent efforts to secure congressional passage of the Trade Expansion Act. Komer to Carl Kaysen, 24 January 1962, NSF, Robert W. Komer Series, Box 410, folder "China (CPR) 1961–1963 (3 of 3)," JFKL.
92 "Chinese communist food deficits and US policy," 5 January 1962, JCT Papers, Box 15, folder "Food for China 1/62–2/62," JFKL.
93 For the reasons behind this shake-up, see Dallek, *An Unfinished Life*, pp. 436–7; Freedman, *Kennedy's Wars*, pp. 38, 337–8.
94 Fetzer, "Clinging to containment," in Paterson (ed.), *Kennedy's Quest For Victory*, pp. 190–1.
95 Draft memorandum, Rusk to JFK, 4 April 1962, FRUS, 1961–1963, vol. 22, pp. 208–10.
96 Harriman to Rusk, 13 April 1962, JCT Papers, Box 15, folder "Food for China 3/62–5/62," JFKL.
97 "Food for China," 24 May 1962, ibid.
98 Thomson, "On the making," p. 228.
99 *FRUS*, 1961–1963, vol. 22, p. 233, n. 2.
100 Kochavi, *A Conflict Perpetuated*, p. 113.
101 For the centrality of India in the Kennedy administration's China mindset, see ibid., pp. 28–9, 40, 145–6.
102 Memorandum of conversation, Rusk–Lord Home, 25 June 1962, JCT Papers, Box 15, folder "Communist China: General, 4/62–6/62," JFKL.
103 William P. Bundy Papers (hereafter WPB Papers), Box 1, ch. 7, p. 6, Lyndon Baines Johnson Library (hereafter LBJL). These papers compile an unpublished manuscript written by Bundy about the 1961–65 Vietnam decisions, and are an invaluable source for the foreign policy establishment's views of China in the mid-1960s. See as well Goh, *Constructing the US Rapprochement with China*, p. 85.
104 Cohen, *Dean Rusk*, pp. 169–70.
105 Quoted in Kusnitz, *Public Opinion and Foreign Policy*, p. 107.
106 Chang, *Friends and Enemies*, pp. 220, 229–32; *FRUS*, 1961–1963, vol. 5, p. 63, n. 1.
107 CIA Memorandum, "The Sino-Soviet dispute and its significance," 1 April 1961, NSF, Countries, Box 21A, folder "China General: The Sino-Soviet dispute and its significance 4/61," JFKL. See as well NIE 10-61, "Authority and control in the communist movement," 8 August 1961,

FRUS, 1961–1963, vol. 22, pp. 116–17. For the causes of the Sino-Soviet schism, the best volume is Westad (ed.), *Brothers in Arms*. See especially Westad's introduction; C. Pleshakov, "Nikita Khrushchev and Sino-Soviet relations"; Chen Jian and Yang Kuisong, "Chinese politics and the collapse of the Sino-Soviet alliance."

108 Kochavi, *A Conflict Perpetuated*, pp. 190–5.
109 For a record of this meeting, see James C. Thomson, Jr to Harriman, 12 January 1962, JCT Papers, Box 15, folder "General 1/62–3/62," JFKL.
110 NIE 11-5-62, "Political developments in the USSR and the communist world," 21 February 1962, *FRUS*, 1961–1963, vol. 5, p. 375.
111 "US policy re the Sino-Soviet conflict," 2 April 1962, enclosed in Rusk to Rostow, 30 April 1962, JCT Papers, Box 14, folder "Sino-Soviet conflict and US policy 4/30/62," JFKL.
112 Charles E. Bohlen to M. Bundy, 25 May 1962, NSF, Countries, Box 178A, folder "USSR General: 5/62 and undated," JFKL. See as well Telegram, no. 3070, Moscow to Department of State, 26 May 1962, ibid.; Telegram, no. 636, Belgrade to Department of State, 11 April 1962, NSF, Countries, Box 178, folder "USSR General: 4/62," JFKL.
113 Rusk to Rostow, 30 April 1962, JCT Papers, Box 14, JFKL.
114 Chang, *Friends and Enemies*, p. 220.
115 Airgram, no. CA-976, Department of State and USIA to All American diplomatic and consular posts, 24 July 1963, Record Group (hereafter RG) 59, Central Files, 1963, Box 3863, POL CHICOM-USSR, National Archives, College Park, Maryland (hereafter NA). See as well JFK's remarks in Summary record of the 516th meeting of the National Security Council, 31 July 1963, *FRUS*, 1961–1963, vol. 22, p. 374.
116 Burr and Richelson, "Whether to 'strangle the baby,'" p. 61. For a summary of Kennedy and Khrushchev's discussions of China at Vienna, see Editorial note, *FRUS*, 1961–1963, vol. 22, pp. 70–2.
117 CIA memorandum, "Soviet policy in the aftermath of the Cuban crisis," 29 November 1962, *FRUS*, 1961–1963, vol. 5, pp. 586–7; CIA memorandum, "Sino-Soviet relations at a new crisis," 14 January 1963, NSF, Countries, Box 180, folder "USSR General: 1/9/63–1/14/63," JFKL.
118 Telegram, no. 2310, Moscow to Department of State, 16 March 1963, NSF, Countries, Box 180A, folder "USSR General: 3/16/63–3/21/63," JFKL; Llewellyn E. Thompson to Rusk, 24 April 1963, ibid., folder "USSR General: 4/15/63–4/30/63," JFKL; Telegram, no. 5505, Department of State to Paris, 21 May 1963, NSF, Countries, Box 181, folder "USSR General: 5/63," JFKL. The skepticism of US officials over the prospects of Soviet-American détente in 1962–63 was well founded. Recent research has shown that Khrushchev attempted to mend fences with the Chinese after the Cuban missile crisis. His concerted push for this objective resulted in a hardened posture toward Washington.

Khrushchev's shift to a more active pursuit of peaceful co-existence with the West in the summer of 1963, culminating in the Partial Test Ban Treaty, occurred only after the Soviet leader realized that Mao was unreceptive to his overtures. See S. Radchenko, "The China Puzzle: Soviet Policy toward the People's Republic of China in the 1960s" (PhD dissertation, London School of Economics and Political Science, 2005), pp. 76–91.
119 Dallek, *An Unfinished Life*, pp. 613–21.
120 Editorial note, *FRUS*, 1961–1963, vol. 22, p. 339.
121 The best sources on this topic are Chang, *Friends and Enemies*, ch. 8; Burr and Richelson, "Whether to 'strangle the baby,'" pp. 54–79; Kochavi, *A Conflict Perpetuated*, ch. 8.
122 Quoted in R. MacFarquhar (ed.), *Sino-American Relations, 1949–1971* (New York: Praeger, 1972), p. 200.
123 On this point, see Kochavi, *A Conflict Perpetuated*, p. 217. Some Kennedy aides have corroborated JFK's militancy on this issue. William C. Foster, head of the Arms Control and Disarmament Agency, recalled the President once remarking, "You know, it wouldn't be too hard if we could somehow get kind of an anonymous airplane to go over there, take out the Chinese facilities – they've only got a couple – and maybe we could do it, or maybe the Soviet Union could do it, rather than face the threat of a China with nuclear weapons." William C. Foster Oral History, p. 37, JFKL.
124 Remarks of President Kennedy to the NSC meeting of 22 January 1963, NSF, Meetings and Memoranda, Box 314, folder "National Security Council meetings, 1963: No. 508," 1/22/63, JFKL.
125 Chang, *Friends and Enemies*, p. 238; M.R. Beschloss, *The Crisis Years: Kennedy and Khrushchev, 1960–1963* (New York: Edward Burlingame Books, 1991), pp. 619–20. Harriman strongly encouraged Kennedy's impression that the Soviets wanted to pressure China. Telegram, no. 195, Moscow to Department of State, 18 July 1963, NSF, Departments and Agencies, Box 263, folder "ACDA – Disarmament: Nuclear Test Ban Cables, Moscow 7/63 Incoming," JFKL.
126 Telegram, no. 191, Department of State to Moscow, 15 July 1963, NSF, Departments and Agencies, Box 263, folder "ACDA – Disarmament: Nuclear Test Ban Cables, Moscow 7/63 Outgoing," JFKL
127 Telegram, no. 365, 27 July 1963, ibid., folder "Incoming," JFKL. An internal review of the Moscow negotiations one year later did not turn up any evidence that Harriman had broached any "proposal for a joint US-USSR effort to slow down Red China's nuclear weapons development." Editorial note, *FRUS*, 1961–1963, vol. 22, p. 370.
128 Burr and Richelson, "Whether to 'strangle the baby,'" pp. 71–5.

129 The Hilsman-led China policy review of 1963 has only very recently received sustained attention in the literature. See Kochavi, *A Conflict Perpetuated*, pp. 225–33; K. Quigley, "A lost opportunity: A reappraisal of the Kennedy administration's China policy in 1963," *Diplomacy and Statecraft* 13:3 (2002), 175–98.
130 Kaiser, *American Tragedy*, p. 153.
131 Hilsman to Rusk, 26 February 1963, NSF, Countries, Box 24, folder "China General: 1/63–3/63," JFKL.
132 SNIE 13-4-63, "Possibilities of greater militancy by the Chinese communists," 31 July 1963, NSF, NIE, Box 4, folder "Communist China (2 of 2)," LBJL; George C. Denney, Jr to Rusk, 22 July 1963, NSF, Countries, Box 24, folder "China General: 7/63–8/63," JFKL; Thomas L. Hughes to Rusk, 10 August 1963, RG 59, Records of the Policy Planning Council, 1963–64, Lot 70D199, Box 250, NA.
133 See Chapter 2 of this volume.
134 Hilsman to John M. Cabot, 25 October 1963, RG 59, Bureau of Far Eastern Affairs, Office of the Assistant Secretary: Subject Files, 1964, Lot 66D93, Box 1, NA.
135 Hilsman, *To Move a Nation*, pp. 349–50.
136 Marshall Green to Bowles, 13 February 1963, attached to Airgram, no. A-755, Hong Kong to Department of State, 1 February 1963, RG 59, Central Files, 1963, Box 3862, POL CHICOM-US, NA.
137 Kochavi, *A Conflict Perpetuated*, pp. 248–9.
138 Paper prepared in the Bureau of Far Eastern Affairs, undated, FRUS, 1961–1963, vol. 22, pp. 397–9.
139 Hilsman to Rusk, 22 October 1963, ibid., p. 403; Hilsman, *To Move a Nation*, pp. 348–9.
140 Roger Hilsman, "United States policy toward Communist China," 13 December 1963, NSF, Country File, Box 237, folder "China memos, vol. I," LBJL.
141 Hilsman to Adlai Stevenson, 19 December 1963, FRUS, 1961–1963, vol. 22, pp. 411–12. Against Hilsman's wishes, Beijing reportedly interpreted the speech as a provocative endorsement of "two Chinas." See Foot, *Practice of Power*, p. 98, n. 42.
142 Quoted in Hilsman, *To Move a Nation*, p. 348.
143 Hilsman's proposal for a modification of the travel ban in October 1963, for example, never even reached Rusk's desk. See Editor's note on source, Hilsman to Rusk, 22 October 1963, FRUS, 1961–1963, vol. 22, p. 403.
144 Kochavi, *A Conflict Perpetuated*, pp. 231–2, 250.
145 Ibid., p. 121.
146 MacFarquhar, *Origins of the Cultural Revolution*, vol. 3; Chen and Yang, "Chinese politics and the collapse of the Sino-Soviet alliance," in Westad (ed.), *Brothers in Arms*.

2 Holes in the dam
French recognition and the Chinese nuclear test, 1963–64

Mounting dismay abroad over the PRC's continued exclusion from the international community and high-level alarm over the mainland's nuclear progress all but ensured that China would figure prominently among the several foreign policy items vying for the attention of Kennedy's successor. Indeed, Lyndon Johnson's first year in power coincided with a dramatic change in China's international relationships. Both French recognition of Beijing and China's explosion of a nuclear device exposed the surreality of ostracizing the world's most populous nation, triggering a torrent of calls from home and abroad for the new administration to reappraise America's traditional approach to the communist regime. In stark contrast to Kennedy, Johnson had evinced minimal interest in Chinese affairs prior to assuming the presidency and approached this question with considerably less ideological baggage. Most tellingly, he soon eschewed the option of an unprovoked military strike against the mainland's nuclear facilities. Despite a moderating presence in the Oval Office, however, there was no commensurate shift in Washington's obstinate posture toward Beijing in 1964.

As this chapter documents, Johnson signed off on initiatives aimed at containing the diplomatic fallout from French recognition and China's nuclear test. This insistence on staying the course was an outgrowth of Johnson's complex China mindset and modus operandi as a foreign policy leader in the early stages of his presidency. Mindful of the political controversy that had almost consumed the Truman administration for the "loss" of mainland China to the communists, preoccupied with securing congressional approval of sweeping domestic reform legislation and winning his own mandate in the upcoming presidential election, dubious of grand departures in foreign affairs, and generally susceptible to the conventional wisdom of a threatening China, LBJ passively deferred to the group of advisers bequeathed by Kennedy.

LBJ, China, and foreign policymaking

Johnson's exposure to the nation's major foreign policy debates as a Congressman, Senator, and Vice President was not inconsiderable. Yet while hardly oblivious to world affairs, the issues that seized his attention and had propelled him into a political career were a product of his own background. Reared in the remote Texas hill country, Johnson channelled his extraordinary energy and uncanny knack for dealmaking into spreading the country's riches to his constituents and integrating the South into the mainstream of American life. Matters of national security and defense appeared on Johnson's congressional agenda more often because a politician of his stature and ambition could ill afford to ignore them than by inclination or choice; Henry Kissinger's rather wry observation that "One never had the impression that he would think about the topic spontaneously – while shaving, for example" was surely not wide of the mark.[1]

LBJ's understanding of international relations was colored primarily by his own reading of the major events that unfolded as he came of age, with historical analogies in particular serving as a central point of reference.[2] As with so many of his generation, the "lessons" of Munich left an indelible mark. From the failure of the Western democracies to deter fascist aggression in the 1930s, Johnson believed that America had an indispensable role to play in ensuring world peace and security, that it had to maintain a high standard of military preparedness, project resolve, and make its determination to protect far-flung interests credible to foe and friend alike. This overriding preoccupation with credibility derived from the belief that tests of American resolve had to be successfully met and aggressive conduct decisively checked so as to avert the horrors of another global conflagration. Firm adherence to this logic had obvious ramifications for views of China. In justifying his decision to intervene in Vietnam to Doris Kearns after he left office, Johnson reasoned that the voices of appeasement and isolationism had conveyed "the wrong messages to Hitler and the Japanese ... I firmly believe we wouldn't have been involved in World War II if it hadn't been for all the vacillation."[3] It therefore followed that failure to take a stand in Vietnam would only whet the appetite of expansionist powers like China and heighten the possibilities of greater conflict.

Another seminal event of the 1930s, this one closer to US shores and to his heart, shaped Johnson's worldview. Constantly exposed to economic hardship – as a child, as a high school teacher of impoverished Mexican Americans, as state director of the National Youth Administration, as congressional representative of a district hit hard by the Depression – his imagination was fired and forever altered by Franklin Roosevelt's New Deal. The idea and example of government playing a positive role in alleviating poverty and giving the underprivileged a new lease on life formed the core of LBJ's political philosophy and the overriding ambition of his own presidency. As one biographer has observed, Johnson "impose[d] his conception of relations within American society onto relations between discordant nations." The populist and American nationalist in Johnson believed that all people – whatever their origin, religion, or ideological affiliation – aspired to a life of wealth and opportunity, just like every Texan.[4]

Johnson's reformist impulse endowed him with an intuitive understanding of the socio-economic maladies that afflicted so many of the newly independent nations of Southeast Asia, and the opportunities that this widespread discontent presented to adversaries such as China in the battle for the "hearts and minds" of Asians. His May 1961 tour of the region as Vice President, which evidently struck an emotional chord, was a perfect demonstration of the Munich-New Deal mindset that defined his own conceptualization of the politico-psychological challenge that China posed to American interests. The greatest threat emanating from the region, LBJ informed Kennedy upon his return, "stems from hunger, ignorance, poverty and disease." American leadership in the Far East rested on making "imaginative use of our scientific and technological capability" in combating these dangers and on fostering "knowledge and faith in United States power, will and understanding." Without an effective courting of local opinion, these disillusioned countries would lose faith in the United States as a guarantor of peace and prosperity and turn to the communists for support. The administration, he concluded alarmingly, would then have to "surrender the Pacific and take up our defenses in our own shores."[5]

Yet if the lessons of Munich demonstrated the imperative of *containing* the PRC, the example of Chinese intervention in the Korean War underlined the risks of *confronting* the mainland. The frightening image of a seemingly endless horde of PLA troops pouring across China's frontier proved to be an enduring one and instilled in Johnson an acute sensitivity to Chinese security interests and an aversion to any scheme that threatened to ignite another Sino-American conflict; when presented with the choice of a potentially provocative course of action vis a vis the PRC or a less combative alternative, LBJ would consistently opt for the latter.[6] The contradictions inherent in Johnson's views of China were displayed during the 1954–55 Taiwan Strait crisis. As a senior member of the Senate Armed Services Committee, he firmly supported President Eisenhower's decision to seek congressional approval of his authority to use American forces in defending the Pescadores and Formosa from Chinese attack. He successfully opposed the efforts of fellow Democrats to exclude the offshore islands from the Formosa Resolution. Johnson's reluctance to challenge a popular commander in chief at a time of heightened international tension was buttressed by his own hostile interpretation of Chinese intentions in the Pacific. These hawkish instincts, however, were tempered by recent memories of Korea. Thus when Eisenhower and Dulles announced in March 1955 that the US might use nuclear weapons in any conflict with the PRC, and Republican Senator William Knowland pressed the administration to resist by force any Chinese assault on Quemoy and Matsu, Johnson cautioned against entanglement in "an irresponsible adventure for which we have not calculated all the risks ... we do not want a war party on the American political scene any more than we want an appeasement party."[7]

Beyond a concern with Chinese subversive activity in Southeast Asia, a vague adherence to the Cold War-infused stereotype of a militant and aggressive PRC, and an overriding determination to avoid a replay of Korea, however, Johnson did not have a distinct China policy agenda of his own in November 1963. His congressional and vice presidential years were characterized by a lack of engagement with the China policy sphere. Kennedy duly included his Vice President in formal discussions of foreign affairs, as in the Cabinet or the NSC, yet never took him into his confidence or showed any interest in granting his subordinate an influential role in the administration's various diplomatic initiatives.[8] It was an uneasy political partnership between the two men, Johnson viewing JFK as an upstart who had punched above his weight into the White House, the President wary of the Texan's oversized ego.[9] LBJ's role in the 1963 deliberations over the possibility of joint Soviet-American action against the PRC's nuclear installations remains unclear. Given the prevailing dynamic of the Kennedy-Johnson relationship, it is likely that LBJ was at most kept abreast of the debate, playing nothing akin to a leading role.[10]

Inherent in this relative aloofness from mainland affairs was a notable reserve of intellectual flexibility toward China. Indeed, holdovers from the Kennedy administration have noted the contrast between JFK's complete absorption with the notion of a Chinese menace and LBJ's more detached perspective.[11] While Johnson's populism alerted him to the potential allure of China's brand of communism to its deprived neighbors, it inspired a corresponding inclination to appeal over the heads of the PRC's leadership to the Chinese masses, whom he condescendingly assumed were desirous of the American way of life. Whereas Kennedy was "a somewhat more precise ideologue," NSC staffer James Thomson later observed, his successor was "less troubled by Maoism's twists and turns and more interested in how you feed and clothe and give schools and clinics and roads to all those kids in China, all those hungry people who have no long-term reason to hate us."[12] Kennedy's acute hostility toward China had rested on the notion of a wayward leadership whose revolutionary worldview and adherence to historic Chinese nationalism compelled it to pursue an expansionist agenda in violation of the American tenets of order and stability; Johnson's general anti-communism was less well defined, deriving more from his regret that regimes like China's tended to devote resources to foreign ambitions at the expense of domestic development.[13]

Of two minds concerning the PRC, Johnson was predisposed to retaining the policy of containment and isolation bequeathed to him, a policy sufficiently firm to check the expansionist tendencies of Communist China's rulers yet prudently measured so as to avert provoking another Sino-American confrontation or antagonizing the Chinese people, presumably natural allies for America. Over time, Johnson hoped a less dogmatic leadership would emerge on the mainland, one that was more preoccupied with tending to the material needs of their populace than with exporting the revolution. Once a more agreeable regime was in place, America could then adjust its own attitudes. According to Walt Rostow, the President's National Security Adviser from April 1966 onwards, LBJ did not believe that Mao and his comrades represented "the last word" on China's relationship with the rest of the world.[14]

More importantly, Johnson's predilection for preserving intact US China policy stemmed from an article of faith that governed his general approach to foreign affairs. As one aide put it most succinctly, "In his opinion, politicians, whether comfortable with foreign policy or not, ventured into the field at their own peril."[15] A veteran of Washington warfare, LBJ was well versed in the ways in which developments abroad could undermine a President's authority at home. "I knew that Harry Truman and Dean Acheson had lost their effectiveness from the day that the Communists took over in China," he later recalled. "I believed that the loss of China had played a large role in the rise of Joe McCarthy."[16] The political fallout from events in the Far East during the early 1950s – the vitriolic "who lost China" debate, the emergence of a China Lobby, the zenith of McCarthyism, public disenchantment with the Korean War, and the Republicans' seizure of the White House in 1952 – underscored the hazards of being branded "soft" on Asian communism, especially for a Democrat with presidential ambitions. Consequently, Johnson was not one openly to question Cold War orthodoxy. For much of his tenure as Senate Majority Leader, he assumed a decidedly discreet stance in foreign affairs, championing a bipartisan foreign policy and recoiling from mounting a major challenge to Eisenhower's diplomatic stewardship. This derived from both a shrewd strategy aimed at exploiting divisions in the Republican party over international affairs and the pitfalls he assumed were associated with too conspicuous a role in questions of national security.[17] In the Kennedy White House, LBJ closely guarded his opinions on foreign matters, rarely offering his thoughts in group meetings, even when given a platform by the President.[18] "If I speak one word of disagreement with the Cabinet and White House staff looking on," Johnson confided to a friend, "then they'll put it out ... that I'm a damned traitor."[19]

Perhaps most famously, LBJ bitterly complained in retirement about how "that bitch of a war on the other side of the world" in Vietnam had diverted attention from "the woman I really loved – the Great Society."[20] Crude and self-pitying, Johnson's remark nevertheless highlighted the priority he assigned to domestic policy as President. It was at home where he believed he could accomplish the most and lay a foundation for the esteemed legacy he so zealously craved. Johnson approached foreign policy from a decidedly negative and defensive perspective, viewing it primarily as a political minefield that could potentially obliterate the capital and prestige required for domestic achievements. His governing instinct beyond American shores was to fulfill the diplomatic commitments of his predecessors and avoid committing any embarrassing or controversial mistakes that could be used as ammunition by enemies of his ambitious legislative agenda.[21] Thus while LBJ intermittently voiced private misgivings over what he saw as some of the anomalous features of China policy, as when he mused to a close confidant in January 1964 that the US should not have forsworn diplomatic relations with the PRC,[22] his conservative estimate of popular sentiment acted as a brake against any risk-taking in this regard.

Continuity in foreign affairs was all the more imperative given the extraordinary circumstances in which Johnson inherited the Oval Office. LBJ was determined to retain the services of Kennedy's senior advisers, both to reassure a shaken nation in the government's stability and to avert the spectacle of an en masse walkout that could be taken as a sign of non-confidence in the new President. "I needed that White House staff," he later explained. "Without them I would have lost my link to John Kennedy, and without that I would have had absolutely no chance of gaining the support of the media or the Easterners or the intellectuals. And without that support I would have had absolutely no chance of governing the country."[23] Or, he might have added, securing his own mandate in 1964. Profoundly insecure and thin-skinned, Johnson was highly sensitive as to how his international leadership was assessed. He harbored a tortured inferiority complex, thinking that his humble Texan origins made him a potential target of ridicule among the media, the Eastern establishment that held sway over American national security, and the public at large for any and every misstep on the world stage.[24] "I don't believe that I'll ever get credit for anything in foreign affairs, no matter how successful it is," the graduate of Southwest Texas State Teachers College once complained to a journalist, "because I didn't go to Harvard."[25] LBJ's worst suspicions were hardly alleviated by the proliferation of press reports in the early months of his presidency that alluded to a perceived lack of surefootedness and interest in diplomacy.[26] In striving to reach foreign policy decisions based on the consensus of his martyred predecessor's hand-picked senior staff, a biographer has noted, Johnson wanted to avoid appearing "foolish or incompetent."[27]

For his advice on international affairs, Johnson depended heavily on Rusk, Bundy, and Secretary of Defense Robert McNamara. Johnson's reliance on a small number of advisers comported with a collegial style of decision-making honed during his years in the Senate;

he shunned large-scale gatherings, such as meetings of the unwieldy NSC, because they did not offer a forum for the intimate discussion that he preferred.[28] While Kennedy shared LBJ's affinity for confidentiality and dislike of press leaks, he had opted for a more freewheeling and disorderly approach to foreign policy management, frequently seeking the input of various subordinates in the State and Defense departments so as to encourage debate and explore different options.[29] Johnson, by contrast, had no wish to enmesh himself in internal disputes at Foggy Bottom or the Pentagon. Consequently, he accorded Rusk and McNamara a considerable degree of leeway in the running of their respective departments, making it a practice not to interact directly with officials below their rank without prior notification.[30] In turn, Rusk, McNamara, and Bundy shared Johnson's impatience with the diplomatic bureaucracy, worked diligently to contain intradepartmental conflicts and present unified views, and were completely deferential to presidential authority.[31] This centralized, hierarchical advisory system enabled LBJ to maintain personal control over policy-making and secure the cherished objective of consensus, yet this came at the expense of limited exposure to the alternative viewpoints of those outside the inner circle.[32]

The pre-eminent role accorded to this select few reflected the high degree of trust and respect that Johnson had for each man. A graduate of Groton and Yale and a former dean of Harvard College, the urbane Bundy was the embodiment of the Eastern elite that LBJ feared and despised. Bundy's privileged upbringing, his close ties with the Kennedy family, and his inability to establish any rapport with the earthy Texan all made for a strained relationship that reached near breaking point by mid-1965, culminating in his departure from government the following February.[33] Personal differences aside, however, Bundy was in constant contact with Johnson and was absolutely pivotal in familiarizing the new President with the foreign policy agenda and in framing his understanding of the issues.[34] Johnson considered McNamara to be the most versatile and impressive member of Kennedy's cabinet. By most accounts, he was in awe of the Secretary's commanding intellect and expended considerable effort in wooing him.[35]

Rusk experienced the greatest change in fortune as a result of the events of November 1963. Derided by contemporaries and many historians as a weak personality, the aloof and soft-spoken Georgian was selected by Kennedy precisely because he did not want an assertive State Department hijacking his diplomatic agenda.[36] Despite even these low expectations, Kennedy evidently grew impatient with Rusk's cautious and deliberate style, to the point where he considered the possibility of replacing him after the 1964 election.[37] However, Rusk's humble southern origins, self-effacing manner, political acumen, and unstinting loyalty earned LBJ's personal regard. Nor did it escape Johnson's attention that his Secretary of State, unlike McNamara or Bundy, had not been an intimate of Kennedy's or that his personal relations with the much-loathed Robert Kennedy were less than cordial. All of this enabled Rusk to acquire vastly more influence with Johnson than he had with JFK.[38] Rusk, the President gushed, "was not a mean, scheming, conniving man ... you could fire Dean Rusk at noon and he would come for dinner at night and be just as nice about it as if it had never happened[,] and for that reason he would be Secretary of State as long as he wished to stay."[39]

Johnson's reliance on this triad had considerable consequences for US China policy. All three men shared Kennedy's heightened threat perception of 1962–63 and drew alarming conclusions from Beijing's nuclear weapons program, its espousal of revolutionary upheaval throughout the Afro-Asian world, and its hostility toward Moscow's search for "peaceful co-existence" with the West; their image of a reckless, militant, and expansionist China with no regard for American conceptions of international order was crystallized well before LBJ assumed office.[40] Bundy, in fact, had been Kennedy's point man in the administration's efforts to counter China's nuclear effort.[41]

Yet it was Rusk who emerged as the most forceful and articulate voice of opposition within Johnson's inner circle to any modification of America's posture toward the PRC. By far the most experienced hand in Asian affairs among Johnson's men, Rusk's unpleasant encounter with Communist China dated back to March 1950, when he commenced an eventful stint as Truman's Assistant Secretary of State for Far Eastern Affairs. Unlike many of the Atlanticists who dominated the Truman administration, Rusk's wartime service in the China-Burma-India theatre imbued him with the conviction that the US had a vital role to play across the Pacific in ensuring peace and security.[42] Evidently susceptible to the romantic, idealized view of China as a land onto which American values and institutions could be projected, he later likened his reaction to the CCP's victory in October 1949 to that of a "jilted lover," taking strong exception to the new regime's efforts to "erase from memory all traces of more than a century of goodwill and friendly relations between the American and Chinese peoples."[43] He was foremost amongst those at State agitating for a more robust commitment to Taiwan to deter a possible communist invasion in the spring of 1950.[44] China's intervention in the Korean War and its accompanying anti-American political campaigns were milestones in Rusk's formulation of a Chinese menace.[45] Over time historians have come to the rescue of this much-maligned figure, absolving him of much of the blame for the paralysis that characterized China policy during the Kennedy years. Rusk seems to have harbored more flexible and subtle views of the PRC than previously assumed; it was ultimately the political timidity and militancy of JFK that shaped his administration's dealings with Beijing.[46] A thorough reading of the documentary record for the Johnson presidency, however, makes it plainly evident that Rusk was by this point deeply hostile to any China policy reform. The decisive consideration here, as explained in the pages to follow, was the mainland's role in furnishing the communist insurgency in South Vietnam. It was not until the closing months of the Johnson administration, when signs emerged of a more accommodating Chinese leadership, that his interest in extending modest feelers toward the PRC was revived.

Johnson did not share his Secretary of State's fixation with the mainland, yet he deeply appreciated his experience. The fact that Rusk had emerged unscathed from the politically sensitive Far Eastern portfolio must have assured LBJ that he was tried and tested in Asian affairs, a seasoned professional who offered sensible counsel. Moreover, as one of the President's most senior aides recalled, there was a "kinship, a kinetic energy between Johnson and Rusk on the issue of the right wing and the injury done to the body politic by that right wing attack over China and Korea."[47] Fearing a renewed domestic backlash, both men were not inclined to reconsider the fundamental tenets of America's China policy.

The fallout from French recognition

The foundations of this policy, which ultimately rested on the mobilization of sufficient international support for isolating the mainland, were steadily eroding as Johnson assumed power. In December 1963, Chinese Premier Zhou Enlai embarked on an extensive tour of Africa. Part of a larger strategy aimed at enhancing the PRC's prestige in the underdeveloped world, Zhou showered his hosts with technical and economic assistance, calls for an Afro-Asian conference, and exhortations to fend off the forces of imperialism and colonialism.[48] US officials regarded Zhou's diplomatic offensive as a considerable success. While China could not match the aid proffered by the Western or Soviet blocs, it compensated for its limited economic clout with the allure of its revolutionary zeal. "Many Africans," an intelligence report concluded, "are attracted by [the] vehemence [of the] Chicom anti-imperialist line and Chicom support for violence in [the] national liberation struggle." In articulating an identity of Chinese and African interests, Zhou had heightened awareness of the mainland throughout the continent and created pressures for African recognition of the PRC.[49] Five more African nations established diplomatic relations with Beijing in January, bringing the number to a total of fourteen. The consequences of this shift in allegiances for the issue of Chinese representation in the UN were self-evident. Exacerbating the problem, Chinese overtures coincided with the landmark French decision to extend recognition to the mainland that same month. In assessing the fallout from this French initiative, State's INR bureau predicted that more African governments, particularly former French colonies (among which Taiwan had its greatest support), would conclude that "time is running out" on the Nationalists and therefore prompt further approaches to Beijing.[50]

Rumors of a Sino-French rapprochement had been rampant since June 1963, when both nations rejected the Limited Test Ban Treaty.[51] Rusk attempted to gauge de Gaulle's intentions toward the PRC during a visit to Paris in December, all to no avail.[52] When the French government informed Ambassador Charles Bohlen on 7 January of its decision to recognize Beijing, the reaction in Washington was one of disdain and outrage. Senior Johnson officials bristled at the French leader's provocation, taking it to be the latest in a long line of attempts to buttress his country's standing as a world power at the expense of America's strategic interests. Harriman vigorously protested to the French ambassador, asserting that Paris was "throwing away a great deal of good will and affection here in the US only for the sake of demonstrating its independence of US policy."[53] State Department analysts provided a more nuanced rationale for de Gaulle's actions, carefully noting that there was a tangible benefit for France that extended beyond any pleasure derived from provoking the ire of the Americans. As the only major Western power to have full political relations with the PRC, France would enhance its diplomatic leverage with both the US and the Soviets. Above all, reconciliation with the mainland tapped into a wider European sentiment that "an isolated China is more dangerous to world peace than one in contact with other states, and that, in any case, China is a power that must be dealt with in world affairs."[54]

Few, if any, of Johnson's advisers expected the headstrong de Gaulle to reverse his decision. Bundy recommended that the President remain above the fray and let the State Department register the administration's complaints in Paris. In the likely event of French defiance, he wrote LBJ, "You yourself will want to be in a position to shrug this off."[55] Johnson needed little convincing. His reaction to French recognition was decidedly mild, bordering on indifference. This posture was a reflection of both his aforementioned detachment from the China policy sphere and of the myriad concerns, many of them related to the recent presidential transition, then competing for his attention. From Johnson's perspective, the greatest potential threat arising from the affair would be the public spectacle of an ally spurning the entreaties of a new President. He was certain that de Gaulle would "pay no attention" to Washington's grievances. In a conversation with his mentor Senator Richard Russell, Johnson remarked that he was inclined "to play it [French recognition] as low key and just make a little protest for the record."[56]

Officials outside the White House were less nonchalant. A CIA estimate postulated that recognition would lead to the severing of ties between France and Taiwan, since neither Beijing nor Taipei would countenance a "two Chinas" scenario whereby one nation enjoyed relations with both claimants to the Chinese government. The reluctance of several nations to discard their present ties to the Nationalists for the sake of establishing relations with the communist regime would still prevent any stampede to recognize Beijing. Nevertheless, the report concluded, the French maneuver would give impetus to the "gradual erosion of Nationalist China's international position ... enhance Communist China's prestige, and would be seen by much of the world as a harbinger of eventual general recognition." Countries such as Belgium, Luxembourg, Austria, Italy, and Canada – unsympathetic to the American conception of an expansionist China and not constrained by the equivalent of a China Lobby – would come under formidable domestic pressure to follow the French example.[57]

It was precisely this prospect of a snowball effect that most alarmed Rusk. Sensing a more immediate threat than that outlined by intelligence analysts, he believed the administration would "be faced probably quite soon with a danger of recognition of Peiping by some African countries, by Belgium, by Canada, by Japan and by other countries." Rusk reasoned that France represented a "special case," as no government of comparable stature had extended such a gesture to the PRC since the beginning of the Korean War. The French action would encourage others to take the same step: "if this hole is made in the dam[,] the prospect is that the water will flood through." With these ominous consequences in mind, he underlined the "importance of doing all we can to frustrate Paris' and Peiping's move."[58]

While confining himself to the sidelines, Johnson acquiesced in efforts aimed at enlisting the services of French allies, notably Italy and West Germany, to dissuade de Gaulle from playing any China card.[59] To minimize the effects of a Sino-French settlement, the administration resorted to both crude arm-twisting and diplomatic maneuver. Rusk allegedly summoned the Belgian Ambassador and warned him that "if France recognized China and other members of the Alliance followed suit[,] there would be neither depth nor warmth in the Alliance."[60] LBJ was encouraged by the State Department to use the occasion of a January 1964 visit by the Canadian Prime Minister to "Warn against closer relations with Peiping."[61] US officials devoted most of their attention to advising their Taiwanese counterparts against any rash decision to cut off relations with France, in the hopes that this would then place the burden on Paris to choose between Beijing or Taipei. According to this logic, if de Gaulle proved reluctant to break relations unilaterally with the Nationalists, the PRC (hostile to a "two Chinas" arrangement) would cancel further negotiations with France. If, on the other hand, the French cast their lot with the mainland, Rusk argued that this would be "very embarrassing for President De Gaulle ... and would tend to discourage other countries from following the French tactic."[62] To the chagrin of the administration, Chiang Kai-shek relieved the French leader of this dilemma by withdrawing Taiwan's diplomats from Paris in early February.

French recognition presented a quandary to many of America's allies, who had to balance carefully the demands of managing ties to the US with their own interests in broadening contacts with the PRC. Canada's China policy, for example, epitomized this dynamic. Wary of antagonizing the White House, Canadian Prime Minister Lester Pearson ruled out any dramatic departure in strategy, such as recognizing the mainland. Yet a combination of factors – pressure from the

Department of External Affairs for the adoption of a "two Chinas" policy, growing public criticism of the US posture, high-level consensus that peace and stability in East Asia rested on an accommodation with Beijing, and the Prime Minister's own conviction that the Americans faced an impending diplomatic debacle at the UN over Chinese representation – moved him to gently prod Johnson for a change in tactics. In his January 1964 visit to Washington, Pearson argued that a continued emphasis on ostracizing the mainland would only imperil Taiwan's seat at the UN, since this would force many countries to opt for relations either with the Nationalists or with the communist regime that was steadily gaining international stature. French recognition provided the necessary political covering for a shift toward a "two Chinas" formula that would preserve Taiwan's status in the General Assembly even as the PRC was integrated into the same body.[63] More bluntly, a senior Canadian official informed the US ambassador in Ottawa that same month that "Canadian policy was not identical with that of the United States ... ultimately it would be necessary for the west to move in the direction of a two-China policy ... [the] GOC (Government of Canada) did not believe Communist China could or should be diplomatically isolated indefinitely." Hints were dropped of a possible Canadian initiative following the American presidential election in November.[64] In the spring, the Department of External Affairs studied the pros and cons of introducing a one-China, one-Taiwan declaratory resolution in the UN.[65]

Reactions in Tokyo to developments in the early months of 1964 opened up a widening rift between the United States and its most significant Asian partner on how best to manage China's growing influence. Throughout the 1950s vocal elements within the business community and the governing Liberal Democratic Party, keen on diversifying Japan's trade, advocated overtures to the mainland in the face of expressed US disapproval. Successive Japanese administrations juggled these competing concerns by fashioning a policy of "separation of politics and economics," that is, permitting private trade with the PRC while maintaining exclusive diplomatic relations with the Nationalists.[66] Striking a discordant note in an otherwise cordial phase in high-level exchanges between Washington and Tokyo, Kennedy's and Rusk's dogged attempts to discourage their counterparts' interests in expanded ties to the PRC and convince them of the gravity of China's challenge to regional stability fell on deaf ears. As Johnson moved into the Oval Office, the primary irritant in Japanese-

American relations was the irreconcilable difference in assessments of China's threat potential.[67]

French recognition stirred concern in Tokyo that Japan's clout in Asia would wane if it continued to remain allied to Taiwan. In January 1964, Foreign Minister Masayoshi Ohira explained to Rusk that his people felt "remote and uninvolved" from the national liberation struggles raging in Southeast Asia and were far more inclined to view the Soviets rather than the Chinese as their primary adversary. "In contrast to [the] US reaction," he continued, "Japanese political parties and newspapers are expressing [the] feeling that [the] French action opens up new opportunities for contacts with [the] mainland."[68] Ohira's remarks were only one of many signs of a new Japanese assertiveness toward the China question. A June 1964 State Department study concluded that "even conservative Japanese governments will give steadily less weight to dependence on the US as a reason for caution in improving relations with Communist China."[69] US officials observed with some disquiet the rapid growth in Sino-Japanese trade during 1963–64. Most agreed that Japan's enthusiasm for reappraising its policy on more sensitive matters such as recognition and Chinese representation in the UN was tempered by the objective of maintaining harmonious relations with Washington. Still, the lure of greater trade, cultural and geographic ties between the two great Asian peoples, and widespread hopes among elite and popular opinion alike in Japan for fresh initiatives toward the PRC portended troubling implications for any long-term American strategy of isolating China. "The basic question" for officials in Tokyo, according to the CIA, was "merely the manner and timing of the inevitable approach to Peiping."[70]

The resentful, at times emotional, reaction of senior US officials to this galloping movement for engaging China starkly illustrated the saliency of anti-reform sentiment. In a consistent refrain, Rusk wondered why "the question of Peking's admission to the United Nations had been renewed without adequate reproaches being made over their policies in South East Asia."[71] Johnson's entourage contrasted America's global responsibilities with the evident unwillingness of their friends to shoulder the burdens of containing Asian communism, a point they never hesitated to raise in diplomatic settings. Alluding to this disparity, a testy Rusk pointedly reminded Ohira in January 1964, "At a time [when] our resources and blood go to [the] support of countries threatened by Peiping, Peiping should not be helped." While the US could "pull out of Southeast Asia" and still "survive ... other Asian states could not."[72] To his Canadian counterpart, Paul Martin, the Secretary sardonically remarked that he could better "understand" Canada's desire to bring the mainland into the UN only if Ottawa was "willing to put a division into Southeast Asia to help contain Peiping's expansion."[73] Seeing no compelling strategic rationale for integrating China into the international community, the Johnson team contemptuously viewed their allies' renewed push for this objective as nothing more than a short-sighted attempt to placate domestic constituencies. When LBJ asked why Canada would contemplate changing its vote on Chinese representation, Bundy explained that this would be "politically popular" at home.[74]

The growing likelihood of a Chinese nuclear test sometime in 1964 confronted Washington with the prospect of another diplomatic coup for the PRC and further tensions with its Western partners. It would also require conclusive deliberation over the option of a pre-emptive military strike against Chinese nuclear installations.

Learning to co-exist with a nuclear China

Even while Kennedy explored the contingency of a forceful response to China's nuclear effort, elements of the US bureaucracy raised doubts about both the feasibility and necessity of such an operation. While it is uncertain whether or not JFK was ever exposed to this line of thinking,[75] the favorable impression it made on several senior decision-makers, including Rusk and most likely Johnson himself, determined the new administration's decidedly restrained reply to China's detonation of a nuclear device in October 1964. The leading voices of caution in 1963 were the State Department's INR bureau and PPC. In assessing the likely consequences of China's acquisition of nuclear weaponry, an INR report in May offered a more sober prognosis than the gloomy forewarnings emanating from the White House. It discounted the military significance of a nuclear test, arguing that Beijing's awareness of its relative impotence and fear of American retaliation would deter it from brandishing a nuclear weapon for any offensive purpose; Chinese foreign policy would continue to be distinguished by its prudence and aversion to risk-taking behavior. The PRC would instead seek to use a nuclear capability as a political instrument to enhance its international standing, promote neutralism among its neighbors, and stiffen the will of national liberation movements.[76]

The INR bureau also poured cold water on any hope of securing Moscow's assent to a US strike against Chinese facilities, much less Soviet-initiated action. While Soviet leaders did not welcome the possibility of Chinese membership in the nuclear club, they would contemplate military measures only if "Chinese behavior were so bellicose, and China's weapons program so advanced, as to constitute a threat to the security of the Soviet Union." According to US intelligence experts, the Kremlin viewed this as a remote prospect and saw no cause for alarm.[77] These estimates of Soviet attitudes, as well as Harriman's failure to elicit Khrushchev's interest in a military operation during the test ban talks, evidently gave those who viewed Soviet cooperation, tacit or otherwise, as a prerequisite for any move against China pause for thought. Rusk noted to the Dutch Ambassador in November that the Soviets "told us that they felt we were overestimating the possibility of China becoming a nuclear power."[78] Walt Rostow, chairman of the PPC, was convinced that the USSR was not prepared "to join with us in a great venture to deny the Chinese Communists a nuclear capability, since such a venture would mean a total denial of ideological commitment to communism."[79]

A major study drafted by PPC staffer Robert Johnson in October 1963 yielded similar conclusions to those reached by the INR. "The great asymmetry in Chinese Communist and US nuclear capabilities and vulnerabilities," Johnson contended, "makes Chinese Communist first-use of nuclear weapons highly unlikely except in the event of an attack upon the mainland which threatened the existence of the regime." Like the INR, Johnson focused on the political and psychological ramifications of a detonation, which were not inconsiderable. Indeed, nuclear status would aid Beijing in "weakening the will of countries resisting insurgency ... inhibiting their requests for US assistance and ... stimulating and exploiting divisions within Asia and between Asian countries and the West." The security demands of America's regional partners in the wake of a test, however, were expected to be modest. Countering Chinese nuclear subversion would likely entail nothing more than reassuring allies of existing US defense guarantees and their applicability to nuclear contingencies, and offering various forms of nuclear cooperation and increased conventional military assistance.[80]

A widely circulated April 1964 report, also prepared by the PPC's Robert Johnson, elaborated on this analysis. Its central finding was that overt military action against Chinese nuclear facilities was inadvisable unless it could be justified as part of a larger response to "potential or actual Chinese Communist aggression" or as enforcement of an international norm that scorned nuclear weapons production and testing.[81] "In the absence of such a basis for action," Johnson wrote, a "U.S. attack is likely to be viewed as provocative and dangerous and will play into the hands of efforts by Peiping to picture U.S. hostility to Communist China as the source of tensions and the principal threat to the peace in Asia."[82] The likelihood of securing the necessary political covering for a strike was deemed remote. In view of the anticipated reluctance of even a nuclear-armed PRC to incur the risk of an "imperialist" counterstrike, the administration faced an uphill task in convincing its allies of the imperative of taking out Beijing's program. Asian and European nations alike would invariably "weigh their interest in not having Communist China become a nuclear power against their interest in avoiding actions which will threaten the possibility of broadened hostilities in Asia."[83]

Moreover, it could not be safely assumed that even if international opinion was successfully mobilized against nuclear proliferation, that this would sanction "unilateral U.S. military enforcement action against a non-participant Communist China." Besides, the establishment of any such consensus would most likely follow the Chinese detonation of a device, at which point the mainland would be seen as a legitimate nuclear power.[84] Covert action against the PRC's nuclear program was identified as "the politically most feasible" option for decision-makers, yet it too carried the risk of being viewed by much of the world as "U.S.-inspired and supported."[85] While the probability of lasting damage to American prestige and moral authority as a result of an unprovoked attack was very real, the advantages accrued from such a drastic step were uncertain. Even a successful campaign against China's nuclear facilities "would, at best, put them out of operation for [only] a few years."[86]

Many were persuaded by the thrust of this analysis. Rostow enthusiastically forwarded a condensed version of Robert Johnson's findings to LBJ in April.[87] A conversation that same month with Chiang Kai-shek in Taipei revealed the extent to which Rusk had been converted to this non-alarmist mode of thinking. Referring to the possibility of a Chinese nuclear test, Rusk explained that he "was not thinking of the military signficance of such an event because it would be many years before Peiping could develop any significant nuclear power and the United States had plenty of nuclear force to counter it.

What he was wondering about was the psychological effect of such an event."[88] Rusk's remarks cannot be dismissed as merely an effort to assuage the concerns of a nervous ally. He had followed the PPC's deliberations with keen interest since the fall of 1963 and, like Rostow, recommended them to the President at the end of April.[89]

The proponents of restraint, however, did not go unopposed. In December 1963, the Joint Chiefs of Staff, displaying none of the misgivings advanced by many in the State Department, concluded that a nuclear attack against Chinese facilities was feasible.[90] McGeorge Bundy, who had been intimately involved in developing the Kennedy administration's response to China's nuclear project and appeared to share JFK's anxieties, favored further examination of the opportunities for a pre-emptive strike in early 1964.[91] He thought that the PPC's April report had "defused the issue too much" and that a Chinese nuclear capability "would have far greater political consequences" than either Rostow or Robert Johnson allowed.[92]

Bundy's interest in obstructing China's effort was shared by others. Alarmed by mounting evidence of an imminent test, the Commander in Chief of US forces in the Pacific (CINCPAC) advised the Joint Chiefs in July 1964 that this event would embolden the PRC and "hurt our cause" throughout Asia. Accordingly, "everything possible should ... be done to defer the day when the Chinese detonation takes place." CINCPAC recommended a covert effort to impede the delivery or sabotage the quality of components essential to the production of a nuclear device.[93] Rostow was sufficiently concerned by the emergence of views, particularly within the Defense Department's Bureau of International Security Affairs (ISA), diverging from those at Foggy Bottom that he brought this to Rusk's attention at the end of September. Rostow insinuated that failure to achieve a high-level consensus would send a mixed message and undermine the administration's efforts to downplay the ramifications of a possible Chinese detonation to its Asian allies.[94]

An interdepartmental meeting held that same month was emblematic of the diversity of opinion among US officials. Henry Rowen of ISA asserted that the State Department had vastly underestimated the "horrendous" long-term consequences of a nuclear China. He drew a parallel with the "immense effect" that Soviet acquisition of these weapons fifteen years earlier had inflicted on American policies, postures, and defense budgets. He predicted that Washington would be inundated with demands for costly new aid commitments from its friends. China's regional rivals, particularly India, would be tempted to embark on their own nuclear projects. Echoing what had been Kennedy's greatest concern, a militant China that espoused a revolutionary foreign policy "might be even more adventuresome once they went nuclear than the Soviets had been." Beijing could cause further mischief by "handing around nuclear technology" to potential clients. Rowen claimed that a "limited non-nuclear air attack" against Chinese installations would secure a crucial two- to five-year delay in the PRC's nuclear development and possibly discourage any attempt to resuscitate it. While the administration could exploit a "major blow-up" in Southeast Asia for this purpose, a military strike did not have to be based solely on the pretext of Chinese aggression. Rowen was confident that the US could "handle this as a completely open matter and justify it at the time" to the rest of the world. The gathering ended with no agreement among the attendees.[95]

On the basis of the available documentation, LBJ's direct participation in this debate is difficult to trace. In contrast to Kennedy, he never made public reference to the PRC's nuclear ambitions.[96] Nor does there appear to be any record of Johnson's private views on an issue that had gripped the attention of his predecessor. It is possible, however, to fill in the blanks by briefly examining the interrelationship between Johnson's relatively moderate China mindset in 1963–64 and those decisions that were ultimately taken regarding the appropriate response to the PRC's program. The most significant decision in this respect was reached on 15 September, during a meeting that the President held with his principal foreign policy advisers (Rusk, McNamara, Bundy, and CIA Director John McCone). In accordance with the State Department's views, it was agreed that the administration would "prefer to have a Chinese test take place than to initiate" a unilateral strike. Left open were the possibilities of "appropriate military action" in the event that the US found itself engaged in hostilities with China or "joint action" with the Soviets.[97] This ambiguous compromise reflected Johnson's penchant for a flexible, consensus-based foreign policy and it undoubtedly satisfied those aides, particularly Bundy and McNamara, who were still troubled by the specter of a nuclear China. Indeed, in a November 1964 meeting with the Joint Chiefs one month following the first Chinese test, McNamara disclosed his continuing interest in a "strike against the Communist nuclear facilities," possibly as part of a bombing campaign against North Vietnam. "What worries me," he mused, "is the long-term picture of the capabilities of the 700 million people within the boundaries of China."[98]

For Johnson, the September decision flowed from the same dynamic – preoccupation with domestic matters and a lack of sustained interest in China policy – that had governed his reaction to the French recognition controversy. As William Burr and Jeffrey Richelson have plausibly surmised, the President's opposition to an unprovoked pre-emptive attack stemmed from his overriding determination to present himself during the presidential campaign as the responsible, statesmanlike alternative to the hawkish Barry Goldwater.[99] The strategic rationale underlying LBJ's decision – that the minimal military significance of a Chinese nuclear capability did not warrant the harm to American diplomatic interests that a preemptive strike would exact – comported with his own relatively mild assessment of Chinese power. Upon entering the Oval Office, Johnson viewed the PRC as primarily a subversive, politico-psychological threat, certainly not a strategic adversary on a par with the Soviet Union. Reinforcing his cautious stance toward an impending Chinese test was an ingrained aversion to confrontation with the mainland, rooted in the horrific precedent of the Korean War. This sentiment governed his behavior in the fall of 1964, just as it would during the Vietnam War. If Kennedy's personal absorption with China's nuclear effort provided impetus to the contemplation of military action in 1963, it can also be said that LBJ's comparatively detached posture left its own imprint on the deliberative process and its ultimate outcome.

Pursuant to the 15 September discussions, Bundy met with Soviet Ambassador Anatoly Dobrynin ten days later and raised the administration's interest in a "private and serious talk on what to do about" China's weapons program. Dobrynin's indifferent reply sealed the fate of the pre-emptive option.[100] High-level attention turned to the implementation of a political plan that had been developed by a PPC-chaired interdepartmental committee during the summer. The plan, as Rostow outlined it, did not necessitate any bold changes in policy. The objective was simply to "minimize the adverse impact" of a detonation by "reassur[ing] other nations" and "insur[ing] that the Chinese do not miscalculate the value of their capability."[101] As part of this strategy, the State Department delivered a background briefing to the press on 29 September. Reporters were informed that the US expected a Chinese test in the very near future, the military value of which would be diminished by the lack of a reliable nuclear delivery system.¹⁰² In presenting a calm statement of anticipation, the administration sought to deny the PRC any diplomatic advantage arising from the element of surprise and to convey an image of steadfast vigilance to the mainland, Asian allies, and domestic critics alike. With the latter particularly in mind, LBJ remarked to his aides, "Our position should not be provocative but we should not give the impression of being unconcerned."¹⁰³ When China tested a nuclear device on 16 October, a White House statement issued the same day covered similar ground, stressing to the same audiences that this "would have no effect upon the readiness of the United States to respond to requests from Asian nations for help in dealing with Communist Chinese aggression."¹⁰⁴

Johnson officials were generally satisfied with the mild reaction of China's neighbors (aside from Taiwan) to the test, attributing this in no small part to their careful preparation of world opinion for the event. Most regional leaders, one report found, "seem to have thought through the implications of a CCNE [Chinese Communist Nuclear Explosion] and to have decided that they could live with them."¹⁰⁵ Yet the scale of China's feat, which dramatically shattered any lingering illusions that the communist regime in Beijing was a passing phenomenon, presented new unsettling strategic realities for an administration that, even as it shunned military conflict with the mainland, was determined to perpetuate its status as an international pariah. A sampling of elite and popular reaction in allied nations by the State Department in late October revealed "renewed calls for admitting Peiping to the United Nations" and for the US to "take the initiative in trying to bring Communist China 'into the community of nations.'"¹⁰⁶ Within a week of the detonation, UN Secretary General U Thant called for the convening of a nuclear disarmament conference, with the PRC's full-scale participation alongside other nuclear nations.¹⁰⁷ Reports from Tokyo pointed to a definitive shift in sentiment in favor of normalizing relations with Beijing and downgrading ties to Taipei.¹⁰⁸ US analysts held out little hope that even the new Prime Minister, Eisaku Sato, reputed to be more sympathetic to the American position than his predecessors, could halt the momentum within conservative political circles toward Sino-Japanese rapprochement; "his practical course of action," an intelligence report speculated, "may be limited to minimizing the effects and extent of such a movement, rather than preventing it completely."¹⁰⁹

The dramatic events of October revived the Canadian government's interest in advancing a one-China, one-Taiwan declaratory resolution at the UN, an initiative that had been shelved during the summer out of concern for the American reaction. This resolution now served as the basis for joint discussions with Italy and Belgium.[110] In a mid-November meeting with Rusk, the Canadian ambassador to Washington, Charles Ritchie, explained that the CCNE had created a swelling of support among the Canadian public for engaging in dialogue with China. He opined that many other countries felt the same way. While his government would continue to support the "important question" formula at the UN, it no longer felt obliged to oppose the Albanian resolution (which would seat the the PRC and expel the Nationalists). To avert Taiwan's possible ejection and a diplomatic debacle for the US at the upcoming vote on Chinese representation in the 19th General Assembly, Ottawa intended to sponsor its own "two Chinas" solution.[111]

Even before receiving this unwelcome news, many in Washington were bracing themselves for a change in fortune. At the end of October, Harlan Cleveland, the Assistant Secretary of State for International Organization Affairs, thought it likely that the administration could eke out a victory on the "important question" resolution in the next few weeks. Without a change in tactics, however, Cleveland glumly forecasted "a serious defeat on the issue in the 20th General Assembly." Many countries that had hitherto upheld Taiwan's status at the UN, partly in deference to the US, were now "impatient to get on some new track that is not vulnerable to the political charge [that] they are 'ignoring' the world's most populous nation," and were inclined to blame "the rigid posture of the United States" for "somehow preventing an accommodation with the CHICOMS."[112]

Just as US decision-makers had weighed world opinion when pondering a pre-emptive strike, they now confronted the prospect of allied resentment and a possible loss of face at the UN if they persisted with a hard-line China policy. In a November 1964 article in the *New York Times Magazine*, George Kennan, one of the nation's most respected authorities on foreign affairs, picked up on this theme. In a "psychological and political sense," he perceived China as posing a challenge more vexing than any in the post-war era. Yet both diplomatic recognition and UN membership were inevitable for a country of its size and influence. For reasons perhaps owing as much to domestic politics as to grand strategy, America could not be expected to take the lead in embracing the PRC. Yet by investing their resources in an indefinite campaign to quarantine the mainland, Kennan warned the Johnson team that they were irritating friends and courting "unnecessary prestige defeats for ourselves in the event the decisions eventually go against our wishes."[113]

Kennan was only one of several public figures voicing growing uneasiness with America's stance toward the PRC. Most significantly, many of these voices emanated from Congress, the bastion of pro-Chinese Nationalist sentiment in the 1950s.[114] In an address delivered shortly after French recognition, Senator J. William Fulbright, the Democratic chairman of the Senate Foreign Relations Committee, affirmed his belief that the prevailing freeze in Sino-American relations was destined to change, "if not to friendship, then perhaps to 'competitive coexistence.'" To facilitate this development, Fulbright, while unprepared to advocate recognition, thought it would be "an extremely useful thing if we could introduce an element of flexibility, or more precisely of the capacity to be flexible, into our relations with Communist China."[115] A May 1965 report from a House subcommittee chaired by Democrat Clement J. Zablocki reached similar conclusions, proposing that the White House give "consideration to the initiation of limited but direct contact with Red China through cultural exchange activities with emphasis on scholars and journalists."[116]

That senior Democrats felt free to express these opinions without any apparent fear of political retribution indicated that the terms of the China debate had subtly evolved in the early 1960s. Polling results in mid-1964 revealed a plurality of Americans identifying the PRC as the greatest danger to world peace. According to a Harris survey in June, support for China's admission to the UN was opposed by a seven-to-one margin. When the question was predicated on the President's approval of the mainland's entry into the world body, however, the gap was substantially reduced to a 53 to 31 majority in favor of the status quo.[117] This dichotomy between widespread antagonism toward the PRC and strong hints of a public willingness to acquiesce in a presidential initiative, Rosemary Foot has explained, resulted from "the growing realization that the Chinese Communist regime was a hard fact of life that had to be accommodated and, after China's 1964 explosion of an atomic bomb, one that would be ignored at America's peril."[118]

Indeed, the Chinese test appeared to elicit from many Americans something akin to the conciliatory sentiment among allied public opinion that so nettled US officials. A steady stream of newspaper editorials pressed the administration for more constructive approaches toward the PRC.[119] Another Harris poll taken at the end of November showed a 15 percent increase in those favoring the mainland's membership in the UN since June, with those opposed to such a move having fallen 17 percent.[120] While anything approaching a consensus remained elusive for an issue as sensitive as Chinese representation, the public displayed greater interest in modest measures that would still go some way in expanding contacts with Beijing and lowering tensions. A study sponsored at the time by the Council on Foreign Relations revealed majority support for a mutual exchange of news correspondents (53 percent), remaining in the UN if the PRC was seated (54 percent), and enhanced dialogue with Chinese representatives (51 percent). Perhaps most startling was the large number (as much as a quarter) of respondents who expressed no opinion or were even unaware that the mainland regime was ruled by communists, all of which suggested a significant degree of indifference toward an issue that had scourged the Democrats in the previous decade. Writing to his politically conscious superiors, an official at State's ACA bureau opined that these numbers suggested that the China problem had been effectively depoliticized: "public 'stickiness' is not a principal deterrent to changes in our China policy, so long as it does not appear that we are selling out to Communism."[121]

To the dismay of the Johnson team, the PRC steadily gained acceptance throughout 1964 as a legitimate member of the international community, a power whose inclusion in the world's deliberative organs was deemed essential to the greater cause of peace and stability. Allied interest in forging economic and political contacts with the mainland, of course, was hardly new. Yet the PRC's growing diplomatic and military clout, coming against the backdrop of mounting tensions in Southeast Asia, highlighted for many world capitals the folly of forgoing relations with Beijing for the sake of what was seen as a corrupt and authoritarian government in Taipei. What was relatively new was the frequency and forcefulness with which a growing number of domestic elites echoed some of this thinking. Moreover, there were indications that sizeable elements of the public had become either more flexible or detached in their views of the mainland.

The administration was not inclined to respond in kind to this sentiment. Instead, Johnson approved a number of initiatives aimed at prolonging the PRC's isolation. His instinctive hostility to China policy reform sprang more from a politically infused aversion to rocking the boat and a determination to preserve his martyred predecessor's record than from any personal fixation with Chinese power. Indeed, when some of his advisers pushed for the option of a preemptive strike against China's nuclear installations, LBJ showed little enthusiasm for militarized containment. A more immediate concern in the fall of 1964, as the President saw it, was not the specter of a nuclear-armed China wreaking havoc, but how to reconcile the escalating pressures for a reassessment of existing China strategy with the communist insurgency engulfing South Vietnam.

Notes

1 H. Kissinger, *White House Years* (Boston: Little, Brown, 1979), p. 18.
2 E.F. Goldman, *The Tragedy of Lyndon Johnson* (New York: Alfred A. Knopf, 1969), p. 380; N.B. Tucker, "Lyndon Johnson: A final reckoning," in Cohen and Tucker (eds), *Lyndon Johnson Confronts the World*, p. 313; Brands, *The Wages of Globalism*, p. 24; Logevall, *Choosing War*, p. 390; T. Preston, *The President and His Inner Circle: Leadership Style and the Advisory Process in Foreign Affairs* (New York: Columbia University Press, 2001), pp. 151–3.
3 Quoted in D.K. Goodwin, *Lyndon Johnson and the American Dream*, Revised ed. (New York: St. Martin's Press, 1991), pp. 329–30.
4 Ibid., pp. 94–7.
5 LBJ to JFK, 23 May 1961, NSF, International Meetings and Travel File, Box 1, folder "VP Johnson's trip to the Far East, May 1961 (2 of 2)," LBJL.
6 For the influence of the Korean analogy on LBJ, see Y.F. Khong, *Analogies at War: Korea, Munich, Dien Bien Phu and the Vietnam Decisions of 1965* (Princeton: Princeton University Press, 1992), ch. 5.
7 T.M. Gaskin, "Senator Lyndon B. Johnson and United States Foreign Policy" (PhD Dissertation, University of Washington, 1989), pp. 294–305.
8 R. Dallek, *Flawed Giant: Lyndon Johnson and His Times, 1961–1973* (New York: Oxford University Press, 1998), p. 16.
9 Beschloss, *The Crisis Years*, pp. 511–12; Reeves, *President Kennedy*, pp. 118–19.
10 See Chang, *Friends and Enemies*, p. 242.
11 WPB Papers, Box 1, ch. 16, p. 15, LBJL; Telephone interview with James C. Thomson, 18 February 2002.
12 James C. Thomson Oral History (hereafter OH), p. 47, LBJL.

13 J. Suri, *Power and Protest: Global Revolution and the Rise of Détente* (Cambridge: Harvard University Press, 2003), p. 147.
14 Author's interview with Walt Rostow, Austin, Texas, 17 January 2002.
15 Goldman, *Tragedy of Lyndon Johnson*, p. 379.
16 Quoted in Goodwin, *Lyndon Johnson and the American Dream*, p. 252.
17 Gaskin, "Senator Lyndon B. Johnson and United States Foreign Policy," pp. 4–5, 293; Dallek, *Lone Star Rising*, p. 433.
18 Heinrichs, "Change and continuity," in Cohen and Tucker (eds), *Lyndon Johnson Confronts the World*, p. 15.
19 Quoted in Beschloss, *The Crisis Years*, p. 513.
20 Quoted in Goodwin, *Lyndon Johnson and the American Dream*, p. 251.
21 Brands, *The Wages of Globalism*, pp. 28–9; Kaiser, "Men and policies: 1961–9," in Kunz (ed.), *Diplomacy of the Crucial Decade*, p. 12.
22 Telcon, LBJ–Richard Russell, 15 January 1964, in Beschloss (ed.), *Taking Charge*, p. 162.
23 Quoted in Goodwin, *Lyndon Johnson and the American Dream*, pp. 177–8.
24 Richard Goodwin, LBJ's chief speechwriter in 1964–65, documented the darker side of the President's infinitely complex personality in his memoirs, claiming that Johnson displayed unmistakeable signs of paranoia. See R.N. Goodwin, *Remembering America: A Voice From the Sixties* (Boston: Little, Brown, 1988), ch. 21. Bill Moyers, one of Johnson's most senior political aides, later confirmed that he shared Goodwin's fears. Dallek, *Flawed Giant*, pp. 280–4.
25 Quoted in T.A. Schwartz, "Lyndon Johnson and Europe: Alliance politics, political economy, and 'growing out of the Cold War,'" in Brands (ed.), *Foreign Policies of Lyndon Johnson*, p. 38.
26 Dallek, *Flawed Giant*, pp. 84–5; Telcon, LBJ–Walker Stone, 31 January 1964, in Beschloss (ed.), *Taking Charge*, p. 200.
27 Goodwin, *Lyndon Johnson and the American Dream*, p. 256.
28 D.C. Humphrey, "Tuesday lunch at the Johnson White House: A preliminary assessment," *Diplomatic History* 8:1 (1984), 83, 93.
29 Bird, *Color of Truth*, pp. 185–6.
30 Heinrichs, "Change and continuity," in Cohen and Tucker (eds), *Lyndon Johnson Confronts the World*, p. 22; G.C. Herring, *LBJ and Vietnam: A Different Kind of War* (Austin: University of Texas Press, 1994), p. 7; Hilsman, *To Move a Nation*, p. 535; P.Y. Hammond, *LBJ and the Presidential Management of Foreign Relations* (Austin: University of Texas Press, 1992), pp. 2, 14.
31 D.L. DiLeo, *George Ball, Vietnam, and the Rethinking of Containment* (Chapel Hill: University of North Carolina Press, 1991), p. 102; D.C. Humphrey, "NSC meetings during the Johnson presidency," *Diplomatic History* 18:1 (1994), 31.

32 Preston, *The President and His Inner Circle*, pp. 139–43.
33 Bird, *Color of Truth*, pp. 189, 299–300, 320–3; A. Preston, *The War Council: McGeorge Bundy, the NSC, and Vietnam* (Cambridge: Harvard University Press, 2006), pp. 195–201.
34 Dallek, *Flawed Giant*, p. 90.
35 D. Shapley, *Promise and Power: The Life and Times of Robert McNamara* (Boston: Little, Brown, 1993), pp. 276–8.
36 Freedman, *Kennedy's Wars*, p. 37.
37 Reeves, *President Kennedy*, p. 561. For JFK's less than flattering assessment of Rusk, see Beschloss, *The Crisis Years*, pp. 356–60.
38 Cohen, *Dean Rusk*, pp. 94–6, 218–21; Brands, *The Wages of Globalism*, pp. 6–7; T. J. Schoenbaum, *Waging Peace and War: Dean Rusk in the Truman, Kennedy, and Johnson Years* (New York: Simon & Schuster, 1988), pp. 409–14; J. Shesol, *Mutual Contempt: Lyndon Johnson, Robert Kennedy and the Fued that Defined a Decade* (W.W. Norton & Company, 1997), p. 297. For Rusk's take on his frosty relationship with Robert Kennedy, see Rusk, *As I Saw It*, pp. 268, 280–1.
39 Diary entry, 12 December 1965, Papers of Orville L. Freeman, Diary, folder "Volume 6: August 28 1965 – May 17 1966," LBJL.
40 Kochavi, *A Conflict Perpetuated*, pp. 153–4, 230–2, 250; Fetzer, "Clinging to containment," in Paterson (ed.), *Kennedy's Quest for Victory*, pp. 193–7.
41 Burr and Richelson, "Whether to 'strangle the baby,'" p. 55.
42 T.W. Zeiler, *Dean Rusk: Defending the American Mission Abroad* (Wilmington: SR Books, 2000), p. 12; Schoenbaum, *Waging Peace and War*, ch. 3.
43 Rusk, *As I Saw It*, pp. 135–6.
44 Accinelli, *Crisis and Commitment*, pp. 17–27.
45 Kochavi, *A Conflict Perpetuated*, pp. 35–6; Cohen, *Dean Rusk*, ch. 4; Schoenbaum, *Waging Peace and War*, pp. 218, 222–5.
46 Kochavi, *A Conflict Perpetuated*; Cohen, *Dean Rusk*, pp. 163–7; Schoenbaum, *Waging Peace and War*, pp. 387–8.
47 Bill Moyers, quoted in Dallek, *Flawed Giant*, p. 88.
48 Kuo-kang Shao, *Zhou Enlai and the Foundations of Chinese Foreign Policy* (New York: St. Martin's Press, 1996), pp. 227–34. For Mao's interest in expanding China's influence throughout the Afro-Asian world, see Radchenko, "The China Puzzle," pp. 105–8.
49 Airgram, no. CA-8112, Department of State to All African posts, 14 February 1964, RG 59, Central Files, 1964–66, Box 2011, POL 7 VISITS CHICOM, NA; Telegram, no. 1231, Department of State to Paris, 27 February 1964, ibid.
50 George C. Denney, Jr to Rusk, 13 February 1964, RG 59, Records of the Policy Planning Council, 1963–64, Lot 70D199, Box 250, NA.

51 Denney to Rusk, 22 January 1964, NSF, Country File, Box 176, folder "Recognition of Communist China, vol. I (3 of 3)," LBJL; Kochavi, *A Conflict Perpetuated*, p. 223.
52 Telegram, Rusk to Department of State, 16 December 1963, *FRUS*, 1961–1963, vol. 22, pp. 409–10.
53 Telegram, Department of State to Paris, 15 January 1964, *FRUS*, 1964–1968, vol. 30, p. 2.
54 Denney to Rusk, 22 January 1964, NSF, Country File, Box 176, LBJL. For a discussion of the motives underlying the Sino-French rapprochement of 1963–64, see Suri, *Power and Protest*, pp. 71–9.
55 M. Bundy to LBJ, 8 January 1964, NSF, Memos to the President, Box 1, folder "Vol. I (2 of 2)," LBJL.
56 Editorial note, *FRUS*, 1964–1968, vol. 30, p. 3.
57 CIA memorandum, "Implications of an assumed French recognition of Communist China," 15 January 1964, NSF, Country File, Box 176, folder "Recognition of Communist China, vol. I (3 of 3)," LBJL.
58 Telegram (unnumbered), Department of State to Tokyo, 24 January 1964, NSF, Country File, Box 176, folder "Recognition of Communist China, vol. I (2 of 3)," LBJL.
59 Telegram, no. 1976, Department of State to Bonn, 16 January 1964, NSF, Country File, Box 176, folder "Recognition of Communist China, vol. I (3 of 3)," LBJL; Telegram, no. 1685, Department of State to Rome, 16 January 1964, ibid.
60 Telegram, no. 35, David Ormsby-Gore to the Foreign Office, 22 January 1964, FO 371/175922, Public Record Office (hereafter PRO).
61 Talking points paper, "Communist China," 17 January 1964, NSF, Country File, Box 167, folder "Pearson Visit Briefing Book 1/21–22/64 (1 of 2)," LBJL.
62 Memorandum of conversation, Rusk–Ambassador Kim Chong-yul, 21 January 1964, RG 59, Office of East Asian Affairs, Lot 66D225, Box 10, NA; Telegram, Department of State to Taipei, 18 January 1964, *FRUS*, 1964–1968, vol. 30, p. 8. For Johnson's approval of this tactic, see Telcon, LBJ–M. Bundy, 15 January 1964, in K.B. Germany and R.D. Johnson (eds), *The Presidential Recordings, Lyndon B. Johnson: The Kennedy Assassination and the Transfer of Power, November 1963–January 1964*, vol. 3 (New York: W.W. Norton & Company, 2005), p. 523.
63 N. St Amour, "Sino-Canadian relations, 1963–1968: The American factor," in P.M. Evans and B.M. Frolic (eds), *Reluctant Adversaries: Canada and the People's Republic of China, 1949–1970* (Toronto: University of Toronto Press, 1991), pp. 106–10.
64 Telegram, no. 928, Ottawa to Department of State, 20 January 1964,

NSF, Country File, Box 176, folder "Recognition of Communist China, vol. I (2 of 3)," LBJL.
65 St. Amour, "Sino-Canadian Relations," in Evans and Frolic (eds), *Reluctant Adversaries*, p. 110.
66 M. Schaller, "Altered states: The United States and Japan during the 1960s," in Kunz (ed.), *Diplomacy of the Crucial Decade*, pp. 269–72.
67 Kochavi, *A Conflict Perpetuated*, pp. 143–5.
68 Telegram (unnumbered), Tokyo to Department of State, 28 January 1964, NSF, Country File, Box 250 (1 of 2), Japan memos, vol. I, LBJL.
69 "Department of State policy on the future of Japan," p. 58, 26 June 1964, NSF, Country File, Box 250 (1 of 2), folder "Japan cables, vol. II (2 of 2)," LBJL.
70 CIA special report, "The China problem in Japanese politics," NSF, Country File, Box 237, folder "China memos, vol. I," LBJL.
71 Record of Rusk–Patrick Gordon Walker meeting, 8 December 1964, FO 371/175095, PRO.
72 Telegram (unnumbered), Tokyo to Department of State, 27 January 1964, NSF, Country File, Box 250 (1 of 2), folder "Japan cables, vol. I," LBJL.
73 Memorandum of conversation, 30 November 1964, *FRUS*, 1964–1968, vol. 30, p. 139.
74 Memorandum for the record, 18 November 1964, ibid., p. 128.
75 Burr and Richelson, "Whether to 'strangle the baby,'" p. 96.
76 Denney to Rusk, 6 May 1963, RG 59, Records of the Policy Planning Council, 1963–64, Lot 70D199, Box 250, NA.
77 Hughes to Rusk, 11 September 1963, ibid.
78 Memorandum of conversation, Rusk–Ambassador J. Herman van Roijen, 1 November 1963, RG 59, Central Files, 1963, Box 3717, DEF CHICOM, NA.
79 Rostow to Harriman, 30 July 1963, Papers of W. Averell Harriman, Box 518, USSR: General, 1963, Library of Congress.
80 "A Chinese communist nuclear detonation and nuclear capability: Major conclusions and key issues," pp. 1–3, 15 October 1963, RG 59, Records of the Policy Planning Council, 1963–64, Lot 70D199, Box 250, NA.
81 "An exploration of the possible bases for action against the Chinese communist nuclear facilities," p. 5, enclosed in Rostow to M. Bundy, 22 April 1964, NSF, Country File, Box 237, folder "China memos, vol. I," LBJL.
82 Ibid., p. 32.
83 Ibid., pp. 11–12.
84 Ibid., p. 26.
85 Ibid., pp. 3, 32.
86 Ibid., pp. 1, 3–4.

87 Rostow to LBJ, 17 April 1964, NSF, Country File, Box 237, folder "China memos, vol. I," LBJL.
88 Memorandum of conversation, 16 April 1964, *FRUS*, 1964–1968, vol. 30, p. 50.
89 Burr and Richelson, "Whether to 'strangle the baby,'" pp. 78, 83.
90 *FRUS*, 1964–1968, vol. 30, p. 24, n. 7.
91 Ibid., p. 24, n. 8.
92 Memorandum for the record, 20 April 1964, ibid., pp. 56–7.
93 CINCPAC to the Joint Chiefs of Staff, July 1964, NSF, Country File, Box 237, folder "China cables, vol. I," LBJL.
94 Rostow to Rusk, 26 September 1964, RG 59, Records of the Ambassador at Large Llewellyn E. Thompson, 1961–1970, Lot 67D2, Box 4, NA.
95 Komer to M. Bundy, 18 September 1964, *FRUS*, 1964–1968, vol. 30, p. 97.
96 Burr and Richelson, "Whether to 'strangle the baby,'" p. 79.
97 Memorandum for the Record, 15 September 1964, NSF, Memos to the President, Box 2, folder "Vol. VI (1 of 2)," LBJL.
98 Quoted in Kaiser, *American Tragedy*, p. 354.
99 Burr and Richelson, "Whether to 'strangle the baby,'" p. 88.
100 Memorandum of conversation, 25 September 1964, *FRUS*, 1964–1968, vol. 30, p. 105.
101 "Program of action: A Chinese communist nuclear detonation and capability," enclosed in Rostow to M. Bundy, 25 September 1964, RG 59, Records of the Policy Planning Council, 1963–64, Lot 70D199, Box 250, NA.
102 Memorandum for the record, 29 September 1964, RG 59, Records of the Ambassador at Large Llewellyn E. Thompson, 1961–1970, Lot 67D2, Box 26, NA; Burr and Richelson, "Whether to 'strangle the baby,'" pp. 89–90.
103 Summary notes of 543rd NSC meeting, 17 October 1964, NSF, National Security Council Meetings (hereafter NSCM), Box 1, folder "Vol. 3, tab 25," LBJL.
104 "Statement by the President on Chinese communist detonation of nuclear devices," 16 October 1964, RG 59, Records of the Policy Planning Council, 1963–64, Lot 70D199, Box 250, NA.
105 Lindsey Grant to William Bundy, 23 October 1964, RG 59, Central Files, 1964–66, Box 1615, DEF 12-1 CHICOM, NA.
106 Hughes to Rusk, 28 October 1964, NSF, Committee File, Box 5, folder "China," LBJL. See as well Carl Rowan to LBJ, 19 October 1964, NSF, Country File, Box 290, folder "United Nations Chinese Representation," LBJL.

107 Waldron, "From nonexistent to almost normal," in Kunz (ed.), *Diplomacy of the Crucial Decade*, p. 236.
108 Telegram, no. 1125, Department of State to Tokyo, 23 October 1964, RG 59, Central Files, 1964–66, Box 2012, POL 16 INDEPENDENCE CHICOM, NA; Airgram, no. A-692, Tokyo to Department of State, 10 December 1964, RG 59, Central Files, 1964–66, Box 1614, DEF 12-1 CHICOM, NA; Telegram, no. 2044, Tokyo to Department of State, 28 December 1964, NSF, Country File, Box 253 (1 of 2), folder "Sato's Visit: Memos & Cables (2 of 4)," LBJL.
109 Hughes to the Acting Secretary, 10 November 1964, NSF, Country File, Box 250 (1 of 2), folder "Japan memos, vol. II (2 of 2)," LBJL.
110 St Amour, "Sino-Canadian relations," in Evans and Frolic (eds), *Reluctant Adversaries*, p. 111.
111 D. Page, "The representation of China in the United Nations: Canadian perspectives and initiatives, 1949–1971," in ibid., p. 92.
112 Harlan Cleveland to George Ball, 31 October 1964, pp. 2–4, NSF, Country File, Box 290, folder "United Nations Chinese Representation 10/65," LBJL.
113 G.F. Kennan, "A fresh look at our China policy," *New York Times Magazine*, 22 November 1964, p. 144.
114 Foot, "Redefinitions," in Ross and Jiang (eds), *Re-examining the Cold War*, p. 278. For a discussion of the 1950s, see S.D. Bachrack, *The Committee of One Million: "China Lobby" Politics, 1953–1971* (New York: Columbia University Press, 1976), chs 3–7.
115 Quoted in Waldron, "From nonexistent to almost normal," in Kunz (ed.), *Diplomacy of the Crucial Decade*, p. 235.
116 James C. Thomson, Jr to M. Bundy, 2 June 1965, NSF, Country File, Box 238, folder "China memos, vol. III," LBJL.
117 Kusnitz, *Public Opinion and Foreign Policy*, p. 109.
118 Foot, "Redefinitions," in Ross and Jiang (eds), *Re-examining the Cold War*, p. 277.
119 Thomson to Douglass Cater, 24 November 1964, White House Central Files (hereafter WHCF), Box 10, folder "Federal Government," LBJL.
120 Kusnitz, *Public Opinion and Foreign Policy*, p. 112.
121 Grant to W. Bundy, 30 October 1964, RG 59, Subject Files of the Office of Asian Communist Affairs, 1961–73, Lot 71D423, Box 1, NA.

3 In Vietnam's shadow
The reaffirmation of US China policy, 1964–65

On the surface, developments in the early stages of the Johnson presidency created an auspicious setting for at least a minor departure in China policy. The positive press reviews of Roger Hilsman's December 1963 address and the muted reaction from a weakened China Lobby indicated a relaxed political climate, while LBJ's sweeping victory in the 1964 election afforded an ideal opportunity for providing substance to Hilsman's words.[1] As Johnson committed his nation to war in Vietnam in July 1965, however, the line of containment and isolation bequeathed by his predecessors remained firmly intact. This chapter links this policy paralysis to the fervently held belief of the President and his closest aides that Beijing's support of the communist insurgency in South Vietnam was part of a larger strategy of indirect aggression aimed at expelling American influence from Southeast Asia.[2]

While establishing the Johnson team's determination to stem communist advances in Vietnam as a decisive determinant of their attitudes toward the PRC, this chapter also underscores how images of China in turn magnified the perceived stakes in defending the embattled regime in Saigon. Indeed, in justifying its growing involvement in Vietnam to the American public, the administration frequently cited the pressing need for containing Chinese expansionism.[3] Curiously, however, in most of the literature pertaining to the pivotal Vietnam decisions of 1963–65, discussion of America's perception of China's role in the conflict has been effectively relegated to the sidelines, lost in a maze of Saigon cables and in meticulous narratives of the events that compelled US decision-makers to seek a military solution in the North in lieu of a political one in the South.[4] The implication here is that on the long list of factors accounting for the commitment of US air and ground forces to the defense of South Vietnam in 1965, containing China ranked near the bottom. Indeed, the author of one very well-received study concluded that geostrategic considerations in general and concerns over Chinese ambitions in particular did not play a decisive role in the decision-making process.[5] No less an authority than John Lewis Gaddis has argued that the PRC was simply too "impotent" to be of any concern to Johnson policymakers, who were far more preoccupied with averting an embarrassing defeat in South Vietnam than with checking a Chinese threat that never in fact existed.[6] Some historians have suggested that those same officials who spoke alarmingly of a Chinese menace may have privately viewed Beijing as little more than a convenient bogeyman for mobilizing popular support for the war.[7] Those who have offered a contrasting view and affirmed that the President and his advisers were genuinely moved to arrest the spread of Chinese influence in Southeast Asia have failed to adequately explore what underpinned this threat perception.[8]

The chapter first examines the spectrum of opinion on China among Johnson officials and the resultant reaffirmation of policy through the summer of 1965. It then elaborates on the basis for the prevailing view of China as a menacing presence in Asia and the impact of this heightened threat perception on the administration's Vietnam discourse. The final section looks at how Washington estimated the prospect of a forceful Chinese rejoinder to American intervention in Vietnam, a consideration that heavily influenced LBJ's cautious escalation of the war effort and that would eventually compel him to modify his stance toward Beijing.

Competing visions of China

The sequence of events outlined in the preceding chapter – French recognition, the Chinese nuclear test, steady pressure from allied nations and elite US opinion for a reappraisal of attitudes – presented the administration with the challenge of how best to respond to the PRC's growing international stature. The fall of 1964 brought a bumper crop of competing policy prescriptions from Johnson officials. The striking divergence of opinion revealed a yawning chasm over the overarching question of whether or not the established strategy of containment and isolation served the purpose of effecting a moderation in China's external behavior.

One well-defined group argued in favor of seizing the initiative and overhauling China policy. Advocates of change during the Kennedy years, they contended that recent international developments underscored the imperative of departing from past practices. James Thomson, a Far East specialist in the State Department until July 1964 and thereafter a China watcher in the NSC, was one of the most vocal and adamant proponents of such a view.[9] The son of China missionaries, raised in China and a student of its history, Thomson's self-admitted "obsession" was "getting back on a better track with China."[10] Unique among many Johnson officials, Thomson dismissed the notion that China was an expansionist threat; ruling the mainland, he thought, was a "full-time job" that did not allow for a bold and ambitious foreign policy.[11] Writing to McGeorge Bundy in October 1964, he warned of the "danger in pushing too far the thesis of Peking's responsibility for the South Vietnam crisis." Urging his superiors to look beyond Vietnam, he asserted that there was little that the United States could do to prevent China's eventual admission to the UN and its wider acceptance as a member of the international community. This presented the administration with a stark choice: "we can either sit tight in increasingly lonely isolation; or we can seek ways to cut our losses."

Thomson proposed a wide range of measures – acquiescence in a "one China, one Taiwan" UN arrangement, the loosening of travel restrictions to the mainland, and the placing of trade in non-strategic goods with China on the same basis as that with the Soviet Union – to deflect escalating allied criticism and thereby shift the blame for poor Sino-American relations. Behind this defensive, short-term tactic was a long-term strategy. Returning to an argument that had won Hilsman's endorsement in 1963, Thomson contended that the "careful use of free world goods, people, and ideas – instruments which have proven their long-term corrosive value in our relations with other totalitarian societies," would expose the PRC to moderating outside influences, encourage the "domestication" of the Chinese revolution, and help erode the distorted worldview of its leadership.[12] One month later, he argued that Johnson's electoral triumph offered an ideal opportunity for enacting these initiatives. As a start, he suggested that the President deliver a briefing to the nation's leading journalists and express both his wish for improved relations with the mainland and a willingness "to search for areas, however small, of mutual self-interest."[13]

Robert Komer joined his fellow NSC staffer in insisting that the domestic and international climate augured well for a shift in course. He interpreted the American public's recent repudiation of Barry Goldwater as "partly a vote for cautious responsibility in a nuclear world." LBJ's mandate at home and his continued support for a non-communist South Vietnam endowed him with the necessary political covering to change tactics on Chinese representation and "retreat gracefully from an increasingly isolated position toward a stance which puts the onus for continued friction more on Peiping and less on us." Komer reasoned that the only way Washington could stem the erosion of Taiwan's international position was to demonstrate greater flexibility by allowing its allies to take the lead in promoting a "two Chinas" solution at the UN. While this shift would buttress America's standing in world opinion, it could also serve as a stepping stone toward the ultimate objective of making "our ChiCom policy more like that toward the USSR – tough where they push us but flexible where there's something to be gained."[14]

Equally enthusiastic in pushing for change was Edward Rice, author of the far-reaching PPC study in October 1961 and now serving as consul general in Hong Kong. Rice maintained that the Chinese threat to US interests had been exaggerated. China's warlike oratory belied tactical caution; its call for wars of national liberation as a means of advancing the revolutionary cause placed the burden on local insurgent groups so as to avert another war with the US. Identifying the Chinese as overt aggressors only served to "blow them up to fearsome size in the eyes of their threatened neighbors" when, in reality, the PRC played "chiefly an off-stage role" in regional affairs. Moreover, Washington's confrontational stance played into Mao's hands, enabling him to use a hostile America as a catalyst for domestic mobilization. As with Thomson and Hilsman, Rice saw a bridge-building opportunity for the administration in China's looming succession struggle. He speculated that the next generation of leadership was likely to be "more concerned with the problems of managing a nation-state than with consummating a revolutionary struggle in the outside world." A unilateral relaxation of trade and travel restrictions would almost certainly be rejected by the "first-generation of religious zealots" currently in power, but these conciliatory gestures could send a message to Mao's successors and thereby "bridge the enormous spiritual gulf between these people and ourselves ... [by] plant[ing] in some of their minds the seeds of doubt as to our irreconcilable enmity."[15]

A second group of Johnson officials was far less ambitious in their policy proposals, recommending only cosmetic and symbolic changes in America's posture, and were far more concerned with what they saw as a menacing Chinese presence in Southeast Asia. This camp was not so much interested in laying the foundation for a new relationship with China as it was in reducing America's growing isolation and re-energizing the policy of containment. Still, even its ambivalent endorsement of change underscored the tenuousness of the US position. In a November 1964 memorandum to LBJ, for example, UN ambassador Adlai Stevenson reasoned that while China would continue to pose the "principal threat" to America's global leadership, the old prescription of containment and isolation was no longer feasible. He envisioned a new strategy that would enlist the support of regional actors such as Japan and India in checking Chinese ambitions by primarily political and economic means. Yet to mobilize support for international vigilance against the PRC, the US had to demonstrate to "potential allies and neutrals" alike that its policy was "directed against Chinese aggressiveness, not against the Chinese people ... and that we are quite ready to negotiate modus vivendi or even real settlements, on a quid pro quo basis, whenever Peiping is ready to accommodate itself to a peaceful world." Chief among Stevenson's recommendations was a "progressive relaxation" of the administration's opposition to the mainland's membership in the UN.[16]

Along somewhat similar lines, Assistant Secretary of State for International Organization Affairs Harlan Cleveland cast doubt on the assumption that the Chinese could be "tamed by the application of sweetness and light." Of greater interest to him was finding a way of "mobilizing all of the world's nations that oppose the way the Chinese Communists are using their power, in a new strategy that puts the primary stress on future improvements in Chinese behavior." Cleveland argued that this did not entail altering China policy in a "fundamental sense;" successful containment merely required the appearance of a change in attitude. Demonstrating a statesman-like willingness to move onto a negotiating track on items such as nuclear testing and Chinese representation would convey a sorely needed image of American flexibility at little expense, since the "implacable hostility" of China's leadership would guarantee minimal progress on these issues. Any deadlock could then be attributed to Chinese intransigence. In this way, a policy of firm containment would be justified and made more palatable to world opinion.[17]

William Bundy, who succeeded Hilsman in the Far East portfolio in March 1964, did not share his predecessor's zeal for new approaches to Beijing. Thomson recollected that his new boss (until July 1964, when Thomson was then assigned to the NSC) regarded him as a "thorn in the flesh."[18] Bundy's China mindset was indelibly influenced by his extensive engagement with Vietnam policymaking. In late 1964, he insisted that the problems of Chinese representation and the insurgency in South Vietnam could not be separated. Beijing's backing of, and potential intervention in, that conflict made this a particularly inopportune time "to add the element – however purely psychological in importance – of international acceptance of Communist China."[19] Even as he favored holding the line on current policy, however, Bundy, somewhat ambiguously, wrote that if this proved counterproductive, Washington would then "have to find ways to preserve the GRC position by rolling with the punch in some fashion." On issues of less symbolic significance, he showed interest in a loosening of travel regulations and initiating limited trade in food and medicines.[20] Indeed, Bundy's evident discomfort with domestic and international criticism of the administration's inflexibility yielded cautious advocacy of policy reform, even if only for defensive purposes. Thus in June 1965, most likely in response to Zablocki's House subcommittee report from the previous month, he proposed broadening the categories of Americans eligible to travel to China to include scholars and graduate students. Bundy argued that this would demonstrate to critics "that it is the Chinese Communists rather than ourselves who fear the exchange of ideas."[21]

Both of these groups, especially the most ardent advocates of reform, lacked the clout and standing of those who had the President's ear. The brash Hilsman had served with the blessing of Kennedy, and the assassination of his patron left him with very few friends in high places. Hilsman's resignation from government in February 1964 stemmed primarily from strained relations with his old colleagues and the new President, particularly over the matter of his hearty encouragement of the overthrow of South Vietnam's President Ngo Dinh Diem the previous November.[22] Yet his views on China were clearly not shared by LBJ's entourage. Hilsman later claimed that he learned through a third party that the President in fact thought the December

1963 speech was "very good," a reaction that would appear to mesh with Johnson's aforementioned intellectual flexibility toward China.[23] This flexibility, however, did not translate into any sustained engagement with China policy in the early months of his administration, and he seemed more willing to defer to the hard-line counsel of his seasoned advisers.[24] According to some accounts, the December 1963 address, by a quirk of bureaucratic politics, never received proper clearance from the White House and Rusk failed to inquire about its content. As one Asian hand in the State Department recalled, it caused the Secretary "considerable agony" and "came as something of a shock to him."[25] Undoubtedly aware of the "uneasy" response of his superiors, Hilsman was forced to backtrack somewhat from the implications of his remarks in subsequent media appearances.[26]

Hilsman's departure from the scene dealt a decisive blow to the policy review he had initiated in the spring of 1963. Those left to champion the cause encountered considerable difficulty. In keeping with his tolerance of dissent within the NSC, McGeorge Bundy gave Thomson free rein to express his thoughts on China.[27] As the President's gatekeeper, however, Bundy was far more circumspect in the information and opinions that he presented to Johnson. Thomson later speculated that his views were not assiduously conveyed to the White House, likely because Bundy did not share them or possibly out of concern for safeguarding his continued access to LBJ.[28] For his part, Bundy thought Thomson was morbidly consumed by the fear of another Sino-American clash. As a result, he tended to "overestimate the likelihood of such a collision and ... underestimate the good sense of others in the Administration ... his estimates of both Chinese and American behavior were consistently too gloomy."[29]

LBJ's inner circle was alarmed by international developments in the fall of 1964. While they eschewed the option of an unprovoked preemptive strike against Chinese nuclear installations, they expressed considerable anxiety over the politico-psychological ramifications of the PRC's successful test on 16 October. Referring to an "intense fear of fallout" throughout Asia over this occurrence at an NSC meeting the following day, Rusk intoned, with no dissension, "Now is no time for a new policy toward Communist China."[30] The simultaneous ouster of Soviet Chairman Nikita Khrushchev, the Kremlin official most identified with Soviet-American détente, exacerbated concerns over China's growing prestige and self-confidence. Few in Washington immediately understood the reasons for Khrushchev's departure, or what this meant for both the future of détente and Sino-Soviet relations. It seemed certain, however, that Beijing's struggle for leadership of the international communist movement had acquired considerable momentum. "The Soviet position has been weakened by the change [in rulers]," the American ambassador in Moscow, Foy Kohler, reported shortly after the purge. "With the disappearance of Khrushchev, Mao ... remains the only old-line world-known communist figure, with no visible Russian rivals of significant stature."[31] This rapid succession of Chinese coups, Rusk remarked to British Foreign Secretary Patrick Gordon Walker, "must have confirmed the Chinese leaders in their view that primitive militancy paid."[32] The State Department's INR bureau noted in November a decidedly "aggressive and uncompromising tone" to Beijing's latest foreign policy pronouncements.[33]

This palpable sense of Chinese ascendancy produced a strong counter-reaction among LBJ's closest aides, especially Rusk. The "central question," as the Secretary defined it, was "the need to influence a half-dozen key people in China on the question of how China is doing, and whether its present policy is or is not on the right track. Such actions as the recognition of China by France or its future admission into the UN would, of course, be very bad in that it would persuade the Chinese that they were being successful. Unless other things demonstrate to the Chinese that they are not on the right track we will be faced with much greater danger in the future."[34] Coming of age at the height of the West's failed policy of appeasement in the 1930s, the Johnson team rejected the notion that the behavior of a brazenly confident and aggressive adversary could be moderated by the extension of olive branches. Gestures of this nature would be misinterpreted as a sign of weakness and would only encourage further probes of American resolve, perhaps setting off another global conflagration. Images of a belligerent China were frequently contrasted with Soviet prudence, as they had been since the beginning of the Kennedy presidency. "The countries of the Warsaw and NATO pacts are now likely to work out their problems without recourse to war," Rusk observed in November. "We can't, however, say the same thing about Communist China."[35] Veterans of the Cuban missile crisis, these Cold War liberals maintained that instilling restraint in an opponent rested on the judicious application of politico-military pressure.[36] This logic underlay Johnson's hard-line proclamation in April 1964: "so long as the Communist Chinese pursue aggression ...

[and] preach violence, there can be and will be no easing of relationships ... It is not we who must reexamine our view of China. It is the Chinese Communists who must reexamine their view of the world."[37]

This policy remained unchanged in the fall, as the administration worked to perpetuate China's international isolation. In September, a State Department circular telegram was sent to all US diplomatic missions in non-communist bloc countries, urging personnel stationed abroad to ensure that those governments now recognizing Taiwan "not move closer" to the PRC at a time when it was "inciting aggression in Asia, encouraging rebellion in Africa and extolling militant revolution in much of the world."[38] Particular attention was paid to Africa, where it was feared that the combined effect of French recognition and loan offers by Beijing would sway opinion on the continent in favor of the PRC's admission to the UN. Some officials cautioned against an overreaction to Chinese activity in Africa, warning that heavy-handed attempts to counter it could alienate sensitive African leaders and enhance the PRC's influence.[39] These sensible objections were overridden by the larger priority of recovering enough votes for the "important question" resolution at the upcoming 19th General Assembly. A number of pressure tactics were reviewed, including letters from the President, high-level missions to critical African nations, and the promise of greater economic aid.[40] To monitor Chinese progress in the region, the State Department established a special monthly series of intelligence studies in January 1965.[41]

In November, Stevenson urged Johnson to approve a "two Chinas" policy, arguing that this would stave off an impending diplomatic defeat and ensnare the PRC in a web of interlocking relations with the world community. A State Department policy paper prepared two months earlier warned that such a move entailed "serious losses and risks," namely the dilution of Taiwan as a diplomatic counter to the mainland. Moreover, a shift in US policy would likely have unsettling effects on the morale of Asian allies – such as South Korea, South Vietnam, and Thailand – and create pressures for their accommodation with the PRC.[42] When the topic came up for discussion at a White House meeting, Rusk objected to Stevenson's proposal on the grounds that it would send the wrong message to China. "If we appeared to falter before ... Communist China," he cautioned, "this would be interpreted as a reward for the track they have been following, and this would increase the chance of war." Remarking that he did not want to be party to "a pay-off for the ... ChiCom hard line," LBJ sided with his Secretary of State.⁴³ The timing of Johnson's decision was particularly noteworthy, coming as it did after being comfortably elected, which leads one to conclude that his motives were not strictly political. Rusk's invocation of the lessons of Munich undoubtedly resonated with the President. McGeorge Bundy fully concurred with this logic, reminding Johnson the following month that China's "nuclear explosion and her aggressive attitudes toward her neighbors make her a major problem for all peaceful people. This is not the time to give her increased prestige or to reward her belligerence – at the UN or elsewhere."⁴⁴

Rusk pressed this theme in conversations with those allies – Britain, Canada, and Japan – seen as increasingly wobbly on the issue of Chinese representation.⁴⁵ Owing in no small part to American pressure, Ottawa dropped its sponsorship of a one-China, one-Taiwan declaratory resolution.⁴⁶ The new Labour government of Harold Wilson, more flexible on Chinese representation than its Conservative predecessor yet just as interested in solidifying the "special relationship" with the US, maintained London's position.⁴⁷ Incidentally, no vote was taken on the question in 1964 because of a crisis over the funding of UN peacekeeping operations. Nevertheless, the administration remained vigilant. In a January 1965 meeting with Japanese Prime Minister Eisaku Sato, Rusk insisted that it was "essential for the United States and Japan to maintain the closest contact" in preventing Beijing's seating at the UN.⁴⁸

In June, the Secretary vetoed William Bundy's aforementioned proposal for the eligibility of scholars and graduate students to travel to China, and grudgingly opted instead for the more limited category of medical doctors and public health specialists. In his recommendation to Johnson, Rusk cited pressures from Congress (the Zablocki House subcommittee) and the academic community for a loosening of travel restrictions, and advanced the negative rationale that Beijing's inevitable refusal to grant any visits would "underline that it is they, not we, who are intractable and perhaps fearful of the contagion of ideas."⁴⁹ At a luncheon with his senior aides, however, LBJ rejected this suggestion as well, explaining that "it would not be wise to change our current policy" at that time.⁵⁰

What accounted for this high-level resistance to altering China policy? LBJ's deference to Rusk on China cannot be separated from his conception of foreign policy as an intensely political process. As discussed in the previous chapter, surveys at this time offered no unambiguous barometer of public attitudes toward the mainland, but there were evident signs that popular hostility toward China had relaxed relative to the obstinate stand voiced by senior administration officials. A majority of Americans continued to identify China as the greatest danger to world peace. In a 1965 Gallup poll, for example, 53 percent held the PRC responsible for Vietcong operations in South Vietnam, an impression no doubt fostered by the administration's rhetoric.[51] Yet even as China's nuclear status and its role in Vietnam cemented impressions of an international pariah, polling results revealed an interest in expanding contacts with Beijing. Whether or not these contradictions in opinion reflected public indifference or genuine recognition of the need for new approaches to China remains unclear. Nor is it clear if Johnson closely monitored this data. LBJ's reading of the politics entwined with China policy was colored by lessons gleaned from the "who lost China" debate of the early 1950s and by his own short-term domestic priorities. By the summer of 1965, the most outspoken critics of the administration's rigid posture were editorialists and academics. If there was indeed greater tolerance among the public at large for rethinking China strategy, this latent sentiment had not been effectively mobilized by the most vocal proponents of reform into any widespread clamoring for change. China policy reform had not been elevated to a pressing item on the American political agenda. Accordingly, a politician as cautious as Johnson, instinctively wary of bold gestures in foreign policy, was inclined to stay the course.

Immediate circumstances recommended this option. Throughout 1964, LBJ's consuming objective was fending off an electoral challenge from the hawkish Goldwater. While Johnson saw advantages in contrasting his prudent statesmanship with the bellicose statements of his opponent, which had likely played a role in his rejection of military action against China's nuclear program, he undoubtedly perceived dangers in creating too much space between himself and the Senator on matters such as Chinese representation. Goldwater had been closely aligned with the China Lobby since the mid-1950s, and he urged withdrawal from the UN if Beijing was ever admitted.[52] Even in the aftermath of his sweeping mandate, Johnson was unwilling to invest substantial political capital in any diplomatic venture that could undermine his domestic authority. He repeatedly stressed to his aides that he viewed the early months of 1965 as a small window of opportunity for enacting his Great Society legislation, knowing full well that his honeymoon with the electorate and Congress would not last indefinitely.[53] On 20 April, 321 legislators – 51 Senators and 270 Representatives – issued a declaration opposing the PRC's admission to the UN, US diplomatic recognition, or trade relations with the mainland.[54] Lingering hostility to China on Capitol Hill, at a time when votes were being courted for crucial domestic bills, could not have escaped the attention of the White House.

China ascendant:
The Johnson team's threat perception, 1964–65

The Johnson team's interpretation of the PRC's role in Southeast Asia contributed decisively to the reaffirmation of China policy through the summer of 1965, and it is to this heightened threat perception that this chapter now turns. Paradoxically, this threat was seen as an outgrowth of China's relative weakness. For while it was acknowledged that China had recovered somewhat by 1964–65 from the disastrous Great Leap Forward, US analysts were more impressed by the "monumental economic problems" still bedevilling Mao and his comrades. China's rapidly growing population, inadequate arable land, low level of technology, and loss of Soviet assistance in 1960 all made for a gloomy forecast. A January 1964 national intelligence estimate asserted that it would be "many years" before the PRC became a modern industrial state.[55] Lacking the economic resources and level of development needed to sustain a modern military machine, senior officials dismissed any notion of a conventional Chinese menace. When Senate Majority Leader Mike Mansfield inquired at one point about the "military strength" of China, McNamara contended that Beijing "presented us with no strategic threat. They cannot touch us with [the] strategic weapons they now possess. We can now counter their non-strategic strength without adding to our existing strength."[56] A steady stream of intelligence analyses all concluded that Chinese leaders respected America's military superiority and were anxious to prevent another Korea-like confrontation. Accordingly, the country's military orientation would remain decidedly defensive for the foreseeable future.[57]

These same officials, however, postulated that the discretion of China's leadership compelled them to adopt alternative methods in pursuit of hostile long-term ambitions. This threat was most coherently and elaborately defined in the administration's June 1966 Long

Range Study on China, prepared jointly by the State and Defense Departments. The mainland's ultimate objective, according to the report, was to make itself "the center and guiding light of a Communist world." The prerequisites for securing this position, and to which the Chinese were now dedicating themselves, were the gradual expulsion of American power and influence from Asia, the strengthening of their own influence among the world's less-developed nations, and the displacement of Soviet leadership of the international communist movement. In lieu of the conventional tactics of invasion and conquest for attaining these ends, the PRC had accommodated itself to its relative impotence vis a vis its Great Power rivals and relied instead on a low-risk strategy of "indirect aggression, subversion and diplomatic maneuver, conceived as a totality and designed to drain the energies of their antagonists." The greatest danger facing Southeast Asia was "militant dissidence within the nations of the area, encouraged, supplied, or fomented by Communist China." In aiding local insurgencies, Beijing aimed to "usurp the functions of legitimate governments, to take them over, and to replace them with regimes permanently sympathetic or subservient to the Chinese Communists."[58] In short, then, the Chinese threat was more a function of its perceived intentions, the zeal with which its leaders were devoted to exporting their values, and the socio-economic vulnerabilities of its neighbors, than it was of any traditional measurement of power and capability.

Communist Chinese ideology, as articulated in speeches and writings, was a critical component of the administration's threat assessment. Bemoaning the importance ascribed to these pronouncements, McNamara later recalled, "we – certainly I – badly misread China's objectives and mistook its bellicose rhetoric to imply a drive for regional hegemony."[59] Correlations were often drawn between the country's recent revolutionary experience and the worldview of its rulers. NIE 13-9-65 "Communist China's Foreign Policy," emblematic of this tendency, makes for interesting reading. Beijing's foreign policy, the authors posited, was "a projection into the world arena of the principles and concepts developed in the prosecution of China's long civil war ... [and] is primarily a strategy for revolutionary war ... conceived in terms of conflict rather than of adjusting relations with other states by negotiations ... International politics is viewed as a great guerrilla struggle in which the opponent is to be constantly harassed and threatened." Infused with this militant philosophy, and with an historic sense of the centrality of their nation and culture, these "dedicated, even fanatic Communists" held no stake in either the Western or Soviet conception of world order and therefore felt "relatively free to encourage and exploit chaos wherever they are able to do so."[60] The publication in September 1965 of Defense Minister Lin Biao's article, *Long Live the Victory of People's War!*, with its call for the "rural areas of the world" (the developing nations) to overtake "the cities" (the industrialized nations) by means of local revolution, confirmed the worst suspicions of Chinese intentions, with many in Washington likening it to a blueprint for aggression on a par with Hitler's *Mein Kampf*.[61]

The challenge posed by China was perceived most acutely in South Vietnam, where a US-sponsored regime was attempting to fend off a ferocious insurgency being waged by the National Liberation Front (NLF) and its patron, communist North Vietnam (the Democratic Republic of Vietnam – DRV). The China dimension had figured prominently in Kennedy's handling of Vietnam, accounting in no small part for the highly ambiguous record he bequeathed to his successor. Firm subscription to the notion of a predatory PRC looking to expand its influence southwards by means of subversion framed his definition of the conflict as a test of America's commitment to containing international communism, his aversion to a negotiated settlement, and his interest in preserving a friendly buffer state in Saigon. Just as significantly, however, Kennedy's grim assumption of Chinese capriciousness and recklessness acted as a brake against any risk-taking action in Vietnam that he feared would only stoke these tendencies. Apprehension over the prospect of renewed Sino-American hostilities, compounded by doubts of the viability of President Diem's regime and of the public's appetite for a substantial devotion of resources to Southeast Asia, undoubtedly influenced JFK's rejection of a major military presence in South Vietnam, as when he spurned a request from some of his closest aides for the introduction of combat troops in November 1961. Torn by conflicting impulses, wary of an open-ended commitment yet fearful of a withdrawal, eager to keep his options open and uncertain about the best course of action to take, Kennedy settled on a middle course. Materiel aid to the South was stepped up, as were the number of US advisers serving in the country. In the hopes of fostering a more vigorous and popular government in Saigon, the Kennedy team acquiesced in Diem's overthrow by his generals in November 1963.[62] In doing so, Washington unwittingly triggered a prolonged period of political turmoil in the South, characterized by a series of military coups, increasingly corrupt and inefficient administration, and mounting discontent among the populace.

In the early months of his presidency, Johnson was inundated with reports of steady progress by the NLF and predictions of an impending collapse in Saigon.[63] Yet the new President balked at recommendations, particularly from the Joint Chiefs of Staff, that he adopt a program of military pressures against the DRV to deter its support of the insurgency. Johnson feared that these escalatory measures would provoke Beijing. It "looks to me like we're getting into another Korea," he frowned to McGeorge Bundy in May 1964. "I believe that the Chinese Communists are coming into it. I don't think that we can fight them ten thousand miles away from home."[64] Determined to preserve Kennedy's commitment to South Vietnam without igniting a wider conflagration that could derail his hopes for election in 1964, LBJ (with the exception of limited air strikes against the North in response to the Gulf of Tonkin incidents of August) deferred a decision for military intervention, opting instead for stopgap measures that aimed to avert disaster for the remainder of the year by expanding economic assistance and the number of US advisers.[65]

The administration's perception of the PRC's role in Vietnam, as with its general assessment of Chinese power, was riddled with contradictions. The most zealous advocates of military intervention in Vietnam frequently cited the imperative of containing Chinese expansionism. Yet in pressing the President for this course of action, they sought to assuage his fears of an enlarged war by calling attention to China's military feebleness and its reluctance to enter the fighting in lieu of a direct threat to its own security.[66] As the application of military pressure against the North was contemplated in the early months of 1964 and afterwards, US officials devoted considerable effort to deciphering the threshold of Chinese restraint and the extent to which action could be safely taken against the PRC's ally without the possibility of setting off a wider conflict. In accordance with the widely accepted image of a cautious, defensive-oriented China, intelligence analysts advanced a consistently optimistic appraisal of the most likely Chinese response to a program of American military coercion against Hanoi. Drawing on these reports, the Joint Chiefs asserted in March 1964 that the mainland viewed the war as a "DRV problem" and was unwilling to introduce significant ground units into North Vietnam; it would offer at most fighter aircraft and volunteers.[67]

In the spring, a national intelligence estimate predicted that, in the event of US air strikes against the North, China would merely deploy forces to areas bordering Vietnam and offer its ally anti-aircraft units. For all of their bravado, the PRC's leaders were determined to avoid a clash with the United States and would only consider direct intervention in response to an unambiguous threat to their own security, such as an attack on Chinese territory or the deep penetration of US ground forces into North Vietnam. Otherwise, Beijing would remain "niggardly with tangible support" for its client.[68] In a similar vein, the CIA interpreted the rapid build-up of Chinese military strength in South China and its moves to bolster Hanoi's air defenses in the aftermath of the Gulf of Tonkin incidents in August as strictly defensive gestures, intended to demonstrate the PRC's continued support for the Vietnamese insurgency and to deter further American military action, all the while keeping itself above the fray with no commitment to enter the fighting.[69]

Many senior US officials doubted that the DRV would welcome such a commitment. This view, commonly espoused by the most hawkish elements of the administration such as the Joint Chiefs and Walt Rostow, rested on the notion of Vietnamese nationalism and the historical enmity existing between the Vietnamese and Chinese. They contended that the DRV's leaders jealously guarded their independence and were loath to request troops from their socialist brethren. Consequently, this camp asserted that this political dynamic created greater leeway for vigorous US military action against the North.[70] Those policymakers less enamored of this option also made reference to Sino-Vietnamese tensions in arguing their case. In a lengthy October 1964 paper, William Bundy explored the ways in which the detrimental effects of a political solution to the Vietnam imbroglio could be blunted. In contemplating a negotiated withdrawal from the war, the Assistant Secretary forwarded the idea of continuing the present course of US assistance to South Vietnam while preserving a credible threat of force against the North to enhance America's bargaining position at the conference table. Bundy fully understood that a "neutralist" outcome in the South would in fact "lead in a period of months ... to a Saigon government dominated by Communists and then to a unified Communist Vietnam." One consolation arising from such an arrangement, however, was that this would amount to "a *Vietnamese* solution without Chinese participation, and almost certainly Hanoi would bend every effort to have it this way ...

China would not have re-entered Southeast Asia in any concrete sense, and there is at least some hope that a Communist Vietnam ... would be to some extent a buffer against [the] further spread of Chinese influence."[71]

Yet those same officials who emphasized China's prudence and the resilience of Vietnamese nationalism elevated the Vietnam War to a textbook case of Chinese strategy, one that sought to extend the mainland's influence across Southeast Asia by furnishing aid and encouragement to communist insurgencies. In Vietnam, Rostow wrote in terms aimed at grabbing Johnson's attention, "we are confronted with the most sophisticated effort mounted by the Communists since the war. They aim, by salami tactics, to produce a climax not in the form of an overt Communist military victory, but in the form of political and psychological fragmentation and collapse in ... Saigon ... and from that political breakdown they plan to move on, via neutralization, to Communist domination."[72] In keeping with the administration's conception of a non-conventional Chinese menace, what was dreaded was not so much Chinese military aggression as the politico-psychological rewards Beijing would accrue from a North Vietnamese victory.

In March 1964, McNamara framed the stakes of America's involvement in Vietnam for the President. The US commitment to preserving a non-communist government in Saigon, he asserted, was regarded by all of Asia, indeed the whole world, "as a test case of U.S. capacity to help a nation meet a Communist 'war of liberation.'" A communist victory in South Vietnam would have a disastrous bandwagon effect throughout the region. Allies confronting similar threats of communist insurgencies would lose faith in American credibility and feel forced to adjust their strategic orientation in line with Chinese interests.[73] McNamara's contention that a toppled Saigon would represent the first in a long line of dominoes falling under China's domination was widely shared. A June 1964 CIA analysis, which the Defense Secretary later cited as "confirming my and others' fear ... that the West's containment policy lay at serious risk in Vietnam,"[74] concluded that China would emerge as the real victor from a North Vietnamese triumph, as it would vindicate Beijing's "thesis that the underdeveloped world is ripe for revolution, that the US is a paper tiger, and that local insurgency can be carried through to victory without undue risk of precipitating a major international war."[75] In losing Saigon without a fight, Washington would send an impression of vacillation and indecisiveness to other governments in the region. When LBJ questioned his advisers in September 1964 whether safeguarding South Vietnam's independence was "worth all this effort," Maxwell Taylor (the US ambassador in Saigon), the Joint Chiefs, CIA Director McCone, and Rusk unanimously concurred that "if we should lose in South Vietnam, we would lose Southeast Asia. Country after country would give way and look toward Communist China as the rising power of the area."[76]

Concurrent events beyond Vietnam's borders shaped an image of Chinese ascendancy in the region. Washington observed with dismay the gradual alignment in the foreign policies of Indonesia and China and the steady rise in political influence of the Indonesian Communist Party (PKI), which was thought to be Beijing's proxy. In Cambodia, the PRC shrewdly exploited that country's traditional fear of its Vietnamese and Thai adversaries by enticing it with promises of aid and assurances of its continued sovereignty. The administration attributed the emergence of a communist insurgency in Thailand in early 1965 to the hidden hand of China. Many US officials believed that these unsettling developments were intertwined with the commitment in South Vietnam, in so far as it was assumed that this multi-front assault on America's interests in Southeast Asia and the lack of a reliable fallback position rendered a retreat from Saigon unthinkable.[77] Even for those policymakers long averse to the notion of a major military commitment in defense of their fledgling Vietnamese ally, such as State's Michael Forrestal, China's growing stature seemed to mandate a greater American effort. Balancing his own ambivalence over an open-ended campaign in Vietnam against the perceived necessity of checking Beijing's drive for regional hegemony, Forrestal noted with some resignation in late 1964 that "if China did not exist, the effect of our withdrawal from a situation in which the people we were trying to help seemed unable to help themselves might not be politically so pervasive in Asia."[78]

With the blessing of the Indonesian army and the PKI, President Sukarno renounced Indonesia's parliamentary system in March 1957 and gradually reinstated presidential rule. Sukarno promoted the aggrandizement of the PKI's influence, appreciating the party as an effective political vehicle that could deliver mass support and serve as a counterweight to the powerful army.[79] The complexities of Sukarno's delicate balancing act frequently resulted in domestic paralysis, and encouraged him to undertake bold initiatives abroad as a means of rallying public opinion and perpetuating his unique leadership role.[80] One such initiative came in 1963, when the Indonesian ruler declared his opposition to British plans for ending its colonial rule in Malaya, Singapore, and two small crown colonies in Northern Borneo by merging them into the new federation of Malaysia. Sukarno's line of "Confrontation" with Malaysia, anti-American diatribes, flirtation with the PKI, and apparent complicity in repeated occurrences of local violence against American offices and business properties distressed officials in Washington. By the time he entered office, Johnson faced growing calls from Congress for barring new aid to Indonesia.[81] Despite their frustration, LBJ's aides cautioned him against rash action, arguing that any severing of American aid would probably have no constructive effect and could provoke hostile countermeasures, such as the seizure of US oil assets or further harassment of diplomatic offices. Moreover, the administration would surrender any leverage it still possessed in that country, thereby crippling efforts to strengthen anti-communist elements (primarily the armed forces). By virtue of its size, resources, and strategic location, Indonesia could not be altogether abandoned.[82]

Developments in 1964 gave little ground for hope that Jakarta's drift away from the West could be reversed. Sukarno's virulently anti-American Independence Day speech on 17 August in particular confirmed for many the clout of the PKI. A CIA memorandum took the address as a sign that the enigmatic leader had irrevocably announced his affiliation with the "anti-Western Asian world" and that he was "well on his way to becoming a captive of the Communists."[83] Sukarno's apparent deference to the PKI was of particular concern because it was commonly assumed that the party took its inspiration and marching orders from China. Indeed, Rusk was convinced that it had "swung from Moscow to Peking" in the Sino-Soviet dispute.[84] Sukarno's decision to withdraw from the UN in January 1965, his efforts to convene a rival Conference of the New Emerging Forces and galvanize international opinion against American actions in Vietnam, and a series of high-level meetings with Chinese representatives were all interpreted as evidence of a flourishing Beijing-Jakarta axis that was working to expunge American influence from Southeast Asia.[85] A major report prepared by roving Ambassador Ellsworth Bunker in April 1965 seconded many of these gloomy forecasts and recommended a sizeable reduction in the American presence in Indonesia, in view of the increasingly inhospitable climate for US diplomats and businessmen.[86] Throughout the summer, an enhanced role for the PKI, the marginalization of the military, and closer ties with China were all seen as foregone conclusions.[87] Yet while it was agreed that a formal communist takeover of the country, an increasing likelihood, would make little difference in terms of the direction and substance of Indonesia's domestic and foreign policies, a special national intelligence estimate in September postulated that such a development could have considerable psychological repercussions for the entire region. Beijing would be greatly encouraged by the triumph of "one of its closest associates." The PKI's accession to power "would be seen as a major change in the international balance of political forces and would inject new life into the thesis that communism is the wave of the future."[88]

Cambodia presented to the Johnson team a variation on the same problem of Chinese preponderance in Southeast Asia. Since gaining its independence from France in 1953–54, Cambodia, under the rule of Prince Norodom Sihanouk, had charted a non-aligned course in foreign affairs. To wean Phnom Penh from deepening its relations with Beijing, both the Eisenhower and Kennedy administrations furnished economic and military assistance. Yet relations between the two countries ultimately deteriorated because the demands of tending to Sihanouk's security concerns clashed with the overriding US priority of containing Asian communism.[89] Incensed by mounting South Vietnamese and Thai incursions into Cambodian territory throughout 1963 and by their support of the rightist Khmer Serei movement, Sihanouk renounced all US aid just days prior to JFK's assassination, evidently under the assumption that the Americans were unwilling or unable to rein in their allies. Washington's complicity in the Diem coup also played a part in the decision, as it stoked the prince's fears of American objectives toward his own leadership. The renunciation was soon followed by a call for the reconvening of the 1954 Geneva Conference to reach an international agreement on Cambodia's neutrality.[90] To induce American participation in such a conference, Sihanouk threatened to recognize North Vietnam and sign a defensive arrangement with the PRC.[91]

US diplomats in the region were sensitive to Sihanouk's predicament, cognizant that his actions stemmed from fears of Cambodia's historic enemies in Thailand and Vietnam. He above all dreaded the prospect of his country becoming engulfed in the Vietnam War and sought an international guarantee of his borders. The embassy in

Phnom Penh, somewhat condescendingly, likened his behavior to that of a "small, intelligent trapped animal desperately seeking exit from [a] trap, dashing back and forth [in] all directions, and keeping up continuous high-pitched shrieking." Superiors in Washington were encouraged to "avoid pushing Sihanouk against [the] wall and driving him into desperation."[92] Johnson's advisers greeted this recommendation with little enthusiasm, due in large part to the objections of Saigon and Bangkok toward an international conference. Any hint of US willingness to discuss Cambodia's neutrality would make it that much more difficult to convince these allies of "our commitments and will to win in Viet-Nam."[93] The administration appeared willing to run the risk of rebuffing the wishes of the mercurial Cambodian ruler and facilitating an accommodation of sorts between Phnom Penh and Beijing for the sake of preserving solidarity with its Cold War partners. "If the issue is whether an unbalanced Sihanouk will irrationally turn to the communist North," Rusk reasoned, "we must balance this against the impact of a complete loss of morale in South Viet-Nam and Thailand."[94]

Washington's stalling on a conference had predictable consequences. Throughout 1964, Sihanouk escalated his anti-American rhetoric and dispatched economic and military delegations to China.[95] Efforts to repair Cambodian-American relations, culminating in ten days of talks in New Delhi during December, came to naught. By the end of the year, the US embassy in Phnom Penh was reduced to only twelve officers. On 3 May 1965, Sihanouk completely severed diplomatic relations following a border incident involving American planes.[96] The prince's pro-Chinese neutrality was widely understood among US officials as a tactical maneuver, owing little to any affinity for Maoist ideology but rather to the practical calculation that the PRC was destined to emerge as the dominant regional power and that Cambodia's sovereignty therefore depended on cooperation with the mainland.[97] "In the longer term," the senior US representative in Phnom Penh wrote in December 1964, "the chance of re-establishing American prestige and influence here continues to be a function of our success (or lack thereof) in South Viet-Nam. If the war there continues to go badly, the process of Cambodian adjustment to the reality of Communist Chinese power in Southeast Asia will almost certainly continue to our detriment."[98] Events in Cambodia were surely viewed with some disquiet by US officials when considered from a regional perspective; however unsavoury or fickle a character Sihanouk might be, his lack of faith in an American victory in Vietnam and his gravitation toward the PRC represented a potentially contagious sentiment.

Indeed, communist advances in South Vietnam, alongside setbacks in Indonesia and Cambodia, convinced the administration of the need to stiffen Bangkok's resolve and encourage its continued allegiance through increased military and economic assistance.[99] Thailand was greatly valued as a staging ground for an ever-expanding number of covert operations in the Vietnam War.[100] The Joint Chiefs of Staff asserted in September 1964 that the "principal US objective for Thailand is to insure that it remains a stable nation, allied to the United States, and available as a forward base for the projection of US power into Southeast Asia. Militarily, Thailand is the only secure mainland base for US operations in that area at this time."[101] Yet Thai cooperation, both as an ally in Vietnam and as a bastion of anti-communism in the region, could not be taken for granted. The American ambassador in Bangkok, Graham Martin, contended that this could only be secured by clarifying the administration's commitment in Saigon. "They are not yet certain whether we are really prepared to use force to achieve our policy aims in Southeast Asia," Martin explained in June 1964. Until "they are certain that we have the will to use such force as appears appropriate, they will wait to see how the situation unfolds. They will not this time be willing to use their real estate as an American base without a clear view of the end of the road."[102] Thai officials wasted no effort in pressing Washington for a vigorous defense of Saigon, even raising the possibility of direct attacks against the DRV. In a December 1964 meeting with LBJ, Thai Foreign Minister Thanat Khoman referred to "the indivisibility of the area and to the fact that any loss of South Viet-Nam would constitute an immediate threat to Thailand." In such an event, Laos and Cambodia "could hardly hold out, and his implication was that Thailand would do its utmost, but that the issue would be in some doubt."[103] Only a few weeks earlier, William Bundy's interagency Vietnam Working Group had broadly reached the same conclusion.[104]

The outbreak of a communist insurgency in northeastern Thailand in early 1965 reinforced concerns about Bangkok's confidence in American leadership.[105] Washington had little doubt that the mainland, in providing direction and support to the newly formed Thailand Independence Movement (TIM) and the Patriotic Front of Thailand (PFT), was opening up another front in the contest for Southeast Asia. Particularly ominous were Chinese Foreign Minister

Chen Yi's alleged remarks to a French diplomat that guerrilla warfare would spread to Thailand in 1965, reports that Beijing was purchasing large sums of Thai currency in Hong Kong, and the new priority assigned to the study of Thai in the PRC's Foreign Language Institute.[106] Johnson officials were cautiously optimistic that Bangkok could counter the subversive threat by diverting its resources to those economically depressed pockets of the country most vulnerable to communist propaganda. Critically, however, Thailand's success in meeting this challenge was seen as directly linked to the outcome of the war in Vietnam. As a CIA estimate noted, "the Thais have a long history of accommodating to external political pressures believed necessary for national survival." Thus if Saigon fell, the Thais, much like Sihanouk's Cambodia, "would almost certainly conclude that the best hope for maintaining a national identity lay in neutralism."[107]

It was against this troubling regional backdrop that the most fateful decisions of America's role in Vietnam were taken. By the end of November 1964, LBJ was presented with a list of options for the bombing of North Vietnam.[108] The Johnson team believed at this point that the only remedy for the malady in the South lay in inflicting punishment on the North and raising the costs of its support for the NLF to an unbearable level. In urging the President to approve bolder actions in defense of the besieged government in Saigon, LBJ's advisers invoked the specter of Chinese expansionism. Typical in this respect was William Bundy's decidedly glum appraisal in the first week of January 1965. By insisting on a more stable South Vietnamese government as a precondition for bombing the North, he observed, "our friends in Asia must well be asking whether we would support them if they too had internal troubles in a confrontation situation." Having insinuated only a few months before that the US could live with a communist outcome in Vietnam, Bundy now maintained that the administration had to at least offer token resistance so as to offset latent neutralist sentiment, bolster the will of Asian governments to resist communist subversion, and prepare the ground for holding "the next line of defense, namely Thailand."[109]

Elaborating on this theme in his landmark memorandum of 27 January, McGeorge Bundy pressed the President to "use our military power in the Far East and to force a change of Communist policy." Continuing the current "passive role" would only court disaster. The problem in Saigon was primarily one of morale and "the spreading conviction that the future is without hope for anti-communists ... they see the enormous power of the United States withheld ... [and] feel that we are unwilling to take serious risks."[110] When he advocated sustained bombing of the North following a Vietcong attack on US Army barracks in Pleiku on 6 February, LBJ's National Security Adviser again made reference to the larger stakes involved. Even if bombing failed to produce the intended effects, "the policy will be worth it. At a minimum it will damp down the charge that we did not do all that we could have done, and this charge will be important in many countries, including our own." Moreover, a forceful reprisal policy would set a precedent by establishing "a higher price for the future upon all adventures of guerrilla warfare."[111]

US officials believed that China, as the standard bearer of national liberation and as the most vocal proponent of upheaval and violent change in the Third World, was ideally positioned to capitalize on the anticipated fallout from an American defeat in Vietnam. A May 1965 NIE affirmed that China's expansionist designs fed on the vulnerabilities and insecurities of its neighbors, whose "weak, inexperienced governments are highly vulnerable to Peiping's line. With large expectations and small capabilities, their people are frustrated by the status quo and naturally inclined to blame their woes on such external factors as colonialist exploitation and racial domination." Under such circumstances, "It is not too hard to sell them radical 'solutions' to their problems."[112] Leaving these governments in the lurch would only exacerbate their grievances, real or imagined, and create an opportunity for Chinese solicitation. In short, the PRC's revolutionary dynamism, both as an instrument of enticement (as with Cambodia, for example) and intimidation (against Thailand), compensated for its own military and economic deficiencies in the pursuit of an ambitious foreign policy agenda. In one of his more morose moods, McGeorge Bundy brooded over the possibility of "a new polarization of the world, which will ... see the poor, restless, non-white peoples, led or pushed by China, isolate themselves from Europe (East and West) and America ... economically if they can, but certainly culturally and politically."[113]

The administration's most senior Vietnam dissident, Under Secretary of State George Ball, believed that the consequences of an American defeat or withdrawal had been vastly exaggerated. He reasoned that reactions across the region to a compromise settlement in Saigon would be "highly parochial," based on each country's calculation of its own interests, its vulnerability to communist insurgency, and its confidence in the sanctity of America's security guarantees. Ball identified only Taiwan and Thailand as favoring "extreme U.S. actions [in Vietnam], including a risk of war with Communist China."[114] American credibility would suffer in the eyes of foe and friend alike more from fruitless engagement in a protracted guerrilla war than from a tactical retreat.[115] Privately, Ball doubted that China posed a serious danger to American interests. He thought "China would like to extend its influence but [only] on a limited liability basis" and "did not think for a minute that China invented the SVN war."[116] In all of his memorandums to Johnson, however, the Under Secretary never directly addressed the validity of the prevailing assumptions of a Chinese threat. It is most likely that he never shared his misgivings out of fear that further questioning of conventional wisdom would only undermine the plausibility of his arguments. As it was, his relatively sanguine appraisal of the consequences of disentanglement from the Vietnam morass had precisely this effect among those more attentive to the imperative of containing the PRC. As one senior participant in the 1965 debates recalled, Ball "just put zero on the China factor ... [which] rendered his analysis much less cogent than it might otherwise have been."[117]

While Beijing's backing of the Vietnamese insurgency held the potential of upsetting the balance of power in Southeast Asia, the administration also believed that the consequences of a setback in Saigon would reverberate further afield. US officials, for example, linked events in Vietnam to the steady deterioration in Soviet-American relations in 1964–65.[118] Following the resolution of the Cuban missile crisis, Washington discerned a decline in Soviet authority (and a worrying commensurate increase in Chinese prestige) among Asian communist parties as the Kremlin pursued détente with the West.[119] In the spring of 1963, Khrushchev informed Averell Harriman that he had effectively "written off and given up" on Southeast Asia, evidently under the assumption that the region was primarily an arena for Sino-American competition.[120] Indeed, on the eve of his removal from power in October 1964, the Soviet leader remained deliberately above the fray in the Vietnam War. Irritated by Hanoi's refusal to side with Moscow in the Sino-Soviet dispute and intent on avoiding another Great Power conflict in the aftermath of his misadventure in the Caribbean, he provided North Vietnam with little more than rhetorical support and limited economic aid.[121]

As a striking measure of how gravely China's apparent sway over the DRV was viewed by US officials, many within the administration welcomed the more assertive efforts of Khrushchev's successors to gain a foothold in North Vietnam and restore Soviet prestige in the region. In January 1965, Moscow began delivering anti-aircraft weaponry to the North, followed the next month by Premier Alexei Kosygin's visit to Hanoi.[122] Many reasoned that the Soviets, as the proponents of a more conciliatory line in foreign affairs, might counter China's belligerent influence and induce Hanoi to curtail its involvement in the South.[123] Some continued to entertain ambitions, stretching back to the Kennedy years, of a Soviet-American identity of interests in blocking Chinese expansionism. With the Soviets "moving with some confidence back into Southeast Asia with the double purpose of expanding their own influence in the East and containing the Chinese," McGeorge Bundy wrote hopefully to LBJ, "we can possibly make a little money on it."[124]

Coupled with these hopes, however, was an understanding that the Kremlin's room for maneuver was small. The Soviets' new activism in Vietnam was widely seen by the Americans as a defensive gesture, compelled by China's ascendancy in the international communist movement and by Beijing's constant taunting of Moscow's reluctance to assist a socialist ally under American bombardment.[125] Ambassador Kohler poured cold water on the notion of any "grand global deal" with the Kremlin, as any sign of Soviet-US collusion in Vietnam would be tantamount to Moscow's "defeat by Peiping for control of [the] world Communist movement."[126] Thus while the Soviets were seen as interested in halting the drift toward an escalation of the conflict, US policymakers realized that Chinese pressure had created an intractable dilemma for the Kremlin. "It is a pity that the U.S. and the USSR are being dragged along by North Vietnam," Rusk remarked in March 1965. "The Soviets are paralyzed by U.S. bombing and, as long as it continues, they cannot take any political action [to encourage negotiations] without exposing themselves to the criticism that they are not defending a socialist country."[127] As American analysts understood it, China's firm support for the DRV had painted Moscow into a corner, forcing it to choose between unmitigated support for Hanoi, even at the risk of war with the US, or disengagement, which would only lend credence to Beijing's charges of a Soviet betrayal.[128]

The Soviets in fact attempted to straddle the issue. Moscow increased economic and military aid to the DRV to preserve its standing among communist allies, while quietly encouraging a peaceful outcome in such a way that would not open it to accusations of coddling the American imperialists.[129] The conflicting demands of Soviet policy, however, produced shifts in behavior which exasperated Johnson officials in 1965. First, the Kremlin rejected US attempts to enlist its assistance in pressuring Hanoi to negotiate. In July, Kosygin, stung by Chinese and Vietnamese criticism of his discreet probing for peace talks earlier that year, insisted to Harriman that he could not serve as an intermediary between the two sides, explaining that the Americans would have to approach the North Vietnamese themselves. Hoping to counter Chinese propaganda of a Soviet willingness to bargain away Hanoi's interests, senior Soviet officials were eager to demonstrate socialist solidarity with the DRV.[130] Second, a gradual freeze in Soviet-American relations took hold. Washington detected a more "militant, anti-Free World position on such issues as colonialism, national liberation wars, [and] Indochina" from the new Soviet leadership "in response to Chinese rivalry for influence ... among radical Afro-Asian states."[131]

In April 1965, Kohler concluded that the imperative of competing with the Chinese for the allegiance of socialist allies had assumed greater priority for the Kremlin than developing relations with Washington. For the foreseeable future, there would be no further movement toward détente, "no new initiatives on [the] Soviet side or acceptance of initiatives from [the] American side."[132] Similarly, a Policy Planning Council paper discerned in recent Soviet actions "an inclination to terminate the post-Cuba phase [of relations] and to return to a harder stance in relations with the West."[133] Johnson's lieutenants held that Moscow's new posture toward the US bespoke Chinese momentum in the Sino-Soviet dispute, with ominous implications for the future. Testifying before the Senate Foreign Relations Committee in March, Rusk observed that "If Peiping can demonstrate that their course of policy is paying substantial dividends, as successes in Southeast Asia ... would indicate, then there is a much greater possibility that Moscow would attempt to close the gap between Moscow and Peiping by moving toward Peiping's more militant attitude toward the world revolution."[134]

What role did images of China play in Lyndon Johnson's most significant Vietnam decisions? LBJ's motives for Americanizing the war were, of course, complex and multifaceted. As the prevailing line of literature has convincingly argued, the President independently reached the conclusion in 1965 that leaving South Vietnam to its fate would be more inimical to his cherished domestic program than the launching of sustained bombing or the dispatch of US combat troops. His decision for intervention stemmed from a thoroughly conservative instinct in foreign affairs, one that placed a premium on the avoidance of errors in the international arena, such as losing "free world" real estate to communism. Burdened by memories of the "who lost China" debate and the ravages of McCarthyism, Johnson was never sufficiently confident that he could continue to govern effectively at home and contain the political firestorm he believed to be inevitable should he cut his losses in Southeast Asia. Tragically, Johnson thought that the road to the Great Society led through the jungles and rice paddies of Vietnam.[135]

Yet it is also evident that LBJ did not dispute the image presented by his most influential advisers of a Chinese menace, propelled by an implacable ideology and an insatiable appetite for expansion, buoyed by a string of promising international developments, and best positioned to take full advantage of the unravelling of America's position in Asia in the event of a defeat in South Vietnam. Johnson assumed the presidency with a set of beliefs – the Munich–New Deal mindset – which alerted him to the challenges posed by the PRC. The common assumption that China's revolutionary élan offered immense appeal to impoverished and malnourished Asians tapped into his own populist impulse. As Vice President, Johnson had urged Kennedy to use all of the economic and technological assets at America's disposal to counter the lure of communism in Southeast Asia. In 1965, he shuddered at the consequences of a wholesale abandonment of Saigon, wondering whether "all these countries [will] say Uncle Sam is a paper tiger – wouldn't we lose credibility [by] breaking the word of three Presidents?"[136]

LBJ's acceptance of McNamara's doom-laden scenario of falling dominoes comported with his own reading of history, which emphasized the need to check aggression before it spawned a wider conflict.[137] "I don't believe I can walk out [on South Vietnam]," he explained. "If I did, they'd [the communists] take Thailand, Cambodia, Burma, Indonesia, India, the Philippines ... I'd be another [Neville] Chamberlain and ... we'd have another Munich."[138] The President and his senior aides were temperamentally inclined to believe that the primary beneficiary of a North Vietnamese victory would be China. Their Cold War mindset tended to underplay the indigenous origins of the insurgency and to inflate the role of their primary adversaries. Barely settled in the Oval Office, Johnson defined Vietnam as a test of American resolve and of his own determination to contain international communism. He remarked to one assistant, "If we don't do something ... it'll [Saigon] go under ... The Chinese. The fellas in the Kremlin ... [will] be taking the measure of us. They'll be wondering just how far they can go."[139] Notwithstanding Hanoi's prickly nationalism, the administration perceived a DRV tilt toward Beijing in the Sino-Soviet contest during 1963–64, citing the North's disenchantment with Moscow's line of "peaceful co-existence" and marginal support for national liberation struggles, its reliance on the mainland for heavier firepower and improved transportation and communications facilities, and the inspiration it took from Maoist war strategy and the Chinese revolutionary experience.[140] North Vietnam's dependence on China and the PRC's objective of undermining US influence in Asia, the Vietnam Working Group concluded in November 1964, had given rise to "close cooperation" between the two countries and frequent consultation "on major decisions regarding South Vietnam."[141]

Developments in the new year crystallized this impression. Frustrated by Hanoi's resilience, even after the initiation of air assaults in February, the Johnson team believed that China's steadfast opposition to any negotiated settlement and its exhortations to the North that it stand firm only stiffened the latter's resolve and encouraged the perpetuation of the conflict.[142] Consequently, the notion of Hanoi serving as Beijing's proxy acquired currency. Rusk, for one, was convinced that "Hanoi seemed now to be coming gradually more under Chinese influence."[143] He saw the PRC as the real enemy in Vietnam and warned Johnson that a defeat there would fan Chinese-inspired subversion: "If the Communist world finds out we will not pursue our commitment to the end, I don't know where they will stay their hand."[144] The President was receptive to this message and dismissed the expressed possibility of a unified, communist Vietnam ever acting as a bulwark against China as "sheer Fulbright nonsense."[145] In a highly publicized address at Johns Hopkins University in April, LBJ contended that China cast a shadow over the war and all of Asia. As part of "a wider pattern of aggressive purposes," the DRV was being "urged on" by the mainland.[146] McNamara recollected that he "totally underestimated the nationalist aspect of Ho Chi Minh's movement. We saw him first as a Communist and only second as a Vietnamese nationalist."[147]

Anticipating China's role in Vietnam

Even as Johnson inched toward taking a stand in South Vietnam to thwart Chinese ambitions, however, his inner circle continued to recoil from any direct confrontation with the mainland. They narrowly defined the objective of any military action as curtailing the North's support of the NLF without provoking Chinese intervention.[148] As throughout 1964, the advocates of escalation in 1965 discounted the possibility of a wider Sino-American war by highlighting the discrepancy between Beijing's effusive rhetorical support for Hanoi and its unwillingness to incur imperialist reprisals for the sake of socialist solidarity. In arguing for the sustained bombing of North Vietnam in February (what would become Operation Rolling Thunder), the Joint Chiefs of Staff maintained that the Chinese remained reluctant to participate in the fighting and at most would reply to this move by dispatching a limited number of volunteers to the North "to raise the specter of further escalation" and ward off the Americans. The Joint Chiefs essentially urged the President to call the PRC's bluff and proceed with the air strikes. In the unlikely event of Chinese intervention, they were confident that "the United States and its allies can deal with them adequately."[149]

Senate Majority Leader Mike Mansfield and George Ball offered a different viewpoint. Mansfield insisted to Johnson that an air offensive was unwise in light of China's substantial military presence on Hainan and its own airfield infrastructure in North Vietnam.[150] Ball supported limited air strikes against the North only as a means of enhancing America's bargaining position in a negotiated withdrawal from Saigon. He was highly dubious, however, of the course of sustained military pressure championed by McNamara and McGeorge Bundy, largely out of fear that this would ignite a conflict with the PRC. Relying heavily on intelligence and analysis provided by Allen Whiting, a State Department expert on China, the Under Secretary was convinced that the recent deployment of 350 Chinese jet fighters to South China conveyed a willingness to deter or engage the United States should the battle line be extended too far northwards.[151] Moreover, Beijing could not be expected to acquiesce in any humiliating setback for Hanoi, simply because this "would mean the collapse of the basic Chinese ideological position which they have been disputing with the Soviets." Considerations of prestige and credibility among their allies, Ball opined, might compel the PRC's leadership to confront the United States on the ground and in the air before the objectives of America's bombing program could be met. Once China had entered the war, he glumly warned LBJ, the administration would then be faced with considerable political pressure to forcefully repel the Chinese – if necessary, by the use of nuclear weapons – so as to avert the spectacle of another Korea-like war of attrition.[152]

Despite these concerns, Johnson sided with his senior civilian and military advisers and authorized the bombing of the North, hopeful that this drastic step would coerce Hanoi into seeking a solution on American terms. At a White House meeting following the Pleiku attack on 6 February, an impatient and testy President bluntly dismissed Mansfield's cautionary counsel, arguing that he "had kept the shotgun over the mantel and the bullets in the basement for a long time." Johnson "realized that there was a risk of involving the Soviets and Chinese but ... neither of these are friendly with us and the problem is to face up to them both."[153] LBJ's bluster belied his own profound anxieties over a wider war in Vietnam. Johnson hedged his bets against Chinese intervention by insisting on a gradual, controlled bombing program that steered clear of sensitive targets. On 6 April, he signed an order that specifically forbade hitting MiG-19 aircraft bases near Hanoi, lest Chinese technicians working there were caught in the line of fire. Similarly, attacks on North Vietnamese airfields and surface-to-air missile (SAM) sites under construction were prohibited. US pilots could not fly over Hanoi or Haiphong without explicit permission from the White House; strikes against either were not authorized until June 1966.[154]

Johnson's cautious escalation of the war was heavily governed by memories of Korea and the failure to anticipate China's entry into that conflict in the fall of 1950. The pressures for firm military measures against a PRC "client" and the promises of Chinese quiescence that LBJ received from his military aides were eerily reminiscent of the same advice given to Truman by General MacArthur.[155] He relied more on his own instincts and preconceptions. Contrary to much of the intelligence he received, Johnson believed that the bonds of ideology overrode any strategic tensions among America's communist adversaries. He thought, for example, that in the event of a Sino-American clash, the Soviets would "go with them [the PRC] as soon as the fight started. They wouldn't forsake that Communist philosophy."[156] It therefore followed that Beijing would not stand idly by while Hanoi was pulverized.

The limits imposed on Rolling Thunder exasperated those within the administration pressing for a more vigorous response. "By limiting our attacks to targets like bridges, military installations and lines of communication," CIA Director McCone advised Johnson in April, "we signal to the Communists that our determination to win is significantly modified by our fear of widening the war." The US could dictate the terms of any settlement in Indochina only by "damaging important economic or military assets in North Vietnam."[157] Throughout the late spring and early summer, the Joint Chiefs pressed for the mining of Northern ports, attacking major bridges along the routes from Hanoi to China, bombing petroleum oil lubricants (POL) storage areas, and raiding airfields and SAM batteries as part of a stepped-up effort to weaken the North's will to resist.[158] LBJ resisted these recommendations, fearful that any bombing near Hanoi "would bring China into the struggle."[159] Johnson's micromanagement of Rolling Thunder was indicative of how he oversaw the larger Americanization of the war effort in 1965, a process which one historian has likened to "an elaborate cat-and-mouse game." Wary of the military's influence on Capitol Hill, the President chose not to challenge the Joint Chiefs directly, giving them "enough to suggest that they might get more later" while, in order to control the risks of escalation, he "denied them several of the items they deemed crucial to their own strategy."[160]

Recent scholarship has confirmed that Johnson did in fact possess some room for maneuver in waging war against the DRV. Mao consistently supported the establishment of a unified Vietnam under communist rule, yet the lengths to which he was willing to go in support of this objective turned on calculations of Chinese strategic interests, relations with the Americans and Soviets, and, not least of all, domestic priorities. Thus for most of the 1950s, particularly during the Geneva Conference in 1954, Beijing counselled caution to its ally in Hanoi, out of concern that forceful prosecution of an insurgency in the South could provoke American intervention and divert Chinese resources from the tasks of economic reconstruction and consolidation of the CCP's rule in the wake of the Korean War.[161] Elements within the Chinese leadership continued to argue in favor of this line well into the next decade. In February 1962, Wang Jiaxiang, head of the CCP's International Liaison Department, contended that China required a stable and peaceful international environment to pursue its recovery from the Great Leap Forward. Mao interpreted

Wang's proposals as a threat to his own leadership and as another disquieting sign of the Soviet-style revisionism that was sapping China's revolutionary vigor.[162]

A fusion of domestic and international concerns elicited Mao's personal interest in a protracted Vietnamese conflict and a shift towards more active support of the North's armed struggle from 1962–63 onwards: the need to counter what was perceived as America's hostile encirclement of China and bleed US resources dry, to promote China's leadership of international communism by cultivating national liberation movements, and to exploit regional tensions as a means of mobilizing domestic support for his vision of "continuous revolution" and vigilance against capitalist restoration at home.[163] The apparent change in US strategy heralded by the air strikes against North Vietnam in August 1964, following the Gulf of Tonkin incidents, alarmed Chinese leaders and galvanized them into delivering on their promises of support to Hanoi. That same month, China delivered fifteen MIG-15 and MIG-17 jets to the DRV, agreed to train North Vietnamese pilots, and initiated the construction of new airfields in areas adjacent to the Vietnamese border. In the aftermath of Rolling Thunder, the PRC sent ground-to-air missiles, antiaircraft artillery, and railroad, engineering, minesweeping, and logistic units to the North.[164] Throughout the first half of 1965, Beijing vigorously opposed Ghanaian, French, and Polish peace initiatives to settle the conflict.[165]

Like its American adversary, however, China's interest in a victory in Vietnam was tempered by its fear of a Great Power collision. Sinologists have argued that Mao's determination to launch the Cultural Revolution, even as early as January 1965, made this a particularly inopportune time for another Korea-like clash. Far from a statement of aggression, Lin's *Long Live the Victory of People's War!* encouraged local insurgency groups to bear the brunt of liberation struggles and "indicated that China would put increasing proportions of its energy not into exporting people's war but in assuring revolutionary continuity inside the country." In these circumstances, Mao sought or at least welcomed assurances of American military restraint in Vietnam.[166]

Even as Beijing increased its aid to Hanoi, it moved to limit its own direct participation in the fighting. Much to the disappointment of the DRV's leadership, China retracted an April 1965 pledge to dispatch volunteer pilots.[167] In June, PLA Chief of Staff Luo Ruiqing and his

North Vietnamese counterpart, Van Tien Dung, finalized an arrangement whereby the North would continue to wage the struggle by themselves, with continued materiel support from China, so long as the US confined itself to bombing only the DRV.[168] Years later, North Vietnam's Prime Minister Pham Van Dong snidely observed that Mao "was always ready to fight to the last Vietnamese."[169] Mao and his comrades evidently hoped that the Korean precedent would serve as a brake against American aggression in the North and deter any action that threatened China's own borders. To heighten the Johnson administration's calculation of risk, they used the Sino-American ambassadorial talks in Warsaw as a forum to issue deliberately vague, ominous warnings against US escalation.[170] On 21 April 1965, Wang Guoquan, the Chinese ambassador to Poland, stated in a typical exchange that "Chinese security was directly threatened by US aggression [in] South Viet-nam [sic] ...[the] Chinese share [the] same destiny with people all over [the] world and must join hands with them."[171]

A joint State-Defense study group, echoing previous findings, concluded barely one week later that China's bark was worse than its bite. While the continued prosecution of an air war against the DRV carried risks of "limited Chinese military involvement," the far more dangerous scenario of a large-scale Chinese offensive in Southeast Asia or an attack on American planes and ships from bases in South China would arise only if the United States "appeared to threaten the very existence of a Communist regime in North Viet Nam [sic] or ... [made] an effort to deal serious blows to China itself."[172] This was ultimately a very accurate reading of Chinese attitudes. The implication here was that China's prudence provided considerable leeway for American operations in the North. Intriguingly, the report went on to argue that should the US find itself engaged in war with China, the initial objective of preserving a non-communist South Vietnam would be "wholly inadequate to the large-scale hostilities going on and some adjustment would have to be made." An expanded conflict would present an opportunity to "'settle' once and for all some of the more troublesome problems facing us in the Far East." Washington could pursue a "restoration of the geographic status quo through elimination of [the] Chinese Communist military presence in all the Southeast Asian countries to reunification, under non-communist regimes, of Viet Nam [sic] and Korea, and ultimately to the extreme objective of destroying communist control of mainland China."[173]

Still, as the State-Defense group acknowledged, the cost of securing any of these goals would "far exceed the level of hostilities experienced in the Korean War."[174] Johnson himself displayed no interest in contemplating such an option. Furthermore, he was far less sanguine than many of his advisers in pinpointing the hair-trigger for Chinese intervention and he took very seriously the warnings issued by Chinese officials. On 31 May, Chen Yi delivered a new message, courtesy of the British Foreign Office, which appeared to be an attempt to establish the ground rules for America's conduct of hostilities in Vietnam. It may have only succeeded in muddying the waters for LBJ. The statement affirmed that (1) China would not provoke war with the United States; (2) what China said counted; (3) China was prepared; and (4) if America bombed China, that would mean war and there would be no limits to the war. The problem with this declaration, McGeorge Bundy wrote, was that "it does not tell us at all at what point the Chinese might move in Vietnam itself in a way which would force us to act against China. And that of course is the $64 question."[175]

Chinese intentions weighed heavily on Johnson as he contemplated the next stage of the war. Within a month of the launching of Rolling Thunder, the President was informed that a bombing offensive alone could not guarantee a reversal of fortunes in the South.[176] In July, the Pentagon, led by McNamara, pushed for an additional 100,000 troops in South Vietnam. In addition to these forces, the White House was urged to place the country on a war footing – by calling up 235,000 Reserves and the National Guard, declaring a state of national emergency, and asking Congress for an increase in taxes – so as to convey a sense of determination and resolve to both the American people and the enemy in Vietnam.[177] Drawing on intelligence analyses, the Defense Secretary assured Johnson that these measures would not trigger Chinese intervention on the ground or in the air provided "we do not invade North Vietnam, do not sink a Chinese ship and, most important, do not strike China."[178]

Following the pattern established in February, Johnson instinctively opted for the middle ground, striking a delicate balance between the imponderability of withdrawal and the intense effort deemed necessary by many to win the war. He approved the request for troops but rejected those other items on the agenda (including an expansion of Rolling Thunder) that he thought unduly provocative to the PRC. LBJ used a meeting with the Joint Chiefs on 22 July to legitimize his preference and foster consensus for a course of measured escalation. Johnson pressed the attendees, asking "If we come in with hundreds of thousands of men and billions of dollars, won't this cause them [China and the USSR] to come in?" When Army Chief of Staff Harold Johnson replied in the negative, the President reminded everyone of the same advice that Truman had received from MacArthur and insisted that he had to "take into account" the possibility that China might intervene militarily.[179]

Johnson's resistance to placing the country on a war footing stemmed in large part from his apprehension that conservative opponents of his domestic legislation might seize a national debate on Vietnam as an opportunity to stifle the Great Society, particularly the Voting Rights and Medicare bills then awaiting congressional approval.[180] Yet as LBJ also told his advisers, he only wanted "to do what is necessary to meet the present situation ... We will neither brag about what we are doing or thunder at the Chinese Communists and the Russians."[181] In August, Johnson chided Senator John Stennis, a senior member of the Senate Armed Services Committee, for publicly speculating on how much the country would have to spend to win the war. He thought that this would only compel Ho Chi Minh to ask Beijing and Moscow for more aid. "I'm trying to keep from forcing the Chinese to come in," the President explained.[182] Thus as Johnson gradually led his nation into war, he deliberately tailored the effort in such a way as to preclude another Sino-American battle whose destructive potential had grown inestimably since the PRC's testing of a nuclear device. In doing so, Johnson consciously accepted the constraints this strategy placed on America's military muscle and underlined his preference for *containing*, rather than *confronting*, China.

As the viability and wisdom of America's China policy of containment and isolation came under attack abroad and increasingly at home, several Johnson officials, to varying degrees, urged a change in approach. The most ambitious advocates of reform contended that the administration's firm posture in South Vietnam provided the necessary political covering to relax trade and travel restrictions and acquiesce in a "two Chinas" arrangement at the UN. An injection of flexibility into America's attitude toward China would shift the blame for continued friction between the two nations in the short term, and pave the way for a long-term reconciliation with a less doctrinaire second generation of Chinese leaders. Far less inclined to view the PRC as an expansionist power and doubtful of any substantial Chinese role in Vietnam, mid-level officials such as James Thomson and Edward Rice reasoned that a policy of engagement – alleviating persistent Chinese fears of American enmity and exposing China to the moderating influences of the world beyond its borders – would effect a gradual whittling away of the mainland's hostility to the international status quo.

For the first two years of his presidency, Lyndon Johnson did not enmesh himself in the details of China policy; he was far more preoccupied with the priorities of election, the passage of domestic legislation, and the unfolding war in Vietnam. Images of the PRC were inextricably linked to all three, which ultimately accounted for his resistance to policy innovation. The perceived political baggage associated with China militated against a departure from his predecessor's record. As this chapter has argued, the reaffirmation of US China policy was also the by-product of the administration's obsession with Vietnam, where Johnson's senior advisers saw Beijing's support of the insurgency in the South as confirmation of a subversive agenda aimed at securing Chinese hegemony in Southeast Asia by means short of war. China's conventional weaknesses – its economic and military feebleness, tactical caution, and tensions between Hanoi and Beijing – were reconciled with, if not overshadowed by, its non-conventional strengths: the capacity to fan anti-Western sentiment, exert politico-psychological pressure against its vulnerable neighbors, undermine the credibility of America's security commitments, and complicate Soviet-American détente.

The Johnson team believed that there was a direct correlation between the international community's conciliatory gestures toward the PRC and China's threatening behavior. As Rusk complained, "the recent reactions of the West – the French recognition of Peking; the gradual strengthening of trade links between the West and China; the relatively mild Western reaction to the recent Chinese detonation of a nuclear device – were ... encouraging ... the Chinese to believe that militancy paid."[183] Frowning upon its allies' tentative engagement with China, Washington worked assiduously to perpetuate the PRC's ostracism from the international system. Seen in this light, the administration had not so much a policy toward China at this time as an attitude. Expressing a view with wide currency among LBJ's inner circle, Walt Rostow asserted, "until it is demonstrated that the game of 'Wars of National Liberation' is not viable and that the borders of China and North Vietnam are firm, the acceptance of Communist China within the world community and in the UN could be a major disaster ... [and] would signal to those on the spot that we have granted Chinese Communist hegemony in Southeast Asia."[184] Any change in attitudes toward the PRC ran contrary to the overriding priority of demonstrating resolve in Vietnam to foe and friend alike. Yet Johnson's decision to commit American forces to the defense of Saigon, the ultimate expression of American credibility and clarity of purpose, would ironically serve as the catalyst for a new approach to China.

Notes

1 Bachrack, *The Committee of One Million*, pp. 210–17; Kusnitz, *Public Opinion and Foreign Policy*, p. 112.
2 Only a handful of historians have alluded to this link. See Tucker, "Threats, opportunities, and frustrations in East Asia," in Cohen and Tucker (eds), *Lyndon Johnson Confronts the World*, pp. 99–111; Foot, "Redefinitions," in Ross and Jiang (eds), *Re-examining the Cold War*, pp. 284–5.
3 A number of Vietnam statements delivered by senior Johnson officials were compiled by the Senate Committee on Foreign Relations in March 1966 and published in a manual entitled "Background Information Relating to Southeast Asia and Vietnam." This may be located in White House Central File (hereafter WHCF), Countries (CO), Box 8, folder "CO 1-3," LBJL. For references to China's role in Vietnam, see Address by McNamara, 26 March 1964, pp. 119–21; Address by William P. Bundy, 23 January 1965, pp. 145–9; Rusk's news conference, 25 February 1965, pp. 166–67; Address by LBJ, 7 April 1965, pp. 206–7; Speech by LBJ, 13 May 1965, p. 232. See as well F.M. Kail, *What Washington Said: Administration Rhetoric and the Vietnam War: 1949–1969* (New York: Harper & Row, 1973), pp. 23–30.
4 Among the more notable volumes covering the 1963–65 Vietnam decisions are L. Berman, *Planning a Tragedy: The Americanization of the War in Vietnam* (New York: W.W. Norton & Company, 1982); Bird, *Color of Truth*; DiLeo, *George Ball, Vietnam, and the Rethinking of Containment*; L.C. Gardner, *Pay Any Price: Lyndon Johnson and the Wars for Vietnam* (Chicago: Ivan R. Dee, 1995); G.C. Herring, *America's Longest War*, Second ed. (New York: Alfred A. Knopf, 1986); Hunt, *Lyndon Johnson's War*; Kaiser, *American Tragedy*; Khong, *Analogies at*

War; Logevall, *Choosing War*; R.B. Smith, *An International History of the Vietnam War, vol. 2: The Struggle for Southeast Asia, 1961–6* (London: Macmillan, 1985); R.B. Smith, *An International History of the Vietnam War, vol. 3: The Making of a Limited War* (London: Macmillan, 1991); B. VanDeMark, *Into the Quagmire: Lyndon Johnson and the Escalation of the Vietnam War* (New York: Oxford University Press, 1990).
5 Logevall, *Choosing War*, pp. 291–2, 388–9.
6 J.L. Gaddis, *Strategies of Containment: A Critical Appraisal of Postwar American National Security Policy* (Oxford: Oxford University Press, 1982), p. 212.
7 Garson, "Lyndon B. Johnson and the China enigma," pp. 63–4, 78.
8 For example, see VanDeMark, *Into the Quagmire*, pp. 121–2; Kaiser, *American Tragedy*, pp. 361–2; Schulzinger, "The Johnson administration, China, and the Vietnam War," in Ross and Jiang (eds), *Re-examining the Cold War*; Goh, *Constructing the US Rapprochement with China*, pp. 38–42.
9 McGeorge Bundy once playfully referred to his aide as "Mao Tse-Thomson." Bird, *Color of Truth*, p. 346.
10 James Thomson OH, p. 5, LBJL.
11 Telephone interview with author, 18 February 2002.
12 Thomson to M. Bundy, 28 October 1964, NSF, Country File, Box 238, folder "China memos, vol. II," LBJL.
13 Thomson to Cater, 24 November 1964, WHCF, Federal Government, Box 10, LBJL.
14 Komer to M. Bundy, 23 November 1964, NSF, Country File, Box 238, folder "China memos, vol. II," LBJL.
15 Airgram, no. A-309, Hong Kong to Department of State, 6 November 1964, NSF, Country File, Box 238, folder "China cables, vol. II," LBJL. Intelligence analyses, which were more widely circulated among senior officials, tended to downplay divisions among China's leaders and to accentuate the uniformity of their radical worldviews. A March 1964 CIA report, for example, concluded that the first generation of leaders were all "intensely nationalistic and appear deeply committed to a militant brand of Communism." As for the leadership-in-waiting, the potentially more pragmatic elements to whom Rice wanted to appeal, their constant subjection to Party indoctrination and limited contact with the outside world likely made them just as dogmatic and impervious to compromise. CIA memo, "The Chinese communist leadership and the succession problem," 19 March 1964, NSF, Country File, Box 237, folder "China memos, vol. I," LBJL. See as well NIE 13-9-65, "Communist China's foreign policy," 5 May 1965, NSF, National Intelligence Estimates (hereafter NIE), Box 4, folder "Communist China (2 of 2)," LBJL.

16 Stevenson to LBJ, 18 November 1964, in W. Johnson (ed.), *The Papers of Adlai E. Stevenson*, vol. 8 (Boston: Little, Brown, 1979), pp. 634–5.
17 Cleveland to Ball, 31 October 1964, NSF, Country File, Box 290, folder "United Nations Chinese Representation 10/65," LBJL.
18 Telephone interview with author, 18 February 2002. In 1991, Bundy stated that, like many in the administration, he viewed China at the time as an "overpowering mass threat." Quoted in T. Gittinger (ed.), *The Johnson Years: A Vietnam Roundtable* (Austin: Lyndon Baines Johnson Library, Lyndon B. Johnson School of Public Affairs, 1993), p. 9.
19 W. Bundy to Arnold Heeney, 21 December 1964, RG 59, Subject Files of the Office of the Assistant Secretary of State for East Asian and Pacific Affairs, 1961–74, Lot 85D240, Box 10, NA.
20 W. Bundy to Rusk, 2 November 1964, RG 59, Bureau of Far Eastern Affairs, Office of the Assistant Secretary: Subject Files, 1964, Lot 66D93, Box 2, NA.
21 W. Bundy to Rusk, 16 June 1965, *FRUS, 1964–1968*, vol. 30, p. 175.
22 S. Karnow, *Vietnam: A History*, Revised ed. (New York: Penguin Books, 1991), p. 356; Bird, *Color of Truth*, p. 275.
23 Roger Hilsman OH, Interview 1, p. 38, LBJL.
24 An excellent illustration of LBJ's deference to his aides on China policy came in an unremarkable, yet revealing, telephone conversation with McGeorge Bundy on 18 April 1964. While being briefed on a major foreign policy address he was to deliver two days later, which included a brief statement on US attitudes toward Beijing, Johnson asked his National Security Adviser, "What are we saying about Communist China," explaining that "I haven't seen it in the speech." Bundy reiterated the hard-line stance: "The speech says that if there's going to be any change [in US policy toward the PRC], it's they who'll have to change." Almost offhandedly, the President remarked, "Yeah, that's good. That's alright." Telcon, LBJ–M. Bundy, 18 April 1964, Recordings of Telephone Conversations and Meetings, WH6404.10 PNO 19, LBJL. In having to ask Bundy what the administration's views on China were, this brief exchange underscores Johnson's passive role in the formulation of China policy during the early months of his administration. It also corroborates Robert Dallek's characterization of the Johnson-Bundy relationship as that of an eager student taking notes from an at times patronizing professor. See Dallek, *Flawed Giant*, pp. 89–90.
25 Marshall Green, quoted in Tucker (ed.), *China Confidential*, p. 196; Thomson, "On the making," pp. 230–1; James Thomson OH, pp. 38–9, LBJL.
26 Thomson to J.C.T. Files, 6 May 1964, JCT Papers, Box 9, folder "12/13/63 San Francisco: Thomson Notes on Genesis and Reaction," JFKL.

27 Bird, *Color of Truth*, p. 18.
28 Telephone interview with author, 18 February 2002.
29 M. Bundy to *New York Times* (Draft Letter), 4 June 1967, NSF, Name File, Box 7, Rostow memos (2 of 2), LBJL.
30 Summary notes of NSC meeting, 17 October 1964, NSF, NSCM, Box 1, folder "Vol. III, tab 25," LBJL.
31 Telegram, no. 1333, Moscow to Department of State, 28 October 1964, NSF, Country File, Box 219, folder "USSR Cables, vol. VI," LBJL. The State Department's Bureau of Intelligence and Research had no doubt that "the retirement of Khrushchev will be interpreted by the Chinese as a victory for their policies." Hughes to Rusk, 15 October 1964, *FRUS*, 1964–1968, vol. 14, p. 121.
32 Record of Rusk–Gordon Walker talks, 26 October 1964, FO 371/175977, PRO.
33 Hughes to Rusk, 27 November 1964, NSF, Country File, Box 238, folder "China memos, vol. II," LBJL.
34 Meeting on China study, 27 August 1965, NSF, Agency File, Box 61, folder "Special State-Defense study group re China," LBJL.
35 Memorandum of conversation, Rusk–Halvard M. Lange, 13 November 1964, RG 59, Central Files, 1964–66, Box 1898, POL 1 ASIA SE, NA.
36 Rusk to Department of State, 16 December 1963, *FRUS*, 1961–1963, vol. 22, pp. 409–10. Also see Rusk's remarks in Minutes of Cabinet meeting, 18 June 1965, p. 28, Cabinet Papers, Box 3, LBJL.
37 Remarks on foreign affairs at the Associated Press luncheon in New York City, 20 April 1964, *Public Papers of the Presidents: Lyndon B. Johnson* (hereafter *PPP:LBJ*), 1963–1964, vol. 1, p. 499.
38 Circular telegram from the Department of State to certain posts, 5 September 1964, *FRUS*, 1964–1968, vol. 30, p. 85.
39 David Dean to Marshall Green, 21 August 1964, RG 59, Subject Files of the Office of Asian Communist Affairs, 1961–73, Lot 72D41, Box 2, NA.
40 Telegram (unnumbered), Department of State to the American Embassy in Bangui, 7 October 1964, NSF, Country File, Box 290, folder "United Nations Chinese Representation 10/65," LBJL; G. Mennen Williams and W. Bundy to Rusk, 19 October 1964, RG 59, Bureau of Far Eastern Affairs, Office of the Assistant Secretary: Subject Files, 1964, Lot 66D93, Box 1, NA.
41 WPB Papers, ch. 21, p. 10, Box 1, LBJL.
42 National policy paper, "The Republic of China," 11 September 1964, *FRUS*, 1964–1968, vol. 30, p. 93.
43 Meeting with the President on United Nations matters, 18 November 1964, ibid., pp. 126–7. In a similar vein, Walt Rostow argued that the US could only "acquiesce in Chinese Communist entrance into the UN after

Southeast Asia was pacified on terms which preserve the independence of Laos and South Viet Nam [sic]." Walt Rostow to Rusk, 17 October 1964, NSF, Vietnam Country File, Box 54, folder "Southeast Asia memos, vol. IV," LBJL.

44 M. Bundy to LBJ, 16 December 1964, NSF, Memos to the President, Box 2, folder "Vol. VII (1 of 2)," LBJL.
45 For Rusk's consultations with the Canadians, see Memcon, Canadian views on Chinese representation at the UN, 14 November 1964, *FRUS, 1964–1968*, vol. 30, pp. 124–5; with the British, see Record of Rusk–Gordon Walker talks, 26 October 1964, FO 371/175977, PRO and Record of Rusk–Gordon Walker meeting, 7 December 1964, PREM 13/104, PRO.
46 St Amour, "Sino-Canadian relations," in Evans and Frolic (eds), *Reluctant Adversaries*, p. 113.
47 Kaufman, *Confronting Communism*, pp. 178–9.
48 Memcon, Rusk–Sato meeting, 12 January 1965, NSF, Country File, Box 253 (1 of 2), folder "Sato's Visit: Memos & Cables (3 of 4)," LBJL. See as well Rusk to LBJ, undated, NSF, Country File, Box 253 (1 of 2), folder "Sato's Visit Briefing Book 1/11–14/65 (1 of 2)," LBJL.
49 Rusk to LBJ, 28 June 1965, NSF, Memos to the President, Box 3, folder "Vol. XI (1 of 3)," LBJL. James Thomson was scornful of Rusk's suggestion, dismissing it as "irrelevant and inadequate." Thomson to M. Bundy, 29 June 1965, *FRUS, 1964–1968*, vol. 30, p. 177.
50 M. Bundy to LBJ, 24 August 1965, NSF, Memos to the President, Box 4, folder "Vol. XIII (3 of 3)," LBJL. Bundy makes reference to the 29 June luncheon in this memorandum.
51 Tucker (ed.), *China Confidential*, p. 202. For the dichotomy between popular and official views of China in the mid-1960s, see Foot, *Practice of Power*, p. 84.
52 Bachrack, *The Committee of One Million*, p. 211.
53 VanDeMark, *Into the Quagmire*, p. 180.
54 Bachrack, *The Committee of One Million*, p. 222.
55 NIE 13-64, "Economic prospects for Communist China," 28 January 1964, NSF, NIE, Box 4, folder "Communist China (2 of 2)," LBJL.
56 President's meeting with Congressional leadership, 22 January 1965, NSF, Files of McGeorge Bundy, Box 18, folder "Miscellaneous Meetings, vol. I," LBJL.
57 SNIE 13-4-63, "Possibilties of greater militancy by the Chinese communists," 31 July 1963, NSF, NIE, Box 4, folder "Communist China (2 of 2)," LBJL; NIE 13-3-65, "Communist China's military establishment," 10 March 1965, ibid.; NIE 13-9-65, "Communist China's foreign policy," 5 May 1965, ibid.; "Communist China – Long Range Study," June 1966, NSF, Country File, Box 245, LBJL.

58 "Communist China – Long Range Study," pp. 35–8, 203.
59 R.S. McNamara, *In Retrospect: The Tragedy and Lessons of Vietnam* (New York: Times Books, 1995), p. 33.
60 NIE 13-9-65, "Communist China's foreign policy," 5 May 1965, pp. 2, 4–5. Underlying this view was the widespread ethnocentric sentiment that the PRC's leadership placed little value on human life and was therefore willing to incur substantial losses in pursuit of external objectives. Kochavi, *A Conflict Perpetuated*, p. 191.
61 McNamara, *In Retrospect*, p. 215; Cohen, *Dean Rusk*, p. 285; WPB Papers, ch. 32, p. 2, Box 1, LBJL; Hughes to Rusk, 24 September 1965, NSF, Country File, Box 238, folder "China memos, vol. IV," LBJL.
62 For the influence of China on Kennedy's policies in Southeast Asia, see Kochavi, *A Conflict Perpetuated*, ch. 6; Kochavi, "Limited accommodation, perpetuated conflict." For Kennedy's Vietnam decisions, see Freedman, *Kennedy's Wars*, pp. 287–413; Kaiser, *American Tragedy*, pp. 58–283; W.J. Rust, *Kennedy in Vietnam* (New York: De Capo Press, 1985); Herring, *America's Longest War*, ch. 3; Logevall, *Choosing War*, chs 1–2.
63 A CIA estimate produced in February 1964 concluded that Saigon "has at best an even chance of withstanding the insurgency menace during the next few weeks or months." SNIE 50-64, "Short-term prospects in Southeast Asia," 12 February 1964, NSF, NIE, Box 7, folder "Southeast Asia," LBJL.
64 Telcon, LBJ–M. Bundy, 27 May 1964, in Beschloss (ed.), *Taking Charge*, p. 370. For the Pentagon's enthusiasm for military pressure against Hanoi in early 1964, see Kaiser, *American Tragedy*, pp. 298–304.
65 Herring, *America's Longest War*, p. 108; Telcon, LBJ–McNamara, 20 February 1964, in Beschloss (ed.), *Taking Charge*, p. 249; Telcon, LBJ–M. Bundy, 2 March 1964, ibid., p. 263; Memorandum of Conversation, 4 March 1964, *FRUS*, 1964–1968, vol. 1, p. 129.
66 In May 1964, LBJ noted that Rusk, McNamara, Bundy, Harriman, and Cyrus Vance were just "like MacArthur in Korea – they don't believe that the Chinese Communists will come into this thing." Telcon, LBJ–Richard Russell, 27 May 1964, in Beschloss (ed.), *Taking Charge*, pp. 364–5.
67 The Joint Chiefs of Staff to McNamara, 2 March 1964, *FRUS*, 1964–1968, vol. 1, p. 117.
68 SNIE 50-2-64, "Probable consequences of certain US actions with respect to Vietnam and Laos," 23 May 1964, NSF, Files of McGeorge Bundy, Box 18, folder "Meetings on Southeast Asia, vol. I," LBJL.
69 CIA memo, "Chinese communists brace for possible spread of Indochina War," 12 February 1965, NSF, Vietnam Country File, Box 48, folder "Southeast Asia Special Intelligence Material, vol. III," LBJL.

70 Rostow to Rusk, 15 February 1964, *FRUS*, 1964–1968, vol. 1, pp. 81–2. In July 1965, General Earle Wheeler, Chairman of the Joint Chiefs of Staff, stated to LBJ that "the one thing all NVN [North Vietnamese] fear is Chinese. For them to invite Chinese volunteers is to invite China's taking over NVN." Meeting on Vietnam, 22 July 1965, Meeting Notes File, Box 1, LBJL.
71 Bundy's emphasis. WPB Papers, ch. 17, pp. 22–4, Box 1, LBJL.
72 Rostow to LBJ, 7 June 1964, NSF, Vietnam Country File, Box 54, folder "Southeast Asia memos, vol. III (B)," LBJL.
73 McNamara to LBJ, 16 March 1964, NSF, NSCM, folder "vol. I, tab 5," LBJL. See as well SNIE 50-64, "Short-term prospects in Southeast Asia," 12 February 1964, NSF, NIE, Box 7, folder "Southeast Asia," LBJL.
74 McNamara, *In Retrospect*, p. 33.
75 Sherman Kent to McCone, 9 June 1964, NSF, Vietnam Country File, Box 54, folder "Southeast Asia memos, vol. III (B)," LBJL.
76 Meeting on South Vietnam, 9 September 1964, NSF, Memos to the President, Box 2, folder "Vol. VI (1 of 2)," LBJL.
77 This critical point is made in Smith, *An International History*, vol. 2, p. 203. Smith's multi-volume work is one of only very few studies that properly places the Vietnam War in a regional context.
78 Michael V. Forrestal to W. Bundy, 4 November 1964, Papers of Paul C. Warnke: John McNaughton Files, Box 8, folder "Book II: Department of State Material (1964)," LBJL. For Forrestal's views on Vietnam, see Preston, *War Council*, chs 5–6.
79 J.D. Legge, *Sukarno: A Political Biography*, Second ed. (Sydney: Allen & Unwin, 1984), pp. 320–8; M. Leifer, *Indonesia's Foreign Policy* (London: George Allen & Unwin, 1983), pp. 54–5.
80 Leifer, *Indonesia's Foreign Policy*, p. 56.
81 Brands, *The Wages of Globalism*, p. 156; A.C. Guan, "The Johnson administration and 'Confrontation,'" *Cold War History* 2: 3 (2002), 111; M. Jones, "US relations with Indonesia, the Kennedy–Johnson transition, and the Vietnam connection, 1963–1965," *Diplomatic History* 26:2 (2002), 249–57.
82 Rusk to LBJ, 6 January 1964, *FRUS*, 1964–1968, vol. 26, p. 6; M. Bundy to LBJ, 7 January 1964, ibid., pp. 13–14; Rusk to LBJ, 29 June 1964, ibid., pp. 116–17. For further discussion of the internal debate over aid to Indonesia in early 1964, see Jones, "US relations with Indonesia," pp. 261–5.
83 Current intelligence memorandum, 20 August 1964, FRUS, 1964–1968, vol. 26, p. 136. For similar assessments, see Marshall Green to Rusk, 19 August 1964, ibid., p. 131; Komer to LBJ, 3 September 1964, NSF, Country File, Box 246, folder "Indonesia memos, vol. III," LBJL.

84 Memorandum of conversation, 27 October 1964, *FRUS*, 1964–1968, vol. 26, p. 175. This perception was widespread. For example, see Ellsworth Bunker to LBJ, undated, ibid., p. 255; M. Green, *Indonesia: Crisis and Transformation, 1965–1968* (Washington, DC: The Compass Press, 1990), p. 25. The PKI's relations with Beijing during this period are covered in D. Mozingo, *Chinese Policy Toward Indonesia, 1949–1967* (Ithaca: Cornell University Press, 1976), pp. 216–20. Even as the PKI's line of a peaceful transfer of power to socialism in Indonesia clashed with China's philosophy, Beijing was willing to overlook these ideological differences to gain the party's support in the Sino-Soviet dispute. The PKI, in turn, tilted toward China in 1963 because it was alienated by Moscow's pursuit of détente with the West.

85 CIA memorandum, "Principal problems and prospects in Indonesia," 26 January 1965, NSF, Country File, Box 246, folder "Indonesia memos, vol. III," LBJL; George Ball to LBJ, undated, NSF, Country File, Box 247, folder "Indonesia memos, vol. IV," LBJL; WPB Papers, ch. 28, p. 12, Box 1, LBJL; Smith, *An International History*, vol. 3, p. 50; Green, *Indonesia*, p. 12; R. Sukma, *Indonesia and China: The Politics of a Troubled Relationship* (London: Routledge, 1999), p. 32. Washington likely exaggerated the degree of convergence between Jakarta and Beijing. Mozingo writes that the 1963–65 relationship was inherently unstable, held together only by shared opposition to the creation of Malaysia. See Mozingo, *Chinese Policy*, pp. 194, 220–30.

86 Report from Ambassador Ellsworth Bunker to President Johnson, undated, *FRUS*, 1964–1968, vol. 26, pp. 255–63.

87 NIE 54/55-65, "Prospects for Indonesia and Malaysia," 1 July 1965, ibid., pp. 270–1.

88 SNIE 55-65, "Prospects for and strategic implications of a communist takeover in Indonesia," 1 September 1965, ibid., pp. 289–92.

89 K.J. Clymer, "The perils of neutrality: The break in US–Cambodian relations, 1965," *Diplomatic History* 23:4 (1999), 612–13.

90 Smith, *An International History*, vol. 2, p. 204; M. Osborne, *Sihanouk: Prince of Light, Prince of Darkness* (St Leonards, Australia: Allen & Unwin, 1994), pp. 161–2.

91 *FRUS*, 1964–1968, vol. 27, p. 260, n. 3.

92 Telegram from the embassy in Cambodia to the Department of State, 26 March 1964, ibid., p. 289. For Sihanouk's hostility toward Vietnam and Thailand, see Osborne, *Sihanouk*, pp. 107–8, 151–5.

93 Telegram, no. 517, Department of State to Phnom Penh, 8 February 1964, NSF, Country File, Box 236, folder "Cambodia cables, vol. I (1 of 3)," LBJL. See as well Clifford L. Alexander, Jr to M. Bundy, 6 December 1963, NSF, Country File, Box 236, folder "Cambodia memos, vol. II," LBJL; Telegram, no. 990, Bangkok to Department of State, 28 December

1963, NSF, Country File, Box 282, folder "Thailand memos, vol. I," LBJ. For a discussion of Cambodia as an irritant in US–Thai relations, see A. Kislenko, "Bamboo in the Wind: United States Foreign Policy and Thailand During the Kennedy and Johnson Administrations, 1961–1969" (PhD Dissertation, University of Toronto, 2000), pp. 192–6.

94 Telegram from the Department of State to the embassy in the United Kingdom, 22 March 1964, *FRUS, 1964–1968*, vol. 27, p. 285.

95 Telegram, no. 737, Phnom Penh to Department of State, 30 January 1964, NSF, Country File, Box 236, folder "Cambodia cables, vol. I (1 of 3)," LBJL; Telegram, no. 775, Phnom Penh to Department of State, 12 February 1964, RG 59, Central Files, 1964–66, Box 1615, DEF 12-1 CHICOM, NA.

96 Clymer, "The perils of neutrality," pp. 620, 628–30.

97 CIA report, "The situation in Cambodia," 20 December 1963, NSF, Country File, Box 236, folder "Cambodia cables, vol. I (2 of 3)," LBJL; Telegram, no. 546, Phnom Penh to Department of State, 19 December 1963, ibid.; Rusk to McCone, 30 June 1964, *FRUS, 1964–1968*, vol. 27, p. 318; Thomson to LBJ, 28 December 1964, ibid., p. 338; Smith, *An International History*, vol. 3, p. 110.

98 Alf E. Bergesen to W. Bundy, 14 December 1964, RG 59, Bureau of Far Eastern Affairs, Office of the Assistant Secretary: Subject Files, 1964, Lot 66D93, Box 1, NA.

99 S.A. Loftus, Jr to John McNaughton, 30 May 1964, *FRUS, 1964–1968*, vol. 27, pp. 584–6; Kislenko, "Bamboo in the Wind," pp. 179–81.

100 Kislenko, "Bamboo in the Wind," pp. 182–3.

101 Joint Chiefs of Staff to McNamara, 23 September 1964, *FRUS, 1964–1968*, vol. 27, p. 609.

102 Martin's emphasis. Memorandum for the record, 1 June 1964, ibid., pp. 590–1.

103 Memorandum of conversation, 11 December 1964, RG 59, Bureau of Far Eastern Affairs, Office of the Assistant Secretary: Subject Files, 1964, Lot 66D93, Box 1, NA. See as well Kislenko, "Bamboo in the Wind," p. 181.

104 Kislenko, "Bamboo in the Wind," p. 180.

105 For example, see W. Bundy to McNaughton, 24 April 1965, *FRUS, 1964–1968*, vol. 27, pp. 625–6. The insurgency is discussed in Kislenko, "Bamboo in the Wind," pp. 217–20.

106 Telegram, no. 948, Bangkok to Department of State, 20 January 1965, NSF, Country File, Box 282, folder "Thailand cables, vol. II," LBJL; CIA memorandum, "The threat of communist subversion in Thailand," 10 September 1965, NSF, Country File, Box 283, folder "Thailand memos, vol. III," LBJL; Memorandum for the record, 29 January 1965, *FRUS, 1964–1968*, vol. 27, pp. 613–15.

107 CIA memorandum, "The threat of communist subversion in Thailand," 10 September 1965.
108 Memorandum for the record, 24 November 1964, NSF, Files of McGeorge Bundy, Box 18, folder "Miscellaneous Meetings, vol. I," LBJL.
109 W. Bundy to Rusk, 6 January 1965, *FRUS*, 1964–1968, vol. 2, pp. 31–2. Bundy later contended, "If it [Vietnam] had stood alone, I have no doubt whatever that the United States would have pulled back and said 'enough' ... [however] it was judged that failure to act would mean a dangerous unravelling of the balance of power in East Asia." WPB Papers, ch. 28, p. 1, Box 1, LBJL.
110 M. Bundy to LBJ, 27 January 1965, *FRUS*, 1964–1968, vol. 2, p. 96.
111 M. Bundy to LBJ, 7 February 1965, ibid., p. 184.
112 NIE 13-9-65, "Communist China's foreign policy," 5 May 1965, NSF, NIE, Box 4, folder "Communist China (2 of 2)," LBJL. This dimension of the Chinese threat is further discussed in Annex V, "Chinese communist efforts to expand their influence by means short of overt aggression, and free world counteraction," in "Communist China – Long Range Study," June 1966, NSF, Country File, Box 245, LBJL.
113 Quoted in L.C. Gardner, "Fighting Vietnam: The Russian-American conundrum," in L.C. Gardner and T. Gittinger (eds), *International Perspectives on Vietnam* (College Station: Texas A & M University Press, 2000), p. 31.
114 Paper by the Under Secretary of State, undated, *FRUS*, 1964–1968, vol. 3, p. 110.
115 See Ball's remarks in Meeting on Vietnam, 21 July 1965, Meeting Notes File, Box 1, LBJL.
116 Telcon, Ball–James Reston, 1 March 1966, Papers of George W. Ball, Box 2, folder "China (Peking)," LBJL.
117 William Bundy, quoted in DiLeo, *George Ball, Vietnam, and the Rethinking of Containment*, p. 121.
118 Hitherto, the only effort that indirectly looks at this angle is Gardner, "Fighting Vietnam," in Gardner and Gittinger (eds), *International Perspectives on Vietnam*.
119 WPB Papers, ch. 7, p. 7, Box 1, LBJL. The steady decline in 1962–63 of Soviet prestige among Asian communist parties and the concomitant rise in China's influence is documented in Radchenko, "The China Puzzle," pp. 93–104.
120 This episode is recounted in Telegram, no. 437, Vientiane to Department of State, 3 November 1965, enclosed in M. Bundy to LBJ, 3 November 1965, NSF, Memos to the President, Box 5, folder "Vol. XVI (2 of 3)," LBJL. For Khrushchev's general ambivalence toward engagement in Asia, see Radchenko, "The China Puzzle," p. 103.

121 Khrushchev's Vietnam policy in the 1960s is covered in I.V. Gaiduk, *The Soviet Union and the Vietnam War* (Chicago: Ivan R. Dee, 1996), pp. 3–19, and D. Pike, *Vietnam and the Soviet Union: Anatomy of an Alliance* (Boulder: Westview, 1987), pp. 45–9, 73–4.
122 Gaiduk, *The Soviet Union and the Vietnam War*, p. 27.
123 WPB Papers, ch. 21, pp. 9, 19, Box 1, LBJL; "Communist China (Short range report)," Section I, p. 6, 30 April 1965, NSF, Agency File, Box 61, LBJL; Hughes to Acting Secretary, 12 May 1965, NSF, Country File, Box 238, folder "China memos, vol. III," LBJL; SNIE 10-9-65, "Communist and free world reactions to possible US course of action," 23 July 1965, *FRUS, 1964–1968*, vol. 3, p. 229.
124 M. Bundy to LBJ, 3 November 1965, NSF, Memos to the President, Box 5, folder "Vol. XVI (2 of 3)," LBJL. For a similar view, see Special report prepared in the CIA, "The Soviet Union since Khrushchev," 9 April 1965, *FRUS, 1964–1968*, vol. 14, pp. 284–5. See as well Dumbrell, *President Lyndon Johnson and Soviet Communism*, pp. 103–4. Bundy and other US officials misread the extent to which increased Soviet assistance to the DRV was undertaken to counter Chinese influence. Indeed, Khrushchev's successors viewed this assistance as an ideological imperative and initially hoped that a joint Sino-Soviet effort could be mounted in support of Hanoi against the US. This is discussed in Radchenko, "The China Puzzle," ch. 3.
125 Telegram, no. 2377, Moscow to Department of State, 15 February 1965, *FRUS, 1964–1968*, vol. 14, p. 241; Special report prepared in the CIA, "The Soviet Union since Khrushchev," 9 April 1965, ibid., p. 278; Policy Planning Council memorandum, "Soviet policy in the light of the Vietnam crisis," 15 February 1965, NSF, Country File, Box 220, folder "USSR memos, vol. VIII," LBJL.
126 Telegram, Moscow to Department of State, 17 April 1965, *FRUS, 1964–1968*, vol. 14, p. 286.
127 Summary notes of 550th NSC meeting, 26 March 1965, NSF, NSCM, Box 1, folder "Vol. III, tab 32," LBJL.
128 SNIE 10-3-65, "Communist reactions to possible US actions," 11 February 1965, *FRUS, 1964–1968*, vol. 2, p. 245; "Communist China – Long Range Study," p. 38, June 1966, NSF, Country File, Box 245, LBJL.
129 Gaiduk, *The Soviet Union and the Vietnam War*, p. 19.
130 M. Bundy to LBJ, 15 July 1965, NSF, Memos to the President, Box 4, folder "Vol. XII (2 of 3)," LBJL; Telegram, no. 216, Moscow to Department of State, 21 July 1965, *FRUS, 1964–1968*, vol. 14, p. 313. For Soviet wariness of playing an intermediary in Vietnam, see Radchenko, "The China Puzzle," pp. 231–2.
131 Background paper, "Soviet bloc situation," 4 January 1965, NSF,

Country File, Box 253 (1 of 2), folder "Sato's Visit: Briefing Book (1 of 2)," LBJL.
132 Telegram, no. 2920, Moscow to Department of State, 6 April 1965, NSF, Country File, Box 220, folder "USSR cables, vol. VIII," LBJL. See as well M. Bundy to LBJ, 7 June 1965, NSF, Memos to the President, Box 3, folder "Vol. XI (3 of 3)," LBJL.
133 Policy Planning Council memorandum, "Soviet policy in the light of the Vietnam crisis," 15 February 1965.
134 Quoted in Gaiduk, *The Soviet Union and the Vietnam War*, p. 26.
135 Logevall, *Choosing War*, pp. 390–3; Berman, *Planning a Tragedy*, p. 146; VanDeMark, *Into the Quagmire*, p. 213; Brands, *The Wages of Globalism*, p. 231; Dallek, *Flawed Giant*, pp. 277–9; J.A. Califano, Jr, *The Triumph & Tragedy of Lyndon Johnson: The White House Years* (New York: Simon & Schuster, 1991), pp. 51–2.
136 Meeting on Vietnam, 21 July 1965, Meeting Notes File, Box 1, LBJL.
137 Goodwin, *Lyndon Johnson and the American Dream*, p. 330.
138 Telcon, LBJ–Drew Pearson, 23 March 1965, in Beschloss (ed.), *Reaching For Glory*, p. 238.
139 Quoted in Dallek, *Flawed Giant*, p. 100.
140 WPB Papers, ch. 16, p. 7, Box 1, LBJL; CIA report, "North Vietnam's military establishment," 27 December 1963, NSF, Vietnam Country File, Box 48, folder "Southeast Asia Special Intelligence Material, vol. I," LBJL; CIA report, "Chinese communist military doctrine," 17 January 1964, NSF, Country File, Box 237, folder "China memos, vol. I," LBJL. Hanoi's tilt toward Beijing is covered in Zhai, *China and the Vietnam Wars*, pp. 122–9; Yang Kuisong, "Changes in Mao Zedong's attitude toward the Indochina War, 1949–1973," pp. 25–9.
141 NSC Working Group on Vietnam, "Section I: Intelligence assessment: The situation in Vietnam," p. 14, 24 November 1964, Papers of Paul C. Warnke: John McNaughton Files, Box 8, folder "Book IV: Department of State Material (1964)," LBJL.
142 Summary notes of 550th NSC meeting, 26 March 1965, NSF, NSCM, Box 1, folder "vol. III, tab 32," LBJL; Summary notes of 553rd NSC meeting, 27 July 1965, ibid., tab 35, LBJL; Telegram, no. 2224, Department of State to Warsaw, 24 June 1965, NSF, Country File, Box 202, folder "Cabot–Wang Talks," LBJL; Hughes to Acting Secretary, 12 May 1965, NSF, Country File, Box 238, folder "China memos, vol. III," LBJL; CIA memo, "Asian communist and Soviet views on the war in Vietnam," 25 May 1965, NSF, Vietnam Country File, Box 50, folder "Southeast Asia Special Intelligence Material, vol. VI (B)," LBJL; "Communist China (Short range report)," Section II, pp. 5–6, 30 April 1965, NSF, Agency File, Box 61, folder "Special State-Defense Study Group re China," LBJL; Memo, Office of Current Intelligence to John McCone,

23 February 1965, *FRUS, 1964–1968*, vol. 2, pp. 360–1; Raborn to LBJ, 12 June 1965, ibid., p. 770.
143 Record of Rusk–Harold Wilson conversation, 14 May 1965, PREM 13/1890, PRO.
144 Meeting on Vietnam, 21 July 1965, Meeting Notes File, Box 1, LBJL.
145 Quoted in Goodwin, *Lyndon Johnson and the American Dream*, p. 330.
146 Address at Johns Hopkins University, 7 April 1965, *PPP:LBJ*, 1965, vol. 1, p. 395.
147 McNamara, *In Retrospect*, p. 33.
148 See McNamara's remarks in Minutes of Cabinet meeting, p. 51, 18 June 1965, Cabinet Papers, Box 3, LBJL; Rusk to LBJ, 1 July 1965, *FRUS, 1964–1968*, vol. 3, pp. 104–5.
149 Joint Chiefs of Staff to McNamara, 11 February 1965, *FRUS, 1964–1968*, vol. 2, p. 241. This assessment was mirrored in SNIE 10-3-65, "Communist reactions to possible US actions," 11 February 1965, ibid., p. 248.
150 Mike Mansfield to LBJ, 8 February 1965, NSF, Name File, Box 6 (2 of 2), folder "Mansfield memo & reply," LBJL.
151 DiLeo, *George Ball, Vietnam, and the Rethinking of Containment*, p. 81.
152 Ball to LBJ, 13 February 1965, *FRUS, 1964–1968*, vol. 2, pp. 252–9.
153 Memorandum for the record, 6 February 1965, ibid., pp. 159–60.
154 Shapley, *Promise and Power*, pp. 324–5; M. Clodfelter, *The Limits of Air Power: The American Bombing of North Vietnam* (New York: The Free Press, 1989), pp. 84–5.
155 For the influence of the Korean analogy on LBJ's Vietnam decisions of 1965, see Khong, *Analogies at War*, ch. 5.
156 Telcon, LBJ–Richard Russell, 27 May 1964, in Beschloss (ed.), *Taking Charge*, p. 368.
157 McCone to LBJ, undated, *FRUS, 1964–1968*, vol. 2, pp. 521–2.
158 Clodfelter, *The Limits of Air Power*, p. 83.
159 Memorandum of Senator Mansfield, 3 June 1965, *FRUS, 1964–1968*, vol. 2, p. 709. See as well Telcon, LBJ–Drew Pearson, 23 March 1965, in Beschloss (ed.), *Reaching for Glory*, pp. 238–9; Telcon, LBJ–Richard Russell, 26 July 1965, ibid., pp. 408–9.
160 Herring, *LBJ and Vietnam*, p. 36.
161 Zhai, *China and the Vietnam Wars*, pp. 4, 49–63; Chen, *Mao's China and the Cold War*, pp. 138–44.
162 Chen Jian and Yang Kuisong, "Chinese politics and the collapse of the Sino-Soviet alliance," in Westad (ed.), *Brothers in Arms*, pp. 276–7; Yang, "Changes in Mao Zedong's attitude toward the Indochina War," pp. 21–2.
163 Zhai, *China and the Vietnam Wars*, pp. 139–52; Chen, *Mao's China and the Cold War*, pp. 209–12. For Mao's dismay with China's internal

direction in the first half of the 1960s, there is no better source than MacFarquhar, *Origins of the Cultural Revolution*, vol. 3, esp. pp. 261–473.

164 Zhai, *China and the Vietnam Wars*, pp. 132–5. For the impact of American intervention in Vietnam on Mao's threat perception in 1964–65, see O.A. Westad, "History, memory, and the languages of alliance-making," in O.A. Westad, Chen Jian, S. Tonnesson, Nguyen Vu Tung, and J.G. Hershberg (eds), "77 conversations between Chinese and foreign leaders on the wars in Indochina, 1964–1977," CWIHP Working Paper 22 (1998), p. 9.

165 Zhai, *China and the Vietnam Wars*, pp. 157–67; Zhai, "Beijing and the Vietnam peace talks, 1965–68," pp. 1–10, 16–18.

166 T. Robinson, "China confronts the Soviet Union: Warfare and diplomacy on China's inner Asian frontiers," in R. McFarquhar and J.K. Fairbank (eds), *The Cambridge History of China, vol. 15: The People's Republic, Part 2: Revolutions within the Chinese Revolution, 1966–1982* (Cambridge: Cambridge University Press, 1991), p. 227. See as well MacFarquhar, *Origins of the Cultural Revolution*, vol. 3, p. 376.

167 Zhai, *China and the Vietnam Wars*, pp. 134–5.

168 Chen, *Mao's China and the Cold War*, pp. 216–21.

169 Quoted in Karnow, *Vietnam*, p. 345.

170 For example, see Telegram from the embassy in Poland to Department of State, 29 July 1964, *FRUS, 1964–1968*, vol. 30, pp. 73–4; Telegram from the embassy in Poland to Department of State, 23 September 1964, ibid., p. 100; Telegram from the embassy in Poland to Department of State, 24 February 1965, ibid., p. 149; M. Bundy to LBJ, 25 May 1965, NSF, Country File, Box 202, folder "Cabot–Wang Talks," LBJL.

171 Warsaw to Department of State, 21 April 1965, NSF, Country File, Box 202, folder "Cabot–Wang Talks," LBJL.

172 "Communist China (Short range report)," Section I, pp. 3–4, 30 April 1965, NSF, Agency File, Box 61, LBJL. See as well Raborn to LBJ, 12 June 1965, *FRUS, 1964–1968*, vol. 2, pp. 768–9.

173 "Communist China (Short range report)," Section I, pp. 1–2, 20.

174 Ibid., Section I, p. 20.

175 M. Bundy to LBJ, 4 June 1965, NSF, Memos to the President, Box 3, folder "Vol. XI (3 of 3)," LBJL. For further discussion of Chen Yi's May 1965 message, see J.G. Hershberg and Chen Jian, "Reading and warning the likely enemy: China's signals to the United States about Vietnam in 1965," *International History Review* 27:1 (2005), 71–9.

176 M. Bundy to LBJ, 6 March 1965, NSF, Memos to the President, Box 3, folder "Vol. IX (3 of 3)," LBJL.

177 Berman, *Planning a Tragedy*, pp. 103–4, 125–6.

178 McNamara to LBJ, 20 July 1965, NSF, Memos to the President, Box 4, folder "Vol. XII (1 of 3)," LBJL.
179 Meeting on Vietnam, 22 July 1965, Meeting Notes File, Box 1, LBJL.
180 Herring, *America's Longest War*, p. 140; Dallek, *Flawed Giant*, pp. 276, 284; Berman, *Planning a Tragedy*, pp. 147–9.
181 Meeting on Vietnam, 27 July 1965, NSF, National Security Council History, Box 43, folder "Deployment of Major US Forces to Vietnam, July 1965: vol. VII, tabs 421–438," LBJL.
182 Telcon, LBJ–John Stennis, 18 August 1965, Recordings of Telephone Conversations and Meetings, WH6508.05 PNO 11, LBJL.
183 Record of Rusk–Gordon Walker meeting, 7 December 1964, PREM 13/104, PRO.
184 Rostow to Rusk, 10 January 1964, NSF, Country File, Box 237, folder "China memos, vol. I," LBJL.

4 The irony of Vietnam
The emergence of a two-pronged China policy, 1965–66

The conventional view of Sino-American relations during the Johnson years holds that Washington's tendency to view China through the prism of Vietnam precluded any policy innovation or movement toward normalization with the mainland.[1] Vietnam did in fact remain a constant determinant of the administration's stance toward Beijing, yet its impact on China policy deliberations changed as conditions on the ground in that war evolved. Indeed, one of the unexamined ironies of Vietnam, a war undertaken in part to check Chinese expansionism, is that it created pressures for an accommodation of sorts with the PRC and encouraged US decision-makers who might not otherwise have been inclined to reassess the tenets of a line of containment and isolation. Only a year after publicly invoking the looming threat posed by China as a contributing factor to his military actions in Vietnam, Johnson affirmed in a nationally televised speech on 12 July 1966 his commitment to an eventual reconciliation with America's greatest Asian adversary and an interest in fostering the free flow of ideas, people, and goods between the two countries. The address followed a relaxation of the travel ban and was the culmination of a new effort to broaden contacts with the communist regime. Revisionist literature has drawn attention to the symbolic and substantive alterations in China policy in 1966, yet it has not adequately tied this critical development to the Johnson team's domestic and strategic objectives in Vietnam.[2]

This chapter traces the thawing of attitudes to LBJ's heightened interest in averting Chinese intervention in the conflict and to his attempts to mobilize public support for a frustratingly prolonged war by burnishing his peace credentials. A concluding section on the administration's simultaneous resistance to seating Beijing in the UN illustrates the tentative nature of this bridge building and the obstacles – firm preconceptions of China as an implacable revolutionary power, alliance politics, and uncertainty over how much anti-Chinese sentiment at home had relented – that continued to impede bolder initiatives at this time.

China stumbles on the world stage: the view from Washington

A rapid sequence of events in the fall of 1965 appeared to undermine one of the primary justifications for the administration's refusal to engage the mainland. As China suffered a number of embarrassing reversals abroad, many of the assumptions underlying the Johnson team's unyielding posture – that the PRC was thrusting forward in pursuit of an expansionist agenda, that it was riding a wave of favorable developments, and that it represented the most pressing threat to the sovereignty of its neighbors – were cast in a new light. The proximity in timing between these events and Washington's China initiatives of 1966, however, was mostly coincidental. As before, China's perceived *intentions* excited as much, if not more, attention and concern as its *actions*. Pressures stemming from Vietnam and shifting political currents at home in fact provided the impetus for bridge-building. The significance of Beijing's stumbling rests not so much on the immediate impact on China policy, but on the administration's evolving threat assessment.

A landmark in this respect was the Indo-Pakistani War of August-September 1965. Alarmed by India's efforts in December 1964 to integrate the disputed territory of Kashmir and by its crash program of military modernization, the Pakistani leadership, sensing a narrowing window of opportunity, launched Operation Gibraltar on 5 August. Utilizing local insurgents in an assault on India's portion of Kashmir, Islamabad evidently hoped to provoke a regional crisis, thereby rallying Muslim opinion throughout the world and forcing the Americans to arbitrate a fair settlement over the state.[3] Pakistan's actions occurred against the backdrop of growing US dismay in South Asia. The Kennedy team's dogged determination to woo New Delhi with economic and military aid, particularly in the aftermath of the Sino-Indian War, had inflicted considerable strain on America's alliance with Pakistan. Disheartened by Washington's courtship of his mortal enemy, President Mohammed Ayub Khan turned to Beijing in his continuing search for security.[4] LBJ had little patience for Pakistan's flirtation with the PRC, and he spared no effort in warning Ayub that this endangered the continued flow of US assistance. Johnson's irritation reached its peak in March 1965, when he abruptly cancelled the Pakistani leader's forthcoming visit to the White House.[5] Ayub's gambit in August raised the prospect of further Chinese meddling in the region. Indeed, he may have felt emboldened to take military action, operating on the (mistaken) assumption that Beijing's anti-Indian rhetoric amounted to a virtual promise of aid in the event of an Indo-Pakistani clash.[6]

The question of Chinese intentions came to the fore when Ayub, in an effort to rescue the floundering infiltration, dispatched a large armoured force on 31 August to cut off the Indian military in Kashmir. New Delhi responded one week later with a drive toward Lahore. Fearful that India would deal a decisive blow to Pakistan, China moved to warn the former and reassure the latter. On 7 September, Foreign Minister Chen Yi affirmed his country's "firm support for Pakistan in its just fight against aggression and solemnly warns the Indian Government that it must bear full responsibility for all the consequences of its criminal and extended aggression."[7] US intelligence analysts saw no cause for alarm and minimized the risks of overt Chinese involvement in the unfolding conflict. A steady stream of reports concluded that Beijing's sabre-rattling amounted to nothing more than an attempt to frighten New Delhi. Beyond this act of deterrence, Chinese leaders had little interest in committing themselves to any action that would divert attention and resources from the far more vital theatre in Southeast Asia. It could therefore be expected that the mainland would exhaust every conceivable option before resorting to force in defense of its ally.[8]

LBJ's inner circle, perhaps unsurprisingly given their China mindset, took a strikingly different view. Rusk took China's bellicose words as confirmation of an understanding between the PRC and Pakistan. Chinese military intervention in the war, he advised the President, was "a clear contingency." Yet even if the mainland remained aloof from the fighting, Rusk estimated that continued Indo-Pakistani hostilities would only benefit Beijing. The fighting would drain both combatants and consequently "negate our effort to build there a viable counterweight to Communist China." An Indian collapse would fan the latent neutralism of powers such as Japan and dramatically enhance the mainland's prestige.[9] Sufficiently concerned by the prospect of a wider conflict, the State Department instructed the American ambassador in Warsaw to caution his Chinese counterpart against any action that "could create a most dangerous situation, [in] which it would be difficult to confine to the areas or parties initially affected."[10]

Tensions escalated on 17 September when Beijing delivered an ultimatum to New Delhi, demanding that it dismantle a string of military structures along the Sikkim-Tibet border within forty-eight hours or face "grave consequences." Johnson immediately ordered the State and Defense departments to prepare a set of military options in the event of a Chinese attack on India, and implored New Delhi and Islamabad to comply with a UN ceasefire resolution before events veered out of control.[11] The crisis over China's ultimatum ended barely after it had begun. The Chinese effectively withdrew their demands on 20 September, dubiously claiming that India had fulfilled its obligations. This decision most likely resulted from a reading of Soviet attitudes; the Kremlin's tacit refusal to lean on India or to promise Beijing support against an American attack apparently convinced the PRC's leadership that they would be completely isolated in a second Sino-Indian war.[12]

US officials interpreted the climb-down as a humiliating admission of impotence. "Our impression of [the] Chicom handling of [the] Sikkim affair is that Peking hardly comes out of this one smelling like a rose," the consulate office in Hong Kong reported. "By acting precipitously and then hastily backing off instead of gradually building up pressure, [the] Chicoms run [the] risk of causing any subsequent threats ... to be heavily discounted by all concerned."[13] Johnson was struck by how the Chinese "have done a great deal of talking in the past week or so, but have not acted, and they have probably lost a great deal of prestige in many quarters."[14]

A more stunning reversal of Chinese fortunes occurred almost simultaneously in Indonesia. On 30 September, a leftist faction within the army, supported by the PKI, launched a revolt against the high command. The abortive coup was ruthlessly suppressed by the Strategic Reserve, headed by Major General Suharto, and then used as the pretext for a bloody purge of the PKI, the army's greatest rival for political influence in the country. The next few weeks and months also witnessed a wave of anti-Chinese demonstrations and a significant downgrading of Sino-Indonesian relations.[15] The affair seemed to have originated from an intra-army dispute rather than from a PKI-inspired plot. Moreover, the army's charges of Chinese complicity, as the US intelligence community eventually acknowledged, could not be corroborated. The mainland's interests had in fact been best served by its existing relationship with Sukarno, not by the orchestration of a violent rift between the PKI and the army.[16]

As reports of the country's anti-communist campaign and Sukarno's marginalization poured in, Johnson officials sensed a major alteration in the balance of forces in the region. By early 1966, the CIA reported that the PKI, whose takeover of Southeast Asia's crown jewel had been glumly predicted only months earlier, had been "reduced to an underground organization of unknown size," with the possibility of any revival "virtually nil for the next few years."[17] Yet it was commonly thought that the greatest loser in this debacle was the party's presumed sponsor. The collapse of the Sino-Indonesian axis, the US ambassador in Jakarta told LBJ, amounted to "a great loss of international prestige for Peking."[18] The dismal fate of the PKI, according to another CIA report, would impair China's standing in the international communist movement: "Communists abroad sympathetic to Peking may begin to have second thoughts about too close an identification with the Chinese."[19]

These dramatic events were seen as part of a wider pattern of Chinese setbacks in the developing world. The limits of China's influence were starkly illustrated in November 1965, when Beijing was forced to abandon its year-long effort to forge a unified bloc opposed to American and Soviet power in the Third World at a new Afro-Asian conference in Algiers. Several of those invited balked at Moscow's exclusion from the proposed meeting, fearful that this would jeopardize future deliveries of Soviet aid. Beijing's latest stumble was enthusiastically welcomed in Washington.[20] By the summer of 1966, it was estimated that Beijing's international status had plummeted to the point where it could rely only on Albania and New Zealand's Communist party for unconditional loyalty in the Sino-Soviet dispute. Moscow's leadership of the communist movement, assumed to be in peril throughout 1964–65, had been restored. This development was attributed to both the PRC's "rigid dogmatism and political ineptitude" and the Kremlin's increased materiel assistance to North Vietnam. By demonstrating their support for armed revolutionary struggle, Khrushchev's successors had neutralized repeated Chinese charges of Soviet collusion with the West.[21]

The Soviet factor figured prominently in Washington's evolving understanding of the Sino-Vietnamese relationship. Hanoi's persistent requests for advanced Soviet weaponry, US analysts opined, bore the hallmarks of a quasi-independent actor striving to lessen its reliance on China and to maintain its freedom of action by assuming a neutral stance in the Sino-Soviet competition for its allegiance.[22] There was speculation by the end of 1965 that the DRV's flourishing ties with the Kremlin signified the ascendancy of the leadership's moderate and pragmatic wing. Led by Premier Pham Van Dong, this pro-Soviet faction was thought to have some interest in an eventual negotiated settlement of the war, which, as one intelligence report noted hopefully, "is a considerable step away from the Chinese Communist position that there should be no talks on any terms, and that the war must be carried through to a complete Communist military victory."[23]

China's foreign policy defeats had a contradictory impact on the administration's thinking. Senior officials, perhaps betraying an ingrained need to highlight any sign of progress amidst the protracted fighting in Vietnam, hailed these developments as a turning point of sorts. As Johnson contemplated the question of American intervention in Vietnam in 1965, his advisers had insisted that a credible defense of Saigon was imperative to alleviating the worries of nervous allies and thwarting the PRC's subversive designs in Southeast Asia. Within a year of making that fateful commitment, the President was now told that "Hanoi's operation, backed by the Chicoms, is no longer being regarded as the wave of the future out there."[24] American resolve in Vietnam and the crushing of the PKI, William Bundy wrote Rusk in March 1966, had created a "markedly healthier" atmosphere throughout the region and restored Asian allies' faith in US leadership.[25]

At the same time, however, decision-makers remained wedded to the long-standing assumption of a Chinese threat. As Bundy recollected, "the fact that China had suffered reverses in 1965 was not seen as changing the basic judgment that she was militant ... Although we in government had followed the Chinese setbacks ... we had also seen more closely the extraordinary stiffness and arrogance of Chinese handling of each situation."[26] The challenge posed by China had never been defined in purely conventional terms. It was deemed primarily politico-psychological in nature, a product of the belligerency of Maoist ideology and the fragility of China's neighbors. Even as the PRC's fortunes soured, Johnson officials held that its hostile intentions and capacity to stir trouble remained virtually unchanged. In a February 1966 speech, Bundy repeated this concern, reminding his audience that Mao was not "another Hitler, building a vast military machine with the aim of conquest by conventional warfare." His ambitions relied instead on "the instigation and support of movements that can be represented as local movements, designed to subvert and overthrow existing governments and replace them with regimes responsive to Peking's will."[27]

Beijing's behavior during the thirty-seven-day bombing pause, initiated by the administration toward the end of December 1965, reinforced these impressions. The sincerity of Johnson's Vietnam "peace offensive" has been disputed by many historians; most likely it was intended to shift the blame for continued hostilities to Hanoi and secure political justification for the sustained military effort that he privately believed to be unavoidable.[28] As anticipated, the DRV was highly suspicious of American motives and spurned offers of negotiation. In assessing North Vietnam's intransigence, US officials apportioned considerable blame to the PRC's militant influence. Beijing was seen as the fiercest opponent of peace talks, including even the North. Its overriding objective of ejecting the US from the Pacific demanded vigorous prosecution of the communist insurgency in the South. By virtue of geography, shared ideology, and the volume of Chinese aid, the mainland was believed to be well positioned to press its views on its ally, notwithstanding the inroads made by Moscow.[29] "Peking has actively intruded on any talks between Hanoi and [the] US," Rusk informed Johnson as the pause came to an end in January. "Hanoi appears to be somewhere between Moscow and Peking – but closer to Peking."[30] Recent Chinese sources have confirmed that there was some basis for this sentiment. Beijing's vehement objection to negotiations appears to have played a significant role in shaping the DRV's decidedly hostile response to an American fourteen-point peace plan delivered by Polish intermediaries.[31]

LBJ's aides continued to point to the threat of Chinese-inspired subversion as a major justification for the war in Vietnam. Despite the improved regional climate, they contended that the strategic considerations undergirding the 1965 decisions were still relevant. As part of a review of Vietnam policy options in April 1966, the State Department advised Johnson that "for the next year or two any chance of holding the rest of Southeast Asia hinges on the same factors assessed a year ago, whether Thailand and Laos in the first instance and

Malaysia, Singapore, and Burma close behind, would – in the face of a US failure for any reason in Viet-Nam – have any significant remaining will to resist the Chinese Communist pressures that would probably then be applied." A defeat in Saigon would be regarded throughout the region as "proof that Communism from the north was the decisive force in the area."[32] Steadfast containment of China remained the most logical course, especially since it could not be taken for granted that the PRC had been chastened by its diplomatic failures. "The Chicoms have had a bad time during the last 15 months," Rusk noted. "The future will turn on whether they become more dangerous and strike out at their opponents or recoup and reconsider peaceful co-existence. We don't know how this will come out."[33]

Averting Chinese intervention in Vietnam

It was precisely this intangible element of Chinese unpredictability or perceived irrationality, rather than any reassessment of Chinese intentions and capabilities, which prompted the administration to supplement containment with new tactics toward the mainland in 1966. From his post in Hong Kong, Edward Rice argued that Beijing's reckless adventurism in the Indian subcontinent and its subversive activity in Indonesia had been concocted by a group of aging ideologues, men distrustful of their successors' revolutionary fervor and therefore desperate for "convincing external successes which would justify keeping China on course towards the same aims they have set after they have passed."[34] Chinese setbacks on the world stage had instilled within the leadership an "emotional state of great frustration," which was only exacerbated by the scale of the American presence in Vietnam.[35]

Rice likened Beijing's profound anxieties in Vietnam to those it had experienced just prior to the fall of Pyongyang to UN forces in 1950. While Mao and his comrades probably hoped to avert any commitment to enter the fighting, further escalation of America's air attacks against the North would only "lend credence to their belief that we are acting under mechanistically increasing pressures to attack their country." Consequently, the administration's war planners were urged to heed the PRC's siege mentality and inherent need for domestic mobilization. The outcome in Vietnam had become so inextricably linked to Mao's revolutionary ambitions at home and abroad that he would ultimately accept the full consequences of assisting Hanoi, even if this led to a clash with the Americans. If it came, Mao might actually welcome an enlarged war, as it would rally the country behind his vision and imbue younger generations with a militant spirit. "Prudence," Rice warned Washington, "requires that we pursue a course designed ... to disappoint any expectations of Communist China's leaders that we will play to their strength by fighting them on their own terrain."[36]

Rice was only one of several officials who had pressed decision-makers throughout 1964–65 to reduce Sino-American tensions by alleviating Beijing's paranoid fears of US intentions. These voices had been effectively relegated to the sidelines as the Johnson team focused their attention on defending the besieged government in Saigon, largely out of concern that any relaxation in the administration's posture toward the PRC would be interpreted as a sign of weakness and encourage further Chinese aggression. Once they had actually committed the US militarily to Vietnam and were confronted with the prospect of another Korea-like war, however, even the most enthusiastic advocates of intervention gradually became more receptive to some of the arguments advanced by the China policy reform camp.

Robert McNamara, for example, expressed growing dismay over the evident stalemate on the battlefield during the latter half of 1965, particularly after a draining fight in the Ia Drang Valley in November, and he wondered whether a military victory could be secured within acceptable risks.[37] In December, he told LBJ that "a substantial number of additional forces" – 200,000 ground troops in 1966 and likely the same figure for the following year – would be needed "if we are to avoid being defeated." Drawing heavily on the latest CIA estimate, McNamara argued that there was only a slightly better than even chance that these deployments would "prevent the DRV/VC from sustaining the conflict at a significant level." If the limits of the North's tenacity were reached, however, there was an "almost equal" chance that the Chinese, with their ideological and emotional interests invested in a North Vietnamese victory, would dispatch their own forces to salvage the situation. Thus there existed the grim possibility, the Defense Secretary concluded, that "we will be faced in early 1967 with a military standoff at a much higher level ... with any prospect of military success marred by the chances of an active Chinese intervention."[38]

McNamara's concerns were buttressed by a number of intelligence reports in the late fall alerting Washington to signs of Chinese unease over US designs in Vietnam. The CIA noted that there had been a steady flow of Chinese military support units into the DRV since the summer. It was also surmised that the construction of new airfields in southern China and the deployment of Chinese jet fighters to Hainan in October had been triggered by the fear that US airstrikes in northeastern North Vietnam would be extended to targets on the mainland.[39] Particularly ominous were reports of Beijing's extensive efforts to prepare the country psychologically for a possible war with the US through an intensification of civil defense and mass propaganda campaigns. The State Department's INR bureau informed Rusk in early December that the regime was evacuating "non-essential persons," small factories, and many government facilities from urban and coastal areas to the remote interior of the country. Regional broadcasts and press reports were issuing frequent warnings to the population that US actions against the DRV threatened Chinese security. Taken together, these actions indicated that "Peking itself estimates the possibility of ... overt involvement [in the war] in 1966 to be a serious one."[40]

Much of this analysis was well informed. These elaborate preparations for war, particularly Mao's Third Front project of industrial development in the interior provinces, were indeed taken in response to Washington's escalation of the fighting after the Gulf of Tonkin incidents in August 1964. The Johnson administration's military maneuvers shook China's leadership and forced them to counter a seemingly renewed US strategic threat. Mao also understood that increased tensions could be exploited in his campaign to organize opposition against domestic "revisionism." As part of his plans for radicalizing China's political and social life, the Third Front was accompanied by a "Resist America and Assist Vietnam Movement" and a series of mass rallies.[41] For senior US officials, however, the distinction between military mobilization and political propaganda remained blurred. At a meeting in early December 1965, both Rusk and McNamara expressed "increasing concern about possible Chinese involvement" in Vietnam.[42]

To defuse tensions, William Bundy successfully proposed that an upcoming meeting in Warsaw on 15 December be used to inform Chinese diplomats that the US was taking a number of unilateral steps to reassure them that "we still seek to avoid a major confrontation." Bundy's suggestions included an initiative to "admit Chinese journalists to the United States without reciprocity" (since 1959, Washington had insisted on only a *mutual* exchange of newsmen) and an offer to "jointly examine their charges of air and sea violations of their territory and attacks on Chinese vessels on the high seas." Most important was a relaxation of travel controls that would permit doctors and scientists in the fields of public health and medicine to visit the mainland.[43] This particular measure, of course, had been vetoed by Johnson in June. Its fortunes were revived when Paul Dudley White, Dwight Eisenhower's physician, wrote LBJ on 10 August, briefly describing his contacts with some Chinese colleagues living on the mainland and offering his services "in helping to break our deadlock with China."[44] Johnson immediately indicated his interest in the travel package.

Why was he now willing to approve a proposal he had rejected five weeks earlier? Part of the answer was provided in a memorandum McGeorge Bundy wrote to the President shortly following the arrival of White's letter. Appealing directly to Johnson's political instincts, he contended that new circumstances – responding to an appeal by a noted Republican "at a time when our policy in Vietnam has reached a new level of clarity and firmness" – augured well for the adoption of an item that would address domestic criticism of the administration's rigid China policy.[45] Indeed, any apprehension of appearing "soft" on Asian communism had been offset by the Vietnam decisions of July. LBJ most likely appreciated this conciliatory measure as a symbolic rebuttal to elements within Congress, the press, and the academic community who bemoaned the President's resort to military force in Southeast Asia.[46] The travel initiative remained holed up in the State Department until late November, when its supporters orchestrated another White letter, this one addressed to Rusk.[47] When finally announced on 29 December, it marked a subtle yet significant departure from the Johnson team's previous insistence that there could be no modification of China policy until the PRC had learned to co-exist peacefully with its neighbors. Taken in part to deflect criticism of this unyielding stance, it was also clearly seen as a way to convey a sense of moderation to Beijing and thereby reduce the chance of any miscalculation or misunderstanding of US intentions igniting a wider conflagration in Vietnam. The ban on travel to the mainland was further relaxed in March 1966, when scholars and writers were exempted from any restrictions.[48]

Historians have argued that both countries, by displaying mutual restraint in Vietnam, reached a tacit understanding by early 1966 that kept the war limited.⁴⁹ A closer look at the record, however, indicates that Johnson and his advisers were still struggling at this time to reconcile the objective of forcing Hanoi to the negotiating table with the strategic imperative of averting Chinese intervention. In a series of meetings in late January, LBJ was encouraged to resume the bombing of the North. McNamara, who had been one of the primary proponents of the pause, reported that the communists had taken advantage of it to build up forces for "intensified action in South Vietnam." Prolonging the pause would only send the "wrong signal to Hanoi, Peking and our own people." Rusk concurred, remarking that without new bombing, the PRC would be led to believe that "a sanctuary has been approved and they can do more than ever."⁵⁰ The President, initially skeptical of the value of a bombing halt and irritated by Hanoi's refusal to respond positively to his overtures, needed little prodding.⁵¹

Yet considerable anxiety was expressed over how Beijing would interpret a renewed offensive. Under Secretary of State George Ball bluntly asserted in a 25 January memorandum to Johnson that a resumption of air attacks against the DRV would "more than likely lead us into war with Red China – probably in six to nine months." As frustration mounted over the North's continued resistance, he warned, the administration would be tempted to include increasingly sensitive targets – such as Haiphong harbor or petroleum, oil, and lubricants supplies – in its bombing program. In such an event, China could hardly be expected "to stand by and let us destroy the industrial life of North Viet-Nam without increasing its assistance to the point where, sooner or later, we will almost certainly collide with Chinese interests." The mainland's ongoing internal war preparations suggested that it was bracing for this possibility.⁵²

While Johnson's inner circle was not prepared to surrender their trump card, they agreed, as Rusk put it, that new bombing should "be kept under firm control ... [because of the] dangers of the Chinese coming in."⁵³ When Rolling Thunder was relaunched on 31 January, LBJ prohibited attacks on any target within a thirty-mile radius from the center of Hanoi and a ten-mile radius from the center of Haiphong.⁵⁴ The uncertainty surrounding Chinese intentions in the war factored heavily in the selection of military targets. Intelligence sources continued to document the PRC's growing military presence in North Vietnam. Johnson was informed at the end of February that as many as 47,000 Chinese military personnel, most of them engineering troops, were now serving in the country. In a calculated act of deterrence, these forces entering the DRV made little effort to conceal their identity and used non-secure methods of communication. It was also revealed that a central authority had been set up in the vicinity of Hanoi, which could possibly be used as "a theater logistic command to support the introduction of a Chinese combat force."[55] The INR bureau reported the following month that there had been a marked increase in the number of official statements making reference to a Chinese obligation to send men to the North. On the basis of this bellicose rhetoric, China's leaders appeared to "consider the danger of an 'imminent' war to be as great as before and ... they are more than ever convinced that some sort of war with the US at some time is 'inevitable.'"[56]

Heightened sensitivity to the PRC's perception of US aggression governed Washington's circumspect handling of a number of other initiatives that were thought to be unduly provocative to China. One such example was Taipei's ongoing efforts to enlist America's support in an invasion of the mainland. During a visit to Washington in September 1965, Taiwan's Defense Minister Chiang Ching-kuo revived his father's plan of seizing the PRC's five southwestern provinces, insisting that Beijing's hold on this region was weak and its rule deeply unpopular. Chiang assured his hosts that there would be no need for extensive American participation, only air and naval cover for the operation. McNamara was cool to the idea, thinking that it eerily resembled the Bay of Pigs disaster, in so far as "it obviously contemplated [a] large scale popular uprising against the Communists" with no palpable evidence that the conditions were ripe for such a revolt.[57] The Joint Chiefs of Staff were no more enthusiastic, branding the plan "militarily unsound." Because of Taiwan's limited capacity to strike airfields in south China, a successful outcome would require the full use of American air and naval power. The Joint Chiefs recommended that the administration continue consultations with its ally, if only to give Chiang Kai-shek the impression that his views were taken seriously and to maintain him as "a fully cooperating partner rather than as a ... potential disruption to our policies and objectives in Asia."[58]

The embassy in Taipei reported at the end of January that this hands-off approach had engendered "considerable disappointment and irritation" among the country's leadership, and counselled Washington to ease this anger by promising to re-examine the question of an assault on the mainland if other options in Vietnam were exhausted and there appeared to be no hope for a peaceful settlement.[59] The suggestion came just as Johnson was hoping to keep a lid on the hostilities in Vietnam. Accordingly, the State Department vetoed this idea on the grounds that it "would not only encourage further GRC mainland attack plans ... but would also be subject to misinterpretation and possible anticipatory action by [the] ChiComs should they learn of [the] statement, as is entirely possible."[60]

Similar considerations derailed plans for the CIA to establish a "gray" radio station targeted at the PRC, a project first proposed in October 1965 and tentatively endorsed the following April.[61] As the project made its way through the bureaucratic channels, however, a number of China hands weighed in with their objections. Both Rice and James Thomson contended that Beijing would regard a new wave of radio propaganda as proof of America's determination to encircle and overthrow the regime, undermining US efforts to head off a possible confrontation.[62] Citing these concerns, as well as the substantial costs of such a large-scale investment, a meeting of the 303 Committee in July 1966 concluded that the project should be shelved and that the United States Information Agency instead continue its broadcasts to the mainland.[63]

Yet what truly distinguished the administration's attempts to prevent China's overt involvement in Vietnam in the early months of 1966, aside from the restrained bombing of the North and attempts to forestall heightened tensions, was a concerted political and diplomatic campaign to disabuse the PRC of its sense of American hostility. To address the troubling questions raised by George Ball's memorandum, McNamara said it was necessary to "tell China we do not intend to destroy the political institutions in NVN [North Vietnam]."[64] The result was a shift from the alarmist, vaguely threatening rhetoric employed against Beijing in 1963–65 to a decidedly more conciliatory tone. Grim warnings of a Chinese menace in Southeast Asia and solemn pledges to contain it were de-emphasized in favor of calming assurances of Washington's limited aims in Vietnam. Directing his remarks toward Beijing, LBJ declared in a speech on 23 February, "We have threatened no one, and we will not. We seek the end of no regime and we will not. Our purpose is solely to defend against aggression."[65] The embassy in Warsaw was instructed to stress the desire for peaceful relations in its periodic meetings with Chinese diplomats.[66]

More importantly, senior US officials signalled their interest in new approaches to Beijing. In a prepared statement to the House subcommittee on the Far East and the Pacific on 16 March, Rusk asserted, "We must avoid assuming the existence of an unending and inevitable state of hostility between ourselves and the rulers of mainland China." He outlined a two-pronged China policy, coupling the traditional goal of containment with a new emphasis on expanding "the possibilities for unofficial contacts between Communist China and ourselves – contacts which may gradually assist in altering Peiping's picture of the United States." As part of the latter strategy, the Secretary advocated steps "to reassure Peiping that the United States does not intend to attack mainland China," continued talks in Warsaw, and a dialogue with Chinese officials on matters concerning disarmament and non-proliferation. Looking toward the future, he speculated that a younger generation of leaders would draw the appropriate lessons from Mao's failed foreign policies and adopt a more pragmatic approach to the world. Rusk assured this leadership-in-waiting that the US would "welcome an era of good relations" with a responsible China.[67] This implicit courting of a less doctrinaire ruling circle broadly resembled Roger Hilsman's landmark address of December 1963, which the Johnson team hitherto had neither repudiated nor embraced. The prevailing view of both the Kennedy and Johnson administrations had rested on the notion that only the firm application of politico-military pressure could instill prudence in Chinese behavior. Rusk's statement suggested that policymakers were now contemplating a mixture of carrots and sticks.

McNamara elaborated on this theme in a speech in May, calling for "practical alternatives" to the current relationship with the PRC and for the adoption of concrete measures to reduce "the danger of potentially catastrophic misunderstandings" between the two nations. He had in mind "properly balanced trade relations, diplomatic contacts, and in some cases ... exchanges of military observers."[68] In September, the State Department reversed previous policy and authorized diplomatic officers abroad to "establish informal social contacts with the Chinese Communists when this can be done without publicity ... [or] conveying the public impression of a change in the US policy of non-recognition of Communist China." The hope here was that increased interaction would enable the US to better gauge Chinese attitudes and provide a forum for countering "the 'devil image' of the United States that Peking inculcates in all its cadres."[69]

The strategic logic of this tentative bridge-building was elucidated in the administration's State-Defense Long Range Study on China, completed in June. This major report examined three options for managing Chinese power: disengagement, showdown, and containment. The drawbacks inherent in the first two choices were thought to outweigh any benefits. A policy of disengagement from the Pacific would effectively "ensure domination of much of Asia by a single hostile power," while the pursuit of a showdown with the PRC would "lead to a war which would impose on us uncertain, but probably large, costs in blood, treasure and prestige for highly uncertain gains."[70] It therefore followed that American objectives in Southeast Asia would best be secured by maintaining a sizeable military presence in the region to check the spread of Chinese influence and by strengthening non-communist Asia to the point where it could successfully repel repeated probes from the mainland. The fight to preserve an independent government in Saigon was seen as consistent with both of these ends. Over time, the authors posited, Mao's successors would discover that there was an unbridgeable gap between Chinese aspirations and capabilities. Greater awareness of this dynamic would bring about "a cautious and conservative approach to problems of foreign policy."[71]

Yet the study also advanced the notion that the administration could facilitate this transition and "induce moderation of Peking's current expansionist policies." Washington could influence the direction of Chinese foreign policy by encouraging present and future leaders to reappraise US intentions and, over the long term, by enhancing the PRC's stake in a constructive relationship. This strategy called for both confidence-building gestures – declaring America's interest in peace and avoiding any actions that would unnecessarily irritate or harass the mainland – and more substantial alterations in policy, such as the gradual loosening of the travel ban and the offer of "a general step-by-step relaxation of our economic controls in the context of reciprocal Chinese moves toward improved relations." Once engaged in commerce with lucrative US markets, Beijing would feel "less free to act in ways which might threaten to cut off that source of scarce foreign exchange" and would therefore develop "a practical interest in developing and maintaining a measure of détente."[72]

To be sure, the report did not advocate immediate implementation of many of these latter initiatives; China's militant conduct precluded such a dramatic shift in policy.⁷³ By conditioning significant policy reform on an improvement in China's behavior, the Long Range Study struck a cautionary note and departed from those China "doves" favoring rapid movement on these items. The most articulate member of this group, ambassador to Japan and prominent Asian scholar Edwin Reischauer, was mildly encouraged by the tentative bridge-building of the first half of 1966, yet still thought the administration's new approach to China, as epitomized by the State-Defense report, too timid. Reischauer ultimately believed that the PRC's myriad diplomatic setbacks and stagnant economy would be of far greater importance in effecting a curtailment of its foreign policy ambitions than any combination of American carrots and sticks. Yet he argued that a fundamental "redefinition of our long-term China policy" would ease this process. Once Beijing understood that the US recognized its legitimacy and was willing to co-exist peacefully, it would then feel sufficiently secure to concentrate its attention on domestic concerns. "For such a stand to have any meaning," he wrote, "we would have to state our readiness to see ... [the mainland] admitted into the United Nations."⁷⁴

Reischauer's disenchantment with the Johnson team's China policy led him to fend off efforts to recruit him in a new role as the administration's senior China watcher. He saw "only futility and frustration" with the proposal, "because I am not enough on the same wave length with the Secretary on this specific subject and not enough of the type to ever develop a close relationship with the President to be at all effective."⁷⁵ Disagreements over China likely played a role in his decision to surrender the Tokyo post in July 1966, yet a more decisive consideration was his gradual marginalization from the policymaking process since Kennedy's assassination.⁷⁶ The administration's thinking on China was in fact starting to move in the direction espoused by officials like Reischauer, albeit at a slower pace than they would have preferred. Interdepartmental endorsement of the broad outlines of an agenda previously associated almost exclusively with this isolated camp signified an important turn in Washington's China debate.

The politics of bridge-building

The second major factor accounting for the emergence of a more flexible China policy was another outgrowth of the Vietnam War, namely, growing public pressure at home. Agitation from some quarters in

Congress and among elite opinion-shapers in the media and the academic community had played a significant role in the adoption of the December 1965 travel package. Samplings of public attitudes throughout 1964–65 hinted at a greater tolerance for a modest opening toward China, a noteworthy evolution from the previous decade yet hardly sufficient to encourage a conservative politician like Lyndon Johnson to make a bold move in this direction.

By 1966, however, popular views of Sino-American relations had become intertwined with Vietnam. Consequently, LBJ's eagerness to sustain backing for the war effort all but demanded that he demonstrate an interest in forging constructive ties to the mainland. One of the administration's pollsters concluded in December 1965 that the American people supported measured military force in Vietnam as a prerequisite for obtaining a position of strength from which to negotiate. A clear majority opposed more provocative actions, such as extending the ground war to the North or bombing the PRC. Blunting the public's mounting frustration and impatience with the indeterminate hostilities required "a series of moves – preferably dramatic – to assure them that we are active in the pursuit of peace."[77] Even as he abandoned the bombing pause at the end of January, his most "dramatic" peace offering to date, Johnson stressed to his aides the political necessity of "keep[ing] [the] peace emphasis on."[78] That this peace emphasis should incorporate China was borne out by popular anxiety over the prospect of an enlarged war. A poll in March 1966, for example, revealed a 46 to 27 percent plurality anticipating Chinese intervention in Vietnam.[79] Thus the constant reiteration of the administration's limited war aims served to relieve the fears of both Beijing and the US population.

That same month, America's China policy was subjected to the most intense public scrutiny in well over a decade. Dismayed by the failure of LBJ's "peace offensive" and alarmed by what he characterized as a drift toward a Sino-American confrontation, Senator Fulbright presided over three weeks of hearings devoted to China in a bid to promote enhanced understanding of the PRC.[80] Among the prominent Sinologists invited to testify were A. Doak Barnett, John K. Fairbank, and Donald Zagoria. While most of the witnesses carefully voiced support for the Vietnam War and underlined Beijing's unremittingly belligerent behavior in their statements, they questioned the wisdom of quarantining the mainland. Barnett in particular articulated a strategy of "containment but not isolation," which would "aim on the one hand at checking military or subversive threats and pressures emanating from Peking[,] but at the same time would aim at maximum contacts with and maximum involvement of the Chinese Communists in the international community." As part of this effort, he advocated removing the embargo on all non-strategic trade and a "two Chinas" solution to Chinese representation in the UN. Like the government's China doves, Barnett did not anticipate reciprocal action from Beijing, yet he believed a new China policy would reap long-term rewards in pacifying the PRC's worldview.[81] These ideas were subsequently endorsed in a declaration signed by 198 academic experts.[82]

Fulbright's China hearings marked something of a watershed. This highly publicized forum effectively legitimized the airing of views that would have been considered heresy in the Red-baiting climate of the 1950s and, as James Thomson recollected, emboldened proponents of China policy reform inside and outside government to press their agenda.[83] Polling results throughout the spring and summer of 1966 revealed growing openness to expanding relations with the PRC. In a Harris survey taken in June, 57 percent of the respondents favored recognizing Beijing, while an identical 55 percent supported the mainland's admission to the UN if this would foster peace in the Pacific.[84]

The spotlight cast on China policy provoked somewhat divergent responses from within the President's entourage. Rusk, Johnson's most influential adviser on Asian affairs, remained fixated with China's obstructionist and bellicose role in Vietnam and was hesitant to alter established strategy toward the mainland for the sake of mollifying public opinion. Just after the beginning of the Fulbright hearings, he confided to Vice President Hubert Humphrey that he was "reluctant to see the Administration involved in this China business."[85] Furthermore, Rusk displayed little enthusiasm for revisiting sensitive matters such as Chinese representation. "With the Southeast Asian situation as it is," he noted, "it remains very difficult for us to see Peiping seated in the United Nations."[86]

Senior White House officials, on the other hand, counselled LBJ to directly address some of the pointed questions raised by the China hearings. When an apparently freelancing Humphrey expressed his approval of Barnett's doctrine on national television, Robert Komer, now serving as McGeorge Bundy's interim replacement, advised Johnson not to disavow the remarks and instead let them stand as a trial balloon. "To withdraw from what was rather grossly overplayed by the press would only start another debate with our VN critics," he reasoned.[87] Komer posited that demonstrating flexibility in relations with Beijing would disarm domestic and foreign critics of US China policy and make some headway in recapturing those elements of the Democratic party disenchanted with the involvement in Vietnam.[88]

Arguably the decisive voice in this internal debate belonged to Johnson's chief political lieutenant, Press Secretary Bill Moyers, whose influence in foreign policy deliberations reached its peak in 1966.[89] The avid interest he took in China policy reflected the extent to which this issue had become politicized and enmeshed with the larger goal of mobilizing domestic support for the fighting in Vietnam. More importantly, Moyers' identification with policy reform exposed LBJ to a view that hitherto had been shunned by his inner circle. As the administration came under fire for its conduct of the war, Moyers became increasingly convinced of the urgency of presenting the peaceful side of America's face in Asia. At the end of February, he notified the President that his approval rating for his handling of the war had fallen from 63 percent to 49 percent in the aftermath of that month's televised Senate hearings on Vietnam.[90] Moyers saw China as one of those "issues that history may judge absolutely critical to the Johnson Administration. How we increased the 'thaw' toward China is just that."[91] The young aide enthusiastically forwarded polling data to the President supporting his claims, and pushed for an infusion of Chinese expertise at Foggy Bottom to assist in the formulation of a new China strategy.[92]

Johnson – less dogmatic than his Secretary of State, still troubled by the prospect of Chinese intervention in Vietnam, acutely sensitive to scrutiny of his foreign policy leadership, and sensing a compelling political need to respond to the shift in popular moods – was receptive to Moyers' arguments. The result throughout the spring and summer was an unprecedented degree of presidential engagement with the China policy sphere. In April, Walt Rostow, the new National Security Adviser, alerted Rusk to Johnson's personal interest in "Imaginative ways of handling the China problem, which would get us off the defensive, and deal with the Chirep issue in the next General Assembly … the President emphasized he wants fresh study groups, including the best people in the country in and out of the government."[93] The idea for a "Chinese Tommy Thompson," a China watcher that would enjoy the President's ear as Llewellyn Thompson did for matters pertaining to the USSR, received "highest level blessing" at the White House in the spring, an offer that was later rebuffed by Reischauer.[94]

When Senator Edward Kennedy called for the establishment of a commission of distinguished academics to make recommendations for fresh approaches to Beijing, LBJ was anxious to nip this implicit criticism in the bud. Through Moyers, he pressed Rusk to speak to journalists about "the Kennedy suggestion re reviewing China policy and point out we have been doing this for a long time ... there was [a] constant review of our relations with China; [the] President thought we should be pretty tough on this at the [press] briefing."[95] For an upcoming Warsaw session on 25 May, Johnson insisted on clearing the instructions to the embassy himself, which were to place special emphasis on "our peaceful intentions toward Communist China."[96]

This same fusion of strategic and domestic factors yielded the most significant bridge-building initiative of the Johnson years, the 12 July 1966 address to the American Alumni Council. As early as March, LBJ was considering a proposal to include POL storage facilities in Hanoi and Haiphong as targets in the bombing of the North, in the hope that this would cripple the enemy's capacity to supply the insurgency in South Vietnam.[97] An escalation of the air war was thought to be feasible in part because of a cautiously optimistic reading of the PRC's intentions in Vietnam. As one China hand in the State Department observed in June, "there had been a significant shift in Chicom attitudes since February, which ... [was] attributed to their belief that we would resume bombing after the [thirty-seven-day] pause with a real 'bang.' When we had not done so ... the Chicoms had drawn the correct conclusion that we were not moving to wipe out North Vietnam, or threaten China, and their 'war warning' propaganda had since become considerably less strident than before."[98]

At a National Security Council meeting on 17 June, both Rusk and CIA Director William Raborn dismissed the possibility of a Chinese military reply to an expansion of Rolling Thunder. Only Arthur Goldberg, the ambassador to the United Nations, dissented from this assessment. Johnson did not respond directly to this point, yet he underscored his determination to secure his military objectives "with minimum loss and minimum danger of escalating the war."[99] It was within the context of these deliberations over increased bombing that the Johnson team saw some value in further signalling American restraint as a hedge against Chinese intervention. When Donald Zagoria sent a proposal to the White House in April for a presidential speech on China, the State Department welcomed the idea as an ideal "opportunity for the United States to demonstrate that its aims toward

Peking are not hostile and belligerent."[100] Similarly, Rostow thought it advisable that the targeting of POL sites be accompanied by a "communication to the Chinese Communists indicating our intentions remain limited."[101]

As expected, China's reaction to the new bombing, launched on 29 June, was relatively mild. While numerous statements from Beijing denounced the action as an act of aggression against the mainland and declared China's readiness to undertake any sacrifice in providing aid to the DRV, US analysts were impressed by the "controlled and hedged nature" of these remarks. They were regarded more as an attempt to deter further American encroachment than as a commitment to enter the war.[102] A Special National Intelligence Estimate concluded in early August that the recent air strikes had not altered the PRC's reluctance to join the fighting. Overt involvement in the war would only be triggered by an American invasion of North Vietnam or the imminent collapse of that regime. At the present level of hostilities, it was thought that China's leaders would limit their role to one of diplomatic and materiel support for their ally and the provision of troops for logistical functions.[103]

Thus Johnson's address in July, delivered at a time when fears of Chinese intervention had somewhat subsided, cannot be explained by strategic considerations alone. Indeed, the idea for a speech on Asian policy took shape as the President's aides were searching for ways to counter popular restlessness over the war and to bolster Johnson's sagging political standing before mid-term congressional elections in the fall. By the summer, Americans were more or less evenly split between those favoring a withdrawal from Vietnam and those who thought it best to stay the course.[104] The protracted fighting, more specifically LBJ's inability to put forward a timetable for its completion or to articulate a statesmanlike vision of peace, pleased neither of these groups and was seen by the White House as a major cause for concern.[105] While new bombing might satisfy those elements who wanted to end the war by force, it raised anew the problem of how to placate those who favored negotiations. As Rostow admitted to Johnson, "Bombing POL will look like an Administration move to the hard side – giving in to the JCS [Joint Chiefs of Staff], etc. We need something new on the dove side to balance our account."[106] In these circumstances, extending the hand of friendship to America's greatest Asian adversary would confirm that Johnson was looking beyond the war and offer dramatic proof of his interest in peace, even as he expanded Rolling Thunder. This sentiment was perhaps best captured in a memorandum Ambassador at Large Averell Harriman wrote to a sympathetic Moyers in June, which forcefully stated that it was "difficult to carry the worldwide unpopularity and misunderstanding of Vietnam along with an unpopular China policy inherited primarily from [John Foster] Dulles. I feel the President could well gain in most parts of the world by a spectacular change in attitude towards Red China. It would then ... be easier to gain better understanding of Vietnam."[107]

LBJ's televised overview of Asian policy, co-drafted by Moyers and Thomson,[108] touched on the importance of events in the region for US security, in particular the campaign to defend Saigon against communist aggression. In the most intriguing passage, he stated that peace and stability in the Pacific ultimately rested on "reconciliation between nations that now call themselves enemies." As a counterpoint to the bloodshed in Vietnam, Johnson affirmed his willingness to utilize diplomatic means in pursuit of this long-term objective. To move the PRC "toward understanding of the outside world and ... policies of peaceful cooperation," he told his audience that "the greatest force for opening closed minds and closed societies is the free flow of ideas and people and goods."[109] This theme, of course, had been propounded in one form or another by senior officials throughout the spring. Moreover, the deliberately vague nature of these remarks comported with the cautious style of a consummate politician who was willing to identify himself with an agreeable principle without committing his prestige to specific proposals that could be potentially controversial. The true significance of the speech is that it represented the first *Presidential* articulation of the rationale for a new China policy. As such, it contributed in no small part to laying the rhetorical foundation and justification for redefining America's relationship with the mainland.

On a tour of Asia in October, highlighted by his attendance at the Manila Conference, Johnson publicly reiterated his hope for a new era in relations with the PRC.[110] While anxious to secure the backing and support of regional allies for the war, the Johnson team made a conscious effort to ensure that the meeting in Manila did not assume anti-Chinese overtones or exacerbate tensions. William Bundy insisted to LBJ's speechwriters that any "references to aggression [in Vietnam] should focus on North Vietnam, with Communist China being referred to only in a supporting role and no implication that the

[Manila] group is a new alliance to combat the over-all menace of Communist Chinese aggression."[111] Keeping the war limited depended as it had before on projecting restraint to Beijing.

The limits of bridge-building: Chinese representation in the UN

While Vietnam defined the imperative of bridge-building, it also imposed clear limits on the process. Even as domestic and strategic pressures arising from the war compelled the Johnson administration to adjust tactics toward China, preoccupation with America's posture in Southeast Asia stifled more substantive policy innovation. Closely related to this concern was the apprehension that any hint of accommodation with Beijing would alarm steadfast Asian allies and undermine their will to withstand Chinese pressure, a consideration that had influenced the decision for military intervention in Vietnam. During the spring of 1966, the embassies in Taipei and Seoul reported that the Fulbright hearings and speculation in the US press of a change in China policy had stirred doubts of the administration's devotion to containing communist expansion.[112] Senior US officials catered to allies' sensitivities by firmly denying the grounds for these charges.[113] The State-Defense Long Range Study pointedly cautioned that any conciliatory moves toward the mainland had to be "applied with proper attention to timing, in order to avoid causing our Communist adversaries to believe that their expansionist policies are succeeding and our Asian friends to fear that we are wavering in our resistance to these policies."[114]

One casualty of this logic was a proposal Bundy sent to Rusk in May for a Sino-American meeting at the Foreign Minister's level. While an affirmative response from Beijing was deemed unlikely, he believed, perhaps with plans for the bombing of POL sites in mind, that some approach was "essential ... to avoid a wider war growing out of tensions or miscalculations in the Far East."[115] Had the idea been approved, it would have accorded the PRC unprecedented diplomatic status and prestige by departing from the established practice of confining official dialogue to the ambassadorial talks in Warsaw. Policymakers, however, were wary of initiatives that, in their eyes, threatened to derail more significant objectives in Vietnam. Upon further reflection, Bundy withdrew the recommendation one week later, noting that "in the existing political circumstances in South

Vietnam such a message at the present time would only be construed as a sign of weakness by Peiping, and would not have the positive effect we had envisaged."[116]

The most glaring example of resistance to policy reform centered on the pivotal matter of Chinese representation, on which Johnson only briefly flirted with a "two Chinas" solution in the spring and summer of 1966. Arthur Goldberg led the charge of those in favor of an overhaul of tactics at the UN. When a vote on the dreaded Albanian resolution to grant China's seat solely to Beijing produced a 47–47 tie (with 20 abstentions) in the General Assembly in November 1965, he saw this as a disquieting harbinger of things to come. The next vote, Goldberg warned the President, could very well result in Taipei's ejection unless the administration shifted its discredited focus on excluding Beijing from the world body to one of guaranteeing Taiwan's inclusion.[117] This pessimism was widely shared. In February, both William Bundy and Assistant Secretary of State for International Organization Affairs Joseph Sisco opined that there was little hope of sustaining majority support in the General Assembly for the notion that changing the China seat was an "important question" requiring two-thirds approval. They suggested to Rusk that Bundy use an impending visit to Taipei to convey this view and float the option of "some arrangement that would reaffirm Taipei's seat but that would permit – by the initiative of others – some form of proposal involving an offer of membership for Peiping as well."[118] The rationale for a "two Chinas" strategy, then, was strictly negative in that it was seen as the only means of averting a diplomatic debacle and a diminution of Taiwan's status as a bulwark of anti-communism. A decidedly skeptical Rusk balked, reasoning that it was not the appropriate time "to take this issue up with the President." He limited Bundy's mandate to one of merely ascertaining the opinions of his hosts in Taipei on the voting prospects at the UN.[119]

This bureaucratic ferment coincided with Johnson's own heightened interest in fresh approaches toward the PRC. He was reminded how a new policy at the UN could advance this objective. A switch to "two Chinas," Komer wrote in April, would "show that 'LBJ is not a stick-in-the-mud' ... all the hints about new flexibility in our China policy have netted out a big plus so far."[120] When Bundy and Goldberg presented their views at a White House meeting, Bundy recollected that Johnson was intrigued and "didn't fight the problem for a minute."[121] At the President's invitation, the UN ambassador set down his thoughts on paper. Once again Goldberg underscored the dismal prospects for maintaining Taiwan's exclusive hold on the China seat, pointing to the enthusiasm of allies such as Japan and Canada for admitting the mainland. To secure Taiwan's membership and to place the burden on Beijing for its isolation, he urged that the US recognize both the PRC and Taiwan as "Successor States" with equal entitlement to representation in the UN.[122]

Goldberg's proposal provoked familiar misgivings. A report prepared by the Far East bureau at Foggy Bottom contended that such a change in policy would "encourage the ChiComs, raise Hanoi's morale, downgrade US prestige and depress Asian and other friendly states. While the ChiComs are aiding and abetting the aggression in Viet-Nam, it would be unthinkable for us to support or 'not oppose' or seek to initiate a proposal to give the ChiComs UN representation."[123] The hawkish Rostow echoed these concerns, alerting Johnson to the potential side-effects of such a move on the alliance with Taiwan and the war in Vietnam.[124]

Evidently struck by the thrust of Goldberg's analysis, however, LBJ leaned on Rusk to review the administration's options at the UN. The result was yet another landmark of sorts, a 14 May memorandum in which the Secretary posited that reliance on previous tactics posed "an unacceptable risk of defeat and expenditure of US influence." As an alternative to the Albanian resolution, a "two Chinas" approach offered the best possibility of preserving Taiwan's presence in the UN. Moreover, Beijing's anticipated rejection of such a compromise would only highlight its own belligerence and deflect growing criticism of the American position. To minimize any fallout among friendly Asian opinion, another government, perhaps Ottawa, could take the lead in guiding such a motion through the General Assembly. Before taking this step, however, Rusk insisted that Taipei had to be convinced of the gravity of the situation and encouraged to "stand steady, rather than withdraw from the UN" as the administration modified its tactics.[125]

What followed illustrated the importance accorded to the views of America's regional partners. The plan foundered in part on the rocks of Chiang Kai-shek's intransigence. At a meeting with Ambassador Walter McConaughy in early July, the Generalissimo expressed his confidence that Washington could keep its Western allies in line on a new vote. More ominously, he warned that passage of a "two Chinas" resolution would "cause disillusionment in Taiwan ... [and] would also be a betrayal of the majority of the people in mainland China who look to [the] GRC as a symbol of hope and steadfastness." Under such circumstances, he would have no other choice but to walk out of the UN.[126] This message remained the same when Rusk visited Taipei only days later. When pressed by his hosts for a public statement reiterating continued US support for the "important question" formula, Rusk demurred, explaining that no commitment to any specific tactic could be made "without a better idea of the outcome."[127] While striving to keep Johnson's options open, Rusk was clearly alarmed by Chiang's threats and by the lukewarm reaction of other Asian allies to a possible change in UN strategy. Relaying his impressions to his Canadian counterpart Paul Martin, he remarked that those "Asian countries who face the militancy of Communist China would feel great pain if she were admitted" to the UN, and wondered whether such an initiative should be taken "merely to please sentiment in Canada and European countries."[128]

Chaotic events on the mainland, the beginnings of what became known as the Cultural Revolution, added an unforeseen element to the administration's deliberations during the summer. Reports of Red Guard assaults on CCP authorities throughout the country were widely perceived as an orchestrated Maoist purge of a party that did not share the Chairman's zeal for continuous revolution.[129] In August, Rostow was notified by Alfred Jenkins, a China hand on the NSC staff, that enthusiasm for a "two Chinas" motion had waned among mid-level officials at Foggy Bottom "at the time when the hard liners are riding high in Peking."[130] The uncertain fate of what appeared to be an intra-party dispute reinforced the inherent caution of senior decision-makers. Rusk, for one, believed it would be "tragic if the militant factions felt that their militancy was rewarded by an embrace in the form of an invitation to the UN, to the detriment of the factions opposing the hard militancy of Peking."[131]

Political considerations, never far from LBJ's mind, served as another inhibitive influence. Instinctively cautious in his reading of the public's foreign policy attitudes and mindful of the upcoming congressional election, Johnson likely saw potential hazards in moving forward on an issue that had for long stirred emotions at home. As he explained to Canadian Prime Minister Lester Pearson in August, "American public opinion had moderated somewhat as a result of the Fulbright hearings ... He thought, however, that opinion could quickly swing back."[132]

All of these factors came into play when the President met with his top aides to discuss UN affairs on 13 September.[133] While no record of this session was kept, US embassies around the world were informed three days later that there would be no change in US policy for the next vote on Chinese representation, and that efforts would be concentrated on defeating the Albanian resolution and affirming the "important question" motion. Among the reasons given for this decision were the "militancy and unyielding mood" of the ascendant Maoist faction in the mainland's political struggle and the "hardening of attitude toward Communist China among those Asian governments which are most directly exposed to [the] dangers of activity advocated and supported by [the] ChiComs as in Vietnam."[134]

Washington's hostile reaction to a Canadian initiative in early November underscored its determination to preserve the status quo as best it could. Ottawa's plan called for the introduction of a one-China, one-Taiwan motion specifically allotting China's seat on the Security Council to the PRC. Alluding to political pressures at home for a fair settlement of the Chinese representation problem, a Canadian official confided to the Americans that his government could no longer justify its opposition to the Albanian resolution without offering a constructive alternative.[135] Rusk was taken aback. A Canadian abstention on the Albanian formula, he wrote Johnson, would trigger a bandwagon effect, encouraging other allies to do the same and thus guaranteeing majority approval of that resolution for the first time. While the administration could fall back on the "important question" procedure to prevent its passage, a dangerous precedent would nevertheless have been set. The challenge, then, was to persuade Ottawa to sponsor a resolution that would be "a less radical departure from past tactics" and ultimately "more palatable to our close Asian allies." Rusk proposed a resolution calling for the formation of a study committee that would examine the issue and report its findings to the General Assembly.[136] He fully understood that this amounted to nothing more than a holding action, and that the committee could very well recommend a variant of "two Chinas." At the very least, however, tying up Chinese representation in deliberations could buy the US some time and perhaps "complicate" the issue for a year or two.[137]

With LBJ's approval, the Secretary sent off an uncharacteristically blunt letter to Pearson outlining Washington's objections to the Canadian idea. An offer of membership to Beijing now, Rusk intoned, would effectively embolden the radical Maoist forces on the mainland

and thereby undermine any prospects for peace in Vietnam. Accordingly, the administration would "exert every ounce of our influence to defeat" Ottawa's proposal "by the heaviest possible margin." Reminding Pearson of "the seriousness of such a split between our two nations," he suggested that the Canadians instead throw their weight behind the study committee, which would still represent "clear forward movement on the issue along the line that your government feels under political pressure to obtain."[138]

This arm-twisting did not have the desired effect. In the end, however, Italy, Belgium, and Chile were recruited as co-sponsors of the study committee option. Sensing that the one-China, one-Taiwan measure would not pass, Ottawa then abandoned its project. The 1966 vote was an entirely satisfactory outcome. In a reversal of the embarrassing results from the previous year, the Albanian resolution was soundly defeated (46 for, 57 against, 17 abstentions) and the "important question" reaffirmed (66–48–7). The victim of competing proposals, the study committee was strongly rejected (34–64–25).[139] The issue of Chinese representation, a nagging concern for the first three years of the Johnson administration that had produced nail-biting votes, would not rear its head for the remainder of the decade. US officials well understood that the turmoil on the mainland had worked to their advantage, helping to dilute the support that had been gaining momentum for Beijing's entry into the UN.[140] The last-minute encouragement of the study committee was consistent with the September decision to hold the line in that it was conceived as an acceptable alternative to a "two Chinas" approach, which the Johnson team, distracted by Vietnam and discouraged by the recent outburst of Chinese militancy, could not countenance. The limits of bridge-building had been established.

America's relationship with China underwent considerable change in the year following the Vietnam decisions of 1965. For some contemporary observers, Beijing's inability to project power on the Indian subcontinent, the destruction of its "proxy" in Indonesia, and the deterioration of its influence in the international communist movement called into question the urgency of checking the PRC's ambitions in Southeast Asia.[141] Yet for senior US decision-makers, China's probes, while a failure, confirmed the image of a bellicose, implacable adversary. According to this prevailing view, the politico-psychological threat posed by the mainland to its neighbors, while perhaps diminished, remained intact. Rusk held in early 1966 that the Chinese leadership's "experience over the past forty years, their deep-seated beliefs, their dispute with the Soviets and their projection of Viet-Nam as a test-case, their vision of the future, and their nationalistic aspirations have combined to convince them that their current policies are right regardless of the consequences."[142]

Of far more importance to the direction of China policy in 1966 was the Johnson administration's realization that containing the spread of Asian communism in Vietnam entailed the risk of unwittingly setting off a region-wide catastrophe. While they were determined to discourage Hanoi's support of the insurgency in South Vietnam through the steady application of America's military might, LBJ and his aides, with memories of Korea still fresh and ominous reports of China's preparations for war, moved to relieve Beijing's evident anxieties over US intentions. At minimum, this required constant assurances that Washington did not harbor designs of toppling North Vietnam or attacking the PRC. These considerations, of course, had in large part determined Johnson's cautious prosecution of the war at the outset. In 1966, the need for *political* signalling to China rose in proportion to the gradual escalation of *military* pressure against its ally, first with the end of the bombing pause in January and then with the targeting of POL facilities in June. These signals took the shape of relaxations of the travel ban, the promotion of expanded contacts, and a striking change in rhetoric.

It was no coincidence that the high-water mark of policy innovation in 1966 dovetailed with LBJ's personal engagement with China strategy, a level of interest that hitherto had been lacking. For some officials, such as the authors of the Long Range Study, a more flexible American stance was a means by which the mainland's foreign policy could be channelled in a more moderate direction. The President's immediate interests were keeping the war limited and selling it to an impatient and confused public. Thus Lyndon Johnson's domestic and strategic objectives in Vietnam increasingly depended on demonstrating restraint and openness toward the PRC. Yet when this accommodation was seen to clash with Asian alliances or the continuing campaign against communist insurgency in South Vietnam, the latter concerns still took precedence, as evidenced by the aborted "two Chinas" initiative. Sensing the tentative nature of the administration's opening to China, James Thomson noted shortly after the 12 July speech that, having established the justification for a new China policy, "Our problem in the months ahead is what kind of substance, and at what pace, to pour into this new rhetorical container."[143] For the duration of the Johnson years, deliberations on this point would continue to be overshadowed by Vietnam and by a new factor: the cataclysm of the Cultural Revolution.

Notes

1 Tucker, "Threats, opportunities, and frustrations in East Asia," in Cohen and Tucker (eds), *Lyndon Johnson Confronts the World*, p. 99.
2 For example, see Waldron, "From nonexistent to almost normal," in Kunz (ed.), *Diplomacy of the Crucial Decade*; Foot, *Practice of Power*; Garson, "Johnson and the China enigma"; Schulzinger, "The Johnson administration, China, and the Vietnam War," in Ross and Jiang (eds), *Re-examining the Cold War*. Brief references to the link between bridge-building and Vietnam in 1966 are provided in Kaufman, *Confronting Communism*, pp. 196–7; Goh, *Constructing the US Rapprochement with China*, pp. 77–8, 88.
3 S. Ganguly, *Conflict Unending: India-Pakistan Tensions Since 1947* (Washington, DC: Columbia University Press, 2001), pp. 31–43; D. Kux, *The United States and Pakistan, 1947–2000: Disenchanted Allies* (Washington, DC: Woodrow Wilson Center Press, 2001), pp. 158–60.
4 For further discussion of JFK's policy dilemmas in South Asia, see McMahon, "Choosing sides in South Asia," in Paterson (ed.), *Kennedy's Quest for Victory*; R.J. McMahon, *The Cold War on the Periphery: The United States, India, and Pakistan* (New York: Columbia University Press, 1994), pp. 272–304; Kux, *United States and Pakistan*, pp. 115–46.
5 McMahon, *Cold War on the Periphery*, pp. 306–22.
6 Ganguly, *Conflict Unending*, pp. 42–3.
7 A.H. Wedeman, *The East Wind Subsides: Chinese Foreign Policy and the Origins of the Cultural Revolution* (Washington, DC: Washington Institute Press, 1987), p. 141.
8 CIA memorandum, "Chinese communist intentions and capabilities with respect to the Kashmir crisis," 7 September 1965, NSF, Country File, Box 244, folder "China vol. I CODEWORD," LBJL; Hughes to Rusk, 6 September 1965, NSF, Country File, Box 238, folder "China memos, vol. IV," LBJL; SNIE 13-10-65, "Prospects of Chinese communist involvement in the Indo-Pakistan War," 16 September 1965, NSF, NIE, Box 4, folder "Communist China (2 of 2)," LBJL.
9 Rusk to LBJ, 9 September 1965, NSF, Country File, Box 129, folder "India memos & misc., vol. V (2 of 2)," LBJL.
10 *FRUS*, 1964–1968, vol. 30, p. 203, n. 3.

11 McMahon, *Cold War on the Periphery*, p. 331.
12 Wedeman, *The East Wind Subsides*, pp. 144–6.
13 Telegram, no. 479, Hong Kong to Department of State, 22 September 1965, NSF, National Security Council History, Box 24, folder "Vol. 3: Indo-Pak War, State Department History [II] (1 of 2)," LBJL. See as well WPB Papers, Box 1, ch. 32, p. 1, LBJL.
14 Memorandum of conversation, 23 September 1965, *FRUS, 1964–1968*, vol. 30, p. 217.
15 Sukma, *Indonesia and China*, p. 33. For the American reaction to these events (and a persuasive case for Washington's passive role in the affair), see H.W. Brands, "The limits of manipulation: How the United States didn't topple Sukarno," *Journal of American History* 76:3 (1989), 785–808.
16 For further discussion, see Mozingo, *Chinese Policy Toward Indonesia*, pp. 235–44. The CIA's dismissal of China's implication in the 30 September coup is in CIA memorandum, "Peking's setbacks in Indonesia," 1 April 1966, NSF, Country File, Box 248, folder "Indonesia memos, vol. VI," LBJL.
17 CIA memorandum, "Indonesian Communist Party," 29 April 1966, ibid.
18 Memorandum of conversation, 15 February 1966, ibid.
19 CIA memorandum, "Peking's setbacks in Indonesia," 1 April 1966, ibid.
20 WPB Papers, Box 1, ch. 28, pp. 7–9, LBJL; Airgram, no. A-431, Hong Kong to Department of State, p. 5, 31 December 1965, RG 59, Central Files, 1964–66, Box 2019, POL CHICOM-US, NA. In February 1966, the State Department's INR bureau prepared an extensive list of Beijing's recent reversals in foreign relations. See Denney to Rusk, 25 February 1966, NSF, Country File, Box 239, folder "China cables, vol. V," LBJL. China's effort to convene the conference is discussed in Wedeman, *The East Wind Subsides*, pp. 119–26.
21 CIA memorandum, "China's growing isolation in the communist movement," 5 August 1966, NSF, Country File, Box 239, folder "China memos, vol. VI (1 of 2)," LBJL.
22 CIA memorandum, "The Chinese position in North Vietnam," 5 August 1966, ibid; CIA memorandum, "The deterioration of Sino-Soviet relations," 22 April 1966, NSF, Vietnam Country File, Box 51, folder "Southeast Asia Special Intelligence Material, vol. IX (1 of 2)," LBJL; CIA memorandum, "Status of Soviet and Chinese military aid to North Vietnam," 3 September 1965, NSF, Vietnam Country File, Box 50, folder "Southeast Asia Special Intelligence Material, vol. VIII," LBJL; Hughes to Rusk, 9 August 1966, RG 59, Central Files, 1964–66, Box 2020, POL CHICOM-VIET N, NA.
23 CIA memorandum, "The militant and moderate elements in the North

Vietnamese Communist Party," 1 December 1965, NSF, Vietnam Country File, Box 25, folder "Vietnam memos (A), vol. XLIII," LBJL.
24 Rostow to LBJ, 25 June 1966, NSF, Vietnam Country File, Box 33, folder "Vietnam memos (A), vol. LV (1 of 2)," LBJL. See as well William J. Jorden to Rostow, 24 June 1966, NSF, Memos to the President, Box 8 (2 of 2), folder "Vol. VII (1 of 2)," LBJL.
25 W. Bundy to Rusk, 14 March 1966, RG 59, Central Files, 1964–66, Box 1897, POL ASIA, NA.
26 WPB Papers, Box 1, ch. 32, pp. 37–9, LBJL.
27 William P. Bundy, "The United States and Communist China," *Department of State Bulletin* (hereafter *DSB*), 28 February 1966, p. 313.
28 Gardner, *Pay Any Price*, pp. 269–80; Dallek, *Flawed Giant*, pp. 342–7.
29 Denney to Rusk, 26 January 1966, *FRUS*, 1964–1968, vol. 4, pp. 148–9; Memorandum by John Whitman and Lou Sandine, 29 December 1965, NSF, Vietnam Country File, Box 25, folder "Vietnam memos (B), vol. XLIII," LBJL; Telegram, no. 1287, Hong Kong to Department of State, 8 January 1966, NSF, Country File, Box 239, folder "China cables, vol. V," LBJL; CIA memorandum, "Communist views of the present state of the conflict in Vietnam," 20 January 1966, NSF, Country File, Box 221, folder "USSR memos, vol. XI," LBJL.
30 Notes of meeting, 28 January 1966, *FRUS*, 1964–1968, vol. 4, p. 179.
31 Zhai, *China and the Vietnam Wars*, p. 164. For the best discussion of China's obstructionist role in various Vietnam peace initiatives, see Zhai, "Beijing and the Vietnam peace talks," CWIHP Working Paper 18.
32 Rusk to LBJ, 24 April 1966, *FRUS*, 1964–1968, vol. 4, p. 365.
33 Memorandum of conversation, Rusk–Paul Hasluck, 11 April 1966, RG 59, Central Files, 1964–66, Box 2006, POL CHICOM 1966, NA.
34 Airgram, no. A-431, Hong Kong to Department of State, p. 2, 31, December 1965, RG 59, Central Files, 1964–66, Box 2019, POL CHICOM-US, NA.
35 Rice to W. Bundy, 2 November 1965, RG 59, Central Files, 1964–66, Box 2006, POL CHICOM 1966, NA.
36 Airgram, no. A-454, Hong Kong to Department of State, pp. 2–4, 6, 7 January 1966, NSF, Country File, Box 239, folder "China cables, vol. V," LBJL.
37 Shapley, *Promise and Power*, pp. 358–9; McNamara, *In Retrospect*, pp. 221–2.
38 McNamara to LBJ, 4 December 1965, NSF, Vietnam Country File, Box 25, folder "Vietnam memos (A), vol. XLIII," LBJL. The analysis from which much of McNamara's report was derived is in Kent to Raborn, 2 December 1965, ibid.
39 CIA memorandum, "Possible change in Chinese communist military posture vis-à-vis Vietnam," 17 October 1965, NSF, Vietnam Country

File, Box 50, folder "Southeast Asia Special Intelligence Material, vol. VII," LBJL; CIA memorandum, "Chinese communist military presence in North Vietnam," 20 October 1965, ibid.

40 Hughes to Rusk, 3 December 1965, NSF, Vietnam Country File, Box 25, folder "Vietnam memos (A), vol. XLIII," LBJL. See as well Hughes to Rusk, 5 November 1965, ibid; Thomson to M. Bundy, 2 December 1965, ibid. In a front-page article, the *New York Times* reported that several Johnson officials feared that the US and China "may be within months of a direct clash." See "Some US aides see risk of direct clash with China," *New York Times*, 3 December 1965, p. A1.

41 Zhai, *China and the Vietnam Wars*, pp. 140–1; Chen, *Mao's China and the Cold War*, pp. 214–15; J.W. Garver, "China and the Revisionist Thesis," in W. Head and L.E. Grinter (eds), *Looking Back on the Vietnam War: A 1990s Perspective on the Decisions, Combat, and Legacies* (Westport: Praeger, 1993), pp. 110–11.

42 M. Bundy to LBJ, 3 December 1965, NSF, Memos to the President, Box 5, folder "Vol. XVII (2 of 3)," LBJL. McGeorge Bundy told Johnson that his own thinking on Chinese intervention diverged somewhat from that of his colleagues. He wrote, "[the] Chinese Communists will not fight for South Vietnam but only for what they regard as [the] survival of North Vietnam."

43 W. Bundy to Rusk, 4 December 1965, RG 59, Central Files, 1964–66, Box 2018, POL CHICOM-US, NA.

44 Paul Dudley White to LBJ, 10 August 1965 (enclosure), NSF, Memos to the President, Box 4, folder "Vol. XIII (1 of 3)," LBJL. For an indispensable insider's account of the 1965 travel initiative and of the political and bureaucratic impediments to China policy reform within the Kennedy and Johnson administrations, see Thomson, "On the making," esp. pp. 232–8.

45 M. Bundy to LBJ, 24 August 1965, NSF, Memos to the President, Box 4, folder "Vol. XIII (1 of 3)," LBJL.

46 For Johnson's concern over domestic criticism of the Vietnam War in 1965, see M. Small, *Johnson, Nixon, and the Doves* (New Brunswick: Rutgers University Press, 1988), ch. 2; Dallek, *Flawed Giant*, pp. 257–62, 285–6; Herring, *LBJ and Vietnam*, pp. 125–6.

47 Thomson, "On the making," pp. 235–8.

48 *FRUS, 1964–1968*, vol. 30, p. 271, n. 2.

49 F.E. Rogers, "Sino-American relations and the Vietnam War, 1964–66," *China Quarterly* 66 (1976) 307–11; Foot, *Practice of Power*, p. 160. Thomas Robinson traces this understanding to as early as mid-1965, arguing that at this point China knew that the US "would likely confine its ground activities to the South and ... Washington had understood and heeded Chinese warning signals." See Robinson, "China confronts the

Soviet Union," in MacFarquhar and Fairbank (eds), *Cambridge History of China*, vol. 15, p. 224.
50 Meeting in the Cabinet room, 22 January 1966, Meeting Notes File, Box 1, LBJL.
51 Dallek, *Flawed Giant*, pp. 349–50.
52 Ball to LBJ, 25 January 1966, NSF, Vietnam Country File, Box 26, folder "Vietnam memos (A), vol. XLVI," LBJL.
53 Notes of meeting, 27 January 1966, *FRUS*, 1964–1968, vol. 4, p. 164. Jack Valenti, one of LBJ'S most trusted political aides, also recommended that renewed bombing be done "on a surgical basis – picking out strictly military targets, and avoid, if we can, any target that summons up a direct response from the Chicoms." Jack Valenti to LBJ, 25 January 1966, ibid., p. 139.
54 Clodfelter, *The Limits of Air Power*, p. 92.
55 CIA memorandum, "Chinese communist military presence in North Vietnam," 28 February 1966 (enclosure), NSF, Vietnam Country File, Box 51, folder "Southeast Asia Special Intelligence Material, vol. IX (1 of 2)," LBJL; Garver, "China and the revisionist thesis," in Head and Grinter (eds), *Looking Back*, p. 109.
56 Hughes to Rusk, 29 March 1966, NSF, Country File, Box 240, folder "China memos, vol. VI," LBJL. See as well "CPR statements on its encirclement," RG 59, Briefing Books, 1958–1976, Lot 70D187, Box 26, Secretary's appearance before the House Foreign Affairs Far East subcommittee, 3/16/66, NA; Telegram, no. 1539, Hong Kong to Department of State, 19 February 1966, NSF, Country File, Box 239, folder "China cables, vol. V," LBJL; Komer to M. Bundy, 16 February 1966, NSF, Files of McGeorge Bundy, Box 14, folder "CHRON File: February 1–28, 1966 (2 of 3)," LBJL. A sampling of letters from mainland residents and refugee reports documented the Chinese propaganda preparing the populace for war. See Denney to Rusk, 25 February 1966, JCT Papers, Box 16, folder "Communist China: General, 1/66–2/66," JFKL.
57 Memorandum of conversation, 22 September 1965, *FRUS*, 1964–1968, vol. 30, pp. 211, 213.
58 Joint Chiefs of Staff to McNamara, 16 November 1965, ibid., pp. 224–5.
59 Telegram, Taipei to Department of State, 25 January 1966, ibid., pp. 242–5.
60 Telegram, Department of State to Taipei, 28 January 1966, ibid., p. 246.
61 Ibid., p. 354, n. 2.
62 Rice to Rostow, 15 April 1966, NSF, Country File, Box 240, folder "China memos, vol. VI," LBJL; Thomson to Rostow, 3 May 1966, NSF, Files of Walt W. Rostow, Box 18, folder "Special Group Memoranda," LBJL.

63 Memorandum for the record, 8 July 1966, *FRUS, 1964–1968*, vol. 30, p. 355.
64 Memorandum of conversation, 26 January 1966, Meeting Notes File, Box 1, LBJL.
65 Lyndon B. Johnson, "Viet-Nam: The struggle to be free," *DSB*, 14 March 1966, p. 393.
66 Telegram, no. 1303, Department of State to Warsaw, 10 March 1966, NSF, Country File, Box 202, folder "Gronouski-Wang Talks 12/65–7/68," LBJL; Telegram, Department of State to Warsaw, 23 May 1966, *FRUS, 1964–1968*, vol. 30, pp. 308–13; Telegram, Department of State to Warsaw, 31 August 1966, ibid., pp. 374–8.
67 Statement by Secretary Rusk, "United States policy toward Communist China," *DSB*, 2 May 1966, pp. 686–95.
68 Robert McNamara, "Security in the contemporary world," *DSB*, 6 June 1966, pp. 880–1. LBJ's resentment over McNamara's 18 May address in Montreal stemmed primarily from the sense that he was being upstaged by his Defense Secretary's peace posturing. The passage concerning China was in fact consistent with the administration's rhetoric at this time. For further discussion, see Shapley, *Promise and Power*, pp. 383–4; Gardner, *Pay Any Price*, p. 305.
69 Administrative History of the Department of State, Box 3, ch. 7, section C, pp. 49–50, LBJL.
70 "Communist China – Long Range Study," pp. 1–2, June 1966, NSF, Country File, Box 245, LBJL.
71 Ibid., pp. 225–6.
72 Ibid., pp. 216–18.
73 Ibid., Annex IV, "Non-military means of influencing the Chinese communists," p. 1.
74 Comments on "Communist China – Long Range Study (Interim report, 1 December 1965)," enclosed in Edwin Reischauer to Thomson, 23 March 1966, JCT Papers, Box 8, folder "Edwin O. Reischauer, 1963–1966," JFKL. Reischauer forcefully repeated this argument in August. See Telegram, Tokyo to State Department, 11 August 1966, *FRUS, 1964–1968*, vol. 30, pp. 366–72.
75 Reischauer to Thomson, 23 March 1966, JCT Papers, Box 8, folder "Edwin O. Reischauer, 1963–1966," JFKL.
76 Schaller, "Altered states," in Kunz (ed.), *The Diplomacy of the Crucial Decade*, pp. 262–3.
77 Hayes Redmon to Bill Moyers, 27 December 1965, Office Files of Bill Moyers, Box 11, Memos to the President, LBJL.
78 Quoted in Dallek, *Flawed Giant*, p. 351.
79 Kusnitz, *Public Opinion and Foreign Policy*, p. 114.

80 R.B. Woods, *Fulbright: A Biography* (New York: Cambridge University Press, 1995), pp. 412–13; W.C. Berman, *William Fulbright and the Vietnam War: The Dissent of a Political Realist* (Kent: Kent State University Press, 1988), pp. 59–60; "Fulbright warns of US-China war as growing peril," *New York Times*, 7 March 1966, p. A1.
81 *China, Vietnam, and the United States: Highlights of the Hearings of the Senate Foreign Relations Committee* (Washington, DC: Public Affairs Press, 1966), pp. 16–17. For the administration's summary of the hearings, see David Dean to W. Bundy, 4 April 1966, RG 59, Office of the Country Director for the Republic of China, 1963–1966, Lot 69D28, Box 1, NA.
82 "Experts on China urge US to seek a Peking accord," *New York Times*, 21 March 1966, p. A1.
83 Telephone interview with author, 18 February 2002.
84 "57% would recognize Mao while keeping Chiang ties," *Philadelphia Inquirer*, 27 June 1966, in Office Files of Fred Panzer, Box 179, folder "China," LBJL.
85 Telcon, Rusk–Hubert Humphrey, 10 March 1966, RG 59, Records of Secretary of State Dean Rusk: Transcripts of Telephone Calls, Lot 72D192, Box 55, NA.
86 Memorandum of conversation, Rusk–Ambassador Ryuji Takeuchi, 13 April 1966, RG 59, Central Files, 1964–66, Box 3330, UN 6 CHICOM, NA.
87 Komer to LBJ, 14 March 1966, NSF, Memos to the President, Box 6 (2 of 2), folder "Vol. XXI (2 of 3)," LBJL. Of twenty-two newspapers that commented editorially on the Vice President's remarks, twenty endorsed them. See Thomson to Komer, 22 March 1966, NSF, Files of Robert W. Komer, Box 2, folder "Memos to the President: March–June 1966," LBJL. Humphrey's comments were reported in "Humphrey hints US is altering policy on China," *New York Times*, 14 March 1966, p. A1.
88 Komer to LBJ, 2 March 1966, NSF, Files of Robert W. Komer, Box 1, folder "Chrono: March 1–20, 1966," LBJL; Komer to LBJ, 27 March 1966, ibid., folder "Chrono: March 21–31, 1966.'
89 J. Prados, *Keepers of the Keys: A History of the National Security Council from Truman to Bush* (New York: William Morrow and Company, 1991), p. 154. For brief references to Moyers' central role in China policymaking during 1966, see Thomson, "On the making," p. 239; Kusnitz, *Public Opinion and Foreign Policy*, p. 115.
90 Woods, *Fulbright*, p. 410.
91 Moyers to Rostow, 17 June 1966, NSF, Name File, Box 7, folder "Moyers memos," LBJL.
92 Moyers to LBJ, 18 January 1966, WHCF, Countries, Box 21, folder "CO 50 China," LBJL.

93 Rostow to Rusk, 23 April 1966, NSF, Files of Walt W. Rostow, Box 15, folder "Non-Vietnam: April–July 1966," LBJL.
94 Thomson to Jorden, 18 May 1966, JCT Papers, Box 8, folder "Edwin O. Reischauer, 1963–1966," JFKL.
95 Telcon, Rusk–Moyers, 3 May 1966, RG 59, Records of Secretary of State Dean Rusk: Transcripts of Telephone Calls, Lot 72D192, Box 56, NA.
96 W. Bundy to Rusk, 20 May 1966, *FRUS, 1964–1968*, vol. 30, p. 306.
97 Clodfelter, *The Limits of Air Power*, p. 95.
98 Paul Kreisberg, quoted in Memorandum for the Record, 22 June 1966, RG 59, Subject Files of the Office of the Assistant Secretary of State for East Asian and Pacific Affairs, 1961–74, Lot 85D240, Box 3, NA.
99 Summary notes of 559th NSC meeting, 17 June 1966, NSF, NSCM, Box 2, folder "vol. 3, tab 41," LBJL.
100 Benjamin Read to Rostow, undated, RG 59, Subject Files of the Office of Asian Communist Affairs, 1961–73, Lot 71D423, Box 1, NA. For Zagoria's proposal, see Valenti to Moyers, 5 April 1966, NSF, Country File, Box 240, folder "China memos, vol. VI," LBJL.
101 Rostow to LBJ, 10 May 1966, NSF, Vietnam Country File, Box 31 (2 of 2), folder "Vietnam memos (A), vol. LII (1 of 2)," LBJL. One day after the intensification of Rolling Thunder, Johnson remarked, "There is nothing we want in Communist China. There is nothing the American people want from Communist China." See "Two threats to peace," 30 June 1966, *PPP:LBJ* 1966, vol. 1, p. 683.
102 Hughes to Rusk, 22 July 1966, NSF, Country File, Box 239, folder "China memos, vol. VI (1 of 2)," LBJL; Telegram, no. 43, Hong Kong to Department of State, 4 July 1966, RG 59, Records of Negotiations About Vietnam, 1965–69, Lot 69D277, Box 6, Communist Positions and Initiatives: Communist China 1966, NA; Telegram, no. 200, Hong Kong to Department of State, 12 July 1966, ibid.
103 SNIE 13-66, "Current Chinese communist intentions in the Vietnam situation," 4 August 1966, RG 59, Policy Planning Council: Subject and Country Files, 1965–1969, Lot 72D139, Box 309, Vietnam 1966, NA.
104 Herring, *LBJ and Vietnam*, p. 138; Dallek, *Flawed Giant*, pp. 364–5.
105 Redmon to Moyers, 9 June 1966, Office Files of Bill Moyers, Box 12, folder "BDM memos June–July 11, 1966," LBJL.
106 Rostow to LBJ, 10 May 1966, NSF, Vietnam Country File, Box 31 (2 of 2), LBJL.
107 Harriman to Moyers, 3 June 1966, Papers of W. Averell Harriman, Box 488, folder "Moyers, Bill D.," Library of Congress.
108 Thomson's account of the 12 July speech is provided in Thomson, "On the making," pp. 241–2.
109 Remarks to the American Alumni Council: United States Asian policy, 12 July 1966, *PPP:LBJ* 1966, vol. 2, pp. 721–2.

110 For references to China during LBJ's tour of Asia, see Manila Summit Conference documents, 25 October 1966, ibid., p. 1259; Remarks upon arrival at Bangkok, 28 October 1966, ibid., p. 1274; Remarks at the State dinner in Parliament House, Kuala Lumpur, 30 October 1966, ibid., pp. 1282–3.
111 W. Bundy to Moyers, John Roche, Harry McPherson, and Douglass Cater, 6 October 1966, NSF, National Security Council History, Box 46, folder "Vol. IV: Backup Material Not Referenced in Narrative [I]," LBJL.
112 Telegram, no. 1086, Taipei to Department of State, 6 April 1966, NSF, Country File, Box 239, folder "China cables, vol. VI (2 of 2)," LBJL; Telegram, no. 1092, Seoul to Department of State, 30 March 1966, RG 59, Central Files, 1964–66, Box 1897, POL ASIA, NA.
113 Telegram, no. 1040, Department of State to Seoul, 22 April 1966, ibid; Telegram, no. 1048, Department of State to Taipei, 14 April 1966, RG 59, Central Files, 1964–66, Box 2018, POL CHICOM-US, NA.
114 "Communist China – Long Range Study," p. 219.
115 W. Bundy to Rusk, 13 May 1966, *FRUS*, 1964–1968, vol. 30, p. 299.
116 W. Bundy to Rusk, 20 May 1966, ibid., p. 307.
117 Arthur Goldberg to LBJ, 20 November 1965, NSF, Agency File, Box 71, folder "Goldberg correspondence (2 of 2)," LBJL.
118 W. Bundy and Joseph Sisco to Rusk, 16 February 1966, RG 59, Office of the Country Director for the Republic of China, 1963–1966, Lot 69D28, Box 1, NA.
119 Samuel Berger to W. Bundy, 23 February 1966, *FRUS*, 1964–1968, vol. 30, p. 261.
120 Komer to LBJ, 19 April 1966, ibid., p. 285.
121 William Bundy OH, Tape 5, pp. 22–3, LBJL.
122 Goldberg to LBJ, 28 April 1966, RG 59, Central Files, 1964–66, Box 3330, UN 6 CHICOM, NA.
123 Ruth Bacon to W. Bundy, 4 May 1966, RG 59, Subject Files of the Office of Asian Communist Affairs, 1961–73, Lot 72D41, Box 2, NA.
124 Rostow to LBJ, 30 April 1966, NSF, Memos to the President, Box 7, folder "Vol. I (1 of 3)," LBJL.
125 Rusk to LBJ, 14 May 1966, *FRUS*, 1964–1968, vol. 30, pp. 301–3.
126 Telegram, Taipei to Department of State, 1 July 1966, ibid., p. 346.
127 Administrative History of the Department of State, Box 4, ch. 10 (2 of 2), pp. 23–4, LBJL.
128 Telegram, Department of State to Ottawa, 25 July 1966, *FRUS*, 1964–1968, vol. 30, p. 359.
129 Rostow to LBJ, 28 July 1966, NSF, Country File, Box 239, folder "China memos, vol. VI," LBJL; Text of Cable from Hong Kong (1988), 19 September 1966 (enclosure), NSF, Country File, Box 240, folder "China

memos, vol. VII," LBJL; ONE (Office of National Estimates) special memorandum 14-66, "The China tangle," 23 September 1966, ibid.
130 Alfred Jenkins to Rostow, 27 August 1966, NSF, Files of Alfred Jenkins, Box 1, folder "CHICOM – General," LBJL.
131 Memorandum of conversation, Rusk–President Senghor, 28 September 1966, RG 59, Central Files, 1964–66, Box 3331, UN 6 CHICOM, NA.
132 Memorandum of conversation, 21 August 1966, *FRUS, 1964–1968*, vol. 30, p. 373.
133 Ibid., p. 387, n. 2.
134 Circular telegram from the Department of State to certain posts, 16 September 1966, ibid., p. 391.
135 Memorandum of conversation, 3 November 1966, ibid., pp. 412–14. For the Canadian perspective, see St Amour, "Sino-Canadian relations," in Evans and Frolic (eds), *Reluctant Adversaries*, pp. 115–21.
136 Rusk to LBJ, 5 November 1966, *FRUS, 1964–1968*, vol. 30, pp. 418–19.
137 Ibid., p. 418, n. 3. As a State Department cable explained, "Our support for [a] study committee resolution was to prevent support building up for [the] Canadian resolution. Our tactic was designed to cut the ground from under the Canadian resolution, which represented a new danger this year." Telegram, Department of State to Taipei, 21 November 1966, ibid., p. 444.
138 Telegram, Department of State to Ottawa, 9 November 1966, ibid., p. 423.
139 St Amour, "Sino-Canadian relations," in Evans and Frolic (eds), *Reluctant Adversaries*, pp. 120–1.
140 Bacon to W. Bundy, 1 December 1966, RG 59, Subject Files of Office of Asian Communist Affairs, 1961–73, Lot 72D41, Box 2, NA.
141 On this point, see George Kennan's Senate testimony in *China, Vietnam, and the United States*, p. 196.
142 Rusk to John Gronouski, 5 February 1966, *FRUS, 1964–1968*, vol. 30, p. 254.
143 Thomson to Jenkins, 25 July 1966, NSF, Country File, Box 239, folder "China memos, vol. VI (1 of 2)," LBJL.

5 Bridge-building in limbo
The impact of the Cultural Revolution, 1966–67

Since the early 1960s, China watchers both inside and outside government had urged that US policy toward the mainland be tailored in such a way as to exploit the apparent differences in perspective between the rigid ideologues ruling the country and the younger, presumably more pragmatic leadership-in-waiting. According to this logic, a more accommodating approach would compel Mao Zedong's potential successors to reconsider their preconception of US hostility, an image inculcated by Maoist dogma and reinforced by America's own obstinacy, and encourage them to concentrate their energies on domestic concerns once the Chairman had departed from the stage. The broad outlines of this strategy were most prominently articulated in Roger Hilsman's December 1963 address. There is little indication, however, that the Johnson team was influenced by these considerations during their first couple of years in office. Images and perceptions of the PRC were strongly conditioned by its threatening external behavior, particularly its role in encouraging and supplying the communist insurgency in South Vietnam. When a two-track China policy of containment and tentative bridge-building took shape in 1966, it was propelled by strategic and domestic objectives closely related to the Vietnam War rather than by any long-term project of engaging moderate elements in Beijing.

The explosion of China's Great Proletarian Cultural Revolution later that same year, however, opened an entirely new dimension to Washington's discourse on the mainland. The distinct possibility of internal tensions spilling over into neighboring countries, most notably Vietnam, meant at minimum that senior decision-makers could ill afford to ignore or overlook political developments on the mainland. Moreover, much as it baffled and even repelled Johnson's inner circle, the anarchy triggered by Mao's attempts to uproot the country's party-state apparatus moved them to consider for the first time what role, if any, the US could play in encouraging the emergence of a more agreeable successor regime.

Literature pertaining to LBJ's reaction to, and handling of, the Cultural Revolution is very sparse and has not made full use of the extensive primary sources now available to scholars. Existing accounts provide only a sketchy overview and adopt a broadly revisionist line, arguing that China's domestic turmoil prompted a reassessment of the conventional view of the PRC as an expansionist menace and a subsequent openness to new approaches to Beijing.[1] A reading of the full documentary record, however, reveals a more complicated story. Mainland affairs were watched intently by US officials and, as the existing scholarship posits, gradually set in motion a reappraisal of the country's political dynamic and threat potential. Yet for at least the first year of the Cultural Revolution, Johnson and his advisers, while not discarding the new emphasis on broadening contacts with Beijing, were disinclined to approve more substantive policy reform.

This chapter focuses on how the administration interpreted the outbreak of virtual civil war on the mainland and examines why bridge-building was relegated to a state of limbo at this time. First, Washington was taken aback by the chaotic and volatile character of China's political struggle; a cautious stance of deferment was a natural reaction for men with little in the way of reliable information at their disposal and little idea of what course events might take. Second, the ongoing war in Vietnam continued to shape policymaking deliberations. While some China watchers feared that the country's mayhem might precipitate an irrational decision for intervention in the conflict, LBJ evidently concluded that the Cultural Revolution had hobbled the PRC and increased the scope for intensified military action against Hanoi, thereby lessening the urgency of reaching out to Beijing. Third, simultaneous efforts to develop détente with the Soviet Union, having as its ultimate objective the Kremlin's assistance in finding a settlement to Vietnam, provided further incentive for postponing any China initiatives that might only exacerbate Moscow's persistent concerns about Sino-American reconciliation.

Interpreting the Cultural Revolution

The Cultural Revolution, one of the most profound political and social upheavals of the twentieth century, stemmed from Mao's "restless quest for revolutionary purity in a postrevolutionary age."[2] In the aftermath of the disastrous Great Leap Forward, the CCP establishment, led by Head of State and Vice Chairman Liu Shaoqi and Party Secretary General Deng Xiaoping, enacted a program of economic recovery that utilized the expertise of former capitalists and technical specialists, reimposed central bureaucratic controls, and catered to the material self-interests of the population. Mao gradually came to view these policies as a threat to both his political authority and utopian socialist ideals. At the heart of the Chairman's estrangement from his colleagues was a divergence of opinion over the severity of the economic crisis gripping China and the degree of retrenchment necessary to overcome it. Mao's vast ambition of continuous revolution and his contention that the country had sufficiently recovered by the early 1960s to withstand another campaign of mass mobilization clashed with the priorities of Liu and Deng. They were decidedly more pessimistic about China's condition, wary of disruptive ideological movements, and determined to pursue political and economic development through Party channels.

Mao's fear of creeping revisionism at home was conditioned in large part by his reading of concurrent events in the Soviet Union. Khrushchev's program of de-Stalinization and his erratic efforts to forge an accommodation of sorts with the "imperialist" West served as a disquieting example of how the agenda of a communist state could be usurped by individuals unsympathetic to the cause. Mao undoubtedly contemplated the uncertain fate of his own legacy if placed in the hands of those who did not share his revolutionary zeal. The Soviet leader's subsequent ouster in October 1964 stirred concerns of a similar end. To counter his own sense of marginalization, he cultivated like-minded allies among the military and radical intelligentsia, and moved to organize a groundswell of opposition from below against those in charge of the Party machine.[3]

China's descent into chaos was triggered by a series of shrewdly choreographed political machinations. In November 1965, Yao Wenyuan, a propagandist based in Shanghai, published a scathing indictment of *Hai Rui Dismissed From Office*, a play written by Wu Han. Wu served as the principal deputy of Peng Zhen, a Politburo member and mayor of Beijing, a powerful Party leader who embodied the bureaucratic stagnation that Mao abhorred. Yao's critique, likely written with the Chairman's tacit approval, branded Wu's work a thinly veiled attack on Mao's purge of Defense Minister Peng Dehuai in 1959. This placed Peng Zhen in the unenviable position of having either to defend his subordinate or admit his own guilt for harboring a revisionist. His ill-conceived attempt to dismiss the entire affair as an academic dispute sealed his fate. Mao seems to have regarded Peng's political demise as the prerequisite for securing the removal of his most formidable opponent and designated heir, Liu Shaoqi. Liu played into Mao's hands when, in June 1966, he dispatched work teams to universities and high schools in an effort to establish Party control over a burgeoning student revolt. Mao seized upon the suppression of the campus movement, which had been stoked by his underlings, as justification for his own offensive. At the Eleventh Plenum of the Central Committee in August, Liu was demoted, his vice chairmanship transferred to Defense Minister Lin Biao. At the same meeting, a Sixteen Point Decision on the Cultural Revolution approved the broad outlines of Mao's program, calling for a "struggle against ... those persons in authority who are taking the capitalist road."[4]

Mao's primary agents of "struggle," those to whom he looked to shake the Party establishment to its foundations and infuse the country with revolutionary fervor, were the Red Guards. Hopes for a unified mass movement, however, came to naught as the Red Guards split into opposing factions. Students from cadre and military families tended to discourage attacks on the Party and instead directed their wrath against intellectuals, former capitalists and landlords, and bourgeois culture. Students from bourgeois backgrounds, on the other hand, were aggrieved by the privileged status accorded to the children of CCP officials and eager to lash out at a system from which they had little to gain. Adding to this confusion were the attitudes of provincial and local leaders, who adopted a variety of tactics to obstruct or divert Red Guard interrogations. Many Red Guard groups were placed under tight restrictions or counterbalanced by the formation of conservative mass organizations. Toward the end of 1966, the Maoists, in a bid to retake the initiative and break the political stalemate, condemned senior Party figures for refusing to subject themselves to mass criticism.[5]

Washington's understanding of the mainland's turmoil was largely framed by reports from the consulate office in Hong Kong. The fluidity of events and backstage political maneuvering baffled even those charged with watching China on a day-to-day basis. "At no time in recent years," Consul General Edward Rice cabled in June 1966, "have there occurred ... developments at once so important and so clouded in obscurity as those of the past few months." He discerned a multidimensional character to the unfolding political drama, one that was at once an ideological purge, a policy dispute, and a power struggle. Rice was sure that recent events were intertwined with the country's looming succession question, yet was uncertain as to who was pulling the strings. Alluding to rumors of Mao's disenchantment with his colleagues, he allowed for the possibility of the leader's involvement, yet noted that the Chairman had remained outside Beijing for much of the past six months and was furthermore disinclined to play a hands-on role. Rice speculated that the assault on the Party apparatus was "spear-headed by or in the name" of Lin Biao, now apparently the new second in command.[6] The passage of time offered a clarified perspective, as analyses from Hong Kong in the fall left no doubt as to Mao's culpability. "Mao to our mind," read a typical assessment, "is architect, authority, and chief executor of the Great Cultural Revolution. It represents his final, and seemingly desperate, attempt to recreate Chinese society in accordance with his own revolutionary model." Mao's actions were placed in the context of his own growing sense of mortality and his despondency over the revisionist course that his rivals were charting.[7]

While Mao's behavior reinforced for most US officials the longstanding image of an implacable, perhaps even unstable, revolutionary, the fierce resistance he faced at home shattered high-level assumptions of a unified Chinese leadership. A July 1966 CIA memorandum, which Rostow forwarded to the President, posited that Peng Zhen's purge had undermined the cohesion and stability of Beijing's ruling circle, creating "deep suspicion and mistrust within the Chinese party from top to bottom'. Any chance of a "peaceful and orderly" succession to Mao had probably been ruined. Just as significantly, the Chinese people were wary of another round of political indoctrination: "Support for the regime will further weaken as the policy of substituting exhortation for material incentives is pushed."[8]

Mao's most immediate concern, as reported from Hong Kong, was the vast majority of CCP functionaries who disapproved of their leader's unholy alliance with the Red Guards. To protect their own institutional interests, this nascent opposition had settled on a low-key strategy of "waiting and blocking in every passive and unobtrusive way possible" the Mao-Lin bid for unencumbered power.[9] Intelligence analysts opined that "even in defeat the former party leaders could throw the nation into great confusion."[10] Indeed, in a brief survey of China's troubled landscape, Rostow wrote Johnson in early 1967 that "Mao's regime is in serious difficulty, to a degree that civil war has become a distinct possibility."[11] The Cultural Revolution had settled into a virtual deadlock, as the obstinacy of "fragmented and embittered leaders" compelled frequent tactical withdrawals by the Maoists. The revered Chairman's own prestige and standing among the Chinese people had been "seriously, perhaps irretrievably, tarnished in this as yet unavailing fracas."[12]

Another strategic retreat, forced on Mao as he confronted the unintended consequences of his own radicalism, occurred soon after Rostow's observation. As provincial authority dissipated in the wake of intensified mass pressure, Mao enthusiastically endorsed the overthrow of the Shanghai Party Committee in January 1967 and the subsequent seizure of power by rebel groups in seven other provinces and cities. When the question arose of what would replace this collapsed apparatus, however, his fear of anarchy took precedence over his revolutionary ardor. Mao most likely envisioned the Cultural Revolution as a campaign of Party rectification whereby those taking the "capitalist road" would be criticized and brought to heel, rather than as an enterprise aimed at creating an entirely new structure of power. Hence his ambivalence toward the notion of a system based on the Paris Commune, an idea favored by many of his allies and which inspired the establishment of the Shanghai People's Commune on 5 February. Mao instead encouraged the creation of a "three-in-one combination" of revolutionary rebels, PLA representatives, and veteran cadres. The intervention of the Red Army in Chinese politics, formalized by a 23 January directive ordering the military to assist "the broad masses of revolutionary Leftists in their struggle to seize power," was an effort to restore order to a process that was quickly spinning out of control.[13]

The administration's China watchers interpreted these developments as a major setback to the Chairman's ambitions and as a decisive shift in favor of the regime's relatively moderate elements. Based on what is now known about the political maneuverings of this period, particularly when senior civilian and military leaders were rebuked during the February Adverse Current for their criticism of the

Cultural Revolution, this was somewhat of a misreading of events.[14] British officials, with whom the Americans often shared information about the PRC, certainly believed that Washington had exaggerated the strength and influence of Mao's opposition in the Party.[15] US analysts were struck by the military's new role. Despite Lin's leadership of the PLA, the office in Hong Kong believed the Red Army to be an unreliable ally for the Maoists. Rice cited the close mutual relationships between many military commanders and the CCP's provincial and municipal leaders as evidence for this view. Moreover, the army's identification with domestic order was at variance with the Red Guards' self-interest in uprooting it.[16] With the PLA's political influence evidently ascendant, the State Department discerned in late February a distinct change in the "pace, intensity and direction" of the Cultural Revolution. The radicalism of the preceding months had been replaced by an emphasis on restoring economic and administrative order, protecting government officials from political attack, and reining in the activities of the Red Guards.[17]

A second factor accounting for this change in course, US officials believed, was the apparent rise in fortunes of Premier Zhou Enlai. Among those in the higher echelons of leadership, Zhou was regarded as the most pragmatic, a statesman with wide exposure to the outside world who was familiar with the give and take of diplomacy, whose Maoist rhetoric belied his conservative instincts and distaste for the Chairman's extremism.[18] Indeed, according to one Swedish source, Zhou had confided to several visitors from Eastern Europe that "while he opposes the cultural revolution personally, he is careful about making public criticism in order to remain in the inner circle, and thereby exercise some degree of moderation."[19] To the extent that China watchers perceived signs of hope in early 1967, they attributed this in large part to the steadying influence of the canny political veteran.[20]

These events provoked considerable speculation as to the likely outcome of the mainland's political conflict. In February, a panel of academic experts on China, which had been established the previous fall by the State Department, listed four possibilities: a Mao-Lin victory, a compromise orchestrated by Zhou, the forging of a triumphant alliance between the Party apparatus and the PLA, or the disintegration of the country into regional units under military leadership. The third scenario was deemed the most feasible, with Mao probably assuming a largely ceremonial position in the hierarchy.[21]

The advantages of a relatively moderate successor regime were self-evident. There was some hope that those same groups who disapproved the Chairman's radicalism at home might exercise similar prudence abroad. Alfred Jenkins, the NSC's China hand, thought that a Zhou-led China would be more preoccupied with internal concerns and therefore less prone to stir up mischief among its neighbors. To the extent that he sought international acceptance and the legitimization of his own rule, Zhou might be tempted to return to the "Bandung spirit" of the mid-1950s and project an image of restraint and "rationality."[22]

In a similar vein, a May 1967 National Intelligence Estimate advanced the possibility that "over the long term, internal changes in the direction of moderation ... will create more favorable conditions for reappraising foreign policy and perhaps for introducing elements of greater moderation."[23] The alternative, a regime dominated by the Mao-Lin partnership, alarmed many in Washington. The enigmatic Defense Minister, "author" of the notorious *Long Live the Victory of People's War!*, was viewed as "a thorough Communist, xenophobic in his nationalism, and lacking in true appreciation of the outside world."[24] Lin, Rostow informed LBJ, was "bad news."[25]

On balance, however, Johnson officials discouraged expectations of a dramatic change in China's foreign policy orientation no matter what the ultimate fate of the Cultural Revolution. The office in Hong Kong postulated that Mao's opposition, while not ideological zealots, were nevertheless "disciplined Marxist-Leninists" whose worldview did not diverge markedly from the Chairman's. Any change in policy by his successors would be "more of style and procedure than in basic goals or priorities."[26] State's Policy Planning Council likened the entire affair to "a domestic squabble among Communists" in which differences over external strategy were not the issue at stake. A relatively moderate successor government, should one emerge, would most likely de-emphasize the primacy of class struggle in the PRC's domestic affairs, yet the implications of such a shift for the country's foreign relations were harder to predict. There was little to suggest that Beijing would relax its hostile attitude toward the US.[27] By the fall of 1967, Jenkins had revised his previous estimate and was less hopeful of a new foreign affairs posture if Zhou was the victor. He noted that there was "very little to substantiate the theory that Chou would wish to deviate in any basic way from the policies he has long mouthed."[28]

Nor did China's troubles diminish in the eyes of senior US decision-makers the continuing relevance of the commitment in Vietnam. In a bid to convince LBJ that international conditions were favorable for a de-escalation of the war, Robert McNamara made the rather startling assertion in May 1967 that "To the extent that our original intervention and our existing actions in Vietnam were motivated by the perceived need to draw the line against Chinese expansionism in Asia, our objective has already been attained" because of the PRC's internal disarray.[29] The Defense Secretary by no means represented high-level thinking. William Bundy thought his comments were "wholly inadequate" and disputed the notion that "we can in any sense rest on our oars." A premature withdrawal from Vietnam would be condemned by Asian opinion and undermine American influence in the region.[30] Even as the Johnson team acknowledged that Mao's own recklessness had hobbled his regional ambitions, they maintained that this unprecedented bout of militancy underscored that China was still a threatening international actor. Just as in 1965, Rostow argued that a US defeat in Vietnam in 1967 would "leave Southeast Asia at the mercy of Communist China. Without the U.S., there is no force ... capable of deterring Communist China."[31] Johnson agreed that a robust American posture in Vietnam "has had its effect. It has hampered China's policy and caused reversals against China in Indonesia and other parts of the world."[32]

Thus while fascinated, even somewhat encouraged, by the turn of events in China, Johnson and his advisers recoiled from any grand departures in policy. The uncertain outcome of China's political struggle and the rampant chaos gripping the country were major factors accounting for this cautious stance. To be sure, long-standing proponents of policy reform within the administration continued to press their case, arguing that this confusion presented Washington with an opportunity to influence modestly the PRC's future orientation to its advantage. James Thomson was convinced that "the present commotion ... makes more desirable than ever U.S. 'intervention' in the Chinese political process through further development of a multiple strategy."[33] In August 1966, he alerted Rostow to a trade initiative that was then in its deliberative stages. Thomson favored White House intervention to give the process a push. A modification of the embargo, besides serving the familiar objective of deflecting domestic and international criticism of American intransigence, would send "a new and supportive message to elements within mainland

China that are pushing for policies of pragmatism and accommodation with the outside world."[34] While mindful of the mainland's unsettled climate, Rice also advised his superiors that this should not halt the momentum toward the eventual normalization of relations with Beijing. With an eye to the future and to the possible replacement of Mao, he stressed how a more flexible policy would "facilitate the possibility of ... a successor regime acting as we would wish a responsible government of the most populous nation in the world to act."[35] Several members of the State Department's panel of China experts were sympathetic to this line of reasoning and pinpointed the loosening of trade restrictions as a means to serve this end.[36]

A far more significant voice in this debate belonged to Alfred Jenkins, who, upon Thomson's departure from government in August 1966, became the NSC's resident China watcher. A former deputy director of Southeast Asian Affairs at Foggy Bottom who had also served in Hong Kong and Taipei, Jenkins played a substantial role in shaping the White House's reaction to the Cultural Revolution. Key to this influence was his access to the President via Rostow, who thought highly of his aide and frequently forwarded his memorandums to Johnson. Rostow counted him among his most trusted sources on Chinese matters; he later contrasted Jenkins' sober judgement with that of his immediate predecessor who, perhaps owing to his background as a missionary offspring, Rostow thought had too much of an emotional investment in advancing the cause of Sino-American reconciliation.[37]

Jenkins' own attitudes evolved slowly. Early in his tenure at the NSC, he believed, much like Thomson, that mainland events demanded a clarification of Washington's benign intentions. Most strikingly, he confided to Rostow that the administration was ill-served by the hardline views of decision-makers like Rusk, whose approach to the PRC "scares me. He is so orderly and judicial and a sheaf of other virtues, that he wants all the returns in before he moves. On China we are not going to get as many returns as we want; and inaction is an act watched by mainlanders, especially, I should think, the ChiCom moderates."[38] Yet Jenkins' enthusiasm for further bridge-building efforts was eventually dampened by the mainland's persistent turmoil and by the sense that any goodwill gesture would be spurned in Beijing. In these circumstances, he argued, any fundamental overhaul of China policy should be postponed "until we can make a much better judgment as to the course of events in China."[39] Rostow saw much to recommend this view. China, as he recollected, "was like a dragon with a bellyache ... They were caught up in a great debate and struggle as to how they should behave with respect to themselves and the rest of the world. They were not in a mood or in a position to talk to us."[40]

Jenkins' advocacy of a posture of "relative silence and careful scrutiny"[41] resonated with senior officials instinctively prone to worst-case assumptions of Chinese intentions, confused by the rush of events, and distracted by more pressing concerns. The mainland's implosion effectively derailed the momentum for further policy revision that had been generated by the President's 12 July speech. As discussed in the previous chapter, deliberations over the merits of adopting a "two Chinas" formula in the UN during the summer and fall of 1966 were influenced by the outbreak of Red Guard violence on the mainland. It was felt by some, notably Rusk, that a conciliatory overture at this point might encourage or reward the country's militant elements and possibly tip the balance in favor of the Mao-Lin faction. In lieu of a settlement of the politically sensitive issue of Chinese representation, many within State's East Asian bureau pushed for alternative means of deepening relations with the PRC. In December 1966, Bundy and Leonard Meeker, the State Department's Legal Adviser, sent Rusk a far-reaching proposal for the removal of all passport restrictions for travel to the PRC. The idea was justified in part as a way of "eventually persuading mainland China to turn its energies into non-aggressive, responsible channels."[42] The measure, however, reached Rusk's desk at a time most analysts recognized as an acutely radical phase in the Cultural Revolution, and was shelved as a result. Bundy evidently had second thoughts, withdrawing the idea a few months later "in view of the unsettled political condition inside China and the xenophobic behavior of the mobs of Red Guards ... committing excesses or threatening foreigners ... in Peking and elsewhere."[43]

Similar logic determined the fate of trade proposals under discussion since the spring of 1966.[44] In September, Bundy, again acting at the behest of his subordinates, recommended that the State, Defense, Treasury, Commerce and Agriculture departments agree to a set of changes in America's trade and transaction controls against Beijing. Among the suggestions were the general licensing of those US citizens with valid passports to China for engagement in all transactions incidental to their travel and the eventual licensing of foodstuffs, medical supplies, and art objects for import and export. The package was framed as a natural extension of the administration's efforts to increase contacts with the PRC. Johnson's 12 July address, with its call for the "free flow of ideas and people and goods" between the two countries, raised expectations of such a move. Whether or not the inclusion of "goods" in the speech was seriously deliberated remains unclear.[45] By the fall, however, events in China had clearly changed minds. Rostow favored deferment of the trade package, thinking it best that Rusk "take this up directly with the President *at the right time*."[46] Reflecting this cautious mood, Under Secretary of State Nicholas Katzenbach suggested that "we should hold this awhile."[47]

Deteriorating conditions on the mainland were in fact the basis for the approval of a modest trade initiative in April 1967. Bundy reported to Rusk at the end of March that the breakdown of order and authority had jeopardized food supplies and contributed to the spread of various diseases. "Neither U.S. public opinion, that of China, or that of the rest of the world," he wrote, "should be presented with a picture of total U.S. indifference to [the] prospect of famine in China." Bundy used the occasion to revive his trade program from the previous fall and to submit a new recommendation for the licensing of medical supplies.[48] In accordance with the prevailing distaste for policy experimentation, Bundy's original proposals were yet again postponed. Yet the compelling humanitarian rationale forced unusually prompt agreement on the latter idea. On 19 April, the administration announced the license for sale to China pharmaceutical and medical supplies directly related to the prevention or treatment of meningitis, cholera, or infectious hepatitis.[49] While noteworthy, the decision was defensive and bore little relation to any long-term strategy. It was motivated mostly by the need to safeguard America's benign international image.

Officials were evidently taken aback by what they characterized as an "overwhelmingly hostile" public reaction to this gesture and were apprehensive that any further trade liberalization would undermine the President's simultaneous efforts to win Congressional approval of an East-West trade bill.[50] In contrast to the spring of 1966, when public perceptions of the PRC were shaped in large part by Fulbright's China hearings and rumors of Beijing's preparations for war, surveys of popular attitudes in 1967 did not reveal widespread support for new bridge-building efforts or offer the Johnson team any direct incentive for overhauling China policy. Media reports of political purges and Red Guard brutality deepened impressions of Chinese irrationality and lawlessness. A Gallup poll taken in March revealed that 71 percent of Americans deemed China to be the major threat to world peace.[51]

Yet the scarcity of policy innovation at this time cannot be solely attributed to political timidity or knee-jerk aversion to Mao's radicalism. Indeed, inherent in the US posture of aloofness toward the Cultural Revolution was a significant degree of sophistication and foresight. Senior officials acknowledged that their capacity to shape events on the mainland to their liking was severely limited, and were fearful lest any hint of American interference in Chinese politics unwittingly sabotaged the chances of a more pragmatic leadership succeeding the Chairman.[52] Jenkins cited the "unpredictability of what effect our actions might have on a Chinese situation which seemed, from our standpoint, to be developing quite satisfactorily without any help from us."[53] This consideration accounted for the calculated decision to refrain from public commentary on either the PRC's state of affairs or the administration's preferred outcome. In February 1967, Bundy cancelled a scheduled speech on China and instead provided an off-the-record session for reporters. As he explained to a colleague, "anything in the nature of an official statement on China at the present time is subject to misconstruction ... [and] will be deemed to thrust our influence one way or the other and to be thus harmful." It was therefore prudent to "stand aside wholly from the current struggle."[54]

In lieu of any forward movement on the policy front, the Johnson team upheld the conciliatory bridge-building rhetoric from the previous year. The embassy in Warsaw was instructed to continue emphasizing Washington's interest in peace during the Sino-American ambassadorial talks. With so few opportunities for interaction with their Chinese counterparts, US officials viewed this forum as a critical "'holding operation' ... to keep open some dialogue with [the] ChiComs."[55] In his January 1967 State of the Union address, LBJ again asserted his "hope for a reconciliation between the people of Mainland China and the world community – including working together in all the tasks of arms control, security, and progress on which the fate of the Chinese people ... depends." Reiterating the broad sentiments of Hilsman's December 1963 speech, he maintained that the US would be "the first to welcome a China which decided to respect her neighbors' rights."[56] That same month, the State Department circulated a set of guidelines for public statements on China to all diplomatic and consular posts. The paper advised US representatives stationed abroad to underline America's limited objectives in Vietnam and to "Seek ways of recognizing the past and potential greatness of China and the history of friendly relations between the American and Chinese peoples." While it was conceded that this would not alter the outlook of the current leadership, it was thought "conceivable that potential future leaders might be influenced."[57]

Most notably, Johnson used the occasion of a visit in June by Romanian Premier Ion Gheorghe Maurer, who remained on good terms with the Chinese and was soon scheduled to travel to Beijing, to convey his good intentions. Adhering to the counsel of his aides that he "*not* get into any discussion on the internal situation in Communist China,"[58] the President asked his guest to relay the message that "we do not want war with China or to change the system of government in China ... We have no designs on her territory or her philosophy. All we want to do is to trade with China and get along with her to the extent that she will permit."[59] In all of these subtle ways, the administration, without overtly involving itself in China's political debate, sought to signal to various contenders for power on the mainland that options existed for improved relations between the two countries.

China and the Vietnam War, 1966–67

The most pressing concern for Johnson and his advisers was whether the pressures emanating from China's domestic crisis portended any change in its willingness to intervene in Vietnam. This consideration, largely overlooked in the existing literature, heavily influenced the administration's conduct of the war in 1967 and its posture toward the PRC. Recent studies have confirmed that the Cultural Revolution, particularly in its early stages, exercised significant influence on the conduct of Chinese foreign relations, lending it a decidedly ideological and revolutionary cast. Contrary to the hopes of professional diplomats like Zhou and Foreign Minister Chen Yi, who sought to insulate the conduct of the nation's diplomacy from Mao's anti-revisionist campaign, the Maoists viewed domestic and international politics as two sides of the same coin. Propagation of Mao Zedong Thought abroad was a means by which popular opinion could be mobilized and their own power consolidated on the mainland. The Ministry of Foreign Affairs became a battleground for these competing moderate and radical visions. In early 1967, the former lost considerable ground to the latter, as Chen was sidelined due to his complicity in the February Adverse Current. Consequently, the Central Cultural Revolution Group assumed a more prominent role in the formulation and implementation of policy. The result was chaos. All but one of the country's ambassadors were recalled for indoctrination. Chinese embassies were instructed to distribute Mao badges, and protests were frequently organized against other countries for minor offenses.[60] John Gronouski, the American ambassador in Poland, observed an unnerving change in the deportment of his Chinese interlocutors at the Warsaw sessions. Officials "all appeared in identical dark blue Chungshan uniforms with Mao Tse-tung buttons on [the] left chest ... Repeated references to 'great leader of [the] Chinese people,' Mao, and to thought of Mao [is] an unusual feature in [the] talks."[61] Alfred Jenkins confirmed reports in the summer of 1967 that "a group of radical Red Guards, who know little about international affairs and diplomacy, but who are letter-perfect in the thoughts of Mao Tse-tung, have taken over the [Foreign] Ministry."[62]

Most US intelligence analysts thought it unlikely that China's foreign policy would be affected for the worse by the country's internal confusion. On the contrary, many speculated that Mao's preoccupation with vanquishing his rivals would reinforce his natural aversion to a major commitment to Hanoi. As a July 1966 CIA report concluded, "it might be prudent for the regime to seek a certain equilibrium abroad, lest foreign developments intrude on internal programs. Recent Chinese propaganda – e.g., that the main enemies are internal ones – seems to point in this direction."[63] The PRC's relatively muted response to the targeting of North Vietnam's POL sites that same month corroborated this view. Observers were careful to note that Beijing's vehement objections to the bombing and its affirmation as "the reliable rear area of the Vietnamese people" were intended primarily to reassure a nervous ally and did not represent any change in strategy. The Chinese would continue to hold their fire unless directly provoked.[64] A Special National Intelligence Estimate attributed this gun-shyness in part to the disarray within the armed forces and throughout the country at large.[65] Similarly, the shift toward an even more radical line in foreign relations in 1967 was calmly assessed. The Maoists' intensified rhetorical support of Asian national liberation movements amounted to little more than "propaganda, political support, limited financial assistance and the training of cadres." In its actions abroad, the mainland would continue to be "guided by a realistic appraisal of feasible courses of action."[66]

The State Department's China hands were not nearly as sanguine as the intelligence community on the question of Chinese intentions in Vietnam. Edward Rice, long a skeptic of Rolling Thunder, strenuously contended that any complacency derived from Beijing's troubles was dangerously misguided. Any estimate of China's intervention in the war could not be attempted without reference to Mao's dogged efforts to instill revolutionary purity into the next generation of leadership, a scheme which called into question his own "sense of mental balance and predictability."[67] Rice advocated greater concentration of the military effort in the South and the avoidance of potentially provocative actions against the DRV; the Chairman's fatalistic belief in the inevitability of a clash with the forces of imperialism and his appreciation of conflict as an instrument of mass mobilization made Chinese entry into the war "a possible contingency."[68]

The mainland's charged political climate evidently gave many senior US decision-makers pause for thought. Shortly following the bombing of the North's POL facilities in July 1966, diplomats were explicitly discouraged from publicly speculating on how the mainland's purges might impair its military preparedness. It was thought that China's "hypersensitivity to mockery of their effectiveness and resentment over [an] outside effort to profit from internal problems ... may only serve to strengthen any Chinese disposition ... to make [a] strong, dramatic display of power."[69] This consideration underpinned Bundy's "grave reservations" the following month over Pentagon proposals for air strikes against steel plants and the Haiphong docks. An expansion of Rolling Thunder, he argued, might be interpreted by the Chinese "as a sign that we thought we could get away with something because of the political confusion in Communist China. This could trigger irrational action."[70] Rusk as well took seriously the possibility that the country's "leaders might react irrationally because of tensions in [the] regime."[71]

The risk of stoking China's siege mentality figured prominently in the administration's heated debate over war planning in the spring and summer of 1967. Seizing upon General William Westmoreland's request in March for an additional 200,000 troops, the Joint Chiefs of Staff pressed the White House for the adoption of several measures designed to dramatically curtail Hanoi's support of the insurgency in the South: ground raids on enemy sanctuaries in Laos and Cambodia and across the demilitarized zone; mobilization of the reserves; bombing military and industrial facilities in the Hanoi-Haiphong area and along the rail lines to China; and mining the DRV's major ports.[72] These proposals provoked considerable unease among Johnson's civilian aides. The long-standing assumption that China would directly intervene in the war only if North Vietnam was invaded or on the verge of collapse remained intact. Yet as both the CIA and State's INR bureau posited in April, mining Haiphong harbor or attacking the rail lines might convince Beijing's leaders that either scenario was imminent and therefore precipitate a decision for a broadened role in the fighting, possibly involving air or ground action.[73]

LBJ's inner circle, while differing over the appropriate bombing strategy, was even more adamant about the dangers inherent in the Joint Chiefs' program. Though predisposed to increased military pressure on the North, Rostow concluded that the advantages of concentrating action against the "top of the funnel" were outweighed by "the risks of Soviet and Chinese countermeasures and heightened world tensions." To encourage Hanoi's continued participation in the war, Beijing would counter any American escalation by introducing additional engineering and anti-aircraft forces. More ominously, he wrote, "given the turmoil inside Communist China, an irrational act ... cannot be ruled out."[74] McNamara, distraught by the seemingly endless stalemate and convinced that American bombing was not producing the desired effect of reducing the North's infiltration into the South, was "appalled" by the military's "continued willingness to risk a nuclear confrontation."[75] In a 19 May memorandum to the President, he asserted that an escalation of the conflict along these lines would have minimal impact on Hanoi's resolve and instead likely provoke "a serious confrontation, if not war, with China and Russia." McNamara recommended an increase of only 30,000 troops, arguing that granting Westmoreland's request would only create pressure for additional forces. He steadfastly opposed expanding the ground war beyond South Vietnam or bombing the DRV north of the twentieth parallel. Fearful of going over the brink, he hoped that these limited steps would prove sufficient in serving as "a lever toward negotiations."[76]

The State Department's position, as articulated by Bundy and Katzenbach, reiterated the argument that the PRC might perceive increased military pressure on Hanoi as a concerted effort to destroy its ally. Among other considerations, the need to avert heightened

Sino-American tensions dictated a "cut back [in Rolling Thunder] in the near future to concentration on supply routes and re-strikes north of the 20th parallel limited to those necessary to eliminate targets directly important to infiltration." The distinguishing feature of Bundy and Katzenbach's paper was its contention that intensified bombing of the North would have detrimental effects on China's internal condition. Relying heavily on reports from Hong Kong, they argued that enacting the Joint Chiefs' recommendations would set off a crisis atmosphere that could unite the mainland's disparate factions, which would either "calm down the Chinese internal situation or … assist Mao to gain control" of the reins of power. Besides undermining the prospects of a moderate post-Mao regime, an easing of China's domestic conflict would increase Beijing's leverage over the North and thereby discourage Hanoi from seeking a negotiated settlement. Put another way, the DRV's interest in peace talks depended in part on continued Chinese disarray.[77]

Whether or not Johnson factored Chinese politics into his military decisions of 1967 remains uncertain. More likely his general fear of triggering a replay of Korea, so prominent since the outset of the war, was a decisive consideration. Swayed by the cautionary advice of his aides, he rejected any mining of the DRV's ports or incursions into Laos, Cambodia, and North Vietnam. Tilting toward his Secretary of Defense, he authorized only 55,000 additional troops, far below what the Joint Chiefs had requested. On the issue of bombing, however, LBJ sought to "steer a course midway between the proposal of those who wanted to cut back our air action and the plan advanced by those who believed we should step up strikes … I felt that a cutback to the 20th parallel at that time would have been misunderstood in Hanoi as a sign of weakness."[78] While Johnson genuinely believed in the utility of new bombing to convince the DRV of American resolve, he was also troubled by the prospect of divisions within his administration being driven into the open. As befitted his consensus-based approach to policymaking, he attempted to juggle competing recommendations by weaving elements of them together. When Senator John Stennis opened public hearings on bombing strategy on 9 August, giving the military a forum for airing their grievances, the approval of expanded bombing became a matter of political necessity. By no coincidence, he selected sixteen new targets on the same day that Stennis called his session into order, ten of which were in the DRV border area with China.[79]

The President took this step despite the opposition of most of his senior civilian advisers. Bundy raised anew his concerns that Beijing "could well see [these] systematic attacks as an attempt by us to take advantage of their internal weakness and confusion, and ... drive them to action however irrational." Moreover, bombing near the border might compel the PLA, a possible agent of moderation, to close ranks with Mao.[80] Yet Johnson believed that circumstances provided some leeway for more vigorous military action. As he explained, "Our strategy, as I see it, is that we destroy all we can without involving China and Russia ... but I do not believe China and Russia will come in." While he agreed that "we must be careful about the [Sino-Vietnamese] buffer zone because of the danger in going over the border," he felt that "targets more than eight to ten miles away from the buffer zone could be hit without danger."[81]

LBJ's confidence likely stemmed in part from the counsel of one his most trusted confidants, Clark Clifford, who, upon returning from a tour of Southeast Asia in early August, urged that "the [bombing] margins be moved closer to Red China and that additional targets be approved." Clifford assured his friend that there was "no concern anywhere in the countries [I] visited about Red China entering the war."[82] Indeed, in an interview that spring with American correspondent Simon Malley, Zhou implied that China did not wish to provoke a war with the US and would only fight if attacked.[83] Johnson may well have been satisfied that he had signalled sufficient restraint through his aforementioned meeting in June with the Romanian Premier. At a press conference on 18 August, he insisted that "these air strikes are not intended as any threat to Communist China ... the United States does not seek to widen the war in Vietnam."[84]

Apparently encouraged by Chinese quiescence during the first wave of new attacks in August, Johnson authorized air strikes on the Phuc Yen airfield in October, once again overruling the reservations of Rusk and McNamara, both of whom raised the possibility of a strong Chinese reaction.[85] Thus while Johnson's continued worries over Chinese intervention led him to rebuff the more belligerent elements of the Joint Chiefs' agenda, his escalation of the air war in the summer and fall of 1967 suggested that this fear had receded somewhat since the previous year. China's internal disorder and the dearth of evidence that it was taking tangible steps to prepare for war contributed to this impression.[86]

The ramifications for China policy were significant. Just as the possibility of Chinese intervention kindled LBJ's personal interest in bridge-building in 1966, the diminished threat of an enlarged war as China turned inward rendered the need for new overtures to the mainland less urgent.[87] With a raging Cultural Revolution and the growing unlikelihood of Sino-American hostilities, substantive policy reform was put on the backburner.

Leaning toward Moscow

While creating an opening for increased military activity against the North, another geopolitical side-effect of the Cultural Revolution offered equally alluring benefits to US policymakers: the intensification of the Sino-Soviet schism. Indeed, Johnson officials were struck by the depths to which relations between the two communist giants plunged. Few events better illustrated this phenomenon than the Red Square incident of 25 January 1967. When Soviet authorities suppressed a gathering of Chinese students for publicly reading quotations from Mao at the tombs of Lenin and Stalin, millions of angry Chinese protested at the Soviet embassy in Beijing. In retaliation, a group of Soviet citizens was dispatched to the PRC's embassy in Moscow one week later, at which point a number of Chinese diplomats were mauled.[88] Even casual observers of mainland affairs could not fail to notice that the tenor of Mao's campaign – the vilification of Liu Shaoqi as "China's Khrushchev" and the exhortations against "revisionism" – was decidedly anti-Soviet. As the Hong Kong office reported in the fall of 1966, "the Soviet Union has matched, if not replaced, the U.S. as Peking's major propaganda target ... an emotional trend of hostility to the USSR has been set off which perhaps over the years will lead to less concentration on Peking's fundamental enmity toward the U.S."[89]

Confounded like their American counterparts by the bizarre turn of events in China, Soviet officials initially responded cautiously to the Cultural Revolution. By ignoring increased Chinese provocation and refusing to engage in polemical exchanges, the Kremlin hoped to remain above the fray and prudently navigate the storm in the hope of de-escalating tensions with its neighbor. As reports of Chinese militancy and harassment of Soviet diplomats in Beijing deluged the Kremlin in the fall of 1966, however, Kosygin and Brezhnev thought it necessary to defend themselves against Chinese accusations, highlight the differences between the Soviet and Chinese conceptions of revolution, and rally the support of allies in the international communist movement. Abandoning previous efforts to maintain a semblance of civility, the Soviet media counterattacked in late 1966 with its own charges of Chinese irrationality and isolation within the communist camp, a significant change in tone that was documented by State's INR bureau.[90] Rostow notified LBJ of rumors that the Soviets were "instigating and aiding anti-Mao resistance in Sinkiang, Manchuria and possibly Inner Mongolia."[91] Inherent in Soviet attitudes, intelligence analysts believed, was profound concern over developments on the mainland and a fear that the breakdown of CCP authority could "set dangerous precedents for other socialist states."[92] There seemed to be few advantageous outcomes to China's political conflict from the Kremlin's perspective. A Maoist victory would only prolong tensions between Moscow and Beijing, while continued disorder threatened the security of Soviet borders. As a hedge against these and other contingencies, the USSR had reinforced armed forces along the frontier it shared with its adversary.[93]

This mutual fear and suspicion took its toll. In its long-term forecast of Sino-Soviet relations, a December 1966 NIE postulated that much would depend on China's future political orientation. Should the Mao-Lin faction triumph, relations would deteriorate even further, possibly leading to "a sudden explosion of the dispute into a new and more virulent form in the near term." Yet even a more accommodating Chinese leadership that was eager to mend fences with its neighbor could not be expected to make major concessions to serve this end, such as recognizing Moscow's leadership of the world revolution. "Divergent Chinese and Soviet national interests" would "remain a source of friction and distrust for many years to come."[94]

As China's prestige in the communist bloc plummeted and Moscow became increasingly preoccupied with the threat on its eastern flank, these same reports surmised, the Kremlin would feel both emboldened and compelled to improve relations with the West.[95] In February 1967, British Prime Minister Harold Wilson relayed to Rostow his impressions of recent talks with Soviet Premier Alexei Kosygin. Most noteworthy was the new "Soviet attitude about involvement in efforts to obtain a [Vietnam] settlement ... Kosygin had clearly revealed in private the extent to which he was now willing to play a role." Wilson attributed this "substantial shift in the Soviet position" to the "almost obsessional concern shown by Mr. Kosygin about events in China."[96]

There is some evidence that suggests Soviet strategy toward the US at this time was influenced in part by the Chinese threat. In January 1967, the Politburo approved a foreign policy memorandum that affirmed the imperative of "avoid[ing] a situation where we have to fight on two fronts, that is against China and the United States. Maintaining Soviet-American relations on a certain level is one of the factors that will help us achieve this objective."[97] An additional concern arguing in favor of engaging the Americans was the specter of an exclusive Sino-American bargain in Vietnam that would eradicate Soviet influence in Southeast Asia.[98]

Some Johnson officials argued that the Sino-Soviet rift could be used as leverage in inducing the Kremlin to apply pressure on North Vietnam to negotiate. Expounding on a strategy in November 1966 that would gain considerable currency during the Nixon presidency, Zbigniew Brzezinski of State's Policy Planning Council opined that "some public intimation ... of a developing US interest in US-Chinese accommodation may spur the Soviet Union into considering the advantages of greater US-Soviet cooperation."[99] Douglass Cater, one of LBJ's most senior political aides, soon picked up on this theme. Without sufficient prodding, he wrote the President, Moscow would have little incentive to help extricate America from the war by facilitating peace talks. A possible solution to this quandary would be to "undertake a series of calculated moves to stimulate anxiety among the Soviets about the state of our conversations with Communist China."[100]

Cater's idea was forwarded to Jenkins and fellow NSC staffer Nathaniel Davis for comment. Their frosty reaction reflected the thinking of their superiors and constituted another reason for the deferment of further bridge-building to China during this period. Jenkins' reservations stemmed from familiar concerns that any new gestures toward the PRC would be inappropriate without "some semblance of order on the mainland."[101] Perhaps more importantly, Davis contended that precisely because the Soviets were in "an emotional lather about China," any attempt to unnerve them would probably have a counterproductive effect and undermine ongoing efforts to engage the Kremlin in talks on Vietnam, non-proliferation, and arms control. As he wrote, "Their response may be more hostility and withdrawal, if they think we are systematically using the Chinese against them."[102] Washington's image of an increasingly militant China dovetailed with heightened expectations that Khrushchev's conservative successors were interested in developing a stable international climate and mediating an end to the hostilities in Vietnam.

The US intelligence community was, on balance, skeptical about the USSR's willingness to play a constructive role in Vietnam. The Soviet attitude toward greater political and diplomatic involvement in the war was depicted as one of ambivalence. On the one hand, it was assumed that Moscow had an obvious stake in containing the fighting, as US escalation or the DRV's stubbornness could force its hand and trigger a superpower confrontation. Balanced against these considerations, however, was the Soviets' appreciation of the war as an open wound that diverted American resources from Europe and alienated world opinion. Moreover, the Kremlin would be loath to forsake its hard-earned influence in Hanoi on behalf of US interests, whether by a cutoff in military aid or the application of crude political pressure.[103] A typical CIA assessment concluded in April 1967, "the Soviets see no feasible alternative but to follow their present policy of continuing the current level of support to Hanoi, while avoiding any great pressure on either North Vietnam or on the US to end the war. The Soviet leaders probably hope that the conflict will ... end without any further substantial escalation."[104]

This was a reasonably accurate reading of Soviet policy. As Ilya Gaiduk's research has shown, the USSR was reluctant to assume a visible and prominent role in the peace process. During the latter half of 1966, Soviet officials believed that China's waning clout in Hanoi afforded an opportunity gently to push their Vietnamese comrades toward negotiations. Yet the DRV proved mostly resistant to this counsel, particularly in the spring of 1967 as it increased its military effort in the South. Aware of its limited influence and protective of its self-image as the guardian of national liberation struggles, Moscow settled on "a consistent though cautious and sometimes ineffective policy of indirect pressure and persuasion [to negotiate] so as not to antagonize its allies."[105]

Yet the Johnson team, anxious to exhaust every option for ending the war on favorable terms, invested considerable faith in the Soviet card. More so than intelligence analysts, they believed that the USSR was displaying greater willingness to cooperate on issues of major concern to the administration toward the end of 1966. Following a meeting with Foreign Minister Andrei Gromyko in October, LBJ thought that "our relations with the Soviet Union were better at present than they have ever been since he assumed the Presidency." He was particularly encouraged by Gromyko's hints that "the Soviets now have some influence in North Viet-Nam and that, if the [US] bombing were to cease, there was reason to hope that this would be followed by positive action on the part of the North."[106]

These hopes were fuelled by numerous indications that the Sino-Vietnamese alliance, assumed to be virtually watertight in 1964–65, was roiled by tension. Hanoi's military and diplomatic ties to the Soviet Union, a source of irritation to the Chinese since Khrushchev's purge, deepened in 1966–67. Efforts to maximize support from both communist patrons and to maintain a neutral stance in the Sino-Soviet dispute were dramatically displayed when the DRV sent a delegation to the Soviets' Twenty Third Party Congress in the spring of 1966. Like their Russian counterparts, Chinese leaders were reluctant to damage their standing in Hanoi by overtly imposing their views. Yet the Maoists were clearly upset by the emergence of elements in North Vietnam favoring a "fighting while negotiating" strategy. Mao's interests rested on a perpetuation of the war, both as a means of bleeding American resources and rallying popular support for his campaign against capitalist restoration at home. China continued to press its ally for vigorous prosecution of the fighting and advised against peace talks.[107] US intelligence reports recognized discord between the PRC and the DRV over Soviet aid and the utility of negotiations.[108] China's intense preoccupation with domestic affairs was seen to be another source of irritation for the North. The CIA surmised that the mainland had been "exposed as a rather uncertain and unstable ally, and the net result may be a loss of Chinese influence in Hanoi."[109] Rusk detected a similar change in the early stages of the Cultural Revolution, noting that "Peiping ... probably had somewhat greater influence than [the] Soviets in Hanoi but [the] latter was rising."[110]

Against this backdrop, the administration believed that the USSR, presumably eager to head off a wider war, was well positioned to exert a moderating influence on the DRV. The most enthusiastic adherent to this view was Averell Harriman, who headed a committee assigned to explore possibilities for negotiations. Convinced that the road to peace went through Moscow, he urged that the Kremlin be offered "compensating inducements" – such as relieving its fears of a nuclear West Germany – for undertaking any mediatory role.[111] While less optimistic than Harriman, Johnson's inner circle saw some merit in canvassing the Soviets for support in Vietnam. Even Rostow, who thought that the Soviets' influence with its ally had been somewhat exaggerated and believed that the firm application of US military power would ultimately prove more decisive, agreed that Moscow preferred a negotiated settlement and that it was therefore necessary to "maintain as close and direct a dialogue with the USSR and Eastern Europe as we can."[112] This consideration factored heavily in the recommendations of LBJ's senior advisers for meeting Kosygin at Glassboro in June 1967.[113]

Johnson himself expressed hope for progress on peace talks once the Kremlin exhibited "the same weight that apparently the Chinese have [in Hanoi]. When the Chinese get a little weaker and the Russians stronger, we're going to have a peace."[114] Indeed, the President placed major emphasis on advancing Soviet-American détente at this time. At the beginning of 1967, he wrote Kosygin to convey "the great importance I attach to the improvement of relations between our two countries," and sent Llewellyn Thompson, the administration's most senior Kremlinologist, as his new Ambassador to Moscow.[115] In pushing aggressively for arms control measures, which would go some way in addressing the USSR's concerns of a costly arms race, Johnson may well have thought that he could encourage Soviet cooperation in securing a settlement in Vietnam.[116]

It is within the context of these efforts to enlist the Kremlin as a potential partner for peace that the Johnson team's resistance to exploiting the Sino-Soviet rivalry can be best explained. The administration in fact took several steps to assuage Soviet anxieties about any hint of Sino-American reconciliation. Rusk cited this as one of many factors in his opposition to a "two Chinas" posture in the fall of 1966. Such a move, he explained to Canadian officials, would "confront the Soviet Union with serious problems. In terms of the really serious interest the USSR and its Eastern European friends now appear to be taking toward peace in Vietnam, I doubt very much if they would feel that a new controversy on this issue would be helpful."[117] Similarly, when Thompson proposed in March 1967 that the US share some of its intelligence on mainland developments with Moscow as a conciliatory gesture to "help allay Soviet suspicions of our relations with the Chinese," senior State officials readily agreed.[118] When Senate Majority Leader Mike Mansfield sought White House approval the following month for a trip to Beijing to gauge China's interest in resolving the war in Vietnam, Rusk once again successfully voiced his misgivings. Aside from unwelcome congressional interference in a matter of national security and the implausibility of China's openness to such a visit, he insisted that even granting the request would only make the Kremlin "upset and suspicious."[119]

In short, LBJ and his advisers implicitly agreed with Brzezinski's diagnosis for peace in Vietnam – the need for Soviet pressure on the North – yet disagreed with his suggested remedy of a policy of ambiguity toward the PRC. Senior decision-makers fully recognized that the Cultural Revolution had irreparably damaged relations between Moscow and Beijing, but decided that an unambiguous tilt toward the former suited the administration's interests, particularly while the latter remained acutely militaristic and unsettled. Events in China strongly reinforced an inherent tendency among US officials, most prevalent since the Kennedy years, to regard the Soviets as the more "civilized" of the communist powers, with whom they could compromise and manage global conflict.

With the benefit of hindsight, the outbreak of the Cultural Revolution in 1966 can be seen as a watershed in US relations with the mainland, the point at which several of the perceptual preconditions for America's eventual opening to China were established. The campaign directed against Mao's "revisionist" colleagues destroyed the myth, based more on preconception than empirical proof, of an impenetrable Chinese leadership that was unanimous in its devotion to the Chairman's vision of continuous revolution. The resistance and obstruction mounted by elements of the regime, while somewhat exaggerated by China watchers, stirred guarded hopes in some quarters that domestic "moderates" such as Zhou Enlai and factions of the PLA would show a concomitant interest in relaxing international tensions. One can plausibly surmise that the decidedly optimistic reading of mainland developments in early 1967 was colored in part by an underlying desire to co-exist peacefully with a reformed China and to search for signs of common interest. The apparent waning of the Maoist forces elevated the question of how best to prepare for a post-Mao China to a pressing consideration on Washington's mainland agenda.

China's disarray, coming on the heels of a series of diplomatic setbacks in the fall of 1965, set in motion a gradual reassessment by US policymakers of the PRC's threat potential. The sole focus of Mao's Cultural Revolution, after all, was internal transformation, a project so sweeping that it dictated a lower profile in international affairs and the country's insulation from the outside world.[120] Among the consequences of this shift in emphasis, Johnson officials noted, was the targeting of domestic opponents and Soviet influence. In 1964–65, the Johnson team resisted domestic and international pressure for the adoption of a more flexible China policy out of a sense that this would be perceived as a sign of weakness by Mao and his comrades, and embolden them to foment more trouble among their neighbors. With the advent of China's intense political and social turmoil, the deferment of substantive policy reform was no longer mandated by an expansionist menace, but by the calculation that a xenophobic, inward-looking leadership would refuse to accept any olive branch offered to them. This marked a subtle, yet significant, evolution in strategic thinking.

Yet while highly significant for altering Cold War images of the PRC, the immediate impact of the Cultural Revolution on US China policy was far more complex. The twists and turns of the mainland's power struggle left most in Washington bewildered. LBJ and his aides opted for a prudent course of awaiting a definitive resolution of these events before proceeding with any major new initiatives. A posture of aloofness and relative silence, it was sensibly judged, would not pose the same risk of discrediting potentially pragmatic factions vying for the reins of leadership in China as would one of overt intervention. More importantly, the imperative of expanding relations with the mainland was gradually deemed to be less urgent. Indeed, as the mainland turned inwards and the contingency of China's military involvement in Vietnam became less apparent, the logic underpinning the extension of tentative feelers to Beijing in early 1966 – the need to relieve its fears of American intentions – lost its momentum. The Johnson team hoped that a combination of American military muscle and Soviet diplomatic pressure would prod Hanoi toward the conference table. Moscow's preoccupation with its increasingly unpredictable neighbor raised expectations among many in Washington that the Soviets would now be more willing to play a constructive role in Vietnam. To the extent that it was felt that a more accommodating stance toward the PRC would alienate the Kremlin, the administration consciously resisted the temptation to exploit the Sino-Soviet split. The cumulative effect of all of these factors, then, was a slowdown in the tentative bridge-building that had been gaining momentum during the first half of 1966. Developments on the mainland would spark Johnson's interest in reviving this very option in early 1968.

Notes

1 Garson, "Johnson and the China enigma"; Schulzinger, "The Johnson administration, China, and the Vietnam War," in Ross and Jiang (eds), *Re-examining the Cold War*, pp. 255–60; Kaufman, *Confronting Communism*, ch. 8.
2 H. Harding, "The Chinese state in crisis, 1966–9," in R. MacFarquhar (ed.), *The Politics of China: The Eras of Mao and Deng*, Second ed. (Cambridge: Cambridge University Press, 1997), p. 148.
3 Leiberthal, "The Great Leap Forward and the split in the Yan'an leadership," in ibid., pp. 87–147; MacFarquhar, *Origins of the Cultural Revolution*, vol. 3, chs 12, 15, 18–19; P. Short, *Mao: A Life* (New York: Henry Holt and Company, 2000), pp. 518–26.
4 Harding, "The Chinese state in crisis," in MacFarquhar (ed.), *The Politics of China*, pp. 165–78; Short, *Mao*, pp. 527–42; MacFarquhar, *Origins of the Cultural Revolution*, vol. 3, pp. 440–7, 452–65; R. MacFarquhar and M. Schoenhals, *Mao's Last Revolution* (Cambridge: Belknap Press of Harvard University Press, 2006), pp. 14–94.
5 Harding, "The Chinese state in crisis," in MacFarquhar (ed.), *The Politics of China*, pp. 159–61, 180–9.
6 Telegram, no. 2327, Hong Kong to Department of State, 25 June 1966, *FRUS*, 1964–1968, vol. 30, pp. 326–32.
7 Airgram, no. A-304, Hong Kong to Department of State, 25 November 1966, RG 59, Central Files, 1964–66, Box 2006, POL CHICOM 1966, NA. For similar assessments of Mao's central role, see Copy of Hong Kong's A-299 to Department of State, 18 November 1966, enclosed in W. Bundy to Rusk, 23 December 1966, RG 59, Subject Files of the Office of Asian Communist Affairs, 1961–73, Lot 71D423, Box 1, NA; Airgram, no. A-432, Hong Kong to Department of State, 27 January 1967, NSF, Country File, Box 240, folder "China cables, vol. VIII," LBJL; Airgram, no. A-478, Hong Kong to Department of State, 17 February 1967, ibid. Recent findings from Chinese archives leave no doubt as to Mao's central role in launching the Cultural Revolution. This is convincingly argued in MacFarquhar and Schoenhals, *Mao's Last Revolution*.
8 Abbot Smith to Helms, 15 July 1966, enclosed in Rostow to LBJ, 25 July 1966, NSF, Country File, Box 239, folder "China memos, vol. VI (1 of 2)," LBJL.
9 Airgram, no. A-304, Hong Kong to Department of State, 25 November 1966, p. 22, RG 59, Central Files, 1964–66, Box 2006, POL CHICOM 1966, NA.
10 ONE special memorandum, no. 14-66, "The China tangle," 23 September 1966, NSF, Country File, Box 240, folder "China memos, vol. VII," LBJL.

11 Rostow to LBJ, 9 January 1967, NSF, Memos to the President, Box 12 (1 of 2), folder "Vol. XVIII (1 of 2)," LBJL.
12 Rostow to LBJ, 13 January 1967, NSF, Country File, Box 240, folder "China memos, vol. VIII," LBJL.
13 Harding, "The Chinese state in crisis," in MacFarquhar (ed.), *The Politics of China*, pp. 190–8; Short, *Mao*, pp. 555–8; MacFarquhar and Schoenhals, *Mao's Last Revolution*, pp. 163–9.
14 For more on the February Adverse Current, see Harding, "The Chinese state in crisis," in MacFarquhar (ed.), *The Politics of China*, pp. 206–11; MacFarquhar and Schoenhals, *Mao's Last Revolution*, pp. 191–7.
15 "Anglo-American discussions on China," 14 February 1967, enclosed in E. Bolland to Nigel Trench, 14 February 1967, FCO 21/23, PRO; Trench to Bolland, 6 June 1967, ibid.
16 Airgram, no. A-432, Hong Kong to Department of State, 27 January 1967, NSF, Country File, Box 240, folder "China cables, vol. VIII," LBJL.
17 Telegram, no. 144624, Department of State to Paris, 27 February 1967, NSF, Country File, Box 240, folder "China memos, vol. VIII," LBJL. See as well Jenkins to Rostow, 15 February 1967, ibid.
18 CIA memorandum, "Chou En-Lai and the Cultural Revolution," 8 September 1967, NSF, Files of Alfred Jenkins, Box 2, folder "CHICOM: Cultural Revolution, July–December 1967," LBJL.
19 Jenkins to Rostow, 9 August 1967, NSF, Country File, Box 241, folder "China memos, vol. X," LBJL.
20 Telegram, no. 5823, Hong Kong to Department of State, 20 February 1967, RG 59, Central Files, 1967–69, Box 1966, POL 15-1 CHICOM, NA; Jenkins to Rostow, 24 February 1967, NSF, Country File, Box 240, folder "China memos, vol. VIII," LBJL.
21 Jenkins to Rostow, 3 February 1967, ibid. William Bundy proposed the creation of a panel of China experts in May 1966. He saw the benefits of setting up a forum for discussion of Chinese affairs, yet was careful enough to suggest that the panel not be empowered to make specific policy recommendations. See W. Bundy to Rusk, 5 May 1966, RG 59, Subject Files of the Office of the Assistant Secretary of State for East Asian and Pacific Affairs, 1961–74, Lot 85D240, Box 9, NA. For the State Department's press release announcing the formation of the panel, see Press Release, no. 270, 10 November 1966, ibid., Box 20, NA.
22 Jenkins to Rostow, 6 March 1967, *FRUS*, 1964–1968, vol. 30, p. 529.
23 NIE 13-7-67, "The Chinese Cultural Revolution," 25 May 1967, ibid., p. 574.
24 Text of Cable from Consul General Rice in Hong Kong (1392), 30 August 1966, NSF, Country File, Box 240, folder "China memos, vol. VII," LBJL.

25 Rostow to LBJ, 30 August 1966, *FRUS, 1964–1968*, vol. 30, p. 374.
26 Airgram, no. A-304, Hong Kong to Department of State, 25 November 1966, p. 29, RG 59, Central Files, 1964–66, Box 2006, POL CHICOM 1966, NA.
27 Ralph Clough to Jacobson, 17 January 1967, RG 59, Subject Files of the Office of Asian Communist Affairs, 1961–73, Lot 71D423, Box 1, NA. For a similar assessment, see Henry Owen to Rusk, 28 February 1967, RG 59, Policy Planning Council: Subject and Country Files, 1965–1969, Lot 72D139, Box 302, NA.
28 Jenkins to Rostow, 28 September 1967, NSF, Country File, Box 242, folder "China memos (continued), vol. XI," LBJL.
29 McNamara to LBJ, 19 May 1967, p. 17, NSF, Vietnam Country File, Box 75 (1 of 2), folder "2EE Primarily McNamara Recommendations re Strategic Actions (1967)," LBJL.
30 W. Bundy, "Comments on DOD first rough draft of 19 May," 30 May 1967, NSF, Vietnam Country File, NSF, Vietnam Country File, Box 55, folder "Vietnam misc. memos (vol. 1)," LBJL.
31 Rostow to LBJ, 8 November 1967, NSF, Memos to the President, Box 25 (1 of 2), folder "Vol. L (2 of 2)," LBJL. For similar assessments of China, see Abe Fortas to LBJ, 5 November 1967, *FRUS, 1964–1968*, vol. 5, pp. 991–2; Clark Clifford to LBJ, 7 November 1967, ibid., pp. 993–4.
32 Notes of meeting, 1 November 1967, ibid., p. 970.
33 Thomson to Jenkins, 25 July 1966, NSF, Country File, Box 239, folder "China memos, vol. VI (1 of 2)," LBJL.
34 Thomson to Rostow, 4 August 1966, NSF, Country File, Box 240, folder "China memos, vol. VII," LBJL.
35 Airgram, no. A-478, Hong Kong to Department of State, 17 February 1967, p. 15, NSF, Country File, Box 240, folder "China cables, vol. VIII," LBJL.
36 W. Bundy to Rusk, 29 March 1967, *FRUS, 1964–1968*, vol. 30, p. 542; Jenkins to Rostow, 23 June 1967, NSF, Country File, Box 241, folder "China memos (1 of 2), vol. IX," LBJL.
37 Author's interview with Rostow, Austin, Texas, 23 January 2002.
38 Jenkins to Rostow, 3 August 1966, NSF, Country File, Box 239, folder "China memos, vol. VI (1 of 2)," LBJL.
39 Jenkins to Rostow, 3 February 1967, NSF, Country File, Box 240, folder "China memos, vol. VIII," LBJL.
40 Rostow OH, Interview 1, pp. 95–6, LBJL.
41 Jenkins to Rostow, 8 November 1967, NSF, Files of Alfred Jenkins, Box 1, folder "CHICOM–Warsaw Talks," LBJL.
42 W. Bundy et al. to Rusk, 1 December 1966, *FRUS, 1964–1968*, vol. 30, pp. 472–3.

43 W. Bundy to Rusk, 6 March 1968, ibid., p. 666.
44 Memorandum of conversation, 12 April 1966, Papers of W. Averrel Harriman, Box 442, folder "China (3)," Library of Congress; Memorandum of conversation, 28 June 1966, ibid.
45 By James Thomson's own account, Moyers (much to his relief) retained the word in his revised version of Thomson's draft without any explanation. As Thomson has noted, however, the President was publicly advocating the exchange of only "ideas and people" with the PRC during his Far East tour in October 1966. See Thomson, "On the making," pp. 241–2.
46 Emphasis added. Rostow's handwritten note, Jenkins to Rostow, 9 September 1966, NSF, Files of Alfred Jenkins, Box 1, folder "CHICOM: Trade," LBJL.
47 *FRUS*, 1964–1968, vol. 30, p. 541, n. 2.
48 W. Bundy to Rusk, 29 March 1967, ibid., p. 542.
49 Administrative History of the Department of State, Box 3, chapter 7, section C, pp. 29–30, LBJL.
50 Talking points: China panel, 5–6 June 1967, RG 59, Subject Files of the Office of the Assistant Secretary of State for East Asian and Pacific Affairs, 1961–74, Lot 73D8, Box 20, NA.
51 Kusnitz, *Public Opinion and Foreign Policy*, p. 117.
52 Rostow to LBJ, 9 November 1966, NSF, Country File, Box 240, folder "China memos, vol. VII," LBJL; Rostow to LBJ, 7 July 1967, NSF, Memos to the President, Box 18 (2 of 2), folder "Vol. XXXIII (2 of 4)," LBJL.
53 Jenkins to Rostow, 8 November 1967, NSF, Files of Alfred Jenkins, Box 1, folder "CHICOM–Warsaw Talks," LBJL.
54 W. Bundy to Paul Nitze, 13 February 1967, RG 59, Subject Files of the Office of the Assistant Secretary of State for East Asian and Pacific Affairs, 1961–74, Lot 85D240, Box 4, NA.
55 Telegram, Department of State to Warsaw, 29 May 1967, *FRUS*, 1964–1968, vol. 30, p. 574.
56 Annual Message to the Congress on the State of the Union, 10 January 1967, *PPP:LBJ* 1967, vol. 1, p. 13.
57 Airgram, no. CA-5240, Department of State to All American Diplomatic and consular posts, 17 January 1967, RG 59, Central Files, 1967–69, Box 1974, POL 1 CHICOM-US, NA.
58 Katzenbach's emphasis. Nicholas Katzenbach to LBJ, 26 June 1967, NSF, Memos to the President, Box 18 (1 of 2), folder "Vol. XXXII (3 of 4)," LBJL.
59 Memorandum of conversation, 26 June 1967, *FRUS*, 1964–1968, vol. 17, p. 432. This peace feeler evidently did not produce the desired effect. When Maurer relayed LBJ's message to his Chinese hosts, he found that

they were still "obsessed that [the] US planned [an] attack and told Maurer [that] they [were] mobilizing 700 million Chinese to resist." Rostow to LBJ, 20 July 1967, NSF, Memos to the President, Box 19 (2 of 2), folder "Vol. XXXV (3 of 4)," LBJL.

60 Barnouin and Yu, *Chinese Foreign Policy During the Cultural Revolution*, pp. vii, 1–2, 16–17, 57–62, 66; Li Jie, "Changes in China's domestic situation in the 1960s and Sino-US relations," in Ross and Jiang (eds), *Re-examining the Cold War*, pp. 307–8.
61 Telegram, Warsaw to Department of State, 25 January 1967, *FRUS, 1964–1968*, vol. 30, p. 511.
62 Jenkins to Rostow, 9 August 1967, NSF, Country File, Box 241, folder "China memos, vol. X," LBJL.
63 Smith to Helms, 15 July 1966, enclosed in Rostow to LBJ, 25 July 1966, NSF, Country File, Box 239, folder "China memos, vol. VI (1 of 2)," LBJL. See as well ONE special memorandum, no. 14–66, "The China tangle," 23 September 1966, NSF, Country File, Box 240, folder "China memos, vol. VII," LBJL; Airgram, no. CA-2109, Department of State to All American diplomatic and consular posts, 15 September 1966, RG 59, Central Files, 1964–66, Box 2006, POL 1 CHICOM, NA.
64 Hughes to Rusk, 22 July 1966, NSF, Country File, Box 239, folder "China memos, vol. VI (1 of 2)," LBJL; "China's reaction bolsters US view it won't fight," 6 July 1966, *New York Times*, p. A1.
65 SNIE 13-66, "Current Chinese communist intentions in the Vietnam situation," 4 August 1966, RG 59, Policy Planning Council: Subject and Country Files, 1965–1969, Lot 72D139, Box 309, NA.
66 Hughes to Rusk, 14 July 1967, NSF, Files of Alfred Jenkins, Box 2, folder "CHICOM: Cultural Revolution, July–December 1967," LBJL.
67 Telegram, no. 2095, Hong Kong to Department of State, 21 September 1966, Papers of W. Averrel Harriman, Box 443, folder "China [8]," Library of Congress.
68 Copy of Hong Kong's A-299 to Department of State, 18 November 1966, enclosed in W. Bundy to Rusk, 23 December 1966, RG 59, Subject Files of the Office of Asian Communist Affairs, 1961–73, Lot 71D423, Box 1, NA.
69 State Department circular telegram, no. 2618, 7 July 1966, RG 59, Central Files, 1964–66, Box 2006, POL 1 CHICOM, NA.
70 W. Bundy to Rusk, 25 August 1966, RG 59, Subject Files of the Office of the Assistant Secretary of State for East Asian and Pacific Affairs, 1961–74, Lot 85D240, Box 3, NA.
71 Telegram, no. 4196, Tokyo to Department of State, 6 December 1966, RG 59, Central Files, 1964–66, Box 2006, POL CHICOM 1966, NA.
72 Dallek, *Flawed Giant*, p. 469.
73 CIA memorandum, "Communist policy and the next phase in Vietnam,"

12 April 1967, pp. 22–3, NSF, Files of Alfred Jenkins, Box 1, folder "Vietnam," LBJL; Hughes to Acting Secretary, 12 April 1967, ibid.
74 Rostow to LBJ, 6 May 1967, NSF, Files of Walt W. Rostow, Box 4, folder "Viet Nam (2)," LBJL.
75 McNamara, *In Retrospect*, p. 275.
76 McNamara to LBJ, 19 May 1967, NSF, Vietnam Country File, Box 75 (1 of 2), folder "2EE Primarily McNamara Recommendations re Strategic Actions (1967)," LBJL.
77 W. Bundy, "Bombing strategy options for the rest of 1967," 9 May 1967, NSF, Files of Walt W. Rostow, Box 4, folder "Viet Nam (2)," LBJL. See as well W. Bundy to Katzenbach, 1 May 1967, RG 59, Subject Files of the Office of the Assistant Secretary of State for East Asian and Pacific Affairs, 1961–74, Lot 85D240, Box 4, NA. For Edward Rice's direct influence on Bundy's thinking, see Telegram, no. 7581, Hong Kong to Department of State, 1 May 1967, NSF, Country File, Box 241, folder "China cables, vol. IX," LBJL.
78 L.B. Johnson, *The Vantage Point: Perspectives of the Presidency, 1963–1969* (New York: Holt, Rinehart and Winston, 1971), p. 368.
79 Herring, *LBJ and Vietnam*, pp. 54–7; Dallek, *Flawed Giant*, pp. 476–8; Clodfelter, *The Limits of Air Power*, p. 109.
80 W. Bundy to Rusk, 14 August 1967, *FRUS*, 1964–1968, vol. 5, p. 688.
81 Notes of meeting, 16 August 1967, ibid., p. 698.
82 Notes of meeting, 5 August 1967, ibid., p. 675.
83 Hughes to Rusk, 3 May 1967, RG 59, Records of Negotiations About Vietnam, 1965–69, Lot 69D277, Box 20, NA.
84 President's news conference of 18 August 1967, *PPP:LBJ* 1967, vol. 2, p. 792.
85 Clodfelter, *The Limits of Air Power*, p. 110. For the concerns of Rusk and McNamara about a strong Chinese reaction to an attack on this particular target, see Notes of Meeting, 24 August 1967, *FRUS*, 1964–1968, vol. 5, pp. 723–5.
86 For example, see Hughes to Rusk, 26 October 1967, RG 59, Central Files, 1967–69, Box 1529, DEF 19-6 CHICOM-VIET N, NA.
87 This crucial point is briefly mentioned in Kusnitz, *Public Opinion and Foreign Policy*, p. 116.
88 Barnouin and Yu, *Chinese Foreign Policy During the Cultural Revolution*, pp. 67–8.
89 Airgram, no. A-303, Hong Kong to Department of State, 29 November 1966, RG 59, Central Files, 1964–66, Box 2006, POL 1 CHICOM, NA.
90 Radchenko, "The China Puzzle,'" pp. 283–95. For the US perception of a shift in Soviet attitudes, see Hughes to Rusk, 29 November 1966, NSF, Files of Alfred Jenkins, Box 1, folder "CHICOM: Sino-Soviet Relations," LBJL.

91 Rostow to LBJ, 20 February 1967, NSF, Memos to the President, Box 13, folder "Vol. XXI (2 of 4)," LBJL.
92 Denney to Rusk, 15 March 1967, NSF, Country File, Box 241, folder "China memos, vol. IX (2 of 2)," LBJL.
93 Hughes to Rusk, 21 September 1967, NSF, Files of Alfred Jenkins, Box 1, folder "CHICOM: Sino-Soviet Relations," LBJL; NIE 11-7-67, "Soviet foreign policy," 28 September 1967, *FRUS*, 1964–1968, vol. 14, p. 590.
94 NIE 11-12-66, "The outlook For Sino-Soviet relations," 1 December 1966, *FRUS*, 1964–1968, vol. 30, pp. 479, 487.
95 Ibid., p. 485; Denney to Rusk, 15 March 1967, NSF, Country File, Box 241, folder "China memos, vol. IX (2 of 2)," LBJL. See as well Llewellyn Thompson to Rusk, 14 October 1966, *FRUS*, 1964–1968, vol. 14, p. 429.
96 Record of conversation, Wilson–Rostow, 24 February 1967, PREM 13/1893, PRO. Kosygin may well have played up his fears of Chinese militancy to Wilson in order to deter any Western interest in reaching an understanding with the PRC. For this view, see Radchenko, "The China Puzzle," p. 313.
97 Quoted in A. Dobrynin, *In Confidence: Moscow's Ambassador to America's Six Cold War Presidents* (New York: Random House, 1995), p. 641.
98 Gaiduk, *The Soviet Union and the Vietnam War*, pp. 111–12.
99 Memorandum by Zbigniew Brzezinski, 17 November 1966, RG 59, Policy Planning Council: Subject and Country Files, 1965–1969, Lot 72D139, Box 308, NA. Brzezinski returned to this idea in December 1967. See Memorandum by Brzezinski, pp. 9–11, 61–62, enclosed in Owen to Rusk, 15 December 1967, ibid.
100 Cater to LBJ, 17 January 1967, NSF, Files of Alfred Jenkins, Box 1, folder "CHICOM: Sino-Soviet Relations," LBJL.
101 Jenkins to Rostow, 19 January 1967, ibid.
102 Nathaniel Davis to Rostow, 19 January 1967, ibid.
103 SNIE 11-16-66, "Current Soviet attitudes toward the US," 28 July 1966, *FRUS*, 1964–1968, vol. 14, p. 409; Hughes to Rostow, 6 August 1966, NSF, Memos to the President, Box 9 (2 of 2), folder "Vol. X (2 of 2)," LBJL; Hughes to Rusk, 25 July 1966, NSF, Vietnam Country File, Box 34, folder "Vietnam memos (C), vol. LVI," LBJL; CIA memorandum, "The war in Vietnam," 9 January 1967, pp. 22–3, NSF, Vietnam Country File, Box 39, folder "Vietnam memos, vol. LXIII," LBJL; CIA memorandum, "Assessment of a postulated agreement on US and Soviet actions in North Vietnam," 4 August 1967, NSF, Vietnam Country File, Box 51, folder "Southeast Asia Special Intelligence Material, vol. XI,"

LBJL; Rostow to LBJ, 5 May 1967, NSF, Memos to the President, Box 16 (1 of 2), folder "Vol. XXVII (3 of 4)," LBJL.
104 CIA memorandum, "Communist policy and the next phase in Vietnam," 12 April 1967, NSF, Files of Alfred Jenkins, Box 1, folder "Vietnam," LBJL.
105 Gaiduk, *The Soviet Union and the Vietnam War*, pp. 79–80, 96–7, 109–12. The quote is taken from p. 111. See as well I.V. Gaiduk, "The Vietnam War and Soviet-American relations, 1964–1973: New Russian evidence," CWIHP *Bulletin* 6–7 (Winter 1995/1996), esp. pp. 253–5.
106 Memorandum of conversation, 14 October 1966, *FRUS*, 1964–1968, vol. 14, p. 427.
107 Zhai, *China and the Vietnam Wars*, pp. 166–71; Xiaoming Zhang, "Communist powers divided: China, the Soviet Union, and the Vietnam War," in Gardner and Gittinger (eds), *International Perspectives on Vietnam*, pp. 90–3.
108 W. Bundy to Rusk, 2 September 1966, enclosed in Leonard Unger to Rusk, 2 September 1966, RG 59, Central Files, 1964–66, Box 2020, POL CHICOM-VIET N, NA; Hughes to Rusk, 24 January 1967, RG 59, Records of Negotiations About Vietnam, 1965–69, Lot 69D277, Box 20, NA; Hughes to Acting Secretary, 21 February 1967, ibid; Rostow to LBJ, 9 June 1967, NSF, Country File, Box 241, folder "China memos (1 of 2), vol. IX," LBJL.
109 CIA memorandum, "The view from Hanoi," 30 November 1966, p. 10, NSF, Vietnam Country File, Box 39, folder "Vietnam memos (B), vol. LXII," LBJL.
110 Telegram, no. 209, Tokyo to Department of State, 9 July 1966, NSF, Country File, Box 251, folder "Japan cables, vol. IV," LBJL.
111 Harriman to LBJ and Rusk, 3 October 1966, NSF, Memos to the President, Box 11 (1 of 2), folder "Vol. XIV (1 of 2)," LBJL. See as well Harriman to LBJ and Rusk, 22 May 1967, NSF, Memos to the President, Box 16 (2 of 2), folder "Vol. XXVIII (1 of 3)," LBJL; Harriman to LBJ, 17 June 1967, W. Averrel Harriman Papers, Box 477, folder "Johnson, Lyndon and Lady Bird 1967," Library of Congress.
112 Rostow, "A strategy for Vietnam, 1967," 28 November 1966, NSF, Files of Walt W. Rostow, Box 4, folder "Viet Nam Strategy," LBJL.
113 McNamara to LBJ, 21 June 1967, *FRUS*, 1964–1968, vol. 14, p. 498; M. Bundy to LBJ, 21 June 1967, ibid., p. 499; Rostow to LBJ, 21 June 1967, ibid., p. 501.
114 Quoted in Gardner, *Pay Any Price*, p. 356.
115 Editorial Note, *FRUS*, 1964–1968, vol. 14, p. 450.
116 Gardner, "Fighting Vietnam," in Gardner and Gittinger (eds), *International Perspectives on Vietnam*, p. 46. For a brief overview of LBJ's

pursuit of arms control and non-proliferation measures in 1966–67, see Schwartz, *Lyndon Johnson and Europe*, pp. 136–8, 181–3.
117 Telegram, State Department to Ottawa, 9 November 1966, *FRUS, 1964–1968*, vol. 30, p. 421.
118 Samuel D. Berger to Rusk, 1 March 1967, RG 59, Central Files, 1967–69, Box 1972, POL CHICOM-US, NA. Rusk's approval of this idea is initialled at the bottom of the page.
119 Rostow to LBJ, 30 April 1967, NSF, Memos to the President, Box 15, folder "Vol. XXVI (1 of 4)," LBJL.
120 Robinson, "China confronts the Soviet Union," in MacFarquhar and Fairbank (eds), *Cambridge History of China*, vol. 15, pp. 218, 231–8.

6 Testing the waters
An aborted policy review and closing moves, 1968–69

As the Johnson administration entered what would be its final year in office, its brief flirtation with policy experimentation had given way to a mostly reactive posture, as both the timing and nature of new approaches to the PRC awaited the outcome of the Cultural Revolution. While it challenged long-held assumptions about the mainland's domestic and foreign politics, the onset of this turmoil in 1966 dislodged China policy from the President's crowded agenda. LBJ was kept fully apprised of mainland developments, yet various trade and travel initiatives that had piqued the interest of the White House were shelved indefinitely. As much as the suspension of further bridge-building was a logical response to the virtual civil war engulfing China, it was also in accordance with the modus operandi of a highly cautious national security team inherently suspicious of bold foreign policy ventures, and whose attention and imagination was consumed by the war in Vietnam. The dominant refrain among US officials throughout 1967 was that the unsettled, inhospitable climate in Beijing militated against any sustained engagement with the mainland. LBJ's National Security Adviser doubted that there would be any "appreciable reciprocation during the Maoist era from any attempted rapproachment [sic]."[1]

This sentiment seemed to imply an openness to Sino-American accommodation should circumstances prove more favorable, as they appeared to in early 1968 when reports of a potential turning point in the Cultural Revolution reached Washington. This chapter discusses LBJ's ensuing interest in exploring means of nurturing moderate elements in Beijing, and the factors – domestic and strategic – that ultimately derailed this policy review. It then looks at a final opportunity for reform in the last few weeks of Johnson's tenure in office, as an intriguing offer by the Chinese to revive the moribund Warsaw talks in late November prompted further consideration of an appropriate response, most prominently from the administration's most ardent hard-liner, Dean Rusk. The moment for major departures, however, proved fleeting as the Johnson team focused on transferring power to their successors. The lack of tangible initiatives notwithstanding, an examination of this period is most instructive, as it marked a further thawing of high-level attitudes toward the PRC and a resultant readiness to ponder alternative approaches.

A turning point in the Cultural Revolution?

Developments on the mainland continued to unfold at a pace that left many in Washington perplexed. While US officials discerned a marked shift toward moderation in early 1967 after the military was invited to assist the masses in "seizing power," the year in fact witnessed several twists and turns in China's domestic crisis. The PLA's intervention in Chinese politics reflected a preference among some central authorities for restoring order and reining in the Red Guards, yet the army's new role was by no means unanimously welcomed by all of the country's contending factions. For the leaders of the Cultural Revolution Group (CRG), whose institutional interests and ideological leanings diverged substantially from those of the army, suspicions were heightened during the so-called February Adverse Current, when senior PLA officials and like-minded allies in the Party voiced their misgivings with the prevailing disorder. Mao viewed this criticism as a challenge to his leadership and an impediment to his ongoing campaign against his revisionist rivals. With the Chairman's tacit support, the CRG exploited the pretext of a counter-revolutionary movement in their own bid for power. Regional military commanders, many of whom sympathized with local veteran cadres, were subsequently ordered to refrain from any harassment of radical mass organizations.

Tensions between the CRG and the armed forces came to a head in July. Emboldened by the exhortations of the former, Red Guards in Wuhan organized protests against local leaders resisting central directives. A conservative group composed mostly of Wuhan's Party members, calling itself the "Million Heroes," emerged to counter these pressures. When a delegation of the CRG arrived from Beijing to endorse the radicals and reprimand the military's region command, they were promptly taken captive by a local garrison. This nascent rebellion against central authority was quickly suppressed, yet the fallout from the Wuhan Incident proved momentous for the direction in which Mao chose to steer his political movement. Returning to a hero's welcome in Beijing, Wang Li, one of those who had been detained, argued that the affair necessitated a decisive push against the Cultural Revolution's enemies. With the apparent backing of Lin Biao and Mao's wife Jiang Qing, Wang outlined his views in an August editorial of *Red Flag*, calling for an offensive against the "handful of military leaders taking the capitalist road."

While the Chairman had expressed his displeasure with the army's support of conservative workers' groups and floated the idea of arming students, Wang's proposal for an assault on the PLA evidently went too far. Denouncing the editorial as a "poisonous weed," Mao ordered the arrest of Wang and his associates. As the only institution capable of bringing an end to the armed struggles raging throughout the country, the military was authorized to use force against radical groups and it increasingly assumed a pre-eminent role in the provincial revolutionary committees. Having rid himself of most of his rivals in the higher echelons of the Party and eager to consolidate his gains, Mao turned his attention in the fall of 1967 toward the reconstruction of China's political system, which was to be pivoted on a cleansed and reformed CCP.[2]

Johnson officials watched these events with great interest. Upon completing his service in Hong Kong in September, Edward Rice delivered a cautious assessment. He believed that China remained mired in a stalemate, with no faction having yet attained a position of supremacy and no consistent or coherent guidance flowing from the center. Still, he saw the PLA's most recent rehabilitation as evidence that pragmatists had mounted a tenacious effort to wrest the reins of power from the CRG. While any definitive reading of China's stormy political climate remained premature, Rice surmised that Mao's excesses had provoked the emergence of an alliance of convenience between the Zhou-led bureaucracy and conservative elements in the army. He was convinced that ultimately Mao "cannot win and consolidate supreme power."[3]

This was the prevailing sentiment in subsequent reports from varying sources, many of which reached LBJ's desk. Indeed, it was commonly assumed that the Chairman's leadership was the primary casualty of this apparent conservative resurgence. Mao, who seems to have deliberately opted for stability as the Cultural Revolution threatened to veer out of control, was seen instead by many US analysts as a senile old man with an irrational and self-destructive predilection for continuous upheaval. The CIA concluded that he "has always been an apostle of violence and revolutionary mass action ... and probably will never be satisfied with stability achieved at the expense of his revolutionary programs."[4] Alfred Jenkins, the principal China watcher for the White House, was struck by what he saw as the Chinese leader's detachment from reality and his stubborn resistance to the advances of the moderate Zhou-PLA camp: "Mao shows no understanding that the Cultural Revolution did not work, cannot work, and already has proven to be a near disaster." Jenkins believed that the "military are still the people to watch. Their power continues to grow. In coming weeks they may well quietly shelve most of the by now probably generally hated group around Mao, declare Mao's thought to have triumphed and proceed to run the country in an un-Mao-like manner."[5] The events of August suggested that the army had already "begun to 'insulate' Mao."[6]

Washington was encouraged in so far as the Chairman's presence was regarded as an impediment to any eventual Sino-American reconciliation. A State Department paper prepared for Johnson in early 1968 affirmed that any change in Chinese attitudes toward the US was highly unlikely as long as the wily revolutionary retained influence. Nevertheless, the moderating trend of recent months was cause for hope. The PLA's assertion of power represented a forceful rejoinder to, and weariness with, Mao's recklessness. As new leaders focused on recovering from the mayhem of the Cultural Revolution and putting the country's house back in order, this preoccupation with domestic concerns raised the probability for "a re-examination of the premises and priorities of China's foreign policy."[7]

The waxing and waning of the Cultural Revolution's fervor naturally spilled over into China's foreign relations. As they maneuvered for advantage in the aftermath of the Wuhan Incident, the CRG radicals, in addition to targeting the army, stepped up their attack on the diplomatic establishment. In an incendiary speech delivered on 7 August without Mao's apparent knowledge or approval, Wang Li encouraged rebels in the Foreign Ministry to weed out their superiors. The words had their effect. Barely one week later, Foreign Minister Chen Yi's deputies were imprisoned and provocative orders issued to Chinese representatives stationed abroad. The chaos peaked with the burning of the office of the British charge d'affaires on 22 August. When finally informed of these actions, Mao reacted swiftly. Alarmed by China's international isolation, particularly as the perceived Soviet threat steadily escalated, he authorized a sharp reversal in the country's diplomacy. Zhou and Chen gradually regained their influence in the latter half of 1967 and ideology was de-emphasized in favor of a more traditional, interest-based policy. Mao specifically forbade agitation by Chinese diplomats and criticized the promotion of Mao Zedong Thought as an unwelcome intrusion in the domestic affairs of other countries.[8]

The Johnson administration was alert to this change in tone and welcomed it as a sign that the "professional" old-line bureaucracy, intent on restoring "some semblance of normalcy and amity to Peking's diplomacy," was in the ascendant.[9] A CIA report in early 1968 quoted Zhou as telling a meeting of Afro-Asian leaders that he had been "greatly disturbed about China's image abroad and ... was now in firm control of China's foreign policy."[10] Most intriguingly, Ambassador Gronouski, who had been discouraged by his conversations with the Chinese in Warsaw throughout 1967, reported directly to Rusk that an encounter in early January had been distinguished by "a sharp downturn in invective as compared to each of the other meetings in which I have participated, and a complete absence of reference to the cultural revolution and the sayings of Chairman Mao." The Chinese had reverted to their traditional position that the dispute over Taiwan was the most pressing issue in Sino-American relations, rather than US opposition to world revolution. Gronouski echoed the findings of the intelligence community, attributing this apparent about-face to the "downgrading of the influence on foreign policy of hard-nosed Cultural Revolution types." As a gesture of goodwill, he suggested that Washington end its stance of silence toward the mainland's political conflict and arrange for either LBJ or Rusk to deliver "a major speech designed to appeal to and encourage the moderate element in Communist China. If the Chinese posture at this meeting was designed to signal a positive change in China's policy toward us ... it is important for us to quickly respond."[11] While somewhat less optimistic, Jenkins agreed that the latest Warsaw session was "an additional indication that the more extreme phase of the Cultural Revolution may be over."[12] Similarly encouraged by signs of a new Chinese approach, Under Secretary of State Katzenbach instructed both the East Asian bureau and the Policy Planning Council to prepare a study on how a Sino-American rapprochement might unfold.[13]

This heightened interest in reappraising the US posture was undoubtedly influenced as well by a more nuanced, less alarmist reading of the PRC's threat potential. Indeed, a notable feature of the various Asian crises confronting the administration in early 1968 was the degree to which the role of a hobbled China, which had for long been seen as the primary instigator or beneficiary of America's troubles in the region, was judged to be marginal. One such example was North Korea's seizure of the USS *Pueblo* on 23 January. As befitted their Cold War mindset, the Johnson team assumed that Pyongyang had coordinated its action with a major communist patron, yet blame was initially cast on the Soviets. When North Vietnam launched the Tet Offensive only days later, senior decision-makers concluded that the *Pueblo* incident had been concocted as a ploy to distract Washington's attention from that impending attack.[14] The PRC did not figure prominently in either interpretation. Intelligence officials carefully noted how relations between China and North Korea had deteriorated since the mid-1960s, as the mainland became engulfed by internal turmoil and Pyongyang expanded links to Moscow to counterbalance Chinese influence. Beijing's delayed public acknowledgement of the *Pueblo* affair only served to confirm how estranged the allies had become from one another.[15] "The Chinese were not involved in the Pueblo thing," William Bundy remarked to Rusk. "They were not the ones that most concern us."[16]

Sino-Vietnamese tensions, bubbling beneath the surface since 1965, broke out into the open in 1968 and offered dramatic evidence of wartime partners working at cross-purposes. Hanoi's decision at the end of January to switch to the offensive by attacking urban centers in the South diverged sharply from Mao's strategy of protracted people's war, which emphasized guerrilla warfare in the countryside. The DRV's change in tactics irritated China's leaders, as it threatened to provoke a strong American counter-response, then forcing them to choose between withdrawing their support of the North or sustaining it at the risk of being drawn into a war with the US. Beijing's sense that it was steadily losing influence over the direction of its ally's policies was sharpened in early April when Hanoi, without consulting the mainland, responded to LBJ's 31 March offer of a partial bombing halt and peace talks by agreeing to negotiations. Mao's unstinting opposition to a peace process stemmed from the same fear that had determined his position since the outset of the war: that it would invariably be dominated by the Soviets and Americans, possibly serving as a launching pad for collusion against regional national liberation struggles or, more ominously, against the PRC itself. China's disillusionment with its ally set in motion a prolonged and subtle process of disengagement from the Vietnam War, beginning with the first withdrawal of Chinese armed forces from the North in the spring of 1968.[17]

The stark divergence of opinion between Beijing and Hanoi on the advisability of peace talks was particularly revealing. As UN Secretary General U Thant noted to Johnson, it was "important that Peking has not broadcast Hanoi's statement [on accepting the US proposal for negotiations] ... Hanoi ignored Peking ... Hanoi doesn't care about Peking's attitude. These are factors that indicate Hanoi is somewhat independent of Peking."[18] The President received the same message from his own advisers. Intelligence information collected throughout the year documented a steep decline in the Sino-Vietnamese relationship, as attested by numerous staged demonstrations against DRV consulates in China, the interruption of Chinese deliveries to the North, and Beijing's less effusive pubic backing of its comrade.[19] High-level assumptions of a close Sino-Vietnamese axis, so prevalent as the pivotal decisions for American intervention were made in 1965, gave way to an understanding that the two communist powers acted according to their own national interests. The notion that North Vietnam served as the PRC's proxy in undermining American influence in Southeast Asia now seemed increasingly far-fetched; Johnson admitted in the summer of 1968, "We cannot certify how much influence on Hanoi China is."[20] Rusk, for whom military involvement in Vietnam had been seen as part of the struggle against international communism, acknowledged in an interview at the time that he no longer regarded Beijing as the "real enemy" in the war.[21]

By this point, reference to China as a justification for continuing the war was almost completely dropped from official pronouncements and appeared with even less frequency within government circles. Vietnam had instead become so inextricably linked to LBJ's political leadership that a withdrawal, as he saw it, would be tantamount to an admission of failure and a humiliation from which he might not recover.[22] The war had developed a momentum of its own, assuming a symbolic status of presidential resolve that was far more important than the strategic factors that had first prompted American intervention. A highly sensitive CIA study prepared specifically for Johnson in September 1967 in fact postulated that the drawbacks of an unfavorable outcome in Vietnam, while potentially serious, could be mostly offset by convincing regional allies that America would remain steadfast in support of their defense. In so far as China was concerned, while it would undoubtedly seek to take advantage of an American setback and displace US influence, its persistent domestic difficulties would hinder any overtly aggressive action.[23] Other analyses reached broadly similar conclusions. A State Department report that Rusk forwarded to the President in early 1968 affirmed that "Peking's internal problems will somewhat reduce the degree of pressure [on its Southeast Asian neighbors] from what would have been foreseen prior to the Cultural Revolution, and specifically in the 1965 period when the US made its major decision on Viet Nam."[24]

The China policy review

Against this backdrop of evolving attitudes, LBJ perceived a sense of opportunity and, for the first time since the spring and summer of 1966, became actively involved in China policy deliberations.[25] Johnson's renewed interest in a push for expanded contacts with Beijing, as outlined in an off the record session with a reporter, was twofold. With relatively moderate factions evidently on the rise, he voiced hope that increased interaction with the outside world might encourage the Chinese to behave more responsibly. More immediately, he entertained the notion that heightened Sino-American dialogue would unnerve Hanoi.[26] Publicly, the President declared that he saw "some very important things taking place right in China today that will contribute to, we hope, a better understanding and a more moderate approach to their neighbors in the world."[27] Johnson's intriguing, if unsuccessful, bid to convey America's benign intentions through Romanian intermediaries in June 1967 was the first indication of a less passive response to the Cultural Revolution. His State of the Union address in January 1968 suggested that the administration was flirting with a strategy of offering tangible bridge-building gestures as a means of signalling to potential successors that the option of a new Sino-American relationship existed. In contrast to the vague aspirations for "reconciliation" with the PRC articulated in the previous year's speech to Congress, delivered at a time when the hope for reciprocity from Beijing was at its nadir, the President outlined specific proposals for "the travel of journalists to both our countries ... cultural and educational exchanges ... [and] the exchange of basic food crop materials."[28]

As a reflection of his heightened interest in Chinese affairs, Johnson met with a group of prominent Sinologists on 2 February to discuss the merits of adopting more ambitious initiatives. Urging LBJ to build on the conciliatory rhetoric of his 12 July 1966 speech, the scholars – among them, Edwin Reischauer, A. Doak Barnett, and Lucian Pye – presented a familiar list of items (trade and travel liberalization, "two Chinas" in the UN) on which action needed to be taken sooner rather than later. Hoping to appeal to Johnson's political instincts, they argued that enacting these measures would display a far-sighted ability to "look beyond present crises" and satisfy the desire of elite and popular opinion alike in the US for "a more flexible approach" to China. Meeting only days after the beginning of the Tet Offensive, however, Johnson was clearly preoccupied with "present crises." Improved relations with the PRC, he replied, "was only one thing the public was interested in ... It was also interested in Vietnam. That is the great cost of Vietnam – because of it we do not get the chance to do some of the other things which would be desirable." Still, he asked the group to set their ideas down on paper, noted his interest in having a senior China expert in government akin to a Llewellyn Thompson or Charles Bohlen for the USSR, and directed both the State Department and National Security Council to offer recommendations.[29]

The President's invitation afforded the academics an opportunity to elaborate on the rationale for substantive policy reform. The resultant memorandum reasoned that the mainland's disorder, precisely the factor cited by many administration officials as cause for caution, called for a bold approach. With the very real possibility of a new leadership emerging in Beijing, one willing to consider departures from Maoist dogma, it was "particularly important for us at this time to exercise imaginative initiatives which will broaden in a desirable way the options open to them." The authors made it clear that inducing Mao's successors to shed the policies of the past required an adjustment in America's own attitude, that is, a willingness "to recognize China's legitimate interests as a major power" and "to diminish the friction and psychological pressures the Chinese feel from what they regard to be our close-in military encirclement."[30] Forwarding his comments on the paper to Johnson, an evidently skeptical Rostow counselled against immediately acting on the Sinologists' agenda. While not averse to demonstrations of flexibility toward the PRC, he believed that much of this had already been accomplished in the last couple of years and that the administration continued to be well served by waiting for a "further maturing of the fundamental changes taking place on the mainland ... [and] staying out of this Chinese muddle."[31]

Rostow's wariness was heavily influenced by Alfred Jenkins' contribution to the administration's review of China policy, an eleven-page paper composed in February. Employing the same logic he had used since the outset of the Cultural Revolution, Jenkins, notwithstanding the perceived glimmer of hope for a moderate successor regime, essentially advocated staying the course and "keeping relatively quiet while mainland China is trying to sort itself out." The option of major policy reform as outlined by many in the academic community was at best futile and at worst counter-productive. While Mao's grip on power appeared to be faltering, he retained, at least in the short term, sufficient clout to reject any US overture. Reconciliation with a Mao-led China was virtually impossible, since this was anathema to the Chairman's raison d'etre: "He believes that he can keep his revolution pure, and wound up, only through class hatred at home and devil hatred abroad." While the scholars insisted that the unlikelihood of Chinese reciprocity should not deter new initiatives, Jenkins reasoned that taking action now could unwittingly undermine the long-term project of Sino-American reconciliation. Should a pattern of repeated Chinese rejection of American feelers be established, this would tie the hands of Mao's heirs in so far as *"a successor regime may well feel sufficient continuity with the present one so as to make renunciation of that record awkward* ... the prospect of a different China to come, possibly readier to respond, recommends the waiting game."

Accordingly, Jenkins' policy recommendations were modest and mostly cosmetic, aimed only at altering some of the atmospherics of the administration's present approach to the PRC. While continuing to oppose Beijing's admission to the UN, he believed that China's international isolation now enabled the US "to twist arms in New York with less ferocity and anxiety on the Chinese Representation issue," as a nod to European and Afro-Asian sentiment. Similarly, he favored retaining most trade controls against the mainland, yet thought that "removing the opprobrious 'trading with the enemy' label" would demonstrate "readiness for *future* flexibility by moving slightly from the total embargo wicket," a welcome departure from the "former black-and-white days in China policy."[32]

The decisive voice, as always, belonged to Dean Rusk, whose sensitive political antennae continued to be a source of comfort and reassurance to Johnson. Rusk is most notoriously remembered for publicly invoking in October 1967 the specter of "a billion Chinese on the mainland, armed with nuclear weapons, with no certainty about what their attitude toward the rest of Asia will be."[33] This remark, uttered in response to a journalist's query about the continuing relevancy of fighting in Vietnam, has been taken out of context and suggests an almost irrational fear and loathing of the Chinese communists that is in fact overstated.[34] While instinctively more predisposed toward a hard-line on China than LBJ or his colleagues, the Secretary had carefully watched events on the mainland. The upheaval reinforced his natural aversion to any major initiative, as evidenced by his firm objection to a "two Chinas" formula during the fall of 1966. Yet it is also clear that the Cultural Revolution effected a significant alteration of Rusk's understanding of the PRC's role in Vietnam, particularly as signs of Sino-Vietnamese differences emerged with greater frequency. He was also converted to the view that the prevailing chaos in China called for restrained force against the DRV, lest the ire of the increasingly erratic Chinese were provoked. Moreover, the apparent ebbing of the Maoists in the latter half of 1967 evidently stirred Rusk's interest in probing the intentions of the Chairman's potential successors. In December, for example, he asked the Policy Planning Council to explore "the feasibility of bringing Peking into international technical organizations, as a means of augmenting mainland China's contacts with the outside world."[35]

Rusk's recommendations to Johnson in February 1968 indicated that he saw some advantage in taking additional steps: discarding the ban on travel to the mainland and modifying trade restrictions, particularly those pertaining to US subsidiaries abroad, and perhaps permitting the export of foodstuffs, fertilizer, insecticides, and farm machinery to the PRC. An accompanying memorandum produced by State Department analysts affirmed that it was in "the interest of the U.S. to present to a potential or emerging Chinese leadership a variety of options and alternatives to their present policies."[36] Yet like Jenkins, although for different reasons, Rusk opposed the wide-ranging program advanced by the academics. He remained irrevocably hostile to seating the mainland in the UN. While Jenkins' misgivings revolved around the matter of proper timing, the Secretary expressed his consistent belief that "we can take only very limited steps since our firm posture in Asia generally remains crucial and any significant 'concessions' to Communist China would be seriously misunderstood in key quarters, not to mention the Congress."[37]

Notwithstanding this tentative endorsement of modest bridge-building, Rusk's proposals for trade and travel liberalization never reached the President's desk.[38] The most obvious explanation for the aborted policy review is that the administration was simply swept up by the extraordinary domestic turmoil of 1968, the search for a negotiated settlement in Vietnam, and the distraction provided by a presidential election. Political calculations, as always, played a major role. Although many in the academic community maintained that the depoliticization of China policy afforded the Johnson team considerable leeway in adopting new measures, there was lingering skepticism within government circles. The contrast in the political contexts of 1966, when public pressure for a relaxation of policy mounted in the aftermath of Fulbright's China hearings, and 1968, when the Cultural Revolution still appeared to be at its zenith, was telling. In lieu of a compelling political rationale for action, some contended that changing policy was not only unnecessary but, as Rusk implied in his memorandum to the President, might only succeed in providing ammunition for the administration's enemies in a heated election year. As one State Department official explained his opposition to lifting the travel ban, "The change being recommended would please certain liberal elements in the Congress, but it is not something they are pressing for ... The only important result would be to stir up certain conservative elements who would have a negative reaction ... we would create more trouble for ourselves ... without in any appreciable way gaining new support for the President."[39]

At any rate, Johnson's landmark address of 31 March 1968, in which he announced his withdrawal from the presidential race, confined him to the unenviable status of a political lame duck for most of the year, which considerably restricted his own authority. Rostow later insisted that had he not been politically handicapped, LBJ would have charted a new course in China policy without hesitation. The President, according to his aide, was sensitive as well to the needs of his successor, whomever that might be, and did not wish to tie his hands by undertaking bold departures so close to the transfer of power.[40] While plausible, Rostow's claim suggests more momentum for advancing relations with the PRC than in fact existed. For example, Johnson seems not to have been discouraged either by his diminished political standing or by the possible concerns of the next administration in his last-ditch efforts to secure a strategic arms deal with the Soviets; his ambitions were crushed only by Moscow's decidedly inconvenient invasion of Czechoslovakia in August 1968.[41]

Even as they detected significant changes taking place on the mainland, US decision-makers continued to view China policy through the prism of Vietnam, as merely one component of a far greater whole. The decisive consideration in the spring of 1968 was the Johnson team's judgement that new initiatives toward the mainland clashed with more pressing regional concerns. LBJ's offer of a partial bombing halt and peace negotiations with the DRV in the aforementioned 31 March speech aggravated old divisions between his civilian and military advisers. Arrayed on one side were Rusk, Rostow, Ellsworth Bunker (the US ambassador in Saigon), and the Joint Chiefs of Staff, all of whom thought that the North had been dealt a shattering blow during the Tet Offensive. Skeptical of the value of peace talks and opposed to any sell-out of South Vietnam, they advised the President to move very deliberately and to sustain military pressure against Hanoi as a means of enhancing America's bargaining position. Newly appointed Defense Secretary Clark Clifford, Katzenbach, and Averell Harriman (the envoy to the talks) were critical of this approach. This camp urged Johnson to disengage gradually from the war and resist any escalatory action that threatened to derail the peace process. Ever the cautious consensus-seeker, LBJ sought to straddle the issue. As George Herring has written, "Torn between wanting out of Vietnam and his fear of losing, he veered erratically between a hard line and a softer position." While the President rejected any expansion of the fighting in the North, he authorized intensified operations in the South. Siding with Rusk and Rostow, he was reluctant to extend any concessions to the DRV without the promise of reciprocation.[42]

The consequent emphasis on a tough negotiating stance dampened any enthusiasm for conciliatory gestures toward Beijing, either from the US or its allies. When the new Canadian government of Pierre Trudeau announced its intention of recognizing the PRC, Johnson officials expressed concern that this move could have damaging effects at the conference table. "Such an initiative," Bundy warned the Canadian ambassador in June, "would give encouragement to hard liners, both within Communist China itself and in Hanoi, and this might well rub off on [the] North Vietnamese position in the Paris talks."[43]

Moreover, many within the administration continued to hold that any change in strategy toward the PRC had to take into consideration the sensitivities of Asian allies. Even as the strategic threat posed by China appeared to recede, US decision-makers were convinced that stability in the Pacific rested, as it had since the end of the Second World War, on these nations having the necessary resolve to rebuff communist subversion. This could only derive from confidence in American credibility and adherence to its security commitments, a perception that had underpinned Washington's decision to take a stand in South Vietnam. Katzenbach touched on this thinking in a speech delivered in early 1968. "Whether China is truly an expansionist country, or whether it is too consumed in its own domestic problems ... to follow its aggressive words with aggressive deeds, is a debatable matter," he noted. "But the nervousness of its neighbors is not debatable at all. It is a very palpable thing."[44]

These words took on added significance in the aftermath of 31 March, as Seoul and Bangkok, among other stalwart allies, openly expressed apprehension that Johnson's declared interest in a Vietnam settlement portended a wider abandonment of the region to the communist powers.[45] In this context, holding the line on China was seen as a means by which a gradual withdrawal from Vietnam could be made more palatable to these governments, charges of appeasement offset, and allegiance to America's regional leadership preserved. Jenkins reported to Rostow in June that a modest trade package was being held "in abeyance largely because of [the] reaction of peripheral friendly countries to the President's March 31 statement and the Paris talks ... i.e., fears that we are becoming soft on communism."[46] Bundy also expressed second thoughts on relaxing the trade embargo in the spring, arguing that this could be "seriously over-interpreted as an indication of a major shift in our East Asian policy."[47]

While the melee of the Cultural Revolution, the imperatives of firm negotiating in Paris, and the concerns of Asian friends made it a highly inauspicious time for major departures in China policy, the Johnson team reverted to their practice of signalling interest in lower tensions and broadened contacts with the mainland through less controversial, symbolic channels. In early May, the US Information Agency issued an invitation to Chinese journalists to cover the presidential campaign.[48] Most significantly, Under Secretary Katzenbach broke the administration's calculated silence on the PRC on 21 May, delivering the first extended remarks on China since LBJ's 12 July 1966 address. This satisfied in part the urgings of officials like Gronouski for a formal high-level response to recent developments. Katzenbach's speech to the National Press Club amounted to a restatement of many of the broad conclusions that had already been reached in private and a justification of Washington's stand pat approach. While taking note of the PLA-led attempts to "reorganize and stabilize political and administrative organizations" throughout the country, he stressed that the "dominant element" in Beijing's leadership still clung to the dogma that "easing tensions with the United States would represent a betrayal of the revolution." Confronted with this intransigence and the PRC's unreasonable demands for the "control" of Taiwan, any movement toward Sino-American diplomatic relations or a loosening of trade controls was simply "unrealistic."

The general thrust of the speech, however, was decidedly mild and in some respects went beyond the conciliatory bridge-building language of recent years. As one British official wrote approvingly, it was "an energetic repudiation of the policy of containment at least in its old and unsophisticated form ... [and] serves as a useful reminder of how far the official attitude to China has evolved during the Kennedy and Johnson administrations."[49] Most pointedly, Katzenbach acknowledged that the threat posed by the mainland "can be, and perhaps at times has been, exaggerated" and recognized that the PRC "has legitimate security interests of its own in Asia." As evidence of Washington's benign intentions, he reminded his audience that the US had not attempted to exploit "the many occasions when the mainland was weak or wracked by internal problems." In what had now become standard procedure, the Under Secretary reiterated the Hilsmanesque line that any Chinese desire for improved relations would be enthusiastically reciprocated, offering as a possible inducement a willingness to issue visas to Chinese visitors.[50]

These soothing words, of course, did not tell the whole story. The speech in part served the defensive purpose of shifting blame for the Sino-American deadlock to the Chinese for domestic and international consumption. And while it was contended, correctly to be sure, that Maoist orthodoxy posed a formidable impediment to a thaw in relations, LBJ's telling remark on "the great cost of Vietnam" to the academics in February suggested that the Johnson team remained hostage to their own mindset, one shaped and framed by that simmering war. American intervention in Vietnam, Jenkins postulated to superiors who needed little convincing, had not only purchased "valuable time for non-communist Asia," but had also "exacerbate[d] policy differences in Peking, contributing to the disunity and weakness of our self-proclaimed adversary." It therefore followed that "the very degree of success of our present policies toward China recommends caution in altering them, until the nature of China itself is more clearly altered."[51] Katzenbach's speech, then, perfectly encapsulated the contradictory forces of change and paralysis that had characterized US China policy since the spring of 1966: bold, forward-looking rhetoric and cautious, minute substantive action.[52]

A new signal from Beijing

The last six months of Lyndon Johnson's presidency witnessed stirrings of change on both sides of the Pacific, with momentous implications for the future. America's prolonged disengagement from Vietnam, set in motion by the President's 31 March announcement, coincided with a dramatic escalation of the Soviet threat to China's security. The invasion of Czechoslovakia in August, the Kremlin's subsequent assertion that it had the right to intervene in the affairs of other socialist states, and mounting tensions on the Sino-Soviet border accelerated a reordering of priorities in the PRC's foreign policy already underway since the waning of the Cultural Revolution. This did not escape the attention of US officials. "In the wake of the Czech developments," Jenkins observed, "the Chinese evidently consider the Soviets rather than the U.S. as the primary threat."[53]

As China's strategic environment changed, so too did the thinking of its leaders. Mao and Zhou came to question the viability of sustaining hostile competition with both Moscow and Washington; a tilt toward the latter could deter a possible Soviet strike against the mainland or, perhaps more importantly, derail what some perceived as an emerging Soviet-American condominium in Asia aimed at containing China.[54] Increasingly concerned about Soviet intentions, Mao asked four senior military commanders in early 1969 to monitor closely international developments. While the outbreak of border clashes in March and August of that year appeared to portend a more aggressive Soviet posture toward the PRC, the marshals concluded in September that Moscow's readiness to attempt a decisive blow ultimately "depends on the attitude of the US imperialists." Indeed, the

Kremlin's persistent worries over "possible Sino-American unity makes it more difficult for them to launch an all-out attack on China." In this context, it made strategic sense to unnerve the Soviets and heighten their calculation of risk by dropping hints of a new approach to the Americans.[55]

Well before he saw this report, Mao demonstrated interest in playing the American card. According to some accounts, he was considerably encouraged by an article that Richard Nixon, the eventual Republican nominee for President in the 1968 election, wrote for *Foreign Affairs* in October 1967.[56] In the chronicling of the thaw in Sino-American relations, Nixon's piece has been accorded prominent symbolic status, a landmark of sorts in America's evolving attitudes toward the PRC and a notable point of departure from the rigid policy stance of his predecessors.[57] Nixon's National Security Adviser Henry Kissinger, unsurprisingly, has encouraged this view. Taking full credit for the opening to China, he claims that Nixon's article was only the first in a series of conscious efforts to change the tenor of Sino-American relations by discarding the Johnson team's confrontational approach.[58]

This line of argument both overlooks the bridge-building initiatives of the Johnson years and exaggerates the groundbreaking nature of Nixon's overture. There was in fact nothing in the article that had not already been articulated by Johnson officials, including the President. In an oft-quoted passage, Nixon wrote, "Any American policy toward Asia must come urgently to grips with the reality of China ... Taking the long view, we simply cannot afford to leave China forever outside the family of nations, there to nurture its fantasies, cherish its hates and threaten its neighbors." Yet he coupled this moderation with an unyielding insistence that the US should not be "rushing to grant recognition to Peking, to admit it to the United Nations and to ply it with offers of trade – all of which would serve to confirm its rulers in their present course." Like those in government, Nixon believed that the Cultural Revolution served as confirmation that Beijing remained a hostile and unpredictable adversary; the imperative of new approaches to the mainland did not obviate the need for its containment. The most pressing objective for US decision-makers was to strengthen the countries of non-communist Asia so as to make them impervious to Chinese-inspired subversion, much like how the consolidation of the Atlantic Alliance had deterred the Soviets from pursuing their expansionist ambitions in Western Europe. In the "short run," a modification of China's threatening behavior could only be effected via "a policy of firm restraint, of no reward, of a creative counter-pressure designed to persuade Peking that its interests can be served only by accepting the basic rules of international civility."[59] Thus Mao's decision to respond positively on 25 November 1968 to a US proposal for resuming the stalled ambassadorial talks in Warsaw likely stemmed not so much from the sense that the newly elected Nixon team, soon set to take office, offered a stark alternative to the Johnson line of "containment without isolation," but from the pragmatic calculation that he would be dealing with this administration for at least the next four years.

The Chinese offer to meet on 20 February 1969, accompanied by a call for agreeing to principles of co-existence, stirred considerable interest among US officials. Did this signify a turning point in Chinese foreign relations and, if so, how should it be reciprocated? The reaction, on balance, was one of cautious optimism. Mid-level China watchers at Foggy Bottom interpreted the development as another welcome sign that moderate elements of the regime had asserted control over Chinese diplomacy. These elements, it was assumed, were preoccupied with breaking out of the international isolation wrought by the PRC's steadfast opposition to the Paris peace talks and "test[ing], at little actual cost, [the] intentions of [the] new US administration by seeming [to] take [a] more conciliatory position."[60] The consulate office in Hong Kong reported that its contacts in Beijing believed the move was a genuine effort to improve relations with the US in view of the heightened Soviet threat.[61] The office was more guarded in its own assessment, agreeing with those at the State Department who regarded the Warsaw offer as a defensive reaction to China's exclusion from regional diplomacy, yet still discerning little in Beijing's attitude that held out the promise for an improvement in Sino-American relations in the short term.[62]

Jenkins echoed this sentiment. While mildly encouraged, he cautioned against investing too much hope in the mainland's action, seeing it more as "a shift in style and tactics away from Cultural Revolution extremism" than as a fundamental change in strategy.[63] A more accurate reading of China's intentions would have to await a resolution of the country's domestic disputes. Until then, "it is obvious that very little indeed is obvious about the policy debate concerning Sino-U.S. relations which must be going on in Peking." To help steer this debate in a favorable direction, however, he thought the timing appropriate to provide "a bit of ammunition for those who may be somewhat less inimical to us than the full-fledged Maoists."[64]

This ammunition came in the form of a memorandum that the Secretary of State sent to Johnson in the first week of January. Indeed, the reaction of Rusk, consistently the most skeptical of LBJ's inner circle toward policy reform, to Beijing's proposal for renewed talks was the most intriguing. His recommendation for permitting US subsidiaries abroad to sell a limited range of non-strategic goods to the PRC, an idea he had first broached a year earlier as part of the policy review, was modest enough. The rationale used to justify the move, however, displayed a notable evolution in thinking. Rusk placed particular emphasis on the timing of this olive branch, coming as it would at "a time when the Cultural Revolution appears to be entering a new stage ... It is possible that something important is brewing in Peking. We should, prior to the February meeting with us at Warsaw ... show that we are listening and interested and capable of being responsive." Besides encouraging Chinese moderation, the Secretary argued that relaxing the trade embargo would "arouse Soviet curiosity" and remind the Russians that "better relations with the United States are very much in their long-run interests."[65]

The latter point was particularly significant, as it suggested that senior decision-makers had come to see the advantage of flirting with the Chinese so as to maximize America's strategic position against the Kremlin and elicit its assistance on a broad range of issues. Existing accounts have credited Nixon and Kissinger for initiating the shift away from the decidedly pro-Soviet bias that had characterized America's Cold War approach toward the two communist powers;[66] a more likely interpretation, based on these new archival materials, is that the duo built on ideas that had already gained high-level credence toward the end of the Johnson administration. Previously advocated by mid-level officials such as Zbigniew Brzezinski of State's PPC as a lever to induce the Kremlin's cooperation in facilitating a Vietnam settlement, the Johnson team had passed on the opportunity to exploit Soviet fears of China throughout 1966–67, largely out of the sense that this would provoke the opposite reaction from Moscow. Underlying this conservatism was an understanding that the lack of receptivity in Beijing rendered any game of triangular politics unviable. The PRC's feeler in November 1968 seemed to provide Washington with new policy options. The suspicions of Soviet officials, who had for long been anxious about any movement toward

Sino-American rapprochement even when the prospect appeared remote, were immediately kindled. They nervously probed their US counterparts for any hints of what approach might be taken toward the mainland by the incoming Nixon administration.[67] Rusk welcomed the Soviets' predicament, noting how "this latest development worries [the] Russians somewhat ... We are not ... trying to straighten out this confusion and do not mind if [the] Soviets and Chicoms sometimes worry about each other."[68]

For reasons that remain unclear, LBJ did not act at Rusk's behest. The trade proposal, advanced on the eve of Johnson's departure from office, may have simply been relegated to the sidelines and lost in the confusion of a transition from one presidency to the next.[69] If one is to believe William Bundy's unsubstantiated account, Nixon personally asked Johnson to refrain from authorizing any change in trade or travel restrictions relating to China, possibly hoping to put his own indelible stamp on this policy sphere.[70] In any case, the only intended audience for Mao's advance was Nixon and it occurred far too late in Johnson's tenure, despite some last-minute consideration, to elicit any major counter initiative. It fell to the new administration to determine the American response.

At quick glance the last year of Lyndon Johnson's presidency brought more of the same on the China front: curious scrutiny of the mainland's mayhem, deliberation over the appropriate response, and deferment of substantive policy reform until the dust had settled. On closer inspection, however, this period offered hints of a new approach. Dramatic events in the latter half of 1967 led many US observers to conclude that revolutionary fervor had peaked and moderate elements had outmaneuvered hard-line Maoists. This domestic realignment and an overriding preoccupation with restoring order was thought to have significant ramifications for Chinese foreign policy, as the ideological imperative of propagating Mao Zedong Thought was set aside in favor of greater attentiveness to narrowly defined security interests. China seemed unusually isolated from regional affairs in 1968, most notably in its increasingly strained relations with Hanoi.

Johnson's keen interest in these events, as measured by the policy review undertaken at his direction, was especially noteworthy. His first sustained engagement with the China policymaking process in 1966 had resulted from fixation with a war that cast a long shadow over all of the administration's diplomatic initiatives. LBJ's personal intervention in early 1968, by contrast, was a response to signs of change in the PRC's orientation and the resultant hope of some that new leaders in Beijing could be cultivated. The magnitude of the Cultural Revolution was such that it compelled US decision-makers to start looking at China from a new perspective, one that was not narrowly defined by the Cold War strategy of containment and isolation. The most ardent advocates of policy reform had for long maintained, as Edward Rice did in his October 1961 study, that America's approach to China was distorted by the single-minded focus on providing for the defense of its neighbors, with scant regard for what occurred inside its borders.

This, of course, was a work in progress. While the initiation of a policy review revealed a groping for departures from old policies and an alertness to evolving conditions on the mainland, the outcome was inconclusive and overshadowed by Vietnam. Interest in modest initiatives gave way to the sense that altering the broad outlines of established China policy would send the wrong message to Hanoi and undermine America's firm negotiating stance at the Paris peace talks. The widespread unease of regional allies that the US harbored plans to curtail its involvement in Southeast Asia, galvanized by the President's 31 March address, served as an additional impediment to change. Closely related to these considerations was the specter of a China that still struck many in Washington as hostile and fanatic. Ironically, the very factor that reduced the PRC's threat potential – its persistent turmoil – argued for continued vigilance and colored the Johnson team's estimation of the prospects for rapprochement.

In short, there were substantial perceptual roadblocks on the American side to reconciliation with the mainland, stemming from enduring Cold War images of China that were only exacerbated by the cataclysmic Cultural Revolution. Yet one can easily run the risk of faulting the Johnson administration with the benefit of hindsight. Mao only seems to have entertained notions of a tilt toward the US in the latter half of 1968. Prior to this point, Beijing vehemently spurned various feelers from Washington. While Mao's suspicion of US motives and influence in Asia was genuine, he also clearly saw America as a convenient bogeyman for whipping up domestic support for his political objectives. Any relaxation of attitudes toward the US in 1966–67 would have undermined his authority and diverted attention from his anti-revisionist campaign. Thus a reorientation of

Chinese foreign policy only became possible once the Chairman became disenchanted with his own grand enterprise of continuous revolution.[71] When a new Chinese position finally became evident toward the end of 1968, senior US officials expressed interest in, as Rostow put it, "a modest response to the faint signals from Peking" and giving the next administration "additional room to maneuver should opportunities present themselves."[72]

Notes

1. Rostow to LBJ, 24 February 1968, NSF, Country File Addendum, Box 295, folder "China: Filed by the LBJ Library (1 of 2)," LBJL.
2. Harding, "The Chinese state in crisis," in MacFarquhar (ed.), *The Politics of China*, pp. 151, 205–23; Short, *Mao*, pp. 564–8; MacFarquhar and Schoenhals, *Mao's Last Revolution*, pp. 199–216, 227–31, 245–52.
3. Text of cable from Hong Kong (1786), 21 September 1967, enclosed in Rostow to LBJ, 25 September 1967, NSF, Country File, Box 242, folder "China memos (continued), vol. XI," LBJL.
4. CIA memorandum, "China's Cultural Revolution in 1968," 6 December 1968, NSF, Country File, Box 243, folder "China (B), vol. XIII," LBJL.
5. Jenkins to Rostow, 5 October 1967, NSF, Country File, Box 242, folder "China memos (continued), vol. XI," LBJL.
6. Jenkins to Rostow, 25 October 1967, NSF, Files of Alfred Jenkins, Box 2, folder "CHICOM-Cultural Revolution, July–December 1967," LBJL. See as well Jenkins to Rostow, 5 December 1967, ibid.; Jenkins to Rostow, 2 January 1968, NSF, Files of Alfred Jenkins, Box 3, folder "CHICOM-Cultural Revolution, January–June 1968," LBJL.
7. "Situation in Communist China and United States policy alternatives," enclosed in Rusk to LBJ, 22 February 1968, NSF, Country File, Box 243, folder "China memos (continued), vol. XII," LBJL.
8. Barnouin and Yu, *Chinese Foreign Policy During the Cultural Revolution*, pp. 27–8, 77–8; Robinson, "China confronts the Soviet Union," in MacFarquhar and Fairbank (eds), *Cambridge History of China*, vol. 15, pp. 245–8; Gong Li, "Chinese decision making and the thawing of US-China relations," in Ross and Jiang (eds), *Re-examining the Cold War*, pp. 322–3; M. Gurtov, "The Foreign Ministry and foreign affairs in the Chinese Cultural Revolution," in T.W. Robinson (ed.), *The Cultural Revolution in China* (Berkeley: University of California Press, 1971), pp. 352–6.
9. Memorandum prepared by the Office of Asian Communist Affairs, "The Cultural Revolution: Spring 1968," 18 April 1968, RG 59, Files of Ambassador at Large Averell Harriman, 1967–1968, Lot 71D461, Box 2, NA. See as well Airgram, no. A-349, Hong Kong to Department of

State, 30 January 1968, RG 59, Central Files, 1967–69, Box 1973, POL CHICOM-US, NA; Hughes to Rusk, 27 February 1968, RG 59, Subject Files of the Office of Republic of China Affairs, 1951–75, Lot 72D140, Box 3, NA.

10 CIA information cable, 15 January 1968, NSF, Files of Alfred Jenkins, Box 3, folder "CHICOM-Cultural Revolution, January–June 1968," LBJL.

11 John Gronouski to Rusk, 11 January 1968, NSF, Country File, Box 243, folder "China memos (continued), vol. XII," LBJL.

12 Jenkins to Rostow, 9 January 1968, NSF, Files of Alfred Jenkins, Box 1, folder "CHICOM-Warsaw Talks," LBJL.

13 Katzenbach to W. Bundy and Owen, 6 October 1967, RG 59, Subject Files of the Office of Asian Communist Affairs, 1961–73, Lot 72D41, Box 2, NA.

14 M. Lerner, "A failure of perception: Lyndon Johnson, North Korean ideology, and the *Pueblo* incident," *Diplomatic History* 25:4 (2001), 647–9. The administration's assumption of Soviet complicity in the *Pueblo* affair was wide of the mark. New research has shown that Soviet leaders were not informed by Pyongyang in advance of the move, and were fearful that Kim Il Sung would drag them into an unwanted war on the Korean peninsula. Although the Kremlin attempted to rein in North Korea in the aftermath of the seizure, its ideological commitments to Kim's regime narrowed its leverage. See S.S. Radchenko, "The Soviet Union and the North Korean seizure of the USS *Pueblo*: Evidence from Russian archives," CWIHP Working Paper 47 (2005).

15 Telegram, no. 4221, Hong Kong to Department of State, 25 January 1968, RG 59, Central Files, 1967–69, Box 2264, POL 33-6 KOR N-US, NA; Hughes to Rusk, 29 January 1968, RG 59, Central Files, 1967–69, Box 1970, POL CHICOM-KOR N, NA; Denney to Rusk, 15 February 1968, ibid.; Telegram, no. 19679, Department of State to Tehran, 5 July 1968, ibid. Kim Il Sung was greatly alarmed by the outbreak of the Cultural Revolution, viewing it as a major external threat to his rule. He responded by reaching out to the Soviets and avoiding any provocative actions toward China. See B. Schaefer, "North Korean 'adventurism' and China's long shadow, 1966–1972," CWIHP Working Paper 44 (2004).

16 Telcon, Rusk–W. Bundy, 15 February 1968, RG 59, Records of Secretary of State Dean Rusk: Transcripts of Telephone Calls, Lot 72D192, Box 61, NA.

17 Garver, "The Tet offensive and Sino-Vietnamese relations," in Gilbert and Head (eds), *The Tet Offensive*, pp. 45–59; Qiang Zhai, "An uneasy relationship: China and the DRV during the Vietnam War," in Gardner and Gittinger (eds), *International Perspectives on Vietnam*, pp. 120–3.

18 Notes of meeting, 4 April 1968, *FRUS*, 1964–1968, vol. 6, p. 532.
19 Telegram, no. 184858, Department of State to Saigon, 17 June 1968, RG 59, Central Files, 1967–69, Box 1976, POL CHICOM-VIET N, NA; Telegram, no. 192062, Department of State to Saigon, 27 June 1968, ibid.; Hughes to Rusk, 29 October 1968, ibid.; Rostow to LBJ, 22 June 1968, NSF, Memos to the President, Box 36, folder "Vol. LXXXIII (2 of 2)," LBJL; CIA intelligence cable, 15 July 1968, NSF, Memos to the President, Box 38, folder "Vol. LXXXIX (3 of 4)," LBJL.
20 Memorandum of conversation, 10 August 1968, Tom Johnson's Notes of Meetings, Box 3, folder "12:25 p.m. President's Briefing of Former VP Nixon and Gov. Agnew," LBJL
21 Secretary Rusk discusses Viet-Nam in Canadian magazine interview, *DSB*, 12 February 1968, p. 208.
22 This particular point is well argued in Dallek, *Flawed Giant*, pp. 460–1.
23 CIA memorandum, "Implications of an unfavorable outcome in Vietnam," 11 September 1967, enclosed in Helms to LBJ, 12 September 1967, NSF, Vietnam Country File, Box 259, folder "Vietnam Outcome (CIA Study)," LBJL.
24 "Situation in Communist China and United States policy alternatives," enclosed in Rusk to LBJ, 22 February 1968, NSF, Country File, Box 243, folder "China memos (continued), vol. XII," LBJL.
25 Author's interview with Rostow, Austin, Texas, 23 January 2002.
26 LBJ's private musings on China are recorded in M. Frankel, *The Times of My Life and My Life with the Times* (New York: Random House, 1999), pp. 295–6.
27 "A conversation with the President," *DSB*, 8 January 1968, p. 38.
28 Annual message to the Congress on the State of the Union, 17 January 1968, *PPP:LBJ*, 1968–69, vol. 1, p. 26.
29 Memorandum for the record, 2 February 1968, *FRUS*, 1964–1968, vol. 30, pp. 634–8.
30 "Memorandum on China policy," enclosed in Reischauer to LBJ, 12 February 1968, NSF, Country File Addendum, Box 295, folder "China: Filed by the LBJ Library (1 of 2)," LBJL.
31 Rostow to LBJ, 22 February 1968, NSF, Memos to the President, Box 30 (1 of 2), folder "Vol. LXIV (2 of 2)," LBJL.
32 "Thoughts on China," by Jenkins, 22 February 1968, NSF, Country File, Box 243, folder "China memos (continued), vol. XII," LBJL. This line of argument is reiterated in Jenkins to Rostow, 8 April 1968, NSF, Files of Alfred Jenkins, Box 1, folder "CHICOM-General," LBJL.
33 Secretary Rusk's news conference of October 12, DSB, 30 October 1967, p. 563.
34 For example, see Cohen, *Dean Rusk*, pp. 288–9.

35 Joseph Yager to Rusk, 22 December 1967, RG 59, Policy Planning Council: Subject and Country Files, 1965–1969, Lot 72D139, Box 302, NA.
36 "Situation in Communist China and United States policy alternatives," enclosed in Rusk to LBJ, 22 February 1968, NSF, Country File, Box 243, folder "China memos (continued), vol. XII," LBJL.
37 Rusk to LBJ, 22 February 1968, ibid.
38 The proposals outlined in Rusk's 22 February 1968 memorandum to Johnson were formally drawn up by State Department officials in subsequent memorandums, yet they did not win the Secretary's approval. See W. Bundy and Anthony Solomon to Rusk, undated, NSF, Country File, Box 243, folder "China (C), vol. XIII," LBJL; W. Bundy to Rusk, 6 March 1968, *FRUS, 1964–1968*, vol. 30, pp. 666–9.
39 William B. Macomber, Jr to Rusk, 8 March 1968, RG 59, Subject Files of the Office of Asian Communist Affairs, 1961–73, Lot 72D41, Box 2, NA.
40 Author's interview with Rostow, Austin, Texas, 17 January 2002.
41 See J. Prados, "Prague Spring and SALT: Arms limitation setbacks in 1968," in Brands (ed.), *Beyond Vietnam*, pp. 19–36; Schwartz, *Lyndon Johnson and Europe*, pp. 205–22.
42 Herring, LBJ and Vietnam, pp. 164–71. The quote is taken from p. 166. See as well R.H. Immerman, "'A time in the tide of men's affairs:' Lyndon Johnson and Vietnam," in Cohen and Tucker (eds), *Lyndon Johnson Confronts the World*, pp. 83–6; Gardner, *Pay Any Price*, pp. 464–83.
43 Telegram, Department of State to Ottawa, 10 June 1968, FRUS, 1964–1968, vol. 30, p. 682. See as well Richard H. Donald to W. Bundy, 6 June 1968, RG 59, Subject Files of the Office of Republic of China Affairs, 1951–75, Lot 72D145, Box 7, NA.
44 Nicholas Katzenbach, "Viet-Nam and the independence of Southeast Asia," DSB, 12 February 1968, p. 203.
45 Editorial note, *FRUS, 1964–1968*, vol. 29, p. 410; Summary of discussion and decisions at the 36th meeting of the Senior Interdepartmental group, 13 May 1968, ibid., p. 874. See as well "Koreans fear Vietnam settlement will bring US pullout from Asia," 5 April 1968, *Washington Post*, p. A25; R.J. McMahon, "Ambivalent partners: The Lyndon Johnson administration and its Asian allies," in Brands (ed.), *Beyond Vietnam*, pp. 181–3.
46 Jenkins to Rostow, 7 June 1968, NSF, Country File, Box 242, folder "China memos, vol. XII," LBJL.
47 W. Bundy to Read, undated, RG 59, Subject Files of the Office of Asian Communist Affairs, 1961–73, Lot 71D423, Box 1, NA.
48 MacFarquhar (ed.), *Sino-American Relations, 1949–1971*, pp. 235–6.

49 James Murray to Wilkinson and Samuel, 28 June 1968, FCO 21/61, PRO.
50 Nicholas Katzenbach, "A realistic view of Communist China," *DSB*, 10 June 1968, pp. 737–40.
51 "Further thoughts on China," by Jenkins, 9 October 1968, NSF, Country File, Box 243, folder "China (A), vol. XIII," LBJL.
52 For contemporary criticism of the administration's reluctance to match deeds with words, see A.S. Whiting, "Time for a change in our China policy," *New York Times Magazine*, 15 December 1968, p. 28; E.O. Reischauer, *Beyond Vietnam: The United States and Asia* (New York: Alfred A. Knopf, 1968), pp. 170–3; A.D. Barnett, *A New US Policy Toward China* (Washington, DC: The Brookings Institution, 1971), pp. 15–19, 52–9.
53 Jenkins to Rostow, 5 October 1968, NSF, Files of Alfred Jenkins, Box 3, folder "CHICOM-Cultural Revolution, July–December 1968," LBJL.
54 J.W. Garver, *China's Decision for Rapprochement with the United States, 1968–1971* (Boulder: Westview, 1982) pp. 5–13, 32–9, 149–57. See as well J.D. Pollack, "The opening to America," in MacFarquhar and Fairbank (eds), *Cambridge History of China*, vol. 15.
55 Quoted in Chen and Wilson (eds), "All under the heaven is great chaos," p. 170.
56 Chen, *Mao's China and the Cold War*, p. 245; Gong Li, "Chinese decision making and the thawing of US-China relations," in Ross and Jiang (eds), *Re-examining the Cold War*, p. 332.
57 In his otherwise excellent study of US China policy, James Mann makes the questionable claim that Nixon's views on the PRC in the mid-1960s "ran contrary to the dogma of the American foreign policy establishment." Mann, *About Face*, p. 18.
58 Kissinger, *White House Years*, pp. 167–8.
59 R.M. Nixon, "Asia after Viet Nam," *Foreign Affairs* 46, no. 1 (October 1967), pp. 121–3.
60 Telegram, no. 279939, Department of State to Hong Kong, Taipei, and Warsaw, 30 November 1968, RG 59, Central Files, 1967–69, Box 1972, POL CHICOM-US, NA.
61 Telegram, no. 10675, Hong Kong to Department of State, 19 December 1968, ibid.
62 Airgram, no. A-25, Hong Kong to Department of State, 24 January 1969, RG 59, Central Files, 1967–69, Box 1973, POL CHICOM-US, NA.
63 Jenkins to Rostow, 4 December 1968, NSF, Files of Alfred Jenkins, Box 1, folder "CHICOM-Warsaw Talks," LBJL.
64 Jenkins to Rostow, 30 December 1968, *FRUS, 1964–1968*, vol. 30, p. 728.

65 Rusk to LBJ, 4 January 1969, enclosed in Rostow to LBJ, 6 January 1969, NSF, Memos to the President, Box 44, folder "Vol. CXIII (3 of 3)," LBJL. Rusk's memo seems to corroborate Noam Kochavi's observation that the Secretary's views on China were more sophisticated and flexible than the prevailing line of historical literature has stressed. As Kochavi concludes, dating back to the 1950s Rusk demonstrated an interest in nurturing moderates in Beijing's ruling circle during periods of relative Chinese quiescence on the world stage. Kochavi, *A Conflict Perpetuated*, pp. 37–8, 81, 111, 247.

66 Goh speculates that had the Johnson team been confronted with the Sino-Soviet border clashes of 1969, they would have remained aloof from the affair rather than opt for Nixon's strategy of moving toward Beijing. Goh, *Constructing the US Rapprochement with China*, pp. 93–4. See as well Chang, *Friends and Enemies*, pp. 283–4; Mann, *About Face*, pp. 21–2; Ross, *Negotiating Cooperation*, p. 30; W. Isaacson, *Kissinger: A Biography* (New York: Simon & Schuster, 1992), ch. 16; M. Schaller, "Détente and the strategic triangle: Or, 'drinking your Mao Tai and having your vodka, too,'" in Ross and Jiang (eds), *Re-examining the Cold War*, pp. 363–4.

67 For example, see Memorandum of conversation, Boris Davydov–Daniel I. Davidson, 21 December 1968, RG 59, Central Files, 1967–69, Box 1972, POL CHICOM-US, NA. For Soviet fears of a Sino-American modus vivendi in 1966–67, see Radchenko, "The China Puzzle," pp. 289, 312–13.

68 Telegram, no. 291080, Department of State to Paris, 21 December 1968, RG 59, Central Files, 1967–69, Box 1972, POL CHICOM-US, NA.

69 Rostow's forwarding memo on Rusk's 4 January 1969 proposal bears the following handwritten note from an unidentified official: "I don't want to rush these and do them in the last two weeks." *FRUS, 1964–1968*, vol. 30, p. 729, n. 1.

70 W. Bundy, *A Tangled Web: The Making of Foreign Policy in the Nixon Presidency* (New York: Hill and Wang, 1998), p. 103.

71 For further discussion, see Chen, *Mao's China and the Cold War*, pp. 239–45.

72 Rostow to LBJ, 6 January 1969, NSF, Memos to the President, Box 44, folder "Vol. CXIII (3 of 3)," LBJL.

Conclusion

The implications of this study for the historiography of both Sino-American relations and the foreign policies of the Johnson administration are far-reaching. Recapitulating the book's central themes and findings, this conclusion accounts for the factors underlying the relaxation of US attitudes toward China in the 1960s, assesses the importance of the Johnson team's tentative bridge-building, identifies points of departure between Johnson's and Nixon's respective approaches to the PRC, and highlights LBJ's strengths and weaknesses as a foreign policy leader within the context of his dealings with Beijing.

By November 1963, US policy toward China had changed very little since the founding of the PRC in 1949. Over time, historians have unearthed fascinating evidence showing that, even at the height of the Cold War confrontation between the two adversaries, American interactions with the mainland were often much more complex than either contemporary appearances or rhetoric suggested. The Truman, Eisenhower, and Kennedy administrations all developed a nuanced understanding of Beijing's immediate intentions and capabilities, implicitly recognized that the communist regime on the mainland was there to stay, sought to keep Chiang Kai-shek on a short leash, and pursued strategies aimed at driving the Soviets and Chinese apart or luring one away from the other. Still, as Robert Ross has reminded us, both the US and China throughout this period were ultimately wedded to "unrealistic and destabilizing foreign policy objectives, which made any negotiated resolution of their conflicts all but impossible ... [and] contributed to avoidable crises and war."[1] The bipartisan line of containment and isolation inherited by Lyndon Johnson derived from the widely shared impression that the PRC was an implacable revolutionary foe, preaching the violent overthrow of governments without any apparent concern that its expansionist ambitions could set off large-scale warfare in a nuclear age. It cannot be depicted as one that a zealously anti-communist public forced on successive administrations against their better judgement. Springing from an expansive conception of US interests and power in Asia, it was an instrument of coercion and pressure designed to teach the unruly Chinese how to behave and accommodate themselves to American preponderance in the region.[2]

At the dawn of the 1960s, a number of China hands and their political sponsors (Stevenson, Bowles, Harriman, Hilsman) in the new Kennedy administration posited that this approach had outlived its usefulness: it alienated allies anxious to broaden contacts with the PRC, projected an unpalatable image of rigidity and stubbornness, and made little headway in moderating Chinese behavior. The rationale advanced for policy reform varied, with some eager to get the US off the defensive, others more interested in courting certain elements of Beijing's ruling circle. Whatever the motive, the persistent appearance on the administration's agenda of such items as "two Chinas," food relief, and the relaxation of trade and travel controls suggested a perceived urgency to redressing tactics toward the mainland that had been lacking during the Truman-Eisenhower years.

Kennedy and his most senior aides proved largely unresponsive to this prodding, intent like their predecessors on building and maintaining positions of strength in Asia, and viewing Beijing as the primary source of inspiration and aid to the region's national liberation movements. A prudent Cold Warrior, Kennedy deserves credit for preventing substantial Sino-American tensions in Vietnam and the Taiwan Straits from escalating into another military confrontation. Yet his aversion to conflict evidently did not translate into any immediate interest in easing the deadlock between Washington and Beijing. Hints of flexibility on JFK's part – his tentative endorsement of "two Chinas" and deft management of another crisis in the Taiwan Straits, for example – were often overtaken by his cautious reading of the political potency of the China issue at home and by his profound conviction that the Chinese posed a grave threat to world peace. The President's interest in modifying the US stance on Chinese representation was motivated solely by the need to bolster Taiwan's sagging international position, and soon gave way to the search for a formula that would raise the bar higher for Beijing's entry to the UN and to the issuance of a secret veto pledge to Chiang. An eagerness to explore means of taking out the PRC's nuclear program stood as the ultimate testament to his hostility toward the communist regime. Contrary to the hopes of contemporary observers and the reminiscences of staunch defenders, Kennedy did not seem inclined to inaugurate a new era in relations with the mainland.

Lyndon Johnson, whose sensitivity to the political baggage tied to China was just as acute as Kennedy's and who came to regard the PRC as a menacing influence in Vietnam, his overriding obsession in foreign affairs, was hardly the ideal candidate to initiate changes in America's relationship with China. It follows that the tentative bridge-building undertaken by a President instinctively wary of bold diplomatic initiatives was facilitated, even prompted, by significant shifts in context at home and abroad. Put another way, the alterations in China policy outlined in this study resulted more from reaction to unanticipated circumstances and events beyond the control of decision-makers than from design or natural inclination.

As scholars like Rosemary Foot have demonstrated, the seeming political imperative of projecting antagonism toward the mainland gradually receded during the 1960s. Samples of public opinion at the time offered contradictory findings. When asked which country posed the greatest threat to world peace, Americans consistently cited China. Yet despite, or perhaps because of, its growing stature, particularly after the explosion of a nuclear device in October 1964, a majority of those polled increasingly expressed a willingness to expand ties to the PRC, possibly with the hope of taming it or arriving at a mutual understanding. Much of this sentiment was latent, reflecting more a mellowing of attitudes than any concerted demand for change. The Johnson team initially proved either unaware of, or unwilling to respond to, the subtle shift in mood. Indeed, as they steadily escalated America's involvement in Vietnam, the harsh rhetoric employed against Beijing bore striking similarity to the language of the past decade; a congenial pose in 1963–65 would have contradicted efforts to mobilize backing for stemming the flow of Asian communism.

The administration shifted course only when Vietnam's critics successfully targeted Johnson's intransigence toward China as emblematic of his misguided overall approach to Asia, culminating in Senator Fulbright's March 1966 hearings. As the war bogged down and settled into a messy stalemate, statesmanlike expressions of support for long-term reconciliation with the PRC became a means by which domestic opponents could be disarmed, and the electorate assured that the White House was planning for peace and thinking beyond the fighting. This was the primary motive for LBJ's landmark address of 12 July 1966. In strictly political terms, China by the late 1960s had ceased remaining, to borrow Thomas Christensen's phrase, a "useful adversary." It was now advantageous to be seen reaching out to the mainland. The appearance of Richard Nixon's *Foreign Affairs* article in 1967 was particularly reflective of the changed environment. Both Nixon and Hubert Humphrey supported the idea of developing a new Sino-American relationship during the 1968 campaign.[3]

A far-reaching reassessment of China's international role coincided with this evolution in domestic attitudes. Successive Cold War administrations had for long insisted that any modification of policy would reward bad behavior and whet an expansionist appetite. These sentiments certainly prevailed during the early stages of Johnson's presidency against the insistence of several mid-level officials who strenuously contended that the apparent threat posed by the PRC had been blown out of proportion. Preoccupied by the growing communist insurgency in South Vietnam and susceptible to the view that it was being stoked by the Chinese, LBJ opposed a switch to "two Chinas" in November 1964 on the basis of such reasoning. US decision-makers, Rusk in particular, regarded a firm stand in Vietnam as pivotal to deterring Chinese aggression. A rapid sequence of Chinese setbacks in South Asia, Indonesia, and Tangiers in the fall of 1965 stirred considerable interest and seemed to indicate that the regime's bark was worse than its bite, yet suspicions lingered that Beijing was testing American resolve while it was distracted elsewhere.

The perceptual breakthrough came with the outbreak of the Cultural Revolution. As the mainland imploded, and the Red Guards directed their attacks against domestic "revisionists" and vestiges of Soviet influence, senior officials gradually amended long-standing assumptions about China's priorities and capacity to project power beyond its borders. Thus Walt Rostow could write Johnson with confidence in February 1967 that "Mao's grand design in foreign policy of two years ago has failed completely, and it now appears that his domestic economy may well be disrupted by the Cultural Revolution as seriously as it was by the Great Leap of 1958–59."[4] No clearer illustration can be found of the President's own view that the PRC's internal turmoil had diminished any remaining enthusiasm for external adventures than his approval of increased bombing against North Vietnam later that year.

Underlying America's shift away from a confrontational stance toward China, aside from political calculations and a substantial downgrading of Beijing's threat potential, were the pressures and strains wrought by its own strategic overextension. While military involvement in Vietnam was certainly the product of decisions made by unique personalities at a particular moment in time, it can also be seen as the logical culmination of Washington's traditional interest, predating the Cold War, in ensuring a stable Asian order responsive to its ideals and leadership. The resultant stalemate and bitter divisiveness on the homefront signified to US policymakers that the militarized containment of the 1950s and 1960s could no longer be sustained by stretched resources or supported by a weary populace.[5] Alternative, less costly, means of securing American objectives in Asia – and grappling with the PRC's own ambitions – had to be found. A new relationship with Beijing, as Rusk insinuated to Johnson at the end of their tenure in office, might also be of use in checking a more conspicuous Soviet threat. These were considerations with which Nixon and Kissinger ultimately had to contend, yet they formed the implicit backdrop to deliberations in the latter stages of the Johnson administration. Repeated assertions by Johnson officials that the defense of Saigon had instilled "greater hope and confidence than ever before" in non-communist Asia expressed their hope that US allies would bear a greater share of the manpower burden in guaranteeing their own security in the future.[6]

The immediate catalyst for effecting the first significant shift in US dealings with the PRC was Vietnam, a war nominally fought to arrest the spread of Chinese-inspired subversion. Neither the Chinese nor the Americans were spoiling for a replay of Korea. A simmering, protracted conflict in Vietnam served Mao's objectives of rallying support for the coming purge of his political enemies and of draining US resources, yet he was careful enough to limit his own country's role on the battlefield. To deter the Americans from bringing the war closer to their border, Chinese officials pursued a two-pronged strategy of deterrence and reassurance. On the one hand, they warned their US counterparts via the Warsaw channel that a major attack on North Vietnam would be considered an attack on the mainland, and little effort was made to conceal the dispatch of Chinese units to the DRV.

On the other hand, Washington was informed through sources such as the British that Beijing would not provoke a clash.

Johnson signalled his own interest in a limited war by cautiously escalating America's military involvement and refraining from those actions that could be misconstrued as a direct threat to Chinese security. These efforts notwithstanding, China's leaders were greatly alarmed by the administration's increased activity in Vietnam; US airstrikes against the North in the wake of the Gulf of Tonkin incidents in August 1964 were particularly unnerving, and compelled Mao to reconsider the image of an American paper tiger that he had harboured and propagated since the late 1950s. Stepped up aid to Hanoi and the relocation of Chinese industrial and governmental facilities to the interior were undertaken with a view to creating a tense climate at home for the coming Cultural Revolution, yet the Chairman's actions also undoubtedly reflected a sense of uncertainty over Washington's intentions. By the spring of 1965, the potential for a misunderstanding or miscalculation erupting into renewed Sino-American hostilities was as pronounced as any time since the Taiwan Strait crises of the previous decade. As reports of Beijing's anxieties accumulated toward the end of the year, the President and his aides determined that a more unambiguous effort to disabuse the PRC of its sense of American antagonism was necessary.

The resultant tentative bridge-building may be viewed with some ambivalence. It was narrowly conceived, forced on decision-makers who were strictly interested in keeping a lid on the hostilities in Vietnam. It did not address the question of formulating a long-term strategy for accommodation with the mainland, for which mid-level China hands had been advocating since the early 1960s. The promotion of expanded contacts and the adoption of conciliatory language, however, went considerably beyond the conflict management tactics of the Eisenhower and Kennedy administrations. Indeed, the most enduring achievement of this process was that it established the rhetorical justification for the American opening that unfolded under Nixon. While the notable change in atmospherics failed to elicit a constructive response from Beijing, it at minimum played a part in checking an expansion of the war. It also evidently made an impression on certain elements of the Chinese hierarchy. Wang Guoquan, China's ambassador in Warsaw and one of the officials most exposed to the change in tone in 1966, recollected with some disappointment that his superiors' radical posturing precluded a reciprocation in sentiment: "We lost a favorable opportunity to give Sino-American relations a timely push. It must be a regretful thing in the history of diplomacy."[7] Had they known of this reaction, even the most zealous proponents of policy reform inside and outside the administration, all of whom had never anyways entertained hopes of appealing to the highest echelons of Chinese officialdom, would have been heartened.

1966 proved to be the high-water mark of policy innovation during the Johnson years. The President's 12 July address hinted at greater changes to come, particularly in the sphere of trade, yet it was delivered just as Washington was receiving reports of extraordinary developments on the mainland. The outbreak of Red Guard violence and the stridently radical line of Cultural Revolution foreign policy served as an unsettling counterpoint to Chinese restraint in Vietnam. Relying on fragmentary, often speculative, reports from the consulate office in Hong Kong and a variety of third party sources, the administration's China watchers came to understand this turn of events as a last-ditch attempt by an ageing Mao to reverse the trend toward moderation and Soviet-style revisionism at home. With these unyielding leaders at the helm, the timing seemed decidedly inauspicious for a new round of bridge-building.

Critically, however, deferment was rationalized not just as a logical response to Chinese radicalism, but as the best means of facilitating an eventual Sino-American reconciliation. Many in Washington expressed hope that out of the chaos of Maoist excess, a more accommodating and pragmatic leadership would emerge. It was determined that waiting out the expected political demise of the Chairman and letting the country stew in its own juice stood a far better chance of securing a favorable outcome than any US effort to influence the mainland's political discourse. The notion that competing factions in the CCP presented opportunities for US patronage, long an article of faith for the administration's China "doves," gradually gained currency among decision-makers as evidence emerged of an apparent counter-attack against the Maoists. The result in 1967–68 was a maturation of high-level attitudes toward Beijing, arguably a more significant development than the tangible bridge-building steps of 1966 that sprang mostly from Vietnam-related objectives. As their tenure in office drew to a close, the Johnson team seriously considered initiatives aimed at influencing the orientation of China's political elite. Recall LBJ's authorization of the policy review in early 1968 and Rusk's January 1969 memorandum advising the President to probe Beijing's intentions following its agreement to reconvene the Warsaw talks.

Johnson's consistent eschewal of military confrontation against the PRC (his decision to forgo a pre-emptive strike against the mainland's nuclear facilities in 1964, his caution in Vietnam) and, moreover, his arrival at a far more measured stance toward China begs the question of how a third Johnson administration would have conducted Sino-American relations. Adding to this intrigue is a central facet of the Texan's political personality: his self-image as a statesman able to bridge gaping differences and outsized ambition to be remembered as a great reconciler, borne out by his masterful bargaining skills as Senate Majority Leader, his momentous civil rights legislation, and his concerted push for an arms agreement with the Soviets in 1968. While an irrefutable answer can never be provided, an eventual bold peace-making offer to Beijing would not have been inconsistent with his instincts, if he judged the domestic and international climate favorable to such a move.

Indeed, it has been contended elsewhere that American thinking had reached a turning point by 1968, that the primary stumbling block to enactment of a more ambitious agenda during the latter stages of the Johnson era was the volatile political climate in China.[8] Landmark studies by Chen Jian and Qiang Zhai have made it abundantly clear that throughout the period under consideration, Mao viewed a revolutionary foreign policy – challenging the Soviets for leadership of the international communist movement and combating American "imperialism" in Vietnam – as a natural complement to his overriding objective of continuous revolution at home. It is highly unlikely that a more forthcoming US attitude would have been reciprocated by the Chinese; there was no "lost chance" for Sino-American rapprochement during the Johnson years. The changes in Chinese orientation that would prove so critical to bringing about the reconciliation with Washington – Mao's determination that the Soviet threat outweighed the American, and his shift toward consolidation and stabilization at home – only came to fruition for Johnson's successor.

But, aside from a very probable loosening of trade and travel restrictions and further efforts at an expanded Sino-American dialogue, does it follow that a full-scale opening to the mainland would have been a foregone conclusion had LBJ won another term in office? It should not be presumed that *American* options and decisions were simply hostage to unfolding events in China. Such an interpretation gives short shrift to American dynamics that shaped the policy-making process and precluded bolder initiatives. As significant as the Johnson years were to framing and adumbrating the Nixon opening, consideration of these dynamics reveals that the obstacles to a substantive thaw in the late 1960s lay on both sides of the Pacific and highlights significant differences in how the Johnson and Nixon administrations approached relations with China.

1. *Domestic politics.* Faulting the Johnson administration for overestimating the political opposition to China policy reform and for failing to adopt measures in accordance with relaxed public sentiment, an argument made most forcefully by Rosemary Foot, overlooks a fundamental point. Most politicians' understanding of popular opinion on a given issue, and LBJ was no exception, is colored more by formative experiences and political lessons of the past than by contemporary polls.[9] Memories of how Truman and Acheson were pilloried for "losing" China to the communists and of McCarthyite witch-hunts guided Johnson's incrementalist approach to China policy throughout his entire presidency. His keenness to hew closely to the bipartisan line of containment and isolation during his first two years in office derived mostly from a consummate politician's instinct for survival than from any ideological commitment to the policy. Even after his sweeping victory in the 1964 election, a time many China hands saw as ripe for movement, Johnson proved highly resistant to any action that would distract attention from his cherished domestic program or provoke the ire of his conservative opponents.

Johnson felt compelled to act only once the spotlight cast on China policy in early 1966 rendered the administration's intransigence untenable. Even so, he was only willing to move as far as he thought public opinion would allow. With an eye on the mid-term congressional elections later that year, for example, he doubted that the "two Chinas" option could be advanced. Once public attention and pressure for change abated after the onset of the Cultural Revolution, so too did the perceived urgency and advantages of more bridge-building. Betraying persistent apprehension of a negative political fallout, many officials, notably Rusk, cautioned the President against major initiatives in early 1968. Thus even as the administration's firm stance in Vietnam afforded some leeway for marginal advancements on the China front, Johnson and his aides could never shake the sense

CONCLUSION

that they remained vulnerable to renewed Republican charges of appeasement.

The divergence in political context between the Johnson and Nixon administrations was striking. Though President Nixon harbored fears of a right-wing backlash against an opening to the communist PRC or an abandonment of a loyal Taiwan,[10] his painstakingly cultivated reputation as an unabashed Cold Warrior meant that his insecurities were not as pronounced as those of his Democratic predecessor. Moreover, Nixon's flair for, and delight in, the dramatic gesture in diplomacy stood in stark contrast to Johnson's conservative predilection for avoiding mistakes in this sphere.

2. *Alliance politics.* Existing accounts of the Johnson period have emphasized the role of international pressure in pushing the US to modify some of the more obdurate elements of its mainland policy. To be sure, as the administration confronted increasing demands from allies like Japan and Canada for engaging the PRC, policymakers sought means of deflecting blame for acrimonious Sino-American relations and stemming the loss of support for Taiwan's international standing; the Nationalists' endangered hold on the Chinese seat in the UN provided the impetus for Johnson's consideration of "two Chinas" in the spring and summer of 1966.

Yet a powerful countervailing current of opinion among its staunchly anti-communist Asian allies, one to which Washington ultimately proved more sensitive, imposed sharply defined limits on any feelers extended to Beijing. Johnson officials constantly felt obligated to demonstrate strength and resolve to Saigon, Bangkok, Seoul, and Manila in the battle against communist subversion, fearful that their friends' loyalties and allegiances were easily transferable. The President's inner circle was profoundly concerned in 1965 that failure to take a stand in South Vietnam would undermine confidence in US credibility and encourage neighboring countries to seek security guarantees through strategic bargains with the mainland. Moves to expand contacts with the PRC the following year were coupled with assurances to this audience that the American will to contain Chinese expansionism remained undiminished. A similar need to placate allied sentiment deterred the administration from approving further China initiatives in 1968, particularly once the decision to deescalate the Vietnam War touched off worries of a wider American pullback from Asia.

The Johnson team's complex relationship with Taiwan, largely unexamined and deserving of a full-length treatment, stood as one of the most imposing barriers to a breakthrough in China policy. Like his predecessors, LBJ strove on many occasions to discourage Chiang from attempting a return to the mainland, all the more so while the war in Vietnam was raging. On balance, however, the conservative Johnson was reluctant to alter the contour of America's diplomatic and military commitment to Taipei. The one major instance to the contrary, the aborted "two Chinas" initiative of 1966, was quickly shelved once the Generalissimo voiced his displeasure and threatened to storm out of the UN. Underlying the administration's deference was the pragmatic concern that the mercurial Chiang might attempt something suicidal or rash, such as military action against the PRC, should he feel that the US was abandoning him. Even more importantly, senior US decision-makers continued to value the Nationalist regime, for all of its deficiencies, as a major Cold War ally and a bastion of anti-communism in the Pacific. While there was certainly no love lost between the mutually suspicious partners, it is nevertheless exceedingly difficult to imagine LBJ or Rusk ever exercising the same ruthlessness and callous disregard for Taipei's interests as Nixon and Kissinger did in 1971–72, particularly since Johnson was acutely averse to acquiescing in any arrangement that could be portrayed by his opponents as a "sell out" of Chiang.[11]

The consequences of Johnson's ties to the Nationalists for Sino-American relations were, of course, toxic. Chinese reunification remained the overriding foreign policy objective of Mao and his comrades throughout the 1950s and 1960s. A reading of the Warsaw talks during the Johnson years reveals that the US attitude toward Taiwan, much more than its activities in Vietnam, was Beijing's greatest grievance. Chinese officials consistently used this forum to castigate their US counterparts for interference in the mainland's domestic affairs, and to inform them that a normalization of relations was out of the question until Washington recognized the PRC's sovereignty over the island. Nixon's willingness to offer overt and covert concessions over Taiwan ultimately proved decisive in convincing Mao to consummate a new relationship with the Americans.

3. *Ideology.* An examination of America's tense encounter with China during the Johnson years highlights the central role that ideology played in framing US perceptions and decisions during the Cold War.[12]

Michael Hunt's observation that reliance on a core set of values and beliefs can offer "simplifying clarity" to leaders confronted by complex and indecipherable problems seems especially relevant to our discussion.[13] The Johnson team's repeated insistence that the US could not deal with China until it learned how to behave, while patronizing and self-righteous to a foreign audience, tapped into an historic American inclination to view the world as divided between forces of good and evil and was consistent with an enduring hostility toward disorderly revolutionary regimes "that failed to conform to the standards of America's own moderate, constitutional beginnings."[14] The same confluence of deeply embedded preconceptions and anti-revolutionary sentiment that precluded bolder initiatives toward China during the Johnson years has continued to bedevil US relations with those governments seen as militant, radical, and alien to American values. Strictly as a reiteration of the moralizing impulse so emblematic of America's approach to world affairs, George W. Bush's infamous invocation in 2002 of an "axis of evil," with which there was little room for compromise, would have undoubtedly resonated with Johnson and his closest aides.

Washington's understanding of its Chinese adversary was bound to be disproportionately influenced by anti-communism; ideology filled a vacuum created by the absence of diplomatic relations, minimal face-to-face contacts, and a dearth of high-level Chinese expertise. The contrast with the administration's dealings with its other major communist competitor was stark. Respected, well-connected Kremlinologists such as Llewellyn Thompson and Charles Bohlen provided their superiors with sophisticated, calm appraisals of Soviet intentions and behavior. Communications between the White House and the Kremlin were facilitated by a number of useful channels, notably Soviet ambassador Anatoly Dobrynin. In short, the avenues for easing misunderstandings and managing crises were not inconsiderable.

Johnson officials were often impressed more by Chinese words than deeds. Militant Maoist rhetoric offended the sensibilities of a liberal, internationalist mindset that placed a premium on global order and stability.[15] This fixation with radical Chinese pronouncements gave rise to striking contradictions in threat perception. Even while the Johnson team recognized the mainland's defensive orientation and distaste for large-scale conflict, they interpreted its vehement endorsement of national liberation struggles and advocacy of revolutionary upheaval as evidence of an expansionist agenda. Recall the decidedly alarmist reaction to Lin Biao's *Long Live the Victory of People's War!* Similarly, Beijing's supply of materiel assistance to, and words of encouragement for, Hanoi convinced the President's lieutenants that China was fuelling and prolonging the communist insurgency in South Vietnam, even though they were vaguely cognizant of historical Sino-Vietnamese friction.

The onset of the Cultural Revolution stirred up familiar images of a reckless, unpredictable outcast. More specifically, US officials consistently misunderstood Mao's role in the unfolding drama. They interpreted China's turn toward moderation in the latter half of 1967 as an unmitigated defeat for the Chairman, when in fact he authorized or at least acquiesced in it. While Mao was seen as fully responsible for subjecting his country to the crazed pursuit of some fanciful revolutionary utopia, few believed he had any stake in reining in the disruptive forces he had unleashed. Policymakers underestimated Mao's tactical flexibility and failed to recognize that he was willing to practice *realpolitik* in safeguarding the security of the Chinese revolution, even if this eventually entailed allying himself with the world's leading "imperialist" power in opposition against another communist state. With profound irony, it was determined that Sino-American rapprochement was impossible so long as Mao, who would of course prove instrumental in bringing about the eventual thaw in relations, continued to rule.

These ideologically tinged attitudes prevented elements of the new Nixon administration from seeing the potential for reconciliation with the mainland. The State Department's China experts, many of them holdovers from the Johnson years, continued to regard the PRC as primarily a revolutionary power opposed to the international status quo. To an audience accustomed to Chinese radicalism, Beijing's various feelers toward the US in 1969–70 were viewed as little more than a tactical ploy intended to upset the Soviet Union rather than an attempt to reach a genuine modus vivendi with Washington. With considerable consequence for the direction of US policy, Nixon and Kissinger disagreed with this line of thinking, maintaining instead that Mao's overriding strategic interest in containing the Soviets would compel him to cast aside any scruples and secure an altogether new relationship with the Americans.[16]

CONCLUSION

While shedding new light on the evolution of Sino-American relations during the 1960s, this study has also built on recent works that offer a new perspective on Lyndon Johnson's foreign policy leadership by looking "beyond Vietnam." In keeping with an infinitely complex character who has always defied easy categorization or unqualified judgement, the evidence presented here provides ammunition for both critics and defenders. The historian H.W. Brands has suggested two useful criteria by which a President's diplomatic performance can be appraised.[17] The first concerns the issue of leadership, that is, whether the policy in question was shaped by presidential initiative or instead represented the handiwork of subordinates. Johnson's role in the decision-making process and his relationship with his advisers, at least within the context of Vietnam, has provoked considerable debate. A consensus on these points, however, remains elusive. To some, LBJ's contribution to the pivotal 1964–65 decisions for war mirrored his intimidating physical presence and larger than life personality. According to this school of thought, Johnson was a domineering figure who demanded conformity from his tight inner circle and brokered no dissent, an unimaginative Cold Warrior who personalized the Vietnam conflict as a challenge to his own manhood and manipulated the advisory process to legitimize a decision – measured military intervention – at which he had arrived independently.[18] An alternative, yet no less harsh, view casts Johnson as insecure and inexperienced, a passive leader who willingly permitted his hawkish lieutenants to frame the terms of debate.[19]

Applied to the China policy sphere, neither interpretation is sufficient. To be sure, much of Johnson's 1963–65 record corroborates the standard image of an excessively cautious, somewhat short-sighted novice lacking a sure touch for foreign affairs in the early stages of his presidency.[20] Assuming the reins of control with neither a China agenda of his own nor an inherent preference for fresh foreign policy initiatives, distracted by domestic political maneuvering and the Vietnam crisis, LBJ passively deferred to his inherited national security team and clung tenaciously to the line of containment and isolation in the face of mounting criticism from home and abroad. His dependence on the views of so few advisers restricted his access to alternative prescriptions for China policy, a problem that was alleviated only when Bill Moyers pressed his own case in 1966.[21] Befitting a leader whose relatively limited exposure to the outside world and sporadic participation in China policymaking resulted in undue reliance on simplistic analogies for his understanding of international events, Johnson uncritically embraced the conventional wisdom, espoused most prominently by Rusk and McNamara, that the communist insurgency in South Vietnam represented the frontline in China's battle for regional hegemony; at best this was indicative of careless and dubious strategic reasoning, at worst a disturbing readiness to deliberately distort and magnify an external threat for domestic consumption. There can also be no doubt, as many have charged, that Johnson's obsession with Vietnam came at the expense of furthering other policy objectives.[22] Indeed, his receptivity to China initiatives in particular depended on his reading of events on the ground in that war. Just as the possible contingency of Chinese intervention yielded the modest bridge-building gestures of 1966, the passing of this threat with the PRC's implosion sapped the President's immediate interest in this project. His preoccupation with peace talks in 1968, and the priority of projecting resolve to Hanoi, derailed further reform.

Yet scrutiny of LBJ's China record hardly reveals an easily impressionable figure who was content to let his underlings set the course. On balance, Lyndon Johnson emerges from this discussion as a forceful, attentive, and informed statesman whose China policy reflected his own preferences and inclinations. A positive consequence of the President's steady hand was the suppression of Sino-American tensions that could just as easily have erupted into another conflagration. In some ways, it is instructive to recall the example of Kennedy, to whom Johnson has often been unfavorably compared. It is no contradiction to say that while Johnson shared many of the most common Cold War stereotypes of the PRC, he was less prone to excitable assumptions about Chinese behavior and demonstrated more intellectual flexibility and nuanced thinking than his predecessor or many of Camelot's leading personalities. While Kennedy's fixation with Beijing's nuclear program propelled him to seriously explore a forceful response, there is no record of Johnson harboring the same interest, even though McNamara and McGeorge Bundy pressed him to keep this option open. Furthermore, while JFK's determination to contain the mainland at times blinded him to the fears and insecurities this instilled in China's leadership,[23] Johnson seems to have empathized with Chinese anxieties to a greater extent and recognized that US actions could trigger a hostile counter-response. The restrained escalation of the American role in Vietnam (against the wishes of his military advisers), the careful selection of bombing targets, and the steps taken to defuse tensions with Beijing were all hallmarks of a prudent, responsible leader fully capable of exercising independent judgement, spurning counsel with which he disagreed, and keenly aware of the dangerous precedent of Korea.

Johnson's initial passivity toward China policymaking gave way to steady engagement once the US became fully embroiled in Vietnam. The most notable developments in this sphere, not coincidentally, occurred when the President intervened in the decision-making process. Johnson's eagerness to keep the war limited and deflect domestic criticism in the spring of 1966 provided decisive momentum to the administration's bridge-building. His prodding of the foot-dragging Rusk to re-examine tactics toward Chinese representation, yielding a brief flirtation with "two Chinas," was one such example. His expressed interest in nurturing Chinese moderates, coming late in his tenure and producing little in the way of a tangible policy outcome, nevertheless demonstrated a capacity to look at mainland affairs in a non-Vietnam context. Johnson's consideration of a departure from traditional approaches in 1968 comports with Mitchell Lerner's model of a leader who had matured and refined his thinking by his final year in office.[24]

LBJ's mode of consuming the intelligence data that crossed his desk provides further insight into his modus operandi as a decision-maker. With Vietnam again in mind, Johnson has come under fire for contemptuously dismissing most reports from the field, demonstrating a limited need for basing his decisions on empirical information, cherry picking only those sources that corroborated his own fanciful views of the war's progress, and discouraging the government's various intelligence organs from producing innovative and imaginative anaysis.[25] The clear implication here, of course, is that independence of mind in this sphere is a virtue only if the neglected product is of doubtful quality. Based on what we now know from Chinese archives, the Johnson team was generally well served by the intelligence community. At each stage of the Vietnam War, it accurately pinpointed Beijing's reluctance directly to enter the fighting short of a discernible threat to the DRV's sovereignty or the expansion of US bombing to the mainland itself. While intelligence officials must bear some blame for reinforcing decision-makers' rather drastic preconceptions of the PRC's intentions and ambitions (NIE 13-9-65 "Communist China's Foreign Policy" and the June 1966 State-Defense Long Range Study on China being prime examples), they were careful enough to draw attention to its limited capacity for immediate aggression and its defensive orientation. China's myriad setbacks on the world stage in 1965–66 were well documented, as were the exacerbation of Sino-Soviet tensions and signs of growing friction between Beijing and Hanoi. Continuing a trend that had been a hallmark of information gathering on China during the Kennedy years,[26] US analysts had minimal success in deciphering political developments on the mainland, especially the dramatic and chaotic events of the Cultural Revolution. After some initial confusion, Mao's culpability in mobilizing the Red Guards against his rivals for power and the bureaucratic stagnation he abhorred was soundly established, yet the influence of his opposition was often exaggerated and, as noted above, the consistent view of the Chairman as an inveterate revolutionary resistant to any slowdown in the assault on the country's party-state apparatus proved mistaken.

Did Johnson incorporate all of this information when formulating policy? The evidence is mixed. His assumption of Chinese responsibility for the Vietnam conflict and of a watertight alliance between Mao and Ho, at least in the first few years of his presidency, could not be corroborated by even the most dire intelligence. On the crucial question of the prospects for Chinese intervention in Vietnam, LBJ, forever mindful of the Korean disaster, was far less confident of Beijing's restraint than his experts and rejected the implication that more vigorous action could be taken against the DRV without the risk of setting off a wider conflict. A President more sympathetic to that line of reasoning would have (and could have) expanded Rolling Thunder and possibly authorized limited incursions into North Vietnam, though whether this would have changed the outcome of the war remains uncertain. Seemingly oblivious to the well-founded skepticism of intelligence sources, Johnson also invested considerable faith in the Soviets as a partner for peace in Vietnam, hopeful that the Kremlin would lean on Hanoi to reduce its support of the insurgency in the South.

On the other hand, the conventional image of a headstrong LBJ presiding over a cloistered decision-making system seems overstated. Reports of the PRC's preparations for war in late 1965 heightened Johnson's inherent fears of Chinese embroilment in Vietnam and lent impetus to subsequent bridge-building measures. His downgrading of China's capacity for mischief was clearly influenced by incoming evidence of its declined standing throughout the Afro-Asian world, particularly its increasingly troubled relations with North Vietnam. Johnson's sustained interest in Chinese affairs can surely be measured by Rostow's voluminous correspondence to the President regarding the Cultural Revolution, which played no small part in stimulating consideration of new China initiatives in early 1968.

A cursory look at Johnson's consumption of China data, then, confirms that he was the administration's ultimate arbiter. In determining action or impressions on those matters of greatest interest to him, invariably those centering on Vietnam, he was very much his own man, relying mostly on his own instincts and preconceptions. It is also clear, however, that his capacity for adjusting his thinking in response to changing variables suggests a degree of suppleness and inquisitiveness that hitherto has not been captured in the existing literature.

On Brands' second yardstick of achievement, whether the policy was successful in attaining its stated objectives, LBJ again scores reasonably well. His primary goal vis a vis China, avoiding another military clash, was met and the steps taken to check the drift toward a wider war in Vietnam were a milestone on the road to Sino-American reconciliation.[27] Yet a more indirect accomplishment has gone relatively unnoticed. Given the minimal potential for a constructive dialogue with the Chinese, Johnson's instinctive caution, particularly his recognition that there was little Washington could do to influence the course of the Cultural Revolution and that any action taken might only backfire, suited the times in which he governed and may well have reaped long-term rewards. Rostow later recalled that Mao was one of two leaders whom Johnson deliberately refrained from condemning in public.[28] By refusing to explicitly take sides in China's domestic conflict or intervene in the country's political affairs, he averted the folly of adding fuel to the fire of Sino-American hostility and nourishing Mao's siege mentality. In doing so, he maximized America's policy options and his successor was well positioned to pursue rapprochement with the PRC if he so chose.[29] As Alfred Jenkins aptly reflected in a fitting epitaph of the Johnson team's record, "our policy toward Communist China in recent years has accomplished in good measure about all that could be expected, short of bilateral accommodations which are just not yet in the cards. Our policy has been consistent but not static. It has steadfastly opposed Chinese meddling and aggression; but it has moved toward seeking contact. The ground is well laid to move further when China is ready, if it seems in our interest."[30]

Notes

1. Ross, "Introduction," in Ross and Jiang (eds), *Re-examining the Cold War*, p. 9.
2. For a good discussion, see Pruessen, "Over the volcano," in ibid., pp. 100–5.
3. For references to China during the 1968 campaign, see Goh, *Constructing the US Rapprochement with China*, p. 112.
4. Rostow to LBJ, 20 February 1967, NSF, Memos to the President, Box 13, folder "Vol. XXI (2 of 4)," LBJL.
5. Gaddis, *Strategies of Containment*, p. 298.
6. For example, see Rusk interviewed by Reader's Digest, 25 November 1967, *DSB*, 18 December 1967, p. 822.
7. Quoted in Zhang Baijia and Jin Qingguo, "Steering wheel, shock absorber, and diplomatic probe in confrontation: Sino-American ambassadorial talks seen from the Chinese perspective," in Ross and Jiang (eds), *Re-examining the Cold War*, p. 193.
8. This argument is made in Goh, *Constructing the US Rapprochement with China*, p. 95.
9. The author is indebted to Professor Steven Casey (London School of Economics) for this insight.
10. R. Accinelli, "In pursuit of a modus vivendi: The Taiwan issue and Sino-American rapprochement, 1969–1972," in W.C. Kirby, R.S. Ross, and Gong Li (eds), *Normalization of US-China Relations: An International History* (Cambridge: Harvard University Press, 2005), pp. 11, 24.
11. For a good discussion of Nixon and Kissinger's willingness to sacrifice Taiwan's concerns for the sake of establishing a new relationship with China, see N.B. Tucker, "Taiwan expendable? Nixon and Kissinger go to China," *Journal of American History* 92:1 (June 2005).
12. A convincing appeal for incorporating ideology as a basis for understanding US foreign policy is made in O.A. Westad, "The new international history of the Cold War: Three (possible) paradigms," *Diplomatic History* 24: 4 (2000), 552–6.
13. M.H. Hunt, "Ideology," in M.J. Hogan and T.G. Paterson (eds), *Explaining the History of American Foreign Relations*, Second ed. (New York: Cambridge University Press, 2004), p. 221.
14. For America's traditional antagonism toward revolutionary activity abroad, see Hunt, *Ideology and US Foreign Policy*, chs 4–5. The quote is taken from p. 174. See as well R.S. Litwak, *Rogue States and US Foreign Policy: Containment after the Cold War* (Washington, DC: Woodrow Wilson Center Press, 2000), p. 9.
15. This is effectively discussed in Cohen, *Dean Rusk*, pp. 280–9.
16. Goh, *Constructing the US Rapprochement with China*, ch. 6.
17. H.W. Brands, "Introduction," in Brands (ed.), *Beyond Vietnam*, p. 4.

18 Logevall, *Choosing War*, pp. 390–4; Berman, *Planning a Tragedy*, ch. 4.
19 On this point, see Kaiser, "Men and policies, 1961–9" in Kunz (ed.), *Diplomacy of the Crucial Decade*.
20 Even Thomas Alan Schwartz, a staunch defender, concedes that LBJ initially displayed these tendencies. Schwartz, *Lyndon Johnson and Europe*, pp. 28–30.
21 The drawbacks inherent in Johnson's hierarchical advisory system are discussed in Preston, *The President and His Inner Circle*, pp. 160–2.
22 Tucker, "Lyndon Johnson: A final reckoning," in Cohen and Tucker (eds), *Lyndon Johnson Confronts the World*, p. 314.
23 Kochavi, *A Conflict Perpetuated*, p. 250.
24 Lerner, *The Pueblo Incident*, pp. 236–7.
25 R. Jeffreys-Jones, *The CIA and American Democracy*, Third ed. (New Haven: Yale University Press, 2003), chs 8–9; Preston, *The President and His Inner Circle*, p. 148.
26 Kochavi, *A Conflict Perpetuated*, p. 247.
27 Hershberg and Chen, "Reading and warning the likely enemy," pp. 83–4.
28 Author's interview with Rostow, Austin, Texas, 17 January 2002. The other leader, unsurprisingly, was de Gaulle.
29 A similar argument is made in Kaufman, *Confronting Communism*, pp. 209–10.
30 "Further thoughts on China," by Jenkins, 9 October 1968, NSF, Country File, Box 243, folder "China (A), vol. XIII," LBJL.

Bibliography

Primary sources (unpublished)

Lyndon Baines Johnson Library (Austin, Texas)
Administrative Histories: Department of State
Cabinet Papers
Meeting Notes File
National Security Files (NSF)
    Agency File
    Committee File
    Country File: Cambodia, Canada, China, France, Indonesia, Japan, Poland, Thailand, United Nations, USSR
    Files of McGeorge Bundy
    Files of Alfred Jenkins
    Files of Robert Komer
    Files of Walt Rostow
    International Meetings and Travel File
    Memos to the President
    Name File
    National Intelligence Estimates
    National Security Council History
    National Security Council Meetings
    Vietnam Country File
Office Files of Harry McPherson
Office Files of Bill Moyers
Office Files of Fred Panzer
Oral Histories: William Bundy, Roger Hilsman, Walt Rostow, Dean Rusk, James C. Thomson
Papers of George W. Ball
Papers of William P. Bundy

Papers of Orville L. Freeman
Papers of Paul C. Warnke: John McNaughton Files
Recordings of Telephone Conversations and Meetings
Vice Presidential Security File
White House Central File (WHCF)
  Confidential File
  Federal Government

John Fitzgerald Kennedy Library (Columbia Point, Boston, Massachusetts)
National Security Files (NSF)
  McGeorge Bundy Correspondence
  Countries: China, USSR
  Departments and Agencies
  Robert W. Komer Series
  Meetings and Memoranda
  Regional Security
Oral Histories: William Foster, Roger Hilsman
Papers of Roger Hilsman
Papers of Arthur Schlesinger, Jr
Papers of James C. Thomson, Jr
President's Office Files
White House Central Files

Library of Congress (Washington, DC)
W. Averell Harriman Papers

National Archives (College Park, Maryland)
Record Group 59, General Records of the Department of State

Public Record Office (Kew, London)
FO 371 Foreign Office, General Political Correspondence
PREM 11 Prime Minister's Office: Correspondence and Papers, 1951–1964
PREM 13 Prime Minister's Office: Correspondence and Papers, 1964–1970

Primary sources (published)

Public Papers of the Presidents of the United States: Lyndon B. Johnson (PPP:LBJ):
1963–64, 2 vols (Washington, DC: GPO, 1965)
1965, 2 vols (Washington, DC: GPO, 1966)
1966, 2 vols (Washington, DC: GPO, 1967)
1967, 2 vols (Washington, DC: GPO, 1968)
1968–69, 2 vols (Washington, DC: GPO, 1970)

US Department of State, *Department of State Bulletin (DSB)*, Washington, DC: US Government Printing Office, 1961–1968

US Department of State, *Foreign Relations of the United States (FRUS)*
1961–1963, vol. 5. "Soviet Union" (Washington, DC: GPO, 1998)
1961–1963, vol. 22. "Northeast Asia" (Washington, DC: GPO, 1996)
1961–1963, vol. 24. "Laos Crisis" (Washington, DC: GPO, 1994)
1964–1968, vol. 1. "Vietnam, 1964" (Washington, DC: GPO, 1992)
1964–1968, vol. 2. "Vietnam, January–June 1965" (Washington, DC: GPO, 1996)
1964–1968, vol. 3. "Vietnam, July–December 1965" (Washington, DC: GPO, 1996)
1964–1968, vol. 4. "Vietnam, 1966" (Washington, DC: GPO, 1998)
1964–1968, vol. 5. "Vietnam, 1967" (Washington, DC: GPO, 2002)
1964–1968, vol. 6. "Vietnam, January–August 1968" (Washington, DC: GPO, 2002)
1964–1968, vol. 11. "Arms Control and Disarmament" (Washington, DC: GPO, 1997)
1964–1968, vol. 14. "The Soviet Union" (Washington, DC: GPO, 2001)
1964–1968, vol. 17. "Eastern Europe" (Washington, DC: GPO, 1996)
1964–1968, vol. 26. "Indonesia; Malaysia-Singapore; Philippines" (Washington, DC: GPO, 2001)
1964–1968, vol. 27. "Mainland Southeast Asia; Regional Affairs" (Washington, DC: GPO, 2000)
1964–1968, vol. 28. "Laos" (Washington, DC: GPO, 1998)
1964–1968, vol. 29. "Part 1: Korea" (Washington, DC: GPO, 2000)
1964–1968, vol. 30. "China" (Washington, DC: GPO, 1998)

Newspapers

New York Times
Washington Post

Interviews with the author

Walt W. Rostow, Austin, Texas, 17 January 2002; 23 January 2002; 31 January 2002
James C. Thomson, Jr, Telephone Interview, 18 February 2002

Articles, books, theses

Accinelli, R., *Crisis and Commitment: United States Policy toward Taiwan, 1950–1955* (Chapel Hill: University of North Carolina Press, 1996)
Bachrack, S.D., *The Committee of One Million: "China Lobby" Politics, 1953–1971* (New York: Columbia University Press, 1976)

BIBLIOGRAPHY

Ball, G.W., *The Past Has Another Pattern* (New York: W.W. Norton & Company, 1982)

Barnett, A.D., *A New US Policy toward China* (Washington, DC: The Brookings Institution, 1971)

Barnett, A.D. and E.O. Reischauer (eds), *The United States and China: The Next Decade* (New York: Praeger, 1970)

Barnouin, B. and Yu Changgen, *Chinese Foreign Policy During the Cultural Revolution* (London: Kegan Paul International, 1998)

Barrett, D.M., *Uncertain Warriors: Lyndon Johnson and His Vietnam Advisers* (Lawrence, Kansas: University Press of Kansas, 1993)

Berman, L., *Planning a Tragedy: The Americanization of the War in Vietnam* (New York: W.W. Norton & Company, 1982)

Berman, L., *Lyndon Johnson's War: The Road to Stalemate in Vietnam* (New York: W.W. Norton & Company, 1989)

Berman, W.C., *William Fulbright and the Vietnam War: The Dissent of a Political Realist* (Kent: Kent State University Press, 1988)

Beschloss, M.R., *The Crisis Years: Kennedy and Khrushchev, 1960–1963* (New York: Edward Burlingame Books, 1991)

Beschloss, M.R. (ed.), *Taking Charge: The Johnson White House Tapes, 1963–1964* (New York: Simon & Schuster, 1997)

Beschloss, M.R. (ed.), *Reaching for Glory: Lyndon Johnson's Secret White House Tapes, 1964–1965* (New York: Simon & Schuster, 2001)

Bird, K., *The Color of Truth: McGeorge Bundy and William Bundy, Brothers in Arms* (New York: Simon & Schuster, 1998)

Borg, D. and W. Heinrichs (eds), *Uncertain Years: Chinese-American Relations, 1947–1950* (New York: Columbia University Press, 1980.)

Brands, H.W., "The limits of manipulation: How the United States didn't topple Sukarno," *Journal of American History* 76:3 (1989)

Brands, H.W., *The Wages of Globalism: Lyndon Johnson and the Limits of American Power* (New York: Oxford University Press, 1995)

Brands, H.W. (ed.), *The Foreign Policies of Lyndon Johnson: Beyond Vietnam* (College Station: Texas A & M University Press, 1999)

Broadwater, J., *Adlai Stevenson and American Politics: The Odyssey of a Cold War Liberal* (New York: Twayne, 1994)

Bundy, W., *A Tangled Web: The Making of Foreign Policy in the Nixon Presidency* (New York: Hill and Wang, 1998)

Burr, W. and J.T. Richelson. "Whether to 'strangle the baby in the cradle:' The United States and the Chinese nuclear program, 1960–64," *International Security* 25:3 (2000/2001)

Califano, J.A. Jr, *The Triumph & Tragedy of Lyndon Johnson: The White House Years* (New York: Simon & Schuster, 1991)

Castle, T.N., *At War in the Shadow of Vietnam: US Military Aid to the Royal Lao Government, 1955–1975* (New York: Columbia University Press, 1993)

Chandler, D., *A History of Cambodia*, Second ed. (Boulder: Westview Press, 1996)

Chang, G.H., *Friends and Enemies: The United States, China, and the Soviet Union, 1948–1972* (Stanford: Stanford University Press, 1990)

Chen Jian, *China's Road to the Korean War: The Making of the Sino-American Confrontation* (New York: Columbia University Press, 1994)

Chen Jian, "The Myth of America's 'Lost Chance' in China: A Chinese Perspective in Light of New Evidence," *Diplomatic History* 21:1 (1997)

Chen Jian, *Mao's China and the Cold War* (Chapel Hill: University of North Carolina Press, 2001)

Chen Jian and D.L. Wilson (eds), "All under the heaven is great chaos: Beijing, the Sino-Soviet border clashes, and the turn toward Sino-American rapprochement, 1968–1969," Cold War International History Project *Bulletin* 11 (Winter 1998–99)

Christensen, T.J., *Useful Adversaries: Grand Strategy, Domestic Mobilization, and Sino-American Conflict, 1947–1958* (Princeton: Princeton University Press, 1996)

Clodfelter, M., *The Limits of Air Power: The American Bombing of North Vietnam* (New York: The Free Press, 1989)

Clymer, K.J., "The perils of neutrality: The break in US-Cambodian relations, 1965," *Diplomatic History* 23: 4 (1999)

Cohen, W.I., *Dean Rusk* (Totowa, NJ: Cooper Square, 1980)

Cohen, W.I. (ed.), *New Frontiers in American-East Asian Relations: Essays Presented to Dorothy Borg* (New York: Columbia University Press, 1983)

Cohen, W.I. (ed.), *Pacific Passage: The Study of American-East Asian Relations On the Eve of the Twenty-First Century* (New York: Columbia University Press, 1996)

Cohen, W.I., *America's Response to China*, Fourth ed. (New York: Columbia University Press, 2000)

Cohen, W.I., "Kennedy's China," *Diplomatic History* 28: 1 (2004)

Cohen, W.I. and A. Iriye (eds), *The Great Powers in East Asia, 1953–1960* (New York: Columbia University Press, 1990)

Cohen, W.I. and N.B. Tucker (eds), *Lyndon Johnson Confronts the World: American Foreign Policy, 1963–1968* (New York: Cambridge University Press, 1994)

Dallek, R., *Lone Star Rising: Lyndon Johnson and His Times, 1908–1960* (New York: Oxford University Press, 1991)

Dallek, R., "Lyndon Johnson and Vietnam: The making of a tragedy," *Diplomatic History* 20: 2 (1996)

Dallek, R., *Flawed Giant: Lyndon Johnson and His Times, 1961–1973* (New York: Oxford University Press, 1998)

Dallek, R., *An Unfinished Life: John F. Kennedy, 1917–1963* (Boston: Little, Brown, 2003)

Day, A.J. (ed.), *China and the Soviet Union, 1949–84* (New York: Facts on File Publications, 1985)

DiLeo, D., *George Ball, Vietnam, and the Rethinking of Containment* (Chapel Hill: University of North Carolina Press, 1991)

Dittmer, L., *Liu Shaoqi and the Chinese Cultural Revolution*, Revised ed. (London: M.E. Sharpe, 1998)

Dobrynin, A., *In Confidence: Moscow's Ambassador to America's Six Cold War Presidents, 1962–1986* (New York: Times Books, 1995)

Dodds, A.I., "The China Opening in Perspective, 1961–1976" (PhD dissertation, Cambridge University, 2002)

Dulles, F.R., *American Policy toward Communist China, 1949–1969* (New York: Thomas Y. Crowell, 1972)

Dumbrell, J., *President Lyndon Johnson and Soviet Communism* (Manchester: Manchester University Press, 2004)

Evans, P.M., *John Fairbank and the American Understanding of Modern China* (New York: Blackwell, 1988)

Evans, P.M. and B.M. Frolic (eds), *Reluctant Adversaries: Canada and the People's Republic of China, 1949–1970* (Toronto: University of Toronto Press, 1991)

Fairbank, J.K., *Chinabound: A Fifty-Year Memoir* (New York: Harper & Row, 1982)

Foot, R., *The Practice of Power: US Relations with China Since 1949* (Oxford: Clarendon Press, 1995)

Frankel, M., *The Times of My Life and My Life with the Times* (New York: Random House, 1999)

Freedman, L., *Kennedy's Wars: Berlin, Cuba, Laos, and Vietnam* (New York: Oxford University Press, 2000)

Fromkin, D., "Lyndon Johnson and foreign policy: What the new documents Show," *Foreign Affairs* 74: 1 (1995)

Gaddis, J.L., *Strategies of Containment: A Critical Appraisal of Postwar American National Security Policy* (New York: Oxford University Press, 1982).

Gaddis, J.L., *The Long Peace: Inquiries into the History of the Cold War* (New York: Oxford University Press, 1987)

Gaddis, J.L., P.H. Gordon, E.R. May, and J. Rosenberg (eds), *Cold War Statesmen Confront the Bomb: Nuclear Diplomacy Since 1945* (Oxford: Oxford University Press, 1999)

Gaiduk, I.V., "The Vietnam War and Soviet-American relations, 1964–73: New Russian evidence," *Cold War International History Project Bulletin* 6–7 (1995/1996)

Gaiduk, I.V., *The Soviet Union and the Vietnam War* (Chicago: Ivan R. Dee, 1996)

Ganguly, S., *Conflict Unending: India-Pakistan Tensions Since 1947* (New York: Columbia University Press, 2001)

Gardner, L.C., *Pay Any Price: Lyndon Johnson and the Wars for Vietnam* (Chicago: Ivan R. Dee, 1995)

Gardner, L.C. and T. Gittinger (eds), *International Perspectives on Vietnam* (College Station: Texas A&M University Press, 2000)

Garson, R., *The United States and China Since 1949: A Troubled Affair* (London: Pinter, 1994)

Garson, R., "Lyndon B. Johnson and the China enigma," *Journal of Contemporary History* 32:1 (1997)

Garthoff, R.L., "A comment on the discussion of 'LBJ, China and the bomb,'" *SHAFR Newsletter* 28: 3 (1997)

Garver, J.W., *China's Decision for Rapprochement with the United States, 1968–1971* (Boulder: Westview, 1982)

Garver, J.W., "Little Chance," *Diplomatic History* 21:1(1997)

Gaskin, T.M., "Senator Lyndon B. Johnson and United States Foreign Policy" (PhD dissertation, University of Washington, 1989)

Germany, K.B. and R.D. Johnson (eds), *The Presidential Recordings, Lyndon B. Johnson: The Kennedy Assassination and the Transfer of Power, November 1963–January 1964*, 3 vols (New York: W.W. Norton & Company, 2005)

Geyelin, P., *Lyndon B. Johnson and the World* (New York: Praeger, 1966)

Giglio, J.N., *The Presidency of John F. Kennedy* (Lawrence: University Press of Kansas, 1991)

Gilbert, M.J. and W. Head (eds), *The Tet Offensive* (Westport: Praeger, 1996)

Gittinger, T. (ed.), *The Johnson Years: A Vietnam Roundtable* (Austin, Texas: Lyndon Baines Johnson Library, 1993)

Goh, E., *Constructing the US Rapprochement with China, 1961–1974: From "Red Menace" to "Tacit Ally"* (New York: Cambridge University Press, 2005)

Goldman, E.F., *The Tragedy of Lyndon Johnson* (New York: Alfred A. Knopf, 1969)

Goodwin, D.K., *Lyndon Johnson and the American Dream*, Revised ed. (New York: St. Martin's Press, 1991)

Goodwin, R.N., *Remembering America: A Voice from the Sixties* (Boston: Little, Brown, 1988)

Gould, L.L., "The Revised LBJ," *The Wilson Quarterly* 24: 2 (2000)

Green, M., *Indonesia: Crisis and Transformation, 1965–1968* (Washington, DC: The Compass Press, 1990)

Green, M., J.H. Holdridge and W.N. Stokes, *War and Peace with China: First Hand Experiences in the Foreign Service of the United States* (Bethesda, MD: Dacor Press, 1994)

Guan, A.C., "The Johnson administration and 'confrontation,'" *Cold War History* 2:3 (2002)
Hammond, P.Y., *LBJ and the Presidential Management of Foreign Relations* (Austin: University of Texas Press, 1992)
Harding, H. and Yuan Ming (eds), *Sino-American Relations, 1945–1955: A Joint Reassessment of a Critical Decade* (Wilmington, DE: SR Books, 1989)
Head, W. and L.E. Grinter (eds), *Looking Back on Vietnam: A 1990's Perspective on the Decisions, Combat, and Legacies* (Westport: Praeger, 1993)
Herring, G.C., *America's Longest War*, Second ed. (New York: Alfred A. Knopf, 1986)
Herring, G.C., *LBJ and Vietnam: A Different Kind of War* (Austin: University of Texas Press, 1994)
Hershberg, J.G. and Chen Jian, "Reading and warning the likely enemy: China's signals to the United States about Vietnam in 1965," *International History Review* 27:1 (2005)
Hilsman, R., *To Move a Nation: The Politics of Foreign Policy in the Administration of John F. Kennedy* (Garden City, NY: Doubleday, 1967)
Hogan, M.J. (ed.), *America in the World: The Historiography of American Foreign Relations Since 1941* (New York: Cambridge University Press, 1995)
Hogan, M.J. and T.G. Paterson (eds), *Explaining the History of American Foreign Relations*, Second ed. (New York: Cambridge University Press, 2004)
Humphrey, D.C., "Tuesday lunch at the Johnson White House: A preliminary assessment," *Diplomatic History* 8:1 (1984)
Humphrey, D.C. "NSC meetings during the Johnson presidency," *Diplomatic History* 18: 1 (1994)
Hunt, M.H., *The Making of a Special Relationship: The United States and China to 1914* (New York: Columbia University Press, 1983)
Hunt, M.H., *Ideology and US Foreign Policy* (New Haven: Yale University Press, 1987)
Hunt, M.H., *Lyndon Johnson's War: America's Cold War Crusade in Vietnam, 1945–1968* (New York: Hill and Wang, 1996)
Immerman, R.H. (ed.), *John Foster Dulles and the Diplomacy of the Cold War* (Princeton: Princeton University Press, 1990)
Isaacson, W., *Kissinger: A Biography* (New York: Simon & Schuster, 1992)
Jeffreys-Jones, R., *The CIA and American Democracy*, Third ed. (New Haven: Yale University Press, 2003)
Johnson, L.B., *The Vantage Point: Perspectives of the Presidency, 1963–1969* (New York: Holt, Rinehart and Winston, 1971)
Johnson, W. (ed.), *The Papers of Adlai E. Stevenson*, vol. 8 (Boston: Little, Brown, 1979)

Jones, M., *Conflict and Confrontation in South East Asia, 1961–1965: Britain, the United States and the Creation of Malaysia* (Cambridge: Cambridge University Press, 2002)

Jones, M., "'Groping toward coexistence:' US China policy during the Johnson years," *Diplomacy & Statecraft* 12:3 (2001)

Jones, M., "US relations with Indonesia, the Kennedy-Johnson transition, and the Vietnam connection, 1963–1965," *Diplomatic History* 26:2 (2002).

Kail, F.M., *What Washington Said: Administration Rhetoric and the Vietnam War, 1949–1969* (New York: Harper & Row, 1973)

Kaiser, D., *American Tragedy: Kennedy, Johnson, and the Origins of the Vietnam War* (Cambridge: Harvard University Press, 2000)

Kang, J.S., "Food for communist China: A US policy dilemma, 1961–1963," *Journal of American-East Asian Relations* 7:1–2 (1998)

Karnow, S., *Vietnam: A History*, Revised ed. (New York: Penguin Books, 1991)

Kaufman, B.I., "John F. Kennedy as world leader: A perspective on the literature," *Diplomatic History* 17:3 (1993)

Kaufman, V.S., "A response to chaos: The United States, the Great Leap Forward, and the Cultural Revolution, 1961–1968," *Journal of American-East Asian Relations* 7:1–2 (1998)

Kaufman, V.S., *Confronting Communism: US and British Policies toward China* (Columbia: University of Missouri Press, 2001)

Keith, R.C., *The Diplomacy of Zhou Enlai* (London: Macmillan, 1989)

Kennan, G.F., "A fresh look at our China policy," *New York Times Magazine* (22 November 1964)

Khong, Y.F., *Analogies at War: Korea, Munich, Dien Bien Phu, and the Vietnam Decisions of 1965* (Princeton: Princeton University Press, 1992)

Kirby, W.C., R.S. Ross, and Gong Li (eds), *Normalization of US-China Relations: An International History* (Cambridge: Harvard University Press, 2005)

Kislenko, A., "Bamboo in the Wind: United States Foreign Policy and Thailand During the Kennedy and Johnson Administrations, 1961–1969" (PhD dissertation, University of Toronto, 2000)

Kissinger, H., *White House Years* (Boston: Little, Brown, 1979)

Kochavi, N., *A Conflict Perpetuated: China Policy During the Kennedy Years* (Westport: Praeger, 2002)

Kochavi, N., "Limited accommodation, perpetuated conflict: Kennedy, China, and the Laos crisis, 1961–1963," *Diplomatic History* 26:1 (2002)

Kuisong, Y., "Changes in Mao Zedong's attitude toward the Indochina War, 1949–1973," Cold War International History Project Working Paper 34 (2002)

Kunz, D.B. (ed.), *The Diplomacy of the Crucial Decade: American Foreign*

Relations During the 1960s (New York: Columbia University Press, 1994)

Kusnitz, L.A., *Public Opinion and Foreign Policy: America's China Policy, 1949–1979* (Westport: Greenwood Press, 1984)

Kux, D., *The United States and Pakistan, 1947–2000: Disenchanted Allies* (Washington, DC: Woodrow Wilson Center Press, 2001)

Lacouture, J., *De Gaulle: The Ruler, 1945–1970* (London: HarperCollins, 1991)

Leffler, M.P., *A Preponderance of Power: National Security, the Truman Administration, and the Cold War* (Stanford: Stanford University Press, 1992)

Legge, J.D., *Sukarno: A Political Biography*, Second ed. (Sydney: Allen & Unwin, 1984)

Leifer, M., *Indonesia's Foreign Policy* (London: George Allen & Unwin, 1983)

Lerner, M., "A failure of perception: Lyndon Johnson, North Korean ideology, and the *Pueblo* incident," *Diplomatic History* 25:4 (2001)

Lerner, M., *The Pueblo Incident: A Spy Ship and the Failure of American Foreign Policy* (Lawrence: University Press of Kansas, 2002)

Lewis, J.W. and Xue Litai, *China Builds the Bomb* (Stanford: Stanford University Press, 1988)

Litwak, R.S., *Rogue States and US Foreign Policy: Containment after the Cold War* (Washington, DC: Woodrow Wilson Center Press, 2000)

Logevall, F., *Choosing War: The Lost Chance for Peace and the Escalation of War in Vietnam* (Berkeley: University of California Press, 1999)

Low, A.D., *The Sino-Soviet Dispute: An Analysis of the Polemics* (London: Associated University Presses, 1976)

MacFarquhar, R. (ed.), *Sino-American Relations, 1949–1971* (New York: Praeger, 1972)

MacFarquhar, R., *The Origins of the Cultural Revolution, vol. 3: The Coming of the Cataclysm, 1961–1966* (New York: Columbia University Press, 1997)

MacFarquhar, R. (ed.), *The Politics of China: The Eras of Mao and Deng*, Second ed. (Cambridge: Cambridge University Press, 1997)

MacFarquhar, R. and M. Schoenhals, *Mao's Last Revolution* (Cambridge: Belknap Press of Harvard University Press, 2006)

MacFarquhar, R. and J.K. Fairbank (eds), *The Cambridge History of China, vol. 15: The People's Republic, Part 2: Revolutions within the Chinese Revolution, 1966–1982* (Cambridge: Cambridge University Press, 1991)

McLean, D., "American nationalism, the China myth, and the Truman doctrine: The question of accommodation with Peking, 1949–50," *Diplomatic History* 10:1 (1986)

McMahon, R.J., *The Cold War on the Periphery: The United States, India, and Pakistan* (New York: Columbia University Press, 1994)

McNamara, R.S., *In Retrospect: The Tragedy and Lessons of Vietnam* (New York: Times Books, 1995)

Mann, J., *About Face: A History of America's Curious Relationship with China, from Nixon to Clinton* (New York: Vintage, 1998)

Mozingo, D., *Chinese Policy toward Indonesia, 1949–1967* (Ithaca: Cornell University Press, 1976)

Niu, J., "1962: The eve of the left turn in China's foreign policy," Cold War International History Project Working Paper 48 (2005)

Nixon, R.M., "Asia after Viet Nam," *Foreign Affairs* 46:1 (1967)

Nixon, R.M., *RN: The Memoirs of Richard Nixon* (New York: Simon & Schuster, 1978)

Offner, A.A., *Another Such Victory: President Truman and the Cold War, 1945–1953* (Stanford: Stanford University Press, 2002)

Osborne, M., *Sihanouk: Prince of Light, Prince of Darkness* (St Leonards, Australia: Allen & Unwin, 1994)

Paterson, T.G. (ed.), *Kennedy's Quest for Victory: American Foreign Policy, 1961–1963* (New York: Oxford University Press, 1989)

Pike, D., *Vietnam and the Soviet Union: Anatomy of an Alliance* (Boulder: Westview, 1987)

Prados, J., *Keepers of the Keys: A History of the National Security Council from Truman to Bush* (New York: William Morrow and Company, 1991)

Preston, A., *The War Council: McGeorge Bundy, the NSC, and Vietnam* (Cambridge: Harvard University Press, 2006)

Preston, T., *The President and His Inner Circle: Leadership Style and the Advisory Process in Foreign Affairs* (New York: Columbia University Press, 2001)

Quested, R.K.I., *Sino-Russian Relations: A Short History* (Sydney: George Allen & Unwin, 1984)

Quigley, K., "The Evolving Consensus: The Development of US China Policy between 1959 and 1972 and the Domestic Influences on it" (PhD dissertation, University of Warwick, 2000)

Quigley, K., "A lost opportunity: a reappraisal of the Kennedy administration's China policy in 1963," *Diplomacy and Statecraft* 13:3 (2002)

Radchenko, S., "The China Puzzle: Soviet Policy towards the People's Republic of China in the 1960s," (PhD dissertation, London School of Economics and Political Science, 2005)

Radchenko, S., "The Soviet Union and the North Korean seizure of the USS *Pueblo*: Evidence from Russian archives," Cold War International History Project Working Paper 47 (2005)

Reeves, R., *President Kennedy: Profile of Power* (New York: Simon & Schuster, 1993)

Reischauer, E.O., *Beyond Vietnam: The United States and Asia* (New York: Alfred A. Knopf, 1968)

Robinson, T.W. (ed.), *The Cultural Revolution in China* (Berkeley: University of California Press, 1971)
Robinson, T.W. and D. Shambaugh (eds), *Chinese Foreign Policy: Theory and Practice* (Oxford: Clarendon Press, 1994)
Rogers, F.E., "Sino-American relations and the Vietnam War, 1964–66," *China Quarterly* 66 (1976)
Ross, R.S., *Negotiating Cooperation: The United States and China, 1969–1989* (Stanford: Stanford University Press, 1995)
Ross, R.S. and Jiang Changbin (eds), *Re-examining the Cold War: US-China Diplomacy, 1954–1973* (Cambridge: Harvard University Asia Center, 2001)
Rostow, W.W., *The Diffusion of Power: An Essay in Recent History* (New York: Macmillan, 1972)
Rusk, D., *As I Saw It* (New York: Norton, 1990)
Rust, W.J., *Kennedy in Vietnam* (New York: De Capo Press, 1985)
Schafer, B., "Weathering the Sino-Soviet conflict: The GDR and North Korea, 1949–1989," Cold War International History Project *Bulletin* 14/15 (2003/2004)
Schafer, B., "North Korean 'adventurism' and China's long shadow, 1966–1972," Cold War International History Project Working Paper 44 (2004)
Schlesinger, A.M. Jr, *A Thousand Days: John F. Kennedy in the White House* (Boston: Houghton Mifflin, 1965)
Schoenbaum, T.J., *Waging Peace and War: Dean Rusk in the Truman, Kennedy, and Johnson Years* (New York: Simon & Schuster, 1988)
Schulzinger, R.D. (ed.), *A Companion to American Foreign Relations* (Malden, MA: Blackwell Publishing, 2003)
Schwartz, T.A., *Lyndon Johnson and Europe: In the Shadow of Vietnam* (Cambridge: Harvard University Press, 2003)
Shao, K., *Zhou Enlai and the Foundations of Chinese Foreign Policy* (New York: St Martin's Press, 1996)
Shapley, D., *Promise and Power: The Life and Times of Robert McNamara* (Boston: Little, Brown, 1993)
Shesol, J., *Mutual Contempt: Lyndon Johnson, Robert Kennedy, and the Feud that Defined a Decade* (New York: W.W. Norton & Company, 1997)
Short, P., *Mao: A Life* (New York: Henry Holt and Company, 2000)
Small, M., *Johnson, Nixon, and the Doves* (New Brunswick: Rutgers University Press, 1988)
Smith, R.B., *An International History of the Vietnam War, vol. 2: The Struggle for South-East Asia, 1961–6* (London: Macmillan, 1985)
Smith, R.B., *An International History of the Vietnam War, vol. 3: The Making of a Limited War, 1965–66* (London: Macmillan, 1991)
Sorensen, T.C., *Kennedy* (New York: Harper & Row, 1965)

Stebenne, D.L., *Arthur J. Goldberg: New Deal Liberal* (New York: Oxford University Press, 1996)

Sukma, R., *Indonesia and China: The Politics of a Troubled Relationship* (London: Routledge, 1999)

Suri, J., *Power and Protest: Global Revolution and the Rise of Détente* (Cambridge: Harvard University Press, 2003)

Thomson, J.C. Jr, "How could Vietnam happen? An autopsy," *Atlantic Monthly* (1968)

Thomson, J.C. Jr, "On the making of US China policy, 1961–69: A study in bureaucratic politics," *China Quarterly* 50 (1972)

Tucker, N.B., *Patterns in the Dust: Chinese-American Relations and the Recognition Controversy, 1949–1950* (New York: Columbia University Press, 1983)

Tucker, N.B., "No common ground: American-Chinese-Soviet relations, 1948–1972," *Diplomatic History* 16:2 (1992)

Tucker, N.B., *Taiwan, Hong Kong, and the United States, 1945–1992: Uncertain Friendships* (New York: Twayne, 1994)

Tucker, N.B. (ed.), *China Confidential: American Diplomats and Sino-American Relations, 1945–1996* (New York: Columbia University Press, 2001)

Tucker, N.B., "Taiwan expendable? Nixon and Kissinger go to China," *Journal of American History* 92:1 (2005)

Tyler, P., *A Great Wall: Six Presidents and China* (New York: Public Affairs, 1999)

VanDeMark, B., *Into the Quagmire: Lyndon Johnson and the Escalation of the Vietnam War* (New York: Oxford University Press, 1990)

Wedeman, A., *The East Wind Subsides: Chinese Foreign Policy and the Origins of the Cultural Revolution* (Washington, DC: Washington Institute Press, 1987)

Westad, O.A., "Losses, chances, and myths: The United States and the creation of the Sino-Soviet Alliance, 1945–1950," *Diplomatic History* 21:1 (1997)

Westad, O.A. (ed.), *Brothers in Arms: The Rise and Fall of the Sino-Soviet Alliance,1945–1963* (Washington: Woodrow Wilson Center Press, 1998)

Westad, O.A., "The new international history of the Cold War: Three (possible) paradigms," *Diplomatic History* 24:4 (2000)

Westad, O.A., Chen Jian, S. Tonnesson, Nguyen Vu Tung, and J.G. Hershberg (eds), "77 conversations between Chinese and foreign leaders on the wars in Indochina, 1964–1977," Cold War International History Project Working Paper 22 (1998)

Whiting, A.S., "Time for a change in our China policy," *New York Times Magazine* (15 December 1968)

Whiting, A.S., *The Chinese Calculus of Deterrence* (Ann Arbor: University of Michigan Press, 1975)

Woods, R.B., *Fulbright: A Biography* (New York: Cambridge University Press, 1995)
Young, J.W., *The Labour Governments, 1964–70, vol. 2: International Policy* (Manchester: Manchester University Press, 2003)
Young, K.T., *Negotiating with the Chinese Communists: The United States Experience, 1953–1967* (New York: McGraw-Hill, 1968)
Zeiler, T.W., *Dean Rusk: Defending the American Mission Abroad* (Wilmington: SR Books, 2000)
Zhai, Q., "Beijing and the Vietnam conflict, 1964–1965: New Chinese evidence," Cold War International History Project *Bulletin* 6–7 (1995/1996)
Zhai, Q., "Beijing and the Vietnam peace talks, 1965–68: new evidence from Chinese sources," Cold War International History Project Working Paper 18 (1997)
Zhai, Q., *China and the Vietnam Wars, 1950–1975* (Chapel Hill: University of North Carolina Press, 2000)
Zhang, S.G., *Deterrence and Strategic Culture: Chinese-American Confrontations, 1949–1958* (Ithaca: Cornell University Press, 1992)
Zhang, S.G., *Economic Cold War: America's Embargo against China and the Sino-Soviet Alliance, 1949–1963* (Washington, DC: Woodrow Wilson Center Press, 2001)

Index

Note: 'n' after a page number indicates the number of a note on that page.

Acheson, Dean 16–17, 58
Africa 62–3, 93
African Americans 6
Albania 141
Albanian Resolution, the 161–5
Algiers conference, 1965 141
alliance politics 249–50
American Alumni Council 157
appeasement 92
arms control 36, 37, 63
Asian Communist Affairs, Office of (ACA) 39
Asia, wars of national liberation 24
Austria 64
Ayub Khan, Mohammed 139

Ball, George 108–9, 114–15, 148, 150
Barnett, A. Doak 154–5, 221
Bay of Pigs 27, 28
Belgium 64, 65, 75, 165
Berlin 27
Bohlen, Charles 35–6, 63, 251
Bowles, Chester 22, 25, 30, 31–3, 40, 241
Brands, H. W. 253, 257
Brezhnev, Leonid 196
bridge-building proposals 87–91, 229, 245–7, 255

Cultural Revolution and 185–90, 220–8, 246–7
limits of 160–5, 248–52
politics of 153–60, 242–3, 248–9
two-pronged China policy 151–3
Brzezinski, Zbigniew 198, 231
Bundy, McGeorge 25, 27, 36–7, 59, 60, 61, 64, 68, 71, 73, 87, 91, 94, 99, 107–8, 110, 114, 119, 124n24, 147
Bundy, William 33, 90, 94, 100, 106, 107, 142–3, 146–7, 159–60, 160–1, 161–2, 185, 187–8, 189, 193–4, 195, 232
Bunker, Ellsworth 103–4
Bureau of Intelligence and Research, Department of State 28, 32, 63, 68–9, 92, 146, 149
Bureau of International Security Affairs, Department of Defense 71
Burma 144
Burr, William 73

Cabot, John Moors 29
Cambodia 102, 104–6, 108, 192
Canada 64, 65–6, 68, 74–5, 94, 163–5, 225–6, 249
Cater, Douglas 198

INDEX

Central Cultural Revolution Group 191
Central Intelligence Agency (CIA) 29, 34, 64, 67, 100, 103, 107, 141, 146, 150, 181, 191, 199, 200, 216, 217, 220
Chen Jian 247
Chen Yi 30, 107, 119, 139, 190, 191, 216–17
Chiang Ching-kuo 149
Chiang Kai-shek 15, 16, 17, 18, 19–20, 27, 28–9, 65, 70, 149, 162–3, 240, 250
Chief of the US forces in the Pacific (CINCPAC) 71
Chile 165
China
   Acheson's view of 17
   adventurism 34
   Africa and 62–3
   aid to North Vietnam 117–18, 146
   American defeat in Vietnam and 108–9
   Cambodia and 105
   change in Soviet leadership and 92
   changing perceptions of 3
   communists assume power 13
   competing visions of 86–96
   conflict with India 33, 38
   declaration on American conduct in Vietnam 119
   diplomatic failures 144
   early American trade with 13–14
   economic embargo 19, 20, 30, 32, 41, 88, 90
   economic problems 96
   economic recovery from the Great Leap Forward 179
   expansionism 85, 87, 108, 121, 138, 152, 226, 251–2
   explodes nuclear device 53, 74, 242
   famine 28
   foreign policy 4, 41, 68, 92, 216–17, 228–9, 232–4
   foreign policy defeats 138–42, 165, 243
   French recognition of 53, 63–8, 121
   growing US hostility towards 19
   hints at moderation of foreign policy, 1962 29–30
   ideology 97–8
   imperialist activity in 14
   increase in international acceptance 74–8
   Indonesia and 103–4
   Indo-Pakistani War and 138–40
   influence in North Vietnam 113, 200, 219–20
   international conciliation of 121–2
   JFK on 25, 34
   JFK on nuclear threat 36–8, 72–3, 254
   JFK's food relief plans 30–4, 35
   JFK's impression of 23–5, 34, 41–2, 57, 241–2
   Korean War and 18–19, 55–6, 62
   LBJ's attitude to 54–7, 73, 253–5
   LBJ's goodwill message, 1967 190
   leadership division 123n15
   leadership's hostility to America 89–90
   leadership's militancy 92
   loss of prestige 141
   military deployment 114
   military personnel in North Korea 148–9
   military strength 96, 99

Ministry of Foreign Affairs 190–1
non-communist elites 23
nuclear program 21, 35, 36–9, 41, 51n123, 61, 68–77, 91, 242, 254
nuclear threat 69–71
objectives 96–7
opposition to peace initiatives 117
paranoia 144–5
peace offensive and 143
pre-1961 American policy towards 13–21
Pueblo affair and 218
recognition of Mao's regime 20
rejects Limited Test Ban Treaty 63
response to the re-launch of Operation Rolling Thunder 158
reunification 250
role in Vietnam War 95, 113–20, 121
Rusk's view of 61–2, 92, 101–2, 113, 144, 155, 166, 219, 223–4, 231–2
Second World War and 15
Sino-American rapprochement offer 228–32
Taiwan's status and 21
Taiwan Strait invasion plan and 29
Thailand and 107
Thomson's proposals for change in policy towards 87–8
threat exaggerated 88–9, 251–2
threat of 4, 55–6, 61–2, 76, 165–6, 242
threat perception 86, 89, 95, 109, 111–13, 218
ultimatum to India, 1965 140
UN membership proposal defeated 161–5
value of human life 127n60
Vietnam strategy 101
Vietnam War policy, 1966-67 190–6
see also containment, Cultural Revolution, Great Leap Forward; Sino-Soviet friction
China Lobby, the 18, 19, 58, 85, 95
China policy review 220–8, 232–3, 246–7
Chinese civil war 16–17
Chinese Communist Party (CCP) 13, 15, 16–17
Christensen, Thomas 243
civil rights 6
Cleveland, Harlan 75, 89–90
Clifford, Clark 195, 225
closed door policy 21
Cold War 15–16, 23–4, 58
colonialism 63
communism, containment of 22
"Communist China – Long Range Study," 1966 96–7, 152–3, 160
"Communist China (Short range report)," 1965 118–19
Conference of the New Emerging Forces 103
confidence-building 152
conflict management 3
Conflict Perpetuated, A (Kochavi) 2
Congress, changing stance of 76
containment 89–90
 under JFK 12, 22, 26, 31, 33, 39–40, 241
 under LBJ 55–6, 78, 85–6, 93, 120–2, 144, 152, 154–5, 233, 240–1

INDEX

containment without isolation
    39–40
Council on Foreign Relations 76
counterinsurgency 23
C-SPAN 6
Cuban missile crisis 33–4, 36, 40
Cultural Revolution 117, 163,
    177–8
    American public opinion and
        188–9
    American view of 180–6,
        215–16, 252
    bridge building and 185–90,
        220–8, 246–7
    Chinese foreign policy and
        190–6, 216–17, 246
    CIA interpretation of 181
    Democratic party and 1
    effect of 3
    February Adverse Current
        182–3, 191, 214
    impact of 202–3, 243–4
    indoctrination 191
    interpreting 179–90, 256
    LBJ's reaction to 184–90
    magnitude of 233
    Mao's intentions 182
    opposition to 181–2, 182–3, 184
    origins 179–80
    overthrow of the Shanghai Party
        Committee 182
    PLA intervention in 214–16
    Red Guards, the 180, 181–2,
        183, 187, 214, 246
    Rice's interpretation of 181
    rise of Zhou Enlai and 183–4
    Soviet Union and 196–8, 202
    turning point 214–20
    Wuhan Incident 214–15
Cultural Revolution Group 214–17

Dallek, Robert 6
Davis, Nathaniel 198

Defense, Department of, Bureau of
    International Security Affairs
    71
De Gaulle, Charles 7, 63, 64, 65
Democratic Party 1, 5
Democratic Republic of Vietnam
    see North Vietnam (Democratic Republic of Vietnam -
    DRV)
Deng Xiaoping 179
disengagement 152
Dobrynin, Anatoly 73, 251
domestic politics 248–9
domino principle, the 101–2,
    112–13
Dulles, John Foster 19–21, 56, 159
Dumbrell, John 7

economic embargo 19, 20, 30, 32,
    41, 88, 90
Eisenhower, Dwight D. 1, 2,
    19–21, 23, 56, 58, 104, 240
Europe, LBJ's policies on 7

Fairbank, John K. 154
Foggy Bottom 19, 39, 60, 156,
    162, 163, 230
Foot, Rosemary 2–3, 76, 242, 248
Foreign Affairs 229, 243
Foreign Ministerial meeting
    proposals 160–1
foreign policy
    central tenet of US 13
    Chinese 4, 41, 68, 92, 216–17,
        228–9, 232–4
    Chinese defeats 138–42, 165,
        243
    continuity in 59
    Cultural Revolution and 190–6,
        216–17, 246
    hints at Chinese moderation,
        1962 29–30
    JFK's troubled 27

LBJ's attitude to 57–60
LBJ's record 6–7
Mao's 247
Formosa 56
Formosa Resolution, the 56
Forrestal, Michael 33, 102
Foster, William C. 51n123
France, recognition of China 53, 63–8, 121
Fulbright hearings, the 154–6, 160, 188, 242
Fulbright, J. William 76, 154–5, 242

Gaddis, John Lewis 86
Gaiduk, Ilya 199
Geneva Conference 104, 116
Germany, Nazi 15
Goldberg, Arthur 157, 161–2
Goldwater, Barry 73, 88, 95
Goodwin, Richard 79n24
Government of the Republic of China-Taiwan (GRC) 26, 28
see also Taiwan
Great Britain 94
Great Leap Forward, the 24, 28, 34, 96, 116, 179
Green, Marshall 39, 40
Gromyko, Andrei 199–200
Gronouski, John 191, 217, 227
Gulf of Tonkin incident 99, 117, 245

Hai Rui Dismissed From Office (Wu Han) 179–80
Harriman, Averell 28, 32, 37–8, 63, 69, 109, 159, 200, 241
Heinrichs, Waldo 6
Herring, George 225
Hilsman, Roger 28, 29, 38–40, 40, 85, 90–1, 151, 177, 241
Hitler, Adolf 15
Holyoake, Keith 25

Humphrey, Hubert 155, 243
Hunt, Michael 251

ideology
  Chinese 97–8
  LBJ and 250–3
imperialism 63
India 23, 26, 33, 38, 40, 138–40, 165
indirect aggression 96–7
Indonesia 102–4, 140–1, 165, 243
Indo-Pakistani War, 1965 138–40
intelligence data, LBJ's consumption of 255–7
Italy 64, 65, 75, 165

Japan 14–15, 26, 65, 66–7, 74, 94, 139, 249
Jenkins, Alfred 163, 184, 186–7, 189, 191, 198, 216, 217, 222–3, 227, 230–1
Jiang Qing 215
Johnson, Harold 120
Johnson, Lyndon B.
  achievements 5–6, 257
  address March, 1968 224–5, 233
  Albanian resolution and 161–2, 163–4
  alliance politics and 249–50
  American Alumni Council address 157
  anti-communism 57
  approval rating 156
  Asia tour, 1966 159–60
  assessment of China policy 2–3, 240–57
  attitude to China 54–7, 73, 253–5
  attitude to foreign policy 57–60
  attitude to Mao 57, 257
  caution 95, 253
  China policy review 220–1, 224–5, 232–3, 246–7

INDEX

China record 253–7
China's nuclear weapons program and 68–77
on China's role in the Vietnam War 111–16, 119–20
on Chinese influence in North Vietnam 219–20
compared to JFK 254–5
concerns 53–4
congressional record 54
containment policy 55–6, 78, 85–6, 93, 120–2, 144, 152, 154–5, 233, 240–1
on cost of Vietnam War 227
Cultural Revolution and 178, 203
custodian of JFK's legacy 12
decision to intervene in Vietnam 54–5, 111–13, 253
definition of Vietnam 113
detachment 57
domestic policy and politics 58–9, 248–9
Edward Kennedy and 157
Eisenhower and 56, 58
election victory, 1964 85
engagement with China policy 254–7
escalates Vietnam War 114–16, 119–20, 122, 194–6, 254–5
European policies 7
final year in office 213–14, 232–4
foreign policy advisors 59–62, 124n24, 253–4
foreign policy leadership 253
foreign policy record 6–7
goodwill message to China, 1967 190
Great Society legislation 95–6, 112, 120
hard-line-proclamation, 1964 92–3

ideology 250–3
impact of view of China on decisions 111–13
Indonesia and 103
Indo-Pakistani War and 139
inferiority complex 59
intelligence data and 255–7
interest in Vietnam peace settlement 226
international pressure and 249–50
July 1966 address 158–9, 243, 246
lack of China agenda 56–7
lack of interest in Chinese affairs 53
as lame duck president 224–5
McGeorge Bundy and 91
micromanagement 116
Nixon and 232
objectives 166–7
overtures to China 3
peace offensive 143
peace talks offer, 1967 218–20
poverty and 55
public opinion and 154
reaction to Cultural Revolution 184–90
reaction to French recognition of China 64, 65
reformist impulses 55
refusal to put country on war footing 119–20
rejects lifting of travel restrictions 94, 147, 224
relationship with JFK 56–7
relationship with Taiwan 250
re-launches Operation Rolling Thunder 148
relaxes travel ban 147
reputation 5–7
response to Fulbright hearings 155–6

Rusk and 62
Second World War and 54–5
self-image 247
as Senate Majority Leader 58
Sikkim affair and 140
situation on taking power 53–4
Southeast Asia tour 55
on Soviet-American relations 199–200, 201–2
State of the Union address, 1967 189
State of the Union address, 1968 220–1
Taiwan Strait crisis and 56
two Chinas arrangement and 243, 249
UN China seat and 93–4
understanding of international affairs 54–9
as vice-president 112
the Vietnam War and 6, 54–5, 58, 99, 102, 185, 242–3, 243–4, 245, 253, 256–7
war aims 150, 166
Johnson, Robert 69–70
Joint Chiefs of Staff 71, 99, 102, 106, 114, 149, 192–3

Kashmir 138–40
Katzenbach, Nicholas 188, 193–4, 217–18, 226, 226–7, 227
Kearns, Doris 54
Kennan, George 16, 25, 34, 35–6, 75–6
Kennedy, Edward 157
Kennedy, John F.
  assessment of China policy 40–1
  Cambodia and 104
  China record 2, 241–2
  China's nuclear weapons program and 36–9, 51n123, 68, 73, 242, 254
  on Chinese attitudes 25

congressional record 22
containment policy 12, 22, 26, 31, 33, 39–40, 241
containment without isolation and 40
Eisenhower's threat to come out of retirement 23
expectations of change 21–2
final press conference 40
food relief plans 30–4, 35
foreign policy 27
hopes for 12
hostility towards China 57
important question formula 27
impression of China 23–5, 34, 41
India policy 23
LBJ compared to 254–5
legacy 41
majority 22
political timidity 22–3, 62
relationship with LBJ 56–7
Rusk and 60–1
significance of 12
Southeast Asia tour 23
Taiwan Strait invasion plan and 28–9
Thanksgiving Day Massacre 32
two Chinas arrangement and 25–8, 40, 241
understanding of China 240
Vienna meeting with Khrushchev 34, 36
Vietnam policy 98
view of Sino-Soviet relationship 36
Kennedy, Robert 61
Khrushchev, Nikita 21, 23, 27, 33–4, 36, 50n118, 69, 91–2, 109, 179
Kissinger, Henry 2, 54, 229, 231, 244, 250, 252

INDEX

Knowland, William 56
Kochavi, Noam 2, 28, 239n65
Kohler, Foy 92, 110, 111
Komer, Robert 25–6, 49n91, 88, 155–6, 161
Korean War 1, 17–19, 55, 58, 62, 144–5
Kosygin, Alexei 110, 111, 196, 197, 201

Laos 27, 106, 143, 192
Leffler, Melvyn 17
Lerner, Mitchell 7, 255
Limited Test Ban Treaty, 1963 36, 51n118, 63
Lin Biao 98, 117, 180, 181, 184, 215, 252
Liu Shaoqi 179, 180, 196
Long Live the Victory of People's War! (Lin Biao) 98, 117, 184, 252
"lost chance" 1, 17
Luo Ruiqing 117–18
Luxembourg 64
Lyndon Johnson and Europe (Schwartz) 7

MacArthur, General Douglas 17, 115
McCarthy, Joseph 58
McCone, John 29, 102, 116
McKinley, William 14
Macmillan, Harold 26
McNamara, Robert 59, 60, 96, 97, 101, 113, 114, 145–6, 148, 149, 151, 185, 193
Malaya 103
Malaysia 103, 144
Malley, Simon 195
Manchuria 14
Manila Conference 159–60
Mansfield, Mike 96, 114, 115, 201

Mao Zedong
  aim of the Cultural Revolution 182
  American view of 215–16, 222
  Bundy on 143
  Chinese reunification and 250
  Cultural Revolution 117, 163
  economic recovery from the Great Leap Forward and 179
  Eisenhower's view of 20–1
  fears 41
  foreign policy 247
  Great Leap Forward 24
  hostility towards America 88
  instigates the Cultural Revolution 179–80
  Korean War and 17
  LBJ's attitude to 57, 257
  opposition to 181–2, 184
  overthrow of the Shanghai Party Committee 182
  recognition of regime 20
  refuses US overtures 17
  rehabilitation of the PLA 214–15
  relaxation of attitude to USA 233–4
  Rice's interpretation of 181
  Sino-American rapprochement and 229, 230, 233–4
  Sino-Soviet friction 24–5
  status 92
  succession 181
  tactical flexibility 252
  Taiwan's status and 21
  Third Front project 146
  Vietnam War and 116–18, 144–5, 200, 244, 245
  view of Soviet Union 179
Marshall, General George 16
Martin, Graham 106
Martin, Paul 163
Matsu 56
Maurer, Ion Gheorghe 190

Meeker, Leonard 187
military strength 96, 99
Moyers, Bill 156, 157, 159, 253
Munich Agreement, 1938 54

National Intelligence Estimates (NIE)
  1962 35–6
  1965 108
  1966 197
  1967 184
Nationalists, the 16, 18, 22, 27, 63, 64, 250
National Press Club 227
National Security Council (NSC) 32, 37, 91
National Youth Administration 55
New Deal, the 55
new look policy 31
New York Times 170n40
New York Times Magazine 75
New Zealand 141
Ngo Dinh Diem 90
NIE 13-9-65 "Communist China's Foreign Policy" 97
Nixon, Richard M. 1, 2, 229–30, 231, 232, 243, 244, 249, 250, 252
North Korea 218
North Vietnam (Democratic Republic of Vietnam -DRV)
  bombing preconditions 107
  Chinese aid to 117–18, 146
  Chinese influence 113, 200, 219–20
  Chinese military personnel in 148–9
  fear of China 128n70
  peace offensive and 143
  peace talks offer, 1967 218–20
  Soviet aid 110, 132n124, 141–2
  Soviet influence 199–202
  support for insurgency 98, 99–100
  tenacity 145
nuclear facilities, Chinese 68–73
nuclear weapons
  China explodes first 53, 74, 242
  China's development program 35, 36–9, 41, 51n123, 61, 68–77, 242, 254
  Eisenhower's threat to use 21
  reaction to China's first nuclear test 74–7, 91

Ohira, Masayoshi 67
oil 103, 148
Open Door, the 14, 40
Operation Gibraltar 138–40
Opium Wars, the 14
Outer Mongolia 27

Pakistan 138–40
Paris peace talks 226, 230, 233
Patriotic Front of Thailand (PFT) 106
Pearl Harbor, attack on 15
Pearson, Lester 65–6, 163, 165
Peng Dehuai 180
Peng Zhen 179–80, 181
People's Liberation Army (PLA) 214–15
Pescadores, the 56
Pham Van Dong 118, 142
Philippines 14
Pleiku US Army barracks 108, 115
Policy Planning Council, Department of State 16, 30, 35, 111, 184, 198
poverty 55
public opinion
  Chinese threat and 76–7, 95, 242
  Cultural Revolution and 188–9
  recognition of China and 155

INDEX

Vietnam War and 153–4
Pueblo, USS 7, 218, 235n14
Pye, Lucian 221

Qiang Zhai 247
Quemoy 56

Raborn, William 157
radio propaganda 150
Red Army, the 182–3
Red Flag 215
Reischauer, Edwin 152, 156, 221
Republican Party, closed door policy 21
"Resist America and Assist Vietnam Movement" 146
Rice, Edward 30–1, 32, 39, 40, 88–9, 121, 144, 150, 181, 183, 186, 192, 215, 233
Richelson, Jeffrey 73
Ritchie, Charles 75
Romania 220
Roosevelt, Franklin D. 14, 15, 55
Ross, Robert 240
Rostow, Walt 30, 31–3, 35–6, 40, 57, 70, 71, 101, 122, 125n43, 156, 158, 162, 163, 182, 185, 186–7, 188, 193, 200–1, 221–2, 224–5, 243
Rowen, Henry 71–2
Rusk, Dean
  Albanian resolution and 161, 162–3, 164–5
  background 60–2
  Cambodia and 105
  China policy review 223–4
  on China's diplomatic failures 144
  China's nuclear weapons program and 35, 68, 69, 70–1
  on Chinese influence in North Vietnam 200
  on Chinese leadership 92

concern about Chinese involvement in Vietnam 146, 192, 243
Cultural Revolution and 187
Edward Kennedy and 157
Hilsman and 91
Indonesia and 103
Indo-Pakistani War and 139
on international conciliation of China 121
on JFK 23
in JFK's administration 25, 26, 30, 31, 32, 36
LBJ's policy advisor 59, 60
meeting with Ritchie 75
reaction to French recognition of China 63, 64, 67–8
re-launch of Operation Rolling Thunder and 148, 157
resistance to change in policy 92
Sino-American rapprochement and 231–2
Soviet-American relations and 201
Soviet Vietnam policy and 110, 111
two-pronged China policy 151–3
UN China seat and 93–4, 155
vetoes lifting of travel restrictions 94
view of China 61–2, 92, 101–2, 113, 144, 155, 166, 219, 223–4, 231–2
Russell, Richard 64
Russo-Japanese War 14

Sato, Eisaku 74
Schwartz, Thomas Alan 7
Second World War 15–16, 54–5
Senate Armed Services Committee 56, 120
Senate Foreign Relations Committee 76

Shanghai Party Committee, overthrow of 182
showdown 152
Sihanouk, Prince Norodom 104–6
Sikkim affair 140
Singapore 103, 144
Sino-American rapprochement 2, 3, 228–32, 233–4, 252
Sino-American relationships 240–8
  change in direction 165–7
  cosmetic change proposals 89–91
  effect of Vietnam War on 137–8, 244–5
  public scrutiny of 154–7
  reform proposals 87–9, 95, 120–1
  resistance to change in policy 92–6
  two-pronged China policy 151–3
Sino-American tension 1, 145–8, 241
Sino-Indian war 33, 38
Sino-Indonesian relations 140–1
Sino-Soviet alliance, 1950 17
Sino-Soviet friction 24–5, 34–8, 37, 196–8, 228–9, 231–2, 247, 256
Sino-Vietnamese relations 100, 142, 218–20, 223
Sisco, Joseph 161
South Korea 93
South Vietnam 93
  American commitment 101–2
  communist advances 106
  overthrow of president 90, 98
  threat perception 98–102, 107–13
  US aid 98–9
Soviet-American relations 7, 198, 199–202, 231, 251
  Kennedy administration 34–8, 50n118
  Vietnam War and 109–11

Soviet Union
  aid to North Vietnam 110, 132n124, 141–2
  channels of communication with 251
  China's nuclear weapons program and 37–8, 69, 73
  Cuban missile crisis and 33–4
  Cultural Revolution and 196–8, 202
  decline in influence in Southeast Asia 109–10
  de-Stalinization 179
  influence in North Vietnam 199–202
  intelligence assessment of, 1961 34
  Khrushchev ousted 91–2
  Korean War and 18
  leadership of Communist movement 141–2
  Mao's view of 179
  Pueblo affair and 235n14
  Sikkim affair and 140
  Sino-American rapprochement and 231–2
  threat in Asia 15–17
  US détente with 21
  Vietnam War and 109–11, 198–202
  see also Sino-Soviet friction
Spanish American War 14
Special National Intelligence Estimates 24, 158, 191
State-Defense study group report, 1965 118–19
State-Defense study group report, 1966 152–3, 160
State, Department of 35, 64, 93, 220, 230
  Bureau of Intelligence and Research 28, 32, 63, 68–9, 92, 146, 149

INDEX

Far Eastern Bureau 38
Policy Planning Council 16, 30, 35, 111, 184, 198
Stennis, John 120, 194
Stevenson, Adlai 22, 25, 89, 93, 241
Suharto, Major General 140
Sukarno, President 102–4, 141

Taiwan 16, 19–20, 21, 25–7, 62, 65, 93, 109, 149–50, 162–3, 250
Taiwan Strait crises 1, 33, 34, 56, 241
Taiwan Strait invasion plan 28–9
Tangiers 243
Taylor, Maxwell 102
Thailand 93, 102, 106–7, 108, 109, 143
Thanat Khoman 106
Thanksgiving Day Massacre 32
Third World, development contest 23–4
Thompson, Llewellyn 34, 35–6, 156, 201, 251
Thomson, James 1, 39, 40, 57, 87–8, 90, 91, 121, 150, 155, 159, 166–7, 185–6
threat perception 96
  Cambodia 104–6
  China 86, 89, 95, 96–7, 109, 111–13, 218
  Chinese ideology and 97–8
  Indonesia 102–4
  Thailand 106–7
  Vietnam 98–102, 107–13
Tito 20
trade
  early 13–14
  easing restrictions 152
  liberalization 187–9, 223–4, 231, 232
  reform proposals 87, 88–9

travel restrictions 90, 94, 137, 147, 152, 221, 224, 232
Trudeau, Pierre 225
Truman, Harry S. 1, 2, 15–17, 53, 58, 115, 240
Tucker, Nancy Bernkopf 2
two Chinas arrangement 20, 25–8, 40, 64, 65, 66, 93–4, 120–1, 160–1, 162–3, 187, 241, 243, 249

United Nations
  19th General Assembly 93
  Albanian resolution 161–5
  China seat 66, 75–7, 87, 93–4, 125n43, 155, 222, 224
  Chinese membership proposal defeated 161–5
  Indonesia's withdrawal from 103
  opposition to PRC admission 18, 19, 25–7, 31, 96
  reaction to China's first nuclear test 74
United States Information Agency 150, 226–7
US Navy, Seventh Fleet 19
U Thant 74, 219

Valenti, Jack 171n53
Van Tien Dung 118
Vienna 34, 36
Vietnam War
  alliance politics and 249
  American commitment 101–2
  averting Chinese intervention 144–53
  Cambodian neutrality 104–6
  China's role 95, 113–20, 121
  Chinese bogeyman 86
  Chinese caution 3
  Chinese declaration American conduct 119
  Chinese policy, 1966-67 190–6

Chinese threat 98–102, 142–4
consequences of American defeat 108–9
costs 119, 145, 221, 227
de-escalation discussion 185
Democratic party and 1
early assessment of role 2
effect on Sino-American relations 137–8, 244–5
escalation 98–102, 107–16, 119–20, 122, 146, 192–6, 254–5
GRC's China mainland invasion plan 149–50
Ia Drang Valley fighting 145
intensified operation in South authorized 225
justification for intervention 85, 143–4
LBJ on 58
LBJ on China's role 113
LBJ's China policy and 242–3
LBJ's decision to intervene 54–5, 111–13, 253
LBJ's interest in peace settlement 226
LBJ's obsession with 253, 256–7
literature 85–6, 111
Mao and 116–18, 144–5, 200, 244, 245
Operation Rolling Thunder 114–16, 117, 119
Operation Rolling Thunder re-launched 148, 157–8
peace hopes, 1966 200–2, 203
peace initiatives 117
peace offensive 143
peace talks offer, 1967 218–20
public opinion and 153–4
Rusk's firm stance on 243
scholars' fixation on 6
Soviet Union and 109–11, 198–202
stalemate 242–3
Tet Offensive 218
Thailand and 106–7
US policy 4
war aims 150, 166
Vietnam Working Group 106

Walker, Patrick Gordon 92
Wang Bingnan 30
Wang Guoquan 118, 245–6
Wang Jiaxiang 116–18
Wang Li 215, 216
Warsaw 30, 31, 32, 33, 118, 150, 214, 230
wars of national liberation 23–4, 88, 122
West Germany 65
Westmoreland, General William 192–3
White, Paul Dudley 147
Whiting, Allen 114
Wilson, Harold 94, 197
Wu Han 179–80
Wuhan Incident 214–15

Yao Wenyuan 179–80

Zablocki, Clement J. 76, 90
Zagoria, Donald 154, 157–8
Zhou Enlai 62–3, 183–4, 190, 195, 202, 217

EU authorised representative for GPSR:
Easy Access System Europe, Mustamäe tee 50,
10621 Tallinn, Estonia
gpsr.requests@easproject.com

www.ingramcontent.com/pod-product-compliance
Ingram Content Group UK Ltd.
Pitfield, Milton Keynes, MK11 3LW, UK
UKHW021832140426
5217IPUK00021B/1402